SHIPWRECKS ON THE CHESAPEAKE

SHIPWRECKS
ON THE
CHESAPEAKE

Maritime Disasters on Chesapeake Bay
and Its Tributaries, 1608-1978

Donald G. Shomette

TIDEWATER PUBLISHERS
Centreville, Maryland

Library of Congress Cataloging in Publication Data

Shomette, Donald.
    Shipwrecks on the Chesapeake.

    Bibliography: p.
    1. Shipwrecks--Chesapeake Bay (Md. and Va.)
I. Title.
G525.S5525   363.1'23'0975518   81-85606
ISBN 0-87033-283-X

Manufactured in the United States of America

First edition, 1982; Second printing, 1983

CONTENTS

LIST OF ILLUSTRATIONS

Each Part of this book is introduced by a map of the Bay showing the sites of the maritime disasters described therein.

The engravings at the heads of chapters are taken from eighteenth and nineteenth century sources and are used merely as decorations, not as depictions of the specific vessels or events described in the chapters themselves.

ACKNOWLEDGMENTS

S IMPLY to acknowledge by name the individuals and institutions that have assisted me in the research, writing, and production of this book does not adequately reflect the deep sense of gratitude and appreciation I feel toward them for their generous contributions. First and foremost I would like to thank the personnel of those great institutions in which the bulk of archival and published data, which it has been my chore and delight to evaluate, rests. The Library of Congress and the National Archives in Washington, D. C., the Maryland Historical Society in Baltimore, and the Pennsylvania Historical Society in Philadelphia must be singled out for their unstinting assistance at every difficult bend in the road toward publication.

Dr. Ferdinand Chatard, of the Radcliff Maritime Museum, Baltimore, Maryland, was of great assistance in helping me locate valuable manuscript sources pertaining to a number of middle nineteenth and early twentieth century shipwreck reports, primarily those in the Granofsky Customs Collection. William Dudley, of the Naval History Division, Department of the Navy, in Washington, D. C., was of considerable aid in helping me locate many of the pictorial materials used to illustrate this work. I would also like to thank my good friend and associate Dr. Fred W. Hopkins, Jr., of the University of Baltimore, for lending me the fruits of his extensive research on the War of 1812 which have been employed in the chapter on the Chesapeake Flotilla. To Fred Tilp I extend my warmest appreciation for permission to employ data from his fine works on the

Potomac River. No study of Chesapeake Tidewater history would be complete without paying homage to the works of Robert Burgess, a maritime historian whose books have been my constant companion and frequent guide. I would also like to thank my friend and waterborne companion Captain Varice Henry, without whom the tale of the Pitcher Wreck would never have been written, and to Nicholas M. Freda, whose own research on that most unfortunate steamboat has richly enhanced my narrative. A special note of appreciation must also be given to Jennifer Rutland for her critical and helpful readings of my initial manuscript drafts and for typing the final copy, and to Brett Topping for her assistance in reviewing the galleys.

And last, but not least, I would like to thank my wife Carol who planted the seeds of this project many years ago.

Donald G. Shomette

FOREWORD

IN THE TERRIBLE WINTER of 1608, less than a year after the founding of the first permanent English colony in America, on the banks of the James River in Virginia, a party of eleven colonists prepared to shove off from the settlement at Jamestown for Hog Island. Their small craft was grossly overladen and the sky was heavy with an impending storm. Despite the efforts of many, including the colony's leader, Captain John Smith, to dissuade the voyagers, and despite the ominous premonition of perils ahead, the party resolutely embarked as planned. It was to be the last time any of the men was seen alive, for their expedition was destined to end, as many had feared, in tragedy. Days afterwards, their bodies were washed ashore below the settlement and discovered by Indians. This sad event was the first recorded maritime disaster in the Chesapeake Tidewater. In the decades and centuries that followed there would be innumerable others, and all would add their own distinctive ripple patterns, some extensive and some minuscule, to the flow of Chesapeake Bay history.

It has been my objective to present here a select review of a number of the more significant catastrophes and military losses on record, all of which are confined within the Bay itself, its approaches, or its myriad tributaries. Some stand out for their singular impact on the course of human events, while others are notable for their immense toll on life and property. Included are tales of incredible bravery, courage, and fortitude, as well as stories of cowardice, stupidity, and ineptitude.

Every account has been drawn from reliable contemporary, and occasionally secondary, sources. A few episodes are well-known while others have languished in obscurity. Some, around which traditions have grown hoary, are presented here for the first time in the light of documentation, the glare of which is often wholly unfavorable to the patina of accepted legend. As far as possible I have tried to include the human side of each narrative, drawing on published interviews, reports, and eyewitness accounts to enhance the historic record.

In the course of my research I have documented the demise of more than 1,800 vessels, and have recorded the data in an extensive appendix at the end of this volume.

Despite the litany of disaster recounted in these pages, there is a uniquely positive aspect to a shipwreck. It is simply that each vessel that sinks may become, in the process, a veritable time capsule dating from the moment of its loss, a vast artifactual storehouse of the technology and culture of its day. The results of the calamities inflicted upon our nautical ancestors by nature and by their own hands have only just begun to provide modern man, through the science of underwater archaeology, with a truly intimate knowledge of his maritime heritage hitherto believed largely lost. Nowhere in American waters is this more true than in the Chesapeake, where no fewer than two entire fleets, one from the American Revolution and one from the War of 1812, have been discovered and are even now being scrutinized, measured, and analyzed by marine archaeologists and historians.

My own interest dates from my encountering, more than thirty years ago, the battered remains of a small, stranded workboat in the sand dunes below Virginia Beach. More recently, my work as a marine archaeologist has permitted me to indulge my curiosities about the lives and deaths of ships in this area, and I have had the opportunity to study, in a professional capacity, a number of the vessels included in this narrative. Since I know that I am by no means alone in being intrigued by shipwrecks, I am happy to share my fascination.

Donald G. Shomette

Upper Marlboro, Maryland
May 1982

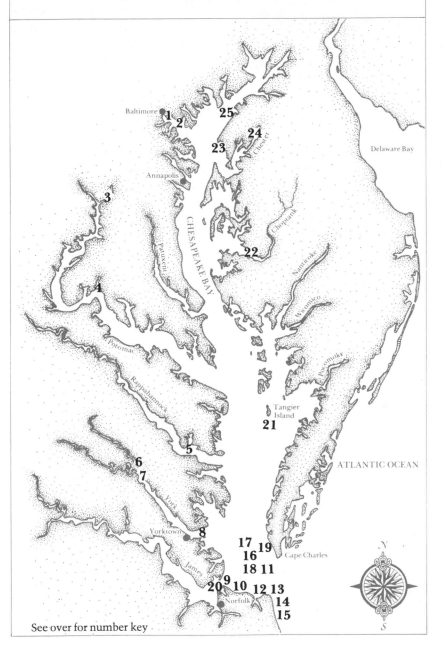

PART ONE
THE COLONIAL ERA

Baltimore **1** **2**
25
24
Chester
23
Delaware Bay
Annapolis
3
CHESAPEAKE BAY
Choptank
22
Patuxent
Nanticoke
4
Wicomico
Potomac
Rappahannock
Pocomoke
Tangier
Island
21
5
ATLANTIC OCEAN
6
7
York
Yorktown
8
17 **19**
16
Cape Charles
18 **11**
James
20 **9** **10** **12** **13**
14
Norfolk
15
N
S

See over for number key

MAP KEY: THE COLONIAL ERA

1. *Unity* (1758)
2. *Boyne* (1770)
3. *Nisbit* (1768)
4. *Susanna* (1749)
5. The Irish Indenture Wreck (1749)
6. *Rose* (1738)
7. *Needham* (1738)
8. The Convict Wreck (1773)
9. *Raleigh* (1747)
10. *Peggy and Nancy* (1752)
11. *Dunlop* (1767)
12. The Switzer Wreck (1738)
13. *Ranger* (1766)
14. Pattison's Wreck (1749)
15. Hunter's Wreck (1749)
16. Unidentified (1746)
17. *Richmond* (1738)
18. *Lucy* (1753)
19. *Success* (1745)
20. *Molly* (1768)
21. The Tangier Island Wreck
22. *Earl of Chatham* (1769)
23. *Swan* (1753)
24. *Sophia* (1759)
25. *Industry* (1753)

Chapter One

THE TANGIER ISLAND WRECK

I T WAS a vague tradition, varying with the narrator but persisting through generations. With each passing year, an increasingly elaborate fabric of romantic folklore was woven about the mysterious, buried shipwreck said to be at the bottom of Chesapeake Bay off tiny, isolated Tangier Island.

Most of the oystermen on the island accepted the notion that the undiscovered hulk was the skeleton of a wooden sailing ship dating from the golden age of galleons and frigates, the days of the earliest European explorations of the Bay. The tale most often told indicated that she was a pirate ship pursued into the Chesapeake by a British warship in 1610, overtaken off Tangier Island, and, after a desperate engagement replete with boarding and bloody hand-to-hand fighting, sent to the bottom.[1]

It was a local legend, kept alive by the islanders—and kept to themselves. Few, if any, expected that the Bay would ever reveal just what it was that she clutched in her dark waters. But often the Chesapeake appears to tease, sometimes given to revealing just enough of her treasure to excite the curiosity of even the most stoic folk. Early in 1926 she provided the hardy Tangier Islanders with just such a glimpse.

At the end of February in that year there was a cold northwest gale so intense that the sturdy roofs of houses on the island groaned and creaked under the strain. By dawn of the next day it was obvious that a major blowout had occurred. So strong, in fact, had been the combination of wind and tide that the water level of the entire Bay was lower than it had ever been in local memory.[2]

Though astonished by this awesome display of nature's power, the watermen nevertheless ventured out in their tiny workboats to begin the daily tonging for oysters, a labor upon which their fortunes rested, as had those of their forefathers. They soon discovered, however, that the blowout revealed the encrusted upper works of a wrecked ship jutting just above the water's surface.[3]

The curiosity of the islanders was piqued, and for once the day's work was forgotten. In sailboats and rowboats they put out for the wreck. Some of the oystermen, it was later claimed, were actually able to tread upon its slippery, worm-eaten decks. No one could identify the hulk as that of any vessel lost in recent memory, and interest continued to grow. With oyster tongs, the watermen dipped into the very depths of the hulk, probing in search of they-knew-not-what.[4]

After a few moments, one of the tongers pulled up the first artifact, a heavily encrusted but obviously ornate copper dish. Then came more beautifully inscribed dishes. But the most exquisite prize of all was a curiously engraved weapon—a battle-ax. It was in an excellent state of preservation, and when the weapon was cleaned, it was found to have a brass shield inlaid upon other metals of the blade. In the uniquely shaped handle of the weapon was concealed a small stiletto.[5]

Time was running out for the islanders; the tide was creeping back over the wreck, sweeping away their slender contact with the past. For most, the Tangier legend was confirmed. The wreck was the only topic of conversation on the island for days on end, but eventually interest waned. The ornate copper dishes were sold to a visiting New York antique dealer. The ax, which was at first of the greatest interest to the islanders, was also forgotten and eventually sold to Lorie Quinn, Sr., of Crisfield, Maryland for $10.[6]

But, in early April of 1926, rumors of the find trickled northward and brought an investigator to the island from a leading Baltimore newspaper. Within a short time the ax was in the hands of the Peabody Institute in Baltimore, and on April 5, was examined by experts. The weapon was found to have been manufactured from Damascus steel, so perfect and strong that it was still, six weeks after its removal from salt water, uninjured by oxidation. The astonished examiners publicly pronounced it "a remarkable specimen of the Medieval pole ax" of a type never employed by the English but used extensively by the Latin nations. The inlaid brass shield on the blade was said to be akin to the hallmark of silversmiths of the Middle Ages but could not be deciphered by the Peabody. The curiously ornate stiletto blade, "another fact which . . . [pointed] to its Latin origin," according to the Peabody, measured eight inches in length. The still-sharp ax blade measured four inches across, with the spearhead adding another eight inches to the overall length of the weapon.[7]

After undergoing further tests and study by Peabody officials, the weapon was scheduled to be taken to New York so that experts could attempt to identify its exact place of origin and age. But mysteriously, at this juncture, the ax vanished. All efforts to pick up its trail failed, leaving the Medieval Wreck of Tangier Island shrouded to this day in a cloak of unanswered questions.[8]

Was the story of the wreck simply a fabrication designed by the normally tight-lipped islanders to hornswoggle an unwary Yankee visitor out of a few dollars, or to excite and perplex a big-city newspaper reporter? Could a vessel of such purported antiquity have survived destruction by the sea, shipworms, and time itself for so long? And, are there historical data to lend credence to the legend surrounding the wreck or to its supposed medieval origin?

The answer to the first question will probably never be known, although the hard-working citizens of Tangier are even today noted for their forthright honesty and no-nonsense stoicism. Regarding the second question, the answers are more reliable. In recent years vessels of great antiquity, some even extending back as early as the Bronze Age, have been discovered by underwater archaeologists, often in excellent states of preservation, even in worm-infested saltwater environments. Entire ships, in fact, such as the seventeenth-century Swedish warship *Wasa,* have been recovered intact. And even in the Bay, in the Patuxent River, vessels of early nineteenth-century origin have been found in the mud in mint condition.[9]

Is it possible, then, that the citizens of Tangier Island actually chanced upon a Spanish ship of great antiquity? There are indeed many indications that Spanish mariners sailed the waters of the Bay well before the first Englishmen. As early as 1529 Spanish maps of the New World portrayed the Chesapeake, or Bahia de Santa Maria, as it was then called; and by 1559-60 Spanish explorers may have touched upon the Bay, extending the province of Spanish Florida northward and giving the region the name Ajacán. Several years later, Spanish colonizing attempts, predating the English settlement at Jamestown by more than three decades, were undertaken but failed. Expeditions to relieve a band of beleaguered priests were dispatched in 1571 and again in 1572, to no avail. Sixteen years later, however, a comprehensive exploration of the Bay as far north as its headwaters was carried out by the Spanish explorer Vincent Gonzales. Confrontations between the English settlers and the Spanish were not long in coming. On July 25, 1609, a scouting expedition commanded by Captain Francisco Fernandez de Ecija entered the Bay but withdrew after encountering an English ship "in the region of the islands." Two years later a Spanish caravel, in search of another vessel reportedly lost in the region, visited Point Comfort, Virginia, to spy on English fortifications supposedly under construction there. Was the vessel she was in search of perhaps the same one lost off Tangier Island? Here, unfortunately, the record of Spanish probes in the Chesapeake ends.[10]

But what of the wreck lying off Tangier Island? Perhaps the Chesapeake will again surprise everyone, and her waters will give us another brief glimpse of this treasure. Until that time, however, the wreck will remain only a legend.

Chapter Two

THREE HUNDRED SWITZERS

T HERE were more than three hundred men, women, and children, staunch German Protestants every one, who cepted Colonel Brown's challenge to establish a new settlement on the southern frontier of the Virginia colony. Brown was ambitious, occasionally called a gentleman of fortune, and the organizer and self-designated leader of the group. He had spent a considerable amount of time, money, and energy in Europe preparing for this, the most daring undertaking of his life.

It was 1738 and the flow of immigrants from the Old World to the New was just beginning to reach the flood stage. Scots, Irish, and German "Switzers," such as those recruited by Brown, formed a sizable body of those choosing to settle on the Virginia frontier. Men like the colonel stood to prosper, and the colony, under the able leadership of Governor William Gooch, encouraged such projects as a means of taming the wilderness.[1]

By early summer most of the eager would-be settlers recruited by the colonel sold or converted into cash all of their lifelong possessions to pay for the trip to America and to purchase the goods that would enable them to begin a new life in the wilderness. For most, however, the new life would never be.

With its name long since lost to history, the ship chartered to carry Brown's Switzers to Virginia set sail from England in early August.[2] Her passengers were packed tightly above and below decks, but their initial discomforts were undoubtedly eased by the excitement of departure and the expectations of the great adventure lying ahead.

Transatlantic voyages in the eighteenth century were expected to be difficult, but they were exceptionally unpleasant aboard the crammed, unsanitary merchantmen specializing in the transport of convict labor, indentured servants, or free immigrants to the English colonies in America. Passengers often fell victim to unscrupulous captains willing to carry as many people as they could squeeze aboard in order to realize the greatest profits possible—regardless of the cost in human life. Misery was a frequent companion to the voyagers. Typical of the excruciating conditions to be suffered during such trips were those described by Gottlieb Mittelberger little more than a decade later. "During the journey," he wrote,

> the ship is full of pitiful signs of distress—smells, fumes, horrors, vomiting, various kinds of sea sickness, fever, dysentery, headaches, heat, constipation, boils, scurvy, cancer, mouth-rot, and similar afflictions, all of them caused by the aged and highly salted state of the food, especially of the meat, as well as by the very bad and filthy water, which brings about the miserable destruction and death of many. Add to all that shortage of food, hunger, thirst, frost, heat, dampness, fear, misery, vexation, and lamentation as well as other troubles. Thus, for example, there are so many lice, especially on the sick people, that they have to be scraped off the bodies. All this misery reached its climax when in addition to everything else one must suffer through two or three days and nights of storm, with everyone convinced that the ship with all aboard is bound to sink. In such misery all the people on board pray and cry pitifully together.[3]

The Switzer ship chartered by Colonel Brown was to be no exception.

A short time after putting to sea, the unsanitary, airless conditions below deck, the putrid food and rancid water, the contagious illnesses, and a hundred other difficulties exacted a shocking toll on the passengers, particularly among the children who sickened and died at an alarming rate. Within a few weeks contagion swept the ship, and fifty to sixty passengers and crew, including the captain and mate, had fallen. Several deaths were an expected occurrence on such voyages, but when both passengers and crew died by the score, the consequences for the survivors were severe.[4]

Normally, a voyage across the "middle passage" lasted from six to eight weeks, but it was not until the beginning of January—five months after the Switzers parted sight of the English coast—that the ship, continually buffeted by adverse winds and violent storms, neared the shores of America. The last of the rotted provisions had long since been consumed; malnutrition, cold, and disease were continuing to take their deadly toll. Among the tormented survivors were Colonel Brown's own four children. The colonel himself, having disembarked from another ship in December well after the expected arrival of the immigrant ship, undoubtedly hoped to find his family and the Switzers awaiting him.[5]

On the morning of Wednesday, January 3, the immigrant ship at long last sighted the low-slung shoulders of the Virginia Capes. The wind was fair as she slipped between them. A few more hours and she would be safely anchored in Hampton Roads. But each minute aboard had become unbearable torture for the emaciated passengers. They could wait no longer; they rose as one and insisted that their appointed replacement for the late captain anchor the ship at once and go ashore to procure provisions.

Despite his better instincts and the darkening gunmetal-gray skies, the new captain immediately ordered the ship to drop anchor in Lynnhaven Bay and the ship's boat to be lowered. The awesome black clouds closing in from the north did not prevent him from boldly setting out to seek provisions for the starving Switzers. "Accordingly," one contemporary report later noted, "the Captain and some of the passengers went ashore, but it being an island, and no house upon it, they walk'd a long time in vain."[6]

As the captain stumbled weakly about the sandspit he had unwittingly mistaken for the mainland, a violent northwest wind arose, mercilessly staving in his boat upon the beach and marooning him and his companions upon the island. As the winds increased to gale proportions, the anchored ship in the Bay strained laboriously at her cables. Suddenly, one of the anchor lines snapped, and the second anchor began to drag along the sandy bottom.

Relentlessly, the ship was driven toward the shore. It was only a matter of minutes before she struck ground with a sickening crunch. Weakened seams along her battered hull stretched and parted almost instantly, and the icy water surged through the gaps, filling her hold and between-decks compartments. Dozens of passengers who had sought shelter from the bitter cold were now trapped. Desperately, they clawed over each other in an effort to reach the ladder. Their efforts were futile. Within minutes nearly fifty people were drowned below decks.[7]

Nearby, two small vessels struggled against the elements to render assistance. In one of the craft was Colonel Brown himself. The colonel had been in the town of Hampton for days awaiting the arrival of the Switzers. Immediately upon receiving notice of their ship approaching the Virginia Capes, he had procured a vessel and provisions and set out to his people's assistance—an expedition which now became a life-and-death race. With great difficulty the wretched survivors, more dead than alive, crowded aboard the two rescue craft, even as their own ship was cruelly battered by the sea. But there were simply too many people for the small boats to carry, and many had to be put ashore at the nearest point in the midst of the freezing gale.

As the tempest grew and the temperatures plunged, even the sanctuary of land held no consolation for the immigrants. Cold, starving, and desperate, those unfortunates who were put ashore quickly became disoriented and were scattered by the storm as they searched aimlessly for shelter. Many froze to death where they stood upon the beach, while others staggered onward into a wild marsh from which there could be no return.

Fewer than sixty of the original three hundred survived long enough to reach shelter and safety, "and those in so low a condition, that it is much doubted, whether some of them will recover." Among those near death who miraculously survived were Colonel Brown's four daughters.[8]

Throughout Princess Anne County the hearts of Virginians opened to the pitiful survivors. Governor Gooch, upon learning of the catastrophe, ordered that everything possible be done to provide for their comfort and for rescue of their property from the wreck. Salvagers scrambled over the remains of the waterlogged death ship which still lay in the Bay where she had been driven aground. Little could be saved.[9]

The loss of the Switzer ship was to prove a tragic setback in privately organized efforts to expand Virginia's frontier. "This ship," the editor of the *Virginia Gazette* wrote only days after the tragedy,

> was reckon'd one of the richest that has come to this colony for many years, and 'tis fear'd that much of her treasure is lost. However, that is but a trifle in comparison to the loss of so many lives, and this loss the colony may sustain, but this disaster's discouraging some thousands of the same country people from coming hither to settle our lands, (which are very rich, and capable of great improvements) who it seems intend it, unless their terror be in some measure mitigated, by the kind, hospitable treatment they met with in their distress.[10]

This marine disaster was, in fact, quite sufficient to restrain further German pioneering attempts in the region Brown had selected along the New River frontier, and attempts at immigrant settlement in this area would not again be considered for at least another half decade.[11]

Chapter Three

A COLONIAL DISASTER LOG

THE MAJORITY of shipping losses in the Chesapeake Bay during the early colonial era will perhaps never be satisfactorily documented due to the paucity of available records. Since 1726, fortunately, a large body of information concerning the comings-and-goings of ships, general maritime and related mercantile activity, and accounts of marine disasters began to appear in the pages of the Annapolis *Maryland Gazette* and later in the Williamsburg *Virginia Gazette.* Most of the shipwreck accounts were brief, often providing just the name of the vessel lost, her master, cargo, and destination. These accounts were usually only intended to inform those who might have had some specific interest or investment in the vessel. When a shipwreck was extremely tragic and involved the loss of more than a few lives or an unusually valuable cargo, the stories could occasionally rival the sensationalist exaggerations of modern yellow journalism.

Most losses could be pinned to specific causes—fire, storm, strandings, collisions, ice, or poor seamanship—although more than a few were simply described as lost, with no explanation offered. The use of navigational aids during the early eighteenth century in the Bay were almost nonexistent, and ships attempting to pass between the broad shoulders of capes Henry and Charles at the mouth of the Bay without a local pilot were tempting the Fates. Besides the deadly shoals of the Capes themselves, the dreaded Middle Ground, which lay squarely between them, soon earned an unenviable reputation as a graveyard of ships, for its shoally sands were constantly shifting, waiting to ensnare even those familiar with them. Yet the bane of wooden ship mariners was fire, a beast which could devour in minutes the vessel upon which they sailed.

One of the first great ships to be lost to fire was the large New England-built merchantman *Needham.* Owned by a London merchant named Jonathan Forward and commanded by one Captain Harwood, *Needham* sailed on her maiden voyage from New England to Virginia late in 1737 to take on a cargo of tobacco for Europe. On Tuesday, February 21, 1738, she lay moored off West Point, Virginia, at the confluence of the Pamunkey, Mattaponi, and York rivers. Only six hogsheads of tobacco had been loaded during the preceding days, and a single crewman was left aboard. The cause of the fire was never determined. The ship burned to the waterline, destroying everything aboard except the sole seaman left to guard her.[1]

Less than two months later, on Sunday, April 16, fire claimed another victim in the Pamunkey, the merchantman *Rose,* Captain Dennis commanding. *Rose* was owned by a certain Mr. Wynch, and had been tied up at Littlepage's Wharf where she loaded more than fifty hogsheads of tobacco destined for Europe. Suddenly, the calamity occurred:

> while the Captain and several others were on board, who perceiving of a sudden, a great Smoak, from below, endeavoured to find out the [source of the] Fire but in vain; for in their Search, they were almost suffocated with Smoak, which soon burst into a Blaze. . . .

Rose, too, was entirely destroyed.[2]

The Bristol merchantman *Richmond* was among the first-named vessels noted as lost on Middle Ground, although a number of unidentified ships had previously suffered a similar fate. Under the command of Captain Smith, *Richmond* had sailed from Bristol bound for the Rappahannock River with "a very considerable Quantity of Goods." On April 4, 1738, with all sails standing, she entered the Virginia Capes. Apparently unaware of the hazards, Smith stood squarely up the center of the Bay and immediately ran aground on the shoals. Within a short time, the ship was buffeted against the bottom so severely that several seams opened and nearly seven feet of water filled her hold. Smith ordered the ship abandoned, and with passengers and crew put out in the longboat. His haste was such that he failed to order the sails lowered. Upon returning with a salvage crew sometime afterward, he failed to locate a trace of the ship, and it was never determined whether she was beaten to pieces or driven off under sail by the wind.[3]

In 1745 another loss, this one more tragic, occurred when the ship *Success* foundered on Middle Ground. *Success* had sailed from her home port of Glasgow, Scotland, for Virginia with a crew of twenty in November, and on December 31, after a voyage of six weeks, came to anchor at the mouth of the York River. Within hours of her arrival, a violent storm struck the lower Bay, and the ship's commander quickly ordered three anchors laid out to secure his vessel. Despite these precautions, the storm's violence was such that *Success* was torn from her moorings and driven nearly two leagues across the Chesapeake, where she struck upon Middle Ground. The effect of the impact was instantaneous, and the ship sank so quickly that the mate and three seamen went down with her. The remainder of the crew managed to secure the ship's longboat. But the storm proceeded to drive them out beyond the Capes. With no provisions to sustain them, and carried ever further out to sea by the elements, the seamen tried to survive. Finally, after unimaginable hardship, the tiny longboat was pulled ashore on Cape Henry where one of the sixteen survivors collapsed and died.[4]

The crew of another merchantman, commanded by a Captain Brown, was more fortunate. Brown's vessel, a new ship, sailed from Maryland for London in April 1746 with a cargo of tobacco. Shortly after leaving the Virginia Capes, the ship was beset with "great distress" and took on water. Fortunately, she fell in with an inward-bound vessel commanded by Captain Preston. Brown's ship was hauled back to the Capes and into ten fathoms of water, where it was thought she could ride out any ill weather while undergoing repairs. Despite the crew's best efforts, the ship seemed determined to sink, and she began taking on water. But, again fortune smiled when another vessel, bound for Nanticoke, took Brown's crew aboard just in time for them to see their ship go down.[5]

The string of shipping losses continued in 1747, when a privateer-turned-merchant brig called *Raleigh*, outward-bound from Williamsburg for Madeira with 5,000 bushels of wheat, ran ashore and bilged on Willoughby Spit, at the entrance to the James River, on March 21. Despite the best efforts of her commander, Captain Samuel Allyn, the vessel's loss was total.[6]

Less than six months later, on September 3, 1747, an unidentified ship carrying a load of "Irish [or, indentured] servants," who sold themselves into years of servitude to pay for passage to America, was lost in the Rappahannock River. Just south of Urbanna, Virginia, she was struck in five fathoms of water by a "sudden violent hurricane" and capsized immediately. The ship's mate and more than fifty others were drowned.[7]

Even ships securely moored in protected anchorages fell victim to the elements. In January 1749, the Glasgow merchant ship *Susanna*, Captain Steel commanding, lay snugly at anchor near Nanjemoy, Maryland, in Port Tobacco Creek. Aboard were 219 hogsheads of tobacco consigned to several of the great merchant houses of Europe. Unfortunately, the winter was one of the worst on record, and most of the rivers and creeks throughout Maryland, and even portions of the Bay itself, had frozen up. Port Tobacco Creek was no exception, and the ice which imprisoned *Susanna* was soon cutting into her hull. The thaw which followed was rapid, and the ship sank at her anchorage, a total loss.[8]

On October 7, 1749, the tidewater was subjected to a terrible thrashing by one of the worst hurricanes in memory. An unrecorded number of ships were driven ashore or destroyed in the southern end of the Bay. At the outset, the region was subjected to violent northeast winds, accompanied by torrential rains. Captain Hunter's inward-bound ship from Glasgow was among the first blown ashore on Cape Henry. Another vessel, Captain Pattison's Glasgow-bound ship, fully laden with tobacco, soon followed. Between 10:00 A.M. and 2:00 P.M. the next day, the storm reached its peak, raising tides more than fifteen feet above normal, destroying waterfront facilities and ships alike. In the Bay, a large unidentified vessel reportedly foundered with all aboard. Bodies from this and other wrecks washed ashore for days afterwards. Fortunately, the storm veered to the east before striking the upper Bay head on, sparing the citizens of Maryland.[9]

Another storm which caused great damage in the southern regions of the Chesapeake occurred on October 22, 1752. Only one ship, however, *Peggy and Nancy*, Captain Isaac Johns, master, was lost in the northeast gale. The ship had sailed only a few hours earlier with 338 hogsheads of tobacco when she was driven ashore on Willoughby Point, Virginia, at about 10:00 P.M. For hours, the ship lay on the shoals, her hull constantly beating against the bottom. The following morning, after incessant torture by the elements, she finally bilged and broke up. The sails, rigging, and five hogsheads of tobacco were all that could be saved, and the ship became a total loss.[10]

In January 1753, the ship *Lucy*, Captain Charles Hargrave commanding, sailed from Annapolis for Lisbon, Portugal, with 9,000 bushels of wheat as cargo. Like many before her, she was unfortunate enough to encounter a Bay storm of vicious proportions which drove her hard on Middle Ground, where she became a total loss.[11]

Not all ships which sank in the Bay were entirely lost. On August 28, 1751, for instance, the ship *Speedwell*, Captain Nicholas Stevenson commanding, a property of the firm of Hunt and Giles, sailed from Annapolis for London with a cargo of 379 hogsheads of tobacco. Not long after departure, the ship sprang a leak. Water began to fill her hold at an extraordinarily rapid rate. Despite the fact that two pumps were kept going, it was soon apparent that she would have to be run ashore or she would sink and be lost. The nearest land was Poplar Island, and Captain Stevenson, realizing that there was more than six feet of water in the ship's hold, determined that it would have to be there or nowhere. Making for the island, he ran upon a shoal and stuck fast. Within a very short time, there was more than eleven feet of water in the hold. Yet the vessel, fast aground, could not sink much more, and efforts were immediately undertaken to salvage whatever was possible. Despite Stevenson's diligent attention to the problems at hand, the greatest part of the cargo was either damaged or spoiled by the salt water. Yet, with the assistance of vessels from Annapolis,

Speedwell was eventually raised and returned to the city dock where repairs were made. The ship was soon back in service and making her transatlantic runs as usual.[12]

Another incident illustrative of how losses were cut despite the apparent total destruction of a ship is shown when the brigantine *Swan,* Captain Clarkson commanding, burned in Swan Creek, Maryland in 1753. On July 21, the vessel lay alongside a wharf in the creek taking on a cargo of tobacco for London. Much of her lading, nearly three hundred ninety hogsheads, was on the dock awaiting transfer. The work was hot and hard. When a round of rum was ordered up, the cabin boy went below to draw a bottle of it from a half-filled hogshead. As he began to draw the spirits, the candle flame ignited the vapors from the hogshead; they were immediately communicated to the container, causing an instantaneous explosion. The cabin boy was "burnt to ashes," and the ship was soon little more than a charred hulk. Yet some of her was saved. Tackle, rigging, portions of her hull, and the tobacco on the wharf were still of sufficient value that her owner, Robert Foster, did not bear an entire loss. Court of Vice Admiralty Judge Benjamin Young ordered that the sale of the remains be held on August 13 near the mouth of Swan Creek. Catalogues of items were posted in Baltimore, Joppa Town, and Bush Town more than a week before the sale, assuring the presence of a sizable crowd, and some return on the loss.[13]

Sometimes, it seems, a vessel was doomed from the start. Such was the case of the new ship *Industry,* built on the Chester River, Maryland, and commanded by Captain George Perkins. In early November 1753, she was dispatched up the Bay to Worton Creek to take on a cargo for her maiden voyage. Unfortunately, as she lay at anchor near the creek, having taken on only a portion of her lading, the butt of one of her planks parted, and the Bay's chilly waters gushed through the·seams in torrents. Pumping was out of the question, and the crew quickly slipped her cable attempting to run her aground on Worton Point. Unfortunately, the ship filled with water too quickly, and was lost.[14]

The next major shipping loss involved the burning of the merchant ship *Unity,* Captain Joseph Richardson commanding, which occurred on May 5, 1758, in the northwest branch of the Patapsco River, Maryland. *Unity*

> by some Accident took Fire in the Fore-Castle, and got to such Head before it was discovered, that she burnt down to the Water's Edge, and the People with much Difficulty saved the Captain's Papers, and narrowly escaped with their Lives.

On May 24, the sails, anchors, guns, running rigging, ship's boats, and other materials from the wreck, as well as the hulk itself, which was still lying in the river, were offered up for sale at public vendue at the house of James Carey in Baltimore.[15]

On May 5, 1759, the merchant ship *Sophia*, of Biddeford, Maine, Captain George Kimber, master, lay at anchor in the Chester River off Chestertown, Maryland. Her cargo consisted of thirty hogsheads of tobacco, three thousand staves, and some pig iron. Only three persons, the ship's carpenter, a seaman, and the cabin boy, were aboard at the time of her destruction. This loss was attributed to the carelessness of the carpenter, who attempted to heat a pitch pot on board rather than ashore, as he should have. The pot accidentally spilled, communicating the fire to the deck. The ship's rigging had been newly tarred, and the fire "ran like lightning, and was almost in an instant up at the masthead." With great difficulty, the three persons aboard managed to save their lives. The ship was a total loss.[16]

In 1766, the Virginia merchantman *Ranger*, Captain Jackson, long noted by mariners as a jinxed ship, met her final demise. Her record of misfortune was well-known. When she had visited Barbados, for instance, the port of Bridgetown was accidentally burned down, and along with it all of *Ranger*'s sails which had been lodged in a warehouse there. When she was finally able to return to Norfolk and turn in for repairs with the ragtag collection of sails she had managed to scrape together in the West Indies, they too were lost when the warehouse in which they were stored, belonging to a certain Colonel Tucker, was burned to the ground. She was eventually refitted and dispatched on a return voyage to Barbados. Unfortunately, the jinx again caught up with her in October. She encountered a storm soon after leaving Norfolk and was driven ashore on Cape Henry where she broke up.[17]

Three months after the loss of *Ranger*, the snow *Dunlop*, Captain William Russel, master, sailed for Glasgow from Baltimore with a cargo of lumber. Encountering rough weather soon after reaching Middle Ground, Russel ordered the anchors let go in an attempt to ride out the storm, but the cables quickly parted, and her rudder was ripped off by the pounding seas. In desperation, he attempted to run before the wind, hoping to get into Hampton Roads for sanctuary and repairs. Like many before and after her, the ship was unfortunate enough to encounter the sandy fangs of Willoughby Spit. She ran aground, quickly bilged, and was lost.[18]

Exactly two years after the loss of *Dunlop*, the snow *Molly* shared the same fate. Bound for Virginia from Antigua, the ship, under the command of Captain Campbell, encountered a violent snowstorm soon after entering the Capes and blindly ran aground on Willoughby Point. Though the vessel's cargo was salvaged, the ship became a total loss.[19]

In the same year one of the most serious shipping losses ever to happen in colonial Maryland occurred. The ship *Nisbit*, a new vessel armed with ten carriage guns and carrying over five hundred hogsheads of tobacco, lay at anchor in the Eastern Branch awaiting a fair wind to sail for Glasgow, Scotland. On October 18, 1768, her captain, Hugh Wylie, went ashore on business. Ten minutes after his departure, the powder in the ship's gun room took fire. The resultant explosion burst out from the stern, instantly killing Archibald Carrie, the Chief Mate; John Morris, the Second Mate; Adam Stewart, the ship's carpenter; John McKinney, a cooper; and Thomas Beck, the cabin boy. Fortunately, most of the crew were forward and were spared as several more explosions ripped the cabin and quarterdeck to pieces. Within a few minutes the ship capsized, and the blaze was extinguished. All that could be saved, however, were mere fragments of the ship and her rigging.[20]

Many vessels of the colonial era, their genealogies occasionally well documented, were sometimes listed as lost without trace. Others were listed as to location of loss, but with no cause given. The 90-ton, square-sterned snow, *Earl of Chatham*, was a case in point. Known to have been built in Maryland in 1767, this particular vessel was documented in that year on

December 4 in the Patuxent Naval District as owned by Hercules Courtney and commanded by Captain George Woolsey. In 1769, on a return voyage from Dublin, Ireland, she sailed into Chesapeake Bay and came to anchor off Cambridge, Maryland, in the Choptank River. Here, she was totally lost—but how and why remains a mystery.[21]

The loss of the brigantine *Boyne* is another case in point. This square-sterned vessel, built in Pennsylvania in 1766 and documented in Philadelphia on October 27 of that year, sailed under the ownership of John Maxwell Nesbit and Company. She was commanded by Captain Caldwell Howard. Her last known voyage was from the island of St. Kitts, in the West Indies, to Baltimore, Maryland, in 1770. Having made the voyage safely, she was inexplicably lost near her final destination, probably in the Patapsco River.[22]

One of the last major losses during the pre-Revolutionary era was that of an unidentified brig en route from Dublin to Virginia. Aboard the ship were more than one hundred fifty indentured servants and convict laborers. The indentured servants, in return for the cost of their passage to America, had been bound by contracts to serve as many as seven years as virtual slaves to those willing to purchase them in the colonies. The convicts, unlike the indentured servants, had little choice in such matters. They were being sent to America not only to provide a labor pool, but primarily to remove the seamier elements from the more "civilized" society of Europe. Under the best of conditions such voyages were worrisome. Sometimes, for the crews of ships carrying such passengers, they turned out to be nightmares. Such was the case of this ship in 1773.

When the brig set sail from Dublin, she carried a crew of seventeen and a captain destined never to see dry land again. While en route the captain and crew became ill and died, reportedly "of jail distemper," possibly meaning, by mistreatment from the indentured servants and convict passengers. In January, when the vessel finally reached the tidewater, she was entirely under the control of the indentured servants and convicts, none of whom had any intentions of spending their time or sentences in servitude. When a pilot boat put out from York River to guide the ship in, she was immediately seized by thirty convicts. The boat was run ashore and the convicts escaped. The remainder of their compatriots, more than one hundred twenty individuals aboard the brig, not being sailors, had little alternative but to try to run their own vessel ashore and escape the best way they could. The vessel was thus hopelessly stranded and bilged near the mouth of the York. Her passengers, for the most part, made their way ashore safely.[23]

As a result of the escape of the 150 convicts and indentured servants, one of the largest manhunts in Virginia history to that date was begun. But the escapees, had apparently prepared well for their flight, probably to the western frontier of Virginia. By January 21 only four men and a single woman were retaken. Others were also undoubtedly taken into custody, but records are not clear. What is certain, however, is that perhaps as many as one hundred individuals eluded the fate of bondage. Freedom, deserved or not, was theirs. The same freedom that their would-be masters soon fought a revolution for.[24]

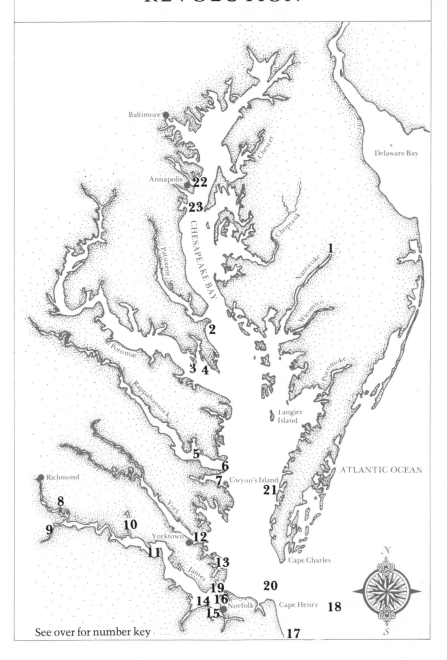

PART TWO

REVOLUTION

Baltimore

Delaware Bay

Chester

Annapolis **22**

23

CHESAPEAKE BAY

Choptank

Patuxent

Nanticoke

1

Wicomico

2

Potomac

3 4

Pocomoke

Rappahannock

Tangier
Island

5

6

ATLANTIC OCEAN

Richmond

7 Gwynn's Island

21

8

York

9

10

Yorktown **12**

11

13

James

Cape Charles

19

20

14 16

15 Norfolk

Cape Henry **18**

N

See over for number key

17

S

MAP KEY: THE REVOLUTIONARY ERA

1. Three unidentifieds (1780)
2. *Cato*, and *Hawk* (1781)
3. Twenty-two unidentifieds (1776)
4. Two unidentifieds (1776)
5. V. S. N. *Lewis* (1778)
6. Unidentified (1776)
7. Four unidentifieds (1776)
8. Virginia State Navy Squadron (1781)
9. Several unidentifieds (1781)
10. Virginia State Navy Squadron of gunboats (1781)
11. Unidentified (1776)
12. Cornwallis Fleet (1781)
13. H. M. S. *Liberty* (1775)
14. Five unidentifieds (1776)
15. One hundred and forty-eight unidentifieds (1779)
16. Twenty-five unidentifieds (1775)
17. Unidentified (1775)
18. V. S. N. *Dolphin* (1778)
19. Three unidentifieds (1776)
20. *Susannah* (1776)
21. Unidentified (1776)
22. *Peggy Stewart* (1774)
23. *Totness* (1775)

Chapter Four

YOU HAVE MADE A BON FIRE

STANDING approximately sixty yards inland from the confluence of the Severn River and Spa Creek, Maryland, on a plat of well-manicured ground lies Luce Hall, a structure glowing with the dignified patina of age, and hoary with tradition. Mounted on the wall of this ivy-covered building is a small plaque, all that is left to denote the final resting place of what was probably the most celebrated ship in Maryland's Revolutionary history, and the focal point of an incident which has come to epitomize the rugged road to independence for the loyalist as well as the patriot. The vessel now lies beneath many feet of soil under Luce Hall, lands reclaimed from the water for the construction of a key factor in the maintenance of that independence, the United States Naval Academy, in Annapolis, Maryland. The ship in question was *Peggy Stewart.*

In the year 1774 Anthony Stewart was a man on the move. Born in Aberdeen, Scotland, in 1738, he was a gentleman of both breeding and industry. Though his father was a member of King George's Court of the Exchequer, young Anthony decided quite early in life to go to America. Arriving in Maryland in 1753 while still in his teens, the hard-working young man soon established himself in the small but powerful merchant community on the Severn River. In 1764 he married the beautiful daughter of one of the city's most wealthy, influential merchants, James Dick. Within a short time Stewart was taken into full partnership in his father-in-law's Annapolis-based export-import operation. In a few years he became a rich man, owning more than 1,500 acres of prime land in Dorchester County, a 300-acre estate, Mount Stewart, a sizable brick warehouse (one of the first of its kind in Maryland) on the South River at London Town, and a spacious home on Hanover Street in Annapolis. His family grew, boasting two sons and three daughters, and he and his wife were expecting yet another child in October. Indeed, the world looked bright for Anthony Stewart. But his days of good fortune and respectability in Maryland were about to come to an end.[1]

The seeds of Anthony Stewart's downfall were planted in 1765, with Parliament's passage of the controversial Stamp Act. In Anne Arundel County, Maryland, as in many sectors of British America, an organization was formed to combat the measure. The Association of Anne Arundel County, as the group was called, quickly resolved not to import any British goods while the Stamp Act continued in force. Though the Stamp Act was soon repealed as a result of the American action, Parliament sought to maintain some vestige of authority by imposing duties on tea, glass, paper, and even paints. Again the Association of Anne Arundel County, along with others across the eastern seaboard of America, agreed to a ban on tea and "foreign luxuries and superfluities." All of the merchants of Annapolis were asked to sign a formal agreement permitting the association to monitor and control the flow of all incoming goods. Most of the merchant community agreed, including Stewart's father-in-law. The outstanding omission on the agreement was the signature of young Stewart himself.[2]

It was unclear whether the signature of Anthony Stewart was withheld as a subtle protest to the association's action, or whether James Dick's signature was sufficient for both men. Whatever the reason, both Stewart and Dick managed to steer clear of any run-ins with the association—that is, until 1770.

When the brigantine *Good Intent,* owned by the Dick and Stewart firm, entered the port of Annapolis, the association refused to permit the cargo to land, contending that it included numerous boycotted items. Each item in the manifest was then "tried" separately and judged either to be "contrary" or "conformable" to the parameters and spirit of the boycott agreement. Ultimately, on February 27, 1770, *Good Intent* was obliged to sail back to England, her bulk largely unbroken, at a great financial loss to Stewart and Dick. Both men were sternly warned that protest would be construed as an attempt to subvert the boycott organization and would be handled accordingly. The warnings were quite clear.[3]

For more than four and a half years, Stewart and Dick managed to obey the law but their continued success became the envy of many. In 1771 the Dick and Stewart firm, in association with one William McGachen, purchased a little 50-ton Bay-built brigantine which Anthony promptly named after his first daughter Margaret ("Peggy") Stewart. Although the vessel had never sailed out of the Chesapeake, the firm boldly proposed to employ her in transatlantic operations. On her first voyage, laden with a cargo of 3,000 bushels of corn, 30 bushels of wheat, 138 barrels of flour, and 30 bushels of beans, she sailed to Madeira and was insured for £900. She managed to return with a valuable cargo of wine. Neither Dick nor Stewart had any intention of paying import duties on the wine. Like many Annapolis merchants, they had regularly dabbled in smuggling, and so cautioned the brig's master, Captain Jackson, to reveal nothing about his cargo to anyone.[4]

In spite of the profits realized from *Peggy Stewart*'s voyage to Madeira, Dick and Stewart soon found themselves in serious economic difficulty because of the failure of the London firm of John Buchanan and Sons, to whom they were more than £6,000 in debt. As a result of the Buchanan bankruptcy, the two merchants, obliged to make good their own debts, tightened their belts, reduced the orders for goods for their various outlets in Annapolis and London Town, and chartered out *Peggy Stewart* to another Annapolis firm, consigning her to the care of one of Buchanan's former partners, James Russell of London.[5]

In February 1774 the *Maryland Gazette* ran an advertisement noting that *Peggy Stewart* would sail for London by the first of March from Selby's Landing on Patuxent River, and was ready to take on tobacco at seven pounds per ton consigned to the firm of Wallace, Davidson, and Johnson, one of Stewart's chief competitors.[6] Significantly, Russell was instructed to sell the brig when she reached London—if he could—for £550. If not able to dispose of her in that fashion, he was to charter her return to Annapolis in the most profitable manner possible.[7]

Unfortunately for Stewart, Russell would do more than that. He would try to ship, at the behest of Annapolis merchant Thomas Charles Williams, seventeen and a half chests of tea, consigned to his brothers and partners-in-business Joseph and James Williams, also occasional rivals of the Dick and Stewart consortium.[8] The attempt, however, did not go unnoticed. In August, after the ship was loaded in London, Joshua Johnson, then the London end of the Wallace, Davidson and Johnson company, sent a letter to Annapolis, undoubtedly with the intention of rousing up the home folk against Russell, one of his own chief competitors.

"I should not be surprized," Johnson wrote on August 4,

> to hear that you have made a Bon Fire of the *Peggy Stewart* as I have a hint that a certain JW [James Williams] has ship'd Tea on Board of her & that Capt. Jackson applied to old Russell & told him that he was suspicious of it but Russell told him it was not his business . . . on Jackson's persisting to be uneasy Russell satisfied him by telling him it was Linens. . . .[9]

This was certainly one way to stir up a hornet's nest. It was soon bandied about Annapolis that Thomas Charles Williams had made no secret of the fact that he would ship whatever items he desired, and he was prepared to tell the association to go to the devil.[10]

Anthony Stewart was blissfully unaware of these goings-on. On the morning of October 14, with his wife expecting their child at any hour, Stewart looked down from his home on Hanover Street and was delighted to see *Peggy Stewart* riding at anchor. His ship had come in, and he was soon going to be a father again at any moment. What happiness he must have experienced.

When Stewart walked down to greet Captain Jackson, however, his world was about to collapse. He was stunned by the news imparted by the good captain. Not only had the ship, which left London on July 23, had a nightmare crossing with fifty-three seasick indentured servants aboard, it was also leaking badly.[11] Worse, there were more than two thousand pounds of tea in the hold. He felt at once duped and frightened. The consequences of having to send this cargo back to London, bulk unbroken, might prove to be a fatal blow to his company, but for the poor humans aboard, in a leaking ship now unfit for sailing on the open seas, the voyage might prove disastrous.

Since customs regulations forbade the landing of any cargo (and the indentured servants were viewed as cargo) without paying import duties on the entire bulk, Stewart was in a dilemma. With characteristic boldness, he resolved to pay the duty on the cargo—tea and all—but to land only the servants. Perhaps, after his wife had the child, he would be able to reason with the hotheaded local boycotters.[12]

The news that a ton of "that detestable weed" was aboard *Peggy Stewart* and that Anthony Stewart had personally paid the duty on it spread throughout Annapolis quickly. Among the first to learn of it were James and Joseph Williams, to whom the consignment was being shipped. Stewart had attempted to have them pay the portion of the duty on their share of the cargo, namely the tea, but they refused. The Williams brothers were in a panic. Aware that they would be obliged to face the wrath of the Annapolis Committee of Safety, the local revolutionists, the two immediately decided to plead for leniency by writing a letter of apology to the committee. After that, everyone in the city was aware of the presence of the tea.[13]

In their letter, they took great pains to express the fact that they informed many Annapolis merchants, including such leading citizens as Thomas Harwood and Samuel and Robert Purviance, that the tea had been ordered prior to the ban, but had been shipped without their knowledge after its imposition. They fully intended on turning it over to the Annapolis Committee to do with as the committee saw fit. They carefully explained that when Stewart requested money from them to pay the duty, they immediately refused until the committee was informed and made its decision known. The Williamses attempted in every way to place the burden of guilt on Stewart by noting that he paid the duty himself, without their knowledge.[14]

By late Friday afternoon the fat was in the fire. Mathias Hammond, a political rival of Stewart's and fiery prorevolutionary leader of the Annapolis Committee, attempted to call a meeting of its members, but with only four persons present, delayed the assembly until the evening. Stewart, Jackson, the Williams brothers, and John Muir, deputy collector of customs, were "requested" to attend. Only Stewart, whose wife was on the verge of childbirth, failed to appear.[15] Despite his absence, and the honest testimony by Muir that the merchant had indeed paid the duties, "it was agreed that this being a weighty Business no further Proceedings should be held," as Stewart later wrote, "'til the sense of the County could be taken at large, or in other Words 'til the Mob be gathered from all Quarters."[16] The meeting, which was held at the Annapolis Playhouse, broke up with little more agreed upon than to post twelve men to guard the ship and insure that the cargo remain aboard. It was adjourned until October 19.[17]

On the day following the Annapolis Playhouse meeting, Mathias Hammond was busy circulating handbills which strongly outlined the case against Stewart and the Williams brothers, and a mob of inflamed Maryland citizenry began to fill the town's inns. Men such as Mordecai Gist, Walter Bowie, and Dr. Charles Alexander Warfield, who had ridden into Annapolis with a label on his hat which read "Liberty and independence or death in pursuit of it, " were well aware of the events in Boston the previous December, when a mob dumped the hated tea into the harbor. Talk of a possible Annapolis Tea Party was on everyone's lips.[18]

Preoccupied with his wife, Stewart did not rouse to his own defense until Sunday, October 16, after the birth of his fourth daughter. Deciding now not to await the upcoming general meeting of the 19th, he began to pen his own side of the story, had handbills printed that evening, and started disseminating them the following morning. It was a masterpiece of an apology which, had it been tendered earlier, might have stemmed the rising tide of public hostility against him.[19]

Despite his efforts, many were publicly calling for tarring and feathering, or worse, hanging. Several of Stewart's friends attempted to have the illustrious Charles Carroll of Carrollton intercede in the merchant's behalf. Carroll, himself a member of the Annapolis Committee, offered the suggestion that perhaps the only way Stewart might save himself would be to burn the ship.[20]

As the hour of the public meeting of the 19th approached, a sizable crowd gathered in front of Stewart's home on Hanover Street. Stewart himself remained inside until solicited by two members of the committee, Gist and Charles Walters. At the appointed time, "a Number of disorderly People under different Ringleaders," Stewart later wrote, "did repair to Annapolis and joining with the Inhabitants of the Town did meet in a tumultuous Manner. . . ."[21]

Anthony Stewart did his best to defend his actions, although his aged partner, James Dick, timidly advised his son-in-law to follow the wishes of the mob. The tumult was great as one fiery impromptu speech followed another. Finally, order was brought by Charles Carroll, the Barrister. A prewritten letter of apology was produced which Stewart and the Williams brothers were directed to sign, giving their consent to burn the tea. One witness to the scene later testified that had Stewart "not complied with the order of the Mob that his life would have been in imminent Danger as their Rage was particularly levelled at him for having paid the Duty on the Tea. . . ."[22] Though Stewart was recalcitrant at first, he and the other two merchants put their signatures to the apology and read it aloud to the howling assemblage.

Then, from somewhere in its midst, a member of the mob shouted that he thought the brig should share the same fate as the tea. Other shouts were raised in agreement, particularly from several citizens of Elk Ridge and Baltimore. Someone asked Dick what he thought of the idea. Timidly, the old man nodded in agreement.[23]

Control was temporarily brought back when one Allen Quynn stood up and noted that "it was not the sense of the majority that the vessel should be destroyed," and made a motion to vote on the matter. The motion was seconded, and the majority voted against the burning of the ship.[24]

Another proposal was offered up that the name of the ship be changed from *Peggy Stewart* to *Wilkes and Liberty*, after the radical Member of Parliament John Wilkes, whose vocal attacks on the government had found favor in the colonies. Doctor Warfield, however, one of those present who adamantly demanded the destruction of the ship, added a twist to the suggestion. Why not burn the ship and make Stewart build a new one which would then be named *Wilkes and Liberty*?[25] Warfield was a strongly persuasive speaker who possessed that rare talent of inflaming an assemblage with oratory alone. For a few fleeting minutes reason was again lost. This time it proved fatal. The mob was Warfield's plaything. James Dick, more concerned for his family's safety than that of his ship, prevailed upon Stewart to turn the brig over to the whims of the mob. Shouts of triumph went up, and under torchlights the crowd marched down to the waterfront with Stewart and the Williams brothers captives in its midst.[26]

The three hapless merchants were soon being carried aboard the brig, and in a few minutes were sailing across the harbor to Windmill Point. There, with all of her sails still set, *Peggy Stewart* was set afire by her owner, Anthony Stewart, and James and Joseph Williams. Within a few hours the entire ship was consumed.[27] The Revolution in Maryland, which was to promise liberty and justice for all, had taken its first faltering steps by withholding justice from Anthony Stewart.

The end for Stewart and Dick was to be painfully drawn out. His company ruined, James Dick retired to his home in London Town where he lived the life of a recluse until his death in 1782, known to all as simply "the old Tory."[28] Stewart attempted to restore his good name and correct the injustices that had been perpetrated, but to no avail. Villified in public, burned in effigy, and hounded by threats on his life, he fled to England, where he applied to the government for compensation for his enormous losses.[29] He received a pension of £200 per year. He later returned to New York where he was joined by his family and became an active member of the Board of Associated Loyalists until that body was forced to flee at the end of the war. By 1781 the state of Maryland, secure enough in its own control to bring an indictment of treason against him, sentenced him to death in absentia, and confiscated all his property. Despite these difficulties, Anthony Stewart reestablished himself in business in Halifax, Nova Scotia, and lived out the remainder of his life as a successful merchant loyal to the King.[30]

And as for the burning of *Peggy Stewart*, it was to become another catchword for revolution in Maryland.

Chapter Five

CONDUCT [TO] ADORN
THE ANNALS OF FAME

B Y 1775 James Gildart and his partner John Gawaith had earned a respected place in the merchant community of Liverpool, England. They owned several fine ships, among them *Totness* and *Johnson,* and despite the recent political upheavals in America established a profitable trade with the colony of Maryland, primarily through the young boomtown port of Baltimore and in Talbot County. Gildart's capable son Johnson Gildart had managed the Baltimore concern and served as his father's attorney with reasonable success, while the Talbot County operation was administered by the firm's factor and agent on the Eastern Shore, James Braddock.

Gildart read with sullen contempt the recent edicts from the upstart committees of safety and correspondence:

> That if any Merchant, residing in Great Britain or Ireland, shall, directly or indirectly, ship any Goods, Wares, or Merchandise, for America, in order to break the Non-Importation Agreement, or in any manner contravene the same, on such unworthy conduct being well attested, it ought to be made publik; and on the same being done, we will not thenceforth have any commercial connexion with such Merchants.[1]

He cared not a whit for such nonsense and cast a blind eye on the tumultuous events of the recent past such as the burning of the *Peggy Stewart.* When one of his captains, Thomas Waring, master of the ship *Totness,* informed him that the Americans meant business and that to send a ship to Maryland at this particular time might be a fatal mistake, Gildart scoffed. There would be ten thousand British regulars there before any of his ships even arrived, and the Americans could eat bayonets if they didn't like it for all he cared.

But the Americans did care. On May 24 the *Maryland Journal* published a letter from a committee of safety correspondent in Philadelphia informing the Baltimore merchants that Gildart had loaded the 200-ton ship *Johnson* with a cargo of salt and dry goods consigned to the firm of Ashburner and Place of Baltimore. There was at least one more vessel preparing to sail from Liverpool for Maryland with salt which might also belong to Gildart. The correspondent was quite clear as to what he expected the Marylanders to do about this.[2]

> I hope your Committee will take care of those going your way. A good lookout ought to be kept, that people acting knowingly, in direct opposition to your engagements, may not escape; and it is well if these ships, on hearing how things are at your Capes, do not land their dry goods in some part of the bay. All goods on board should be taken possession of by the Committee, and indeed ship and all be sent back; the salt at least thrown into the sea, and the goods returned by ship.[3]

The news was received in Baltimore with considerable concern and was immediately relayed by the Baltimore Committee of Safety to the Talbot County Committee of Observation. The latter promptly appointed a deputation of eleven men to "wait" on Gildart's agent, James Braddock, and to "advise" him against accepting cargo from the *Johnson*, or even allowing the ship to break bulk. Furthermore, he was ordered outright not to advertise the sale of such goods. The committee then demanded an inventory and satisfactory accounting of the goods already in his possession. The factor was given a week in which to prepare a list and inform the committee of all matters concerning the *Johnson*.[4]

Braddock was terrified. A week passed and he failed to appear before the committee. Another deputation was sent to his store to fetch him, but he was not to be found. Several strong letters were left for him there, including a copy of the Baltimore Committee's orders to the Talbot Committee concerning *Johnson*. Finally, intimidated, Braddock appeared before the committee that same afternoon, and agreed to its original demands. He also informed the committee that the ship was due to arrive at any time in the Miles River with a cargo of dry goods and salt. The committee ordered the whole proceedings to be published in the *Maryland Gazette* as a warning to all those who would ignore its authority.[5]

Within a month *Johnson* entered the Virginia Capes. Braddock dutifully notified the Talbot Committee, and on the morning of June 28 a deputation boarded her while she lay at anchor in Western Bay. The four committeemen examined her manifest, cocket, and log book and found she carried a cargo of salt, dry goods, fourteen convicts, two indentured servants, and minor miscellaneous items. They informed her master, Captain Jones, that she would not be permitted to break bulk in Maryland. Incredulous, Jones took Braddock aside and told him that he could not possibly take the salt back to Liverpool.[6] "Do with it as you please," the nervous factor replied, undoubtedly recalling the *Peggy Stewart* incident, "just take it back to where it came from."

Jones had little choice, and with the exception of the convicts and servants, which the committee allowed to be landed, *Johnson* was sent back to England fully laden.

As a consequence of the *Johnson* incident the jubilant Talbot Committee came to a unanimous opinion: James Gildart and John Gawaith, by sending goods from England to be landed in Maryland, were in direct violation of the American Association's nonimportation agreement. Henceforth, they declared, all ties between themselves and their "constituents" and the firm of Gildart and Gawaith and Company were to be severed—forcibly, if necessary.[7]

Johnson had been fortunate, for though she returned fully laden, she returned intact. *Totness*, sent out from Liverpool in her wake, would not be so lucky.

Captain Waring had been master of *Totness* since February 1774, when he had taken over command from Captain John Hudson. His ship, though only 130-tons burthen, was a sturdy craft, built in England in 1765, square-sterned, and well cared for. She had been employed in the Liverpool-Baltimore trade for the better part of ten years, usually carrying produce to England and returning with dry goods, salt, and convict labor. On his last voyage, for instance, he had carried a cargo of 600 bushels of wheat and 6,100 bushels of corn. Her crew of eleven were among the most reliable to be found in the trade, though there was some question about their ability to bring the ship into the Bay without a pilot, a situation which had become common in recent times as a result of the political convulsions underway throughout the area.[8]

About July 7, 1775, *Totness* passed between the Virginia Capes and by the evening of July 9 was scudding along approximately twelve miles below Annapolis, directly off several pancake-flat islets off West River called the Three Sisters. Suddenly, there was a terrible grinding sound and the forward motion of the ship ceased with a series of rude bumps. *Totness* had run aground on the shoals of Three Sisters. And there she remained.[9] [The Three Sisters Islands no longer exist; by the first quarter of the twentieth century, the Bay had completely eroded them.]

The reason that Thomas Waring failed to lighten his ship in order to get her off the shoals is unknown. Perhaps he did not want her off. Perhaps he never meant for her to reach Baltimore. Perhaps he was, in fact, in full sympathy with the American Association. Whatever the reason, it is clear that he made no attempt whatsoever to free *Totness* from her imprisonment in the shallows.

The results were inevitable. After several days aground, the vessel was boarded by a deputation, "some Gentlemen, who had been chosen by the Inhabitants of that part of the Province to see that the Association relative to the Non-Importation of Goods from Great Britain should be strictly observed. . . ."[10]

Waring was questioned about his cargo and destination. The deputation learned that the ship was carrying more than four thousand bushels of salt, a large quantity of cheese, and an assortment of dry goods and earthenware, all bound for Baltimore. They were assured by the captain that it was not his intention to land the cargo in West River. The deputation then agreed to let the captain proceed to his destination if he thought it proper to do so.[11] In all probability, however, the deputation simply wished that the touchy problem of what to do with *Totness* be dropped in the laps of the Baltimore Committee.

News of *Totness*'s arrival and grounding in the Bay spread about the region rapidly. Within a day, the Baltimore Committee was apprised of her presence. On July 11 a special meeting of the committee convened and Thomas Place, one of the consignees of Gildart's cargo, was summoned. Place informed the committeemen that he and his partner, Mr. Ashburner, had received a letter sometime earlier from James Gildart, informing them that he would be dispatching *Totness*, ballasted in salt, in twelve days from the date of his communication. Upon her arrival, Place said, he had fully intended that her papers be laid before the committee. He would have informed them sooner, he claimed, but had failed to believe the initial reports of her arrival and grounding.[12]

Johnson Gildart was summoned. The committee, he was informed, had just learned that the young merchant had dispatched a boat to meet *Totness*. Was it, by chance, to warn her, or perhaps guide her to a secluded cove to unload? Gildart retorted that he had, in fact, sent a boat down the Bay with a letter for *Johnson* (which, though he did not know it, was already on her way back to England). The messenger also carried a letter for Captain Waring should the *Totness* be encountered.[13]

The skipper who had carried the message was also summoned. He informed the committee that he had failed to find *Johnson*, but on his way back up the Bay had come upon *Totness* firmly aground off West River. Upon delivering the letter to Waring, he was informed that the captain was not going to do anything with his ship without direct orders. Waring told the messenger that he would have to leave the ship and return to Baltimore or remain on board until orders were sent.[14]

Johnson Gildart was then recalled and ordered by the committee to go down to the ship and direct Waring to bring her to Baltimore to await the committee's determination. The committee, unfortunately, had not the slightest idea what should be done.[15]

While the Baltimore Committee fussed and fumed over the fate of *Totness*, the ship was kept under close scrutiny by the more excitable elements of the Anne Arundel County population. She had been boarded time and again, and it soon became apparent to the West River locals that Waring had no intention of getting her off the shoals until he received direct orders from her owners. A rumor circulated that there were goods aboard other than those reported by the captain. To prohibit the discovery of such goods, it was said, Waring was obliged to remain aboard. He certainly did not want to bring her into Baltimore if that was the case. Or so the rumormongers claimed.[16]

Local animosity was growing by the hour, against Gildart, against Waring, and against that supposed symbol of British arrogance, *Totness*. Stories circulated that the ship's arrival was Gildart's third attempt to land cargo in Maryland, a direct refutation of the American Association. Several persons recently arrived from Liverpool were quick to point out the merchant's avowed intention to pay the boycott no heed.[17]

The Baltimore Committee again summoned Thomas Place and ordered him to produce the ship's invoice. The invoice listed her cargo as salt and earthenware valued at over £220, just as claimed. It was not enough. Public sentiment toward Gildart and the consignees was becoming heated.[18]

On July 19, the heat was no longer confined to rumors. An aroused party of Baltimoreans determined that *Totness*, like *Peggy Stewart*, would have to be made an example of and destroyed. Johnson Gildart was immediately seized, so that "he might share a Stewart's Fate."[19]

The Baltimoreans, however, were just a bit too late; a band of local West River folk, stirred to a fever pitch, had decided on the same objective. The ship was boarded by a company of local militiamen under the direction of their captain. Waring and his men were permitted to remove their personal belongings and property, including twenty wheels of cheese. Then "the ever revered and glorious People," as one local wag later wrote, jubilantly set fire to both the ship and her cargo.[20]

"The ship had not long been burning," noted the wag, "before the *magnanimous Baltimoreans* arrived with a professed design to execute the glorious deed, in which they had been anticipated." Young Gildart would thus not provide the association with the triumph of humiliation that Anthony Stewart had eight months before, but his father would, he knew, most assuredly feel the searing penalty for his arrogance. "This," wrote one citizen to Samuel Chase, Maryland's delegate to the Continental Congress, "has been the conduct of the Marylanders, who I hope will adorn the Annals of Fame."[21]

Chapter Six

LORD DUNMORE'S FLOATING TOWN

THE American Revolution did not initially thrust itself upon the Maryland-Virginia tidewater region with the wholesale thunder and tumult of war as it did in New England. Indeed, many Marylanders and Virginians considered themselves, at least at the outset, loyal Englishmen. Yet a chain of events which openly began with Virginia Royal Governor Lord Dunmore's seizure of a small powder supply in Williamsburg on the night of April 20-21, 1775[1] (less than two days after the Battles of Lexington and Concord) proved irrevocable. The course of Revolutionary history soon became intrinsically linked to this region and to the naval actions carried out on its waters. The resultant losses of ships and men in the tidewater theater of operations (culminating in the British defeat at Yorktown in 1781) were perhaps as closely tied to the achievement of American independence as any other event of the war.

The first naval casualty in the tidewater, though apparently insignificant, was a direct result of the opening of outright hostilities. His Majesty's Sloop *Liberty*, a small tender to the sloop-of-war *Otter*, was a lightly armed vessel, probably commandeered for service in the Chesapeake prior to 1775. Little of her history is documented, yet that which is known is noteworthy. On April 23, 1775, while moored off Burwell's Ferry in the James River, *Liberty* was boarded by Captain George Montagu and ordered to take aboard a quantity of powder from H. M. Armed Schooner *Magdalen*—powder which had been confiscated from Williamsburg two days earlier by *Magdalen*'s crew.

Liberty was then directed to sail for Hampton Roads where she would be secured from the outcry of rage that was certain to follow.[2] As a consequence of the civil unrest and mob action which did ensue, Governor Dunmore prepared to flee at a moment's notice, and *Liberty*, along with H. M. S. *Fowey*, was dispatched on May 4 under the command of Captain Matthew Squires, commander of H. M. S. *Otter*, to Queens Creek, near Yorktown, to assist in his escape.[3] On June 8 the governor, fearing for his life, finally boarded *Fowey*.[4] As late as July 3, the little sloop *Liberty* was still on patrol in the York River.[5] Then Mother Nature took a hand in events.

On August 29 a heavy rainstorm struck Virginia, increasing in intensity until it became apparent that the tidewater region was in for a full-blown hurricane. On September 2 the main storm ravaged the coast from Currituck to Chincoteague. In Norfolk, the waterfront, including wharves and storehouses, was devastated. Milldams for miles up the James were wiped out. In the harbor of Norfolk, "four or five and twenty sail of vessels are run on shore there, many of which are irrecoverably gone." Reports of shipping losses trickled into Williamsburg from everywhere. At Currituck, North Carolina, for instance, an unidentified brig was reported driven ashore, stove to pieces, and entirely lost with all of her passengers and crew excepting the captain and an apprentice.[6] H. M. S. *Mercury*, 20 guns, Captain John McCartney commanding, was driven hard aground on Portsmouth Point in the Elizabeth River. Despite throwing over casks of food, iron ballast, and much artillery to lighten ship, *Mercury* remained stranded in two feet of water (at low tide) for eight days.[7] She was finally refloated after the most trying of ordeals. *Liberty* was not so fortunate.

Like a number of vessels, *Liberty* was cast away, in Back River near Hampton, where she became helplessly stranded.[8] On September 3, after the passage of the storm, a number of local inhabitants, ardent foes of Lord Dunmore, boarded the vessel, captured her crew, secured her guns, rigging, and other goods, and set her afire in the first outright act of war. She was soon little more than a burnt-out hulk. The gauntlet had been flung. Captain Squires barely escaped capture by jumping overboard and hiding in the nearby woods.[9] Mortified over the indignity, he returned several days later aboard *Otter* and threatened to blow the town of Hampton off the map unless full restitution for the loss was made.[10] Although *Liberty*'s crew was returned, a full blockade of Hampton Roads was soon instituted as a result, bringing shipping to a complete halt for more than three months.[11]

On October 25 while in command of a squadron of five ships Captain Squires exacted further revenge when he conducted a bombardment of the town.[12] Hostilities escalated. Again, on New Year's Day, 1776, Squires must have secretly relished his role in the bombardment and what became the near total destruction of Norfolk.[13]

Exiled aboard a fleet of Royal Navy warships and an enormous flotilla of loyalist refugee vessels, Lord Dunmore refused to submit to the rapidly spreading rebel dominance ashore and prepared to fight with every means at his disposal. On February 9, with the arrival of Captain Andrew Snape Hamond's 44-gun floating fortress H. M. S. *Roebuck*, his military strength was appreciably bolstered.[14] Soon after Hamond's arrival, information was received of "several Vessels being in the James River and a quantity of Provisions and Stock on a Farm, that were intended for the Rebel Army." Captain Hamond promptly fitted out several recently captured prize ships with cannons, embarked units of the 14th Regiment of Foot aboard, and dispatched them up the James on March 15 to capture or destroy the rebel shipping.[15]

Hidden shoals and foggy conditions made passage up the river difficult. As the little squadron reached the stretch immediately below Jamestown, "within a small distance of the shore . . . just under one of the Rebel Guard Houses," it ran aground. Within a short time, the rebels, fully aware of the invaders' presence, opened up a sporadic but often hot fire upon the stranded ships. Nevertheless, by ebb tide, all but one armed schooner had managed to float free. Despite the rebel fire, the freed vessels loyally hovered about the remaining grounded schooner, attempting to help her off the shoal. By daybreak of March 2, however, it was apparent that their efforts were in vain. Now under an intense bombardment, the raiders proceeded to remove the schooner's guns and crew, leaving behind only a quantity of cannonballs, salt, and clothing. Their last act, before abandonment, was to set the ship afire.[16]

By mid-May 1776 a ragtag armada of more than ninety vessels, mostly refugee merchant ships, but including a number of prizes and regular Navy warships, was gathered together under Dunmore's banner in Hampton Roads.[17] Acting upon Captain Hamond's wise recommendation that his position was untenable, Dunmore, expecting reinforcements at any minute from New York, decided to evacuate to a more secure location. Yet with so great a number of vessels in his charge, "for want of materials to navigate them," the governor was obliged to have three schooners and a sloop hauled onto Norfolk Flats near Millpoint and scuttled on May 22.[18] Three days later, as the great bulk of the armada prepared to sail from Hampton Roads, a party was sent by Captain Squires "onboard a Sloop scuttled & set her on fire, she having neither Sails nor Men." Several other large vessels were also destroyed.[19]

Dunmore's fleet sailed on the evening of May 25, ostensibly bound for the Atlantic, but at the last minute it was spotted by rebel lookouts turning northward near the mouth of York River. On the afternoon of the 26th the fleet came to anchor off a tiny islet at the mouth of the Piankatank River called Gwynn's Island. Dunmore's feeble detachment of marines and a corps of freed black soldiers were sent ashore the next morning along with many of the sick and starving refugees in his care.[20]

Mosquito-ridden Gwynn's Island was perhaps one of the poorest choices the governor could have made as a place to rebuild his little army, now riddled by smallpox and less than two hundred effectives strong. The island's nearest point to the mainland was barely two hundred yards across and quite fordable at low water. Yet there was a supply of cattle on the island, and the sound between it and the mainland permitted the stationing of a number of ships which could protect, if necessary, its several-miles-long coast from assault by boat.

While Dunmore lay ensconced on Gwynn's Island, the Virginia Convention adopted the Declaration of Rights and a new constitution.[21] On July 8 General Andrew Lewis, at the head of an army of Virginia militiamen and a 14-gun battery of

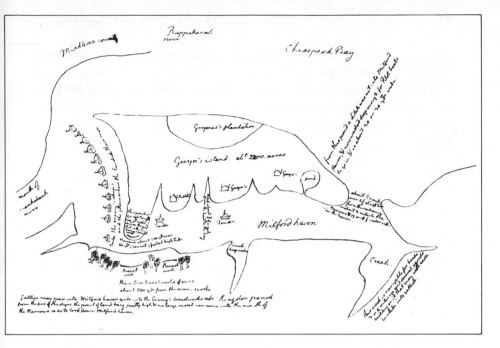

Thomas Jefferson's sketch map of British and American positions at Gwynn's Island, Virginia, in 1776. Note the positions of Lord Dunmore's armada north of the island (left) and the guard tenders in Milford Haven Sound. Manuscript map from the Thomas Jefferson Papers. Courtesy: Library of Congress.

artillery, marched from Williamsburg prepared to banish the royal governor forever. Upon arriving at Gwynn's Island, Lewis soon discovered that there were but a few hundred men bivouacked in a tent encampment at the west end of the island, and a strong artillery battery constructed by Captain James Parker guarding the channel at its narrowest point only a few hundred yards from the mainland. He also discovered that Milford Haven, the narrow sound between the island and the mainland, was strongly protected by *Otter* and several armed tenders. Stationed off the island's north shore and Captain Parker's battery was the remainder of the fleet.[22]

Despite Dunmore's strong defensive position, Lewis promptly proceeded to erect his own batteries. These were placed under the direction of a Frenchman, Dohicky Arundel, and consisted of two 18-pounders, two 12-pounders, five 9-pounders, three 6-pounders, and a few field pieces.[23] Orders were also issued to collect as many canoes, rowboats, and small craft as possible from the surrounding area for an amphibious assault against the island.[24]

On the morning of July 9 Lewis discovered that the ship *Dunmore* had shifted position with *Otter* and lay openly exposed, less than five hundred yards from his two main batteries. *Dunmore,* upon which the governor himself had taken residence, mounted four 6-pounders to a side but would, Lewis realized, be entirely at his mercy should she be caught by surprise. Without waiting for enough boats to be collected for the grand amphibious assault, he ordered his batteries to open on the unsuspecting royalists.[25]

According to H. M. S. *Roebuck's* log, at 5 A.M. the Virginians' battery opened with stunning effectiveness on *Dunmore* and the tenders in Milford Haven.[26] Completely surprised, the governor's forces had few, if any, guns in place which were strong enough to reply. Shot after shot smashed into the governor's ship and its tenders. From their near-point-blank range, the Virginians were making every shot count. One double-ended cannonball crashed through *Dunmore's* cabin, wounding the governor in the leg with a splinter and destroying his personal set of china.[27]

"I got our raw and weak Crew to fire a few Shott at them," he later reported to the Prime Minister. "I soon perseived that our Six Pounders made no impression on their Batteries, our Boatswain being killed and several of the People Wounded, we were therefore obliged to cut our Cable." *Dunmore* fired her own guns less than half a dozen times, while being struck by more than a dozen rebel shot. Though there was not a breath of air stirring, the ship drifted slowly away from shore with the tide, until she and several other vessels were taken under tow by boats from *Roebuck*.[28]

The rebel fire continued, seriously damaging the warships *Otter*, *Fowey*, and *William*, wounding several crewmen and killing others. Four armed tenders in Milford Haven were driven ashore. Fearing an amphibious assault at any moment, the British set three of the stranded ships afire. The 3-gun schooner *Lady Charlotte* and a pilot boat were captured intact by the rebels. Within an hour, the British land battery on the point, commanded by Captain James Parker, was also totally silenced.[29]

Dunmore's alternatives were few. Within a few hours, he knew, the rebels would gather enough small boats to attack the island directly—an attack he felt powerless to repel. Retreat was imperative. "It is impossible," recalled Captain Andrew Snape Hamond of *Roebuck*,

> to describe the distress & confusion that this floating Town was thrown into, upon the sudden order for quitting the Island and preparing to sail; most of them were entirely without free water, and thus the Man of War was under the necessity of supplying them with [it] as well as Seamen to Navigate them.[30]

General Lewis refused to permit Dunmore or his bedraggled armada of Norfolk refugees the least respite. On the morning of July 10, having assembled a force of thirty canoes, he again opened his batteries, this time directly on several more tenders the governor had newly stationed in Milford Haven. The suddenness and accuracy of the firing made it necessary for the tenders to be abandoned, but not before one 6-gun sloop was set ablaze to prevent capture. The second vessel, a 2-gun schooner commanded by Midshipman Thomas of the *Fowey* man-of-war, found herself completely surrounded by rebel boats and had to be abandoned intact for the crew to save their own skins.[31]

Before he could even begin to mount a landing on Gwynn's Island, General Lewis was amazed to see Dunmore's forces abandon their base in a blind panic.[32] Convinced that help would not be forthcoming, either from Tory sympathizers in Virginia or from General Clinton in New York, Dunmore resolved to leave Virginia, dragging his ragtag armada behind him. But for the moment, even that would be impossible. Many of the ships were too worm-eaten to withstand the rigors of an ocean voyage, and almost all lacked sufficient sails and rigging, much of which had been left on the island. The entire fleet was without water, and smallpox was running rampant. It was thus deemed absolutely necessary that they retire to some isolated place where water could be procured in safety, and each vessel could be carefully examined. The nearest such place likely to answer these needs, Dunmore believed, was St. George's Island, in the Potomac River.[33]

Even the simple undertaking of sailing up the Bay was fraught with difficulty. As the poorly manned ships got underway, a strong gale struck, driving one flour-laden supply ship aground and wreaking havoc with others which had reached the mouth of the Potomac.[34] One large ship, injured in the gale and at first thought to be Dunmore's own, was so badly damaged that she was obliged to keep herself afloat by lashing empty casks and hogsheads to her sides. In desperation she sought the aid of H. M. S. *Otter*, which then lay near the mouth of the Rappahannock River, but "after puting her loading on Board the *Oatter* [sic] [she] sunk and totally disappeared."[35]

Another ship, commanded by Captain Parker of Norfolk, mounting two carriage guns and twelve swivels and manned by a crew of eighteen, was driven across the Bay to the Eastern Shore and stranded. Parker and his crew wisely surrendered to the local militia. Soon after Parker's surrender, a boat from his ship's consort attempted to cut her out of the creek before the rebels could secure her, or before she broke up entirely. Perceiving the consort's designs, the militiamen lay in ambush on either side of the creek. When a boat party from the consort entered the creek, the militiamen rushed into the water, muskets ablaze, killing five of the consort's crew and driving off their ship.[36]

Many ships suffered damage to their precious rigging and sails in the storm, and many more lost anchors and small boats while trying to ride it out. Two vessels were driven ashore in St. Mary's County, their smallpox-ridden crews too weak to fight the gale. "This Misfortune," Hamond noted, "to a Fleet ill provided before, was not to be remedied, so that many Vessels were condemned to be destroyed in consequence of it."[37]

Despite the gale's shattering effects on the fleet, on the morning of July 13, Southern Maryland was astonished to see fifty-eight sail in the Potomac, eight in the Bay, and more coming up every hour.[38] Within two days, the number would increase to nearly eighty.[39] Reconnaissance landings on St. George's were soon underway. On July 16, protected by harassing gunfire from a hastily contrived but effective row galley, Dunmore's troops were landed on the island. They proceeded to throw up a breastwork, and began in earnest the search for fresh water.[40] Much to Dunmore's distress, none was found.

On July 20, Hamond and Dunmore, with a force consisting of the warships *Roebuck, Dunmore, William,* the row galley *Anna,* and a prize vessel, sailed from St. George's, leaving the armada under the protection of the frigate *Fowey.*[41] By 10:00 A.M. the following morning, the squadron was off Cedar Point in the Potomac River. After dispatching the row galley to Ladler's Ferry to capture three ferryboats there, the little flotilla proceeded upriver.[42] Finally the expedition came to anchor two miles below the port of Dumfries, Virginia, and began watering. A brief foray ashore against rebel militia units gathered at Brent's Plantation ensued but Dunmore, having gathered the necessary water supply, retired downriver.[43] Though it was a five-day voyage, past the treacherous Kettle Bottom Shoals, off Cedar Point, the governor's squadron arrived just in time to thwart an attack against his floating town precariously anchored off St. George's by the Maryland State Navy warship *Defence.*[44]

It now seemed that he was being hounded by the rebels at sea as well as by those on the land. "I do declare I know not where we can go with our present force to make a Harbour of any tolerable safety."[45] Again, he succumbed to Hamond's advice. H. M. S. *Otter* was directed to escort as many refugee vessels as possible down the coast to St. Augustine, Florida.[46] Nearly fifty went; the remainder would sail with the governor to New York or be disposed of.

From those which were to be destroyed, everything of value was removed, so far as possible. On July 31, a brig was hauled alongside *Roebuck* and portions of her cut up for firewood. The remainder of the vessel was scuttled.[47] Twenty more ships were hauled onto the shoals at the eastern end of the island, dismasted, and burned on August 2.[48] Within hours, the remnants of Dunmore's floating town—once ninety ships strong but now reduced to nine vessels—hoisted anchors and set sail down the Bay.[49] Near the mouth of the Chesapeake, the final sacrifices were made when the sloop *Susannah*, prize to the ship *Pembroke*, was stripped and ignominiously scuttled. Three miles from Cape Henry, two more ships were burned and sunk.[50]

Having lost in battle or destroyed a total of forty-five ships belonging to the most unusual armada ever assembled, John Murray, Fourth Earl of Dunmore, sailed from the Virginia Capes on August 5 with only six vessels. The last Royal Governor of Virginia had been evicted forever.

Chapter Seven

CATO, HAWK, AND NAUTILUS

HENRY HOOPER of Dorchester County, Maryland, was exasperated when he sat down on the evening of July 26, 1780, to write a letter to the governor of Maryland. Almost since the beginning of the Revolution, the Eastern Shore of both Maryland and Virginia had been a battleground where an unending series of raids and skirmishes between the strong Tory element and the weaker patriot Americans took place. Usually the Tory raids were conducted by waterborne "picaroons," and resulted in large property losses. Commerce between Maryland and Virginia had come to a standstill. Occasionally, the Maryland state government responded by sending several of the state navy's armed barges down to chase the Tories away, but as soon as the state vessels had departed, the enemy returned. And now, they were at it again.

"Sir," Hooper began,

> I would begg Leave to inform your Excellency that there are several small Tory-Boats cruising in Hoopers Streights and Tangier Sound that are daily taking some of our Craft. I am informed that they plunder our Islands of Cattle and Sheep. I have sent Capt. Smoot with a party of Militia in quest of these Banditti but from the Want of a proper Boat I apprehend he will not be able to effect anything. Wicomico and Nanticoke Rivers are intirely block'd up by these Picaroons. If your Excellency would be pleased to dispatch one of the State Boat's to Hooper's Streights to Act in Consort with Capt. Smoot I think they may probably capture some of these Pirates . . . One of the Tory Boats is a Barge of thirty two Oars and thirty men, mounts one or two Swivel Guns and the Crew generally lay on Baron Island at Night. . . .[1]

Hooper's plea was typical of those dispatched with irritating regularity to Annapolis, and just as typically acted upon with little or no haste.

In September a Tory force of sloops and barges ascended the Potomac, entered the Wicomico, plundered the inhabitants, and then struck at Point Lookout on their return.[2] On September 29 it was reported that the flotilla had ascended the Nanticoke to the town of Vienna where they landed, though only thirty-two men in number, without the slightest opposition from the local militia or the residents. While at Vienna the picaroons went about their business of destruction. A new brigantine belonging to Robert Dashiell, and another belonging to Joseph Dashiell, a ship belonging to James Shaw, and another belonging to a certain Mr. Travers, were seized in the river and burned to the waterline. They "hove down a New Vessel Belonging to Prichet Willeis that was Building and Destroy'd all the Tools the poore man had & did him much more Damage. . . ."[3] Within a short time similar raids were being carried out on the Pocomoke and Annemessex Rivers, with equally saddening results.[4]

Despite the urgent requests for assistance from Eastern Shore inhabitants, the Maryland government was nearly powerless to act. Several state navy boats, an armed barge, and a whale boat were sent down, but they were so weakly manned that the local population had to be enlisted to fill out their complements. And when they did arrive, the enemy had long since departed. The results were usually not worth the effort.[5]

In early November, the picaroons struck again. This time they entered the Patuxent River with a force of three armed schooners and proceeded as far as Point Patience, where they burned the plantation of John Parran and carried off two tobacco-laden vessels.[6] Again a request for assistance was forwarded to Annapolis. This time the government directed that a substantial naval force be sent to cruise against the enemy. Due to inhospitable weather conditions, however, the squadron's departure was delayed. Finally, on November 14 a little flotilla of the Maryland State Navy was ready to sail from Baltimore.[7] Unfortunately, there was an inexplicable delay of another five days before sailing orders reached the squadron commander, Commodore James Tibbett.

Tibbett's orders were open-ended. He was directed to take his "Fleet," consisting of the hired privateer *Cato*, the armed schooner *Nautilus*, and two armed boats "to cruise down the Bay to protect the Trade of the State and defend the Inhabitants thereof, most exposed to the Depredations of the Enemy." Should any unforeseen events arise, Tibbett was directed to "be governed by [his] own Judgement and Discretion."[8]

By November 25 the Maryland squadron reached Tangier Island, thought to be a picaroon stronghold. The weather was rough, *Cato* was undermanned, and the picaroons were, of course, nowhere to be seen. Tibbett's "Judgement and Discretion," seconded by seven of his ten officers, was to return up the Bay![9]

Less than two weeks after his departure, the picaroons attacked again.[10] This time the privateer sloop *Porpoise*, hired by the frustrated state government, and the Maryland Navy barge *Dolphin* were sent out.[11] Their expedition was no more fruitful than Tibbett's.

In early January 1781 the Maryland government found a more positive use for its ships. *Cato*, *Nautilus*, and the schooner *Hawk* were loaned to the Maryland Council of Safety to carry several thousand barrels of flour to the Continental Army. It was an important chore, for the flour was a scarce commodity and valuable. *Cato*'s cargo alone was valued at £3,000.[12] But the transit, at least in the Bay, was expected to be fairly safe. No one, least of all the commanders of the three ships, expected to encounter anything more than a few picaroons who, if past accounts proved reliable, were not likely to engage a regular Maryland navy warship. No one considered that the Royal Navy might have an interest in the backwater war on the upper Chesapeake.

On January 22 *Cato*, *Nautilus*, and *Hawk* were plodding along off the western shore of the Bay on a southerly course. They were heavily laden which slowed their speed considerably. Suddenly, the lookout aboard the lead ship spotted the sails of a large vessel. The mystery ship's sheets were billowed out, and she was bearing down fast. It was soon apparent to the three astonished Maryland ships that they had run into an enormous British man-of-war. She proved to be H. M. S. *Isis*, of 50 guns and 350 men. With the warship making directly for them under full sail, there was little Captain Bull, of *Hawk*, or his fellow masters aboard *Nautilus* and *Cato*, could do but run their ships ashore and save what they could before the enemy arrived.[13]

The three vessels were just past the mouth of the Patuxent when the warship was spotted and approximately midway between Cedar Point and St. Jerome's Creek when the decision to run them ashore was made. Within a few minutes the ships took a landward tack and simultaneously ran aground near the plantation of a Mr. Bellwood. *Nautilus*, being the shallower of the three vessels, was able to get closer into the shore than the deep-draft *Cato* before she struck. It was a stroke of fortune probably saving many of her men's lives.[14]

Heaving to, *Isis* immediately dispatched boarding parties to capture the three stranded ships. *Hawk*, which was further out, proved to be the first target of convenience. Captain Bull had no intention of giving up the ship without a fight, but he lacked enough ammunition to make a stout resistance, and the vessel was set afire and burned to the waterline. Whether what occurred in the next few minutes was planned by Bull, or whether it resulted from an accident is unknown. What happened, however, had tragic consequences for both sides.[15]

The British paid scant attention to the burning ship, and moved quickly to capture the next closest vessel, Captain Benjamin Wicks's brig *Cato*. This ship was carried with little difficulty. As soon as the ship was taken, they immediately set about plundering whatever they could. Then several seamen entered the ship's magazine, "which blew up carrying 10 of theirs & six of our people." The explosion was so great that the vessel's stores were blown as far forward as the pumps, and in some cases entirely to pieces. More than a third of the ship had been destroyed. Within a few minutes of the explosion, the Chesapeake's muddy waters claimed the remaining two thirds.[16]

In the meantime, Captain James Kiersted, commander of *Nautilus*, had landed his guns and established shore batteries to protect his stranded ship. Satisfied that *Cato* and *Hawk* were done for, and unable to safely attack *Nautilus*, H. M. S. *Isis* departed. Captain Bull, who had managed to escape ashore, did his best to salvage whatever he could of the valuable cargo, but succeeded in recovering barely two hundred barrels of flour.[17] On January 27 Colonel Samuel Smith, from Baltimore, arrived to take charge of the salvage operations. Most of the ships' crews were still in the area, but Smith found them unwilling to preserve anything but rigging and furniture. Yet, buoyed by the fact that Bull had managed to recover some of the cargo intact, and by the hope that the remainder might not be too badly damaged by the seawater, Colonel Smith proceeded zealously with his task.[18]

On the 28th, enlisting the aid of a local militia commander, Major Ignatius Taylor, Smith offered every eighth barrel of flour saved as payment if the St. Mary's County Militia could be induced to help. Unfortunately, "the avarice, avidity & Lazyness of the Inhabitants" prohibited a quick operation. While engaged in the recovery, he learned that *Cato*'s somewhat surly crew had already embezzled much of the cargo for their own profit before his arrival. The local population, having seen little flour since the war began, was willing to pay inflated prices to the crew, knowing full well that the cargo still belonged to the Maryland Council of Safety or to the Continental Army.[19]

Smith persevered. He discharged the ships' crews and a party of black slaves provided by the locals and hired another crew of twenty white laborers. By January 28 nearly seven hundred barrels were saved and piled high on the beach in Mr. Bellwood's yard.[20] On February 7 the Maryland Council of Safety determined to have the flour removed to Baltimore where it was to be sifted, baked, and repacked for shipment.[21]

Though *Cato* and *Hawk* were lost beyond hope, pumping to refloat their consort *Nautilus* was started in earnest on January 27. It was said that the vessel "[was] high up & [would] be saved."[22] By February the brig had been refloated and returned to Baltimore.[23] By the end of the month she was back in service, again carrying flour and corn on government business.[24]

Chapter Eight

SO MANY ARMED VESSELS

O N JANUARY 11, 1776, the Virginia Convention resolved:
That the Committee of Safety shall, and they are hereby
empowered and required to provide, from time to time, such and
so many armed vessels as they may judge necessary for the
protection of the several rivers in this colony, in the best manner
the circumstances of the country will admit. . . .[1]

With these few words the Virginia State Navy was created,
a force destined to grow inordinately large, in numbers if not in
accomplishments, by the end of the American Revolution.
After one year it consisted of five brigs, one sloop, seven row
galleys, and two armed boats. Over the next three years, an
additional nine ships, three brigs, two galleys, and four armed
boats would be commissioned and added to the force. Despite
its size, the Virginia Navy was no more successful in its mission than its smaller sister to the north, the Maryland State
Navy. Its losses, however, would be substantially greater.
Strangely enough, the Virginia Navy's first loss resulted not
from combat but from a simple foundering.

Norfolk Revenge was a row galley fitted out in May 1776
under the command of Captain John Calvert.[2] On July 12 the
vessel was formally commissioned, and on the following day
ordered to harass the enemy's shipping, namely the fleet of Lord
Dunmore, which had been operating with impunity in Chesapeake Bay.[3] Calvert had little success along these lines, and was
ordered to proceed to Hampton on October 26 where he was to
refit. He was then to begin another cruise of the Bay to annoy

the enemy and provide convoy to friendly vessels headed for the Capes.[4] The galley saw little service throughout 1777, and in the spring of 1778 was anchored in the Nansemond River, Virginia, while apparently serving as a prison ship under the command of Captain Wright Westcott. On May 28 *Revenge* foundered in the river with the loss of many of her prisoners and crew. Captain Westcott and the few survivors were immediately directed to proceed to Jamestown for a hearing. Salvage operations, carried out by state navy schooner *Peace and Plenty*, were immediately begun, but apparently little of value could be recovered.[5]

The galley *Lewis* was the first Virginia Navy vessel to be lost as a result of a military action. This vessel, taken into service around the middle of June 1776 under the command of Captain Celey Saunders, was in September directed to proceed in company with the galleys *Page* and *Defiance* and the sloop *Hornet* to Yorktown to embark North Carolina troops being sent to join Washington's army in New Jersey.[6] The soldiers were transported up the Chesapeake to the Head of Elk where they were to be disembarked.[7] In December *Lewis* was employed in transporting munitions on the York River.[8] Two months later, in February 1777, in company with the galley *Page,* she cruised about the mouth of the Rappahannock for the purpose of annoying the enemy, protecting friendly craft, and preventing the defection of black slaves to the British.[9]

The end for *Lewis* came in 1778, when she was stationed in the Rappahannock River. There she was attacked by a large enemy naval force and obliged to retreat upriver. The British followed in hot pursuit. Hoping to elude her pursuers, *Lewis* fled into Carter's Creek and, by favor of an extremely high tide, ran into a millpond which was at that time on a level with the outer waters as a result of the recent collapse of its dam. Despite the uniqueness of her hiding place, the galley was discovered and captured, but not before her master and crew escaped into the nearby woods. Unable to carry off their prize, probably because of the ebb of the tide, the British set her afire and retired down the river.[10]

One of the largest setbacks for the Virginia navy, and, indeed, the entire state of Virginia, came in May 1779, when

British General Sir Henry Clinton dispatched an expedition to attack the Gosport Navy Yard. Twenty-two transports convoyed by a flotilla of Royal Navy warships commanded by Vice Admiral Sir George Collier sailed from Sandy Hook, New Jersey, with 1,800 men under the command of Brigadier General Edward Mathew to carry out the task. On May 10 the British sailed with impunity into the Elizabeth River, attacked and captured tiny Fort Nelson, and on the following day seized Portsmouth, Gosport, Suffolk, and several other small towns in the vicinity.[11] General Mathew found that the retreating rebels had burned the 28-gun Virginia State Navy ship *Virginia*, then abuilding on the stocks, and two French merchantmen in Norfolk harbor, one of which was laden with bale goods and the other with over a thousand hogsheads of tobacco. The British efficiently did the rest. Eight warships were taken intact while on the stocks, along with several merchantmen in the roads. Many privateers which had fled up the different branches of the river, along with a number of merchant craft, were captured and destroyed. All told, an incredible total of 137 ships fell into the enemy's hands, many of them laden with tobacco, tar, and turpentine. Since there were not enough seamen for so many prizes, most were burned, scuttled, or otherwise destroyed. At Suffolk, 1,000 barrels of salted pork, 8,000 barrels of tar, pitch, and turpentine, and a vast quantity of miscellaneous stores and merchandise (much of it earmarked for the Virginia Navy) were set ablaze. More than 3,000 hogsheads of tobacco were also destroyed. After pillaging Portsmouth, putting Suffolk to the torch, and inflicting a loss estimated at £2,000,000, Collier and Mathew prepared to sail back to New York loaded with an enormous amount of plunder. But not before the Gosport Navy Yard, the target of their attack, and the eight ships on the stocks there, were totally destroyed.[12]

"The conflagration in the night," wrote one eyewitness,

> appeared great beyond description, though the sight was a melancholy one. Five thousand loads of fine seasoned oak-knees for ship-building, an infinite quantity of plank, masts, cordage, and numbers of beautiful ships of war on the stocks, were all at one time in a blaze, and all totally consumed, not a vestage [sic] remaining but the ironwork that such things had been.[13]

The destruction of Portsmouth was a hard pill for Virginia to swallow, especially the loss of the eight warships nearing completion, the largest of which would have mounted thirty-six guns. And bad news seemed to beget bad news.[14]

At about the same time as the loss of the Navy Yard, the Virginia State gunboat *Dolphin*, Captain John Cowper commanding, set off from Nansemond River on a cruise in search of Tory privateers and picaroons near the Virginia Capes. Cowper's crew of seventy-five were ready for anything, and the captain himself had nailed the ship's flag to the mast, vowing, "cost what it might, never to strike to an enemy."[15]

Dolphin stood away toward the mouth of the Bay, skirting Cape Henry into the Atlantic. Observers ashore soon noted three sails on the horizon with the gallant little gunboat bearing down on them. The action which ensued, witnesses reported, was long and doubtful. When the firing ceased, three sails bore away to the east. Neither *Dolphin* nor any of her crew were seen again. The gunboat was presumed sunk in battle with all hands.[16] Cowper had been as good as his word.

The following year Virginia was again to be ravaged, this time by a 1,200-man enemy force commanded by the American traitor, General Benedict Arnold. The purposes of Arnold's invasion were the destruction of all military stores in the state, the rallying of Tories to the British flag, and the prevention of Virginia reinforcements reaching the army of General Nathanael Greene, then locked in combat against Cornwallis in the Carolinas. On December 30 the invasion fleet sailed into Hampton Roads, and with little opposition landed Arnold's troops. The British marched boldly across Virginia and entered Richmond without the loss of a single man. The work of destruction, at which Arnold had achieved a noted mastery, was carried out with speed and efficiency. Public and private buildings, military stores, and munitions were put to the torch and the town was sacked. The traitor retired his army to winter at what was left of Portsmouth. Despite a French naval force under the command of Le Bardeur de Tilly, which had been sent out to destroy his naval support, an effort ending in miserable failure, Arnold's army remained secure at Portsmouth until spring.[17]

In March 1781 the British were joined by a major reinforcement of 2,600 under Major General William Phillips which had been sent down from New York. Learning that a force of 1,200 men under the Marquis de Lafayette was on the march to attack him, Arnold moved to counter. On April 18, with a force of 2,500, he embarked his flotilla of transports at Portsmouth, dropped down to Hampton Roads, and then set sail up the James. Six days later he disembarked at City Point and commenced a march on Petersburg, a small town on the Appomattox River where tobacco and munitions in large amounts were stored. After defeating a force of American militiamen under the command of General Peter Muhlenberg, he took Petersburg, burning more than four thousand hogsheads of tobacco and a number of ships lying in the Appomattox River.[18]

Arnold then turned his attention to the Virginia State Navy, several vessels of which lay anchored off the little village of Osborne's, fifteen miles down the James from Richmond. The Americans had assembled the flotilla there sometime earlier in anticipation of conducting a concerted attack with the French fleet against Portsmouth. Arnold marched on Osborne's with the 76th and 80th Regiments of Foot, the American Legion, a detachment of German jägers, and the Queen's Rangers.[19]

Every precaution was taken to insure surprise, and the British were successful in coming up on the fleet without being detected. The Americans were more than a little astonished to see an army appear as if from nowhere. Arnold immediately dispatched a flag of truce to the Americans, offering to take only half the contents of their cargoes if they did not destroy any part. The Americans replied that they were determined and ready to sink their ships rather than surrender to the hated traitor.[20]

The general did not persist in negotiation and promptly ordered two 3-pounders stationed near the stern of the 20-gun ship *Tempest*. The warship had been anchored with springs on her cables to permit rapid maneuvering while at anchor but was only able with great difficulty to bring her broadside to bear on the battery. For a few minutes the fire was both hot and smart, until another British battery of two 6-pounders was unmasked

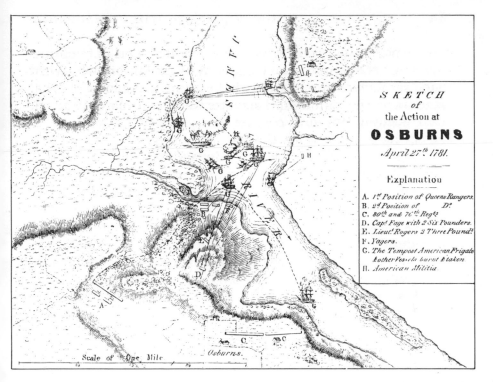

A contemporary sketch plan of the action at Osborne's, Virginia, and the destruction of the Virginia State Navy squadron in the James River. From Simcoe's *Military Journal*. Courtesy: Library of Congress.

and opened with great effect from a different quarter. Unfortunately for the Americans, their guns were loaded only with
round shot, for they had been expecting an attack by water
rather than land. Had grapeshot been used, as even the British
acknowledged, the gun crews at the two batteries would have
been quickly killed or driven off.[21]

In an effort to drive the Americans from the decks, Arnold
directed Lieutenant Colonel John Simcoe to have the Queen's
Rangers and a party of jägers rake the decks with musket fire. As
Simcoe prepared to carry out the order, a lucky shot cut *Tempest*'s spring, and the ship swung around, a helpless slave to the
river current. The vessel now became subject to a raking fire
from the battery of 3-pounders. Her situation was hopeless, and
her crew quickly took to their boats. At that point Simcoe's
Rangers and jägers opened up on the fleeing crew with a deadly
fire. Many of the American sailors chose to jump overboard
rather than risk the killing fire. Suddenly, the musketry
stopped, and a British officer parleyed with the boat crews to
surrender. There was little choice, and the Americans
accepted.[22]

As a British party rowed out in the newly captured boat to
take command of the *Tempest*, the rest of the fleet panicked,
and the Americans began to sink or burn their ships. Desperately, the British tried to stem the tide of destruction. One
officer, Lt. Fitzpatrick of the Queen's Rangers, under a blinding
hail of musket fire from the shore, cut the cable of one ship,
placed a prize party aboard, moved on to another, and then to
another. Reaching the headmost vessel in the line, he seized her
forward gun and turned it on the terrified Americans.[23]

The scene was one of complete pandemonium. One ship
which had been anchored near the *Tempest* was blown up, and
the fire transmitted to the captured warship's topgallant and
forestay sails. Captain McKay, an officer of the 76th Foot,
MacDonnell's Highlanders, managed to cut the burning ship's
cable, permitting the current to drive her aground on the eastern shore of the river, which was occupied by the King's troops.
The Britishers immediately boarded her and extinguished the
flames.[24]

One band of rangers, led by a young soldier named Armstrong, had been deposited onboard another of the burning ships by Lt. Fitzpatrick. Unfortunately, the soldiers discovered that the fire aboard the abandoned warship had grown to such proportions that it could not be brought under control. Yet without a boat they found themselves trapped. Armstrong immediately plunged into the river, swam ashore to procure the only boat available, rowed back out, and took his men off, none too soon. Just as the last man was off, the fire reached the ship's magazine, blowing her to bits.[25]

Such scenes were repeated throughout the fleet as British soldiers braved fire and shot to save what they could. Ultimately, one 20-gun ship, a 16-gun brig, two lesser brigs, and a sloop were captured. The losses in ships by burning or sinking were disastrous to the Virginia Navy. Four ships, including the 20-gun *Tempest* and the 26-gun *Renown*, five brigs, including the 14-gun *Jefferson* and a number of lesser vessels were totally destroyed.[26]   Elated by their victory, the British sent their prizes down to Portsmouth, leaving behind them more than half of the Virginia navy on the bottom of the James.

In May, the British moved toward the Chickahominy, where many of the remaining Virginia Navy galleys lay, along with the 20-gun ship *Thetis*, which had just been launched. The Virginia State Navy Yard on the river was under the command of Captain William Saunders. Learning of the threat imposed by the approaching force, Saunders determined to save his fleet and their cargoes by concealing them further up the river. Unfortunately, wind and tide conspired against him, and his whole force was obliged to come to. Springs were put on the cables of each vessel, and the last of the Virginia State Navy quietly awaited the enemy. The British were not long in coming, and after a brief skirmish, it was soon apparent that the vessels could not be saved. *Thetis* was captured by the enemy and burned, but to Captain Saunders fell the sad task of sinking the fleet. Thus virtually ended the short-lived Navy of Virginia.[27] Six months later, however, America would have her revenge at a small Virginia port town—Yorktown, on the York River.

Chapter Nine

THUNDER AND LIGHTNING

THE TINY schooner had paid scant homage to the turbulent seas as she scudded through the predawn blackness a few miles north of Cape Charles. She had been in pursuit of a barely defined line of ghostly lights all night and not about to retard her progress when the gap was closing so rapidly. The three men aboard the craft, James Robinson, Jonas Rider, and Robert Moyse, were exhausted after six days at sea, constantly dodging the dangerous shoals of the Virginia Capes to elude French naval patrols. The sighting of the lights a few hours earlier had given them new hope and courage, for they fully expected them to belong to a mighty fleet of British warships.[1]

Two of the three men, Robinson and Rider, were free black seamen. Robinson had been a pilot aboard the *Charon*, a three-year-old British frigate, while Rider had served as a seaman aboard the private sloop *Tarlton*, belonging to a Mr. Young of New York. The third man, Moyse, was a white man who had belonged to the dispatch boat *Lapwing*. Ever since August, the men shared a common enemy and a common dilemma. And now, they were joined together to achieve a common goal—escape from American military imprisonment.[2]

It is impossible to know exactly what passed through the minds of these wet and weary seamen as they closed with the long line of lights off the Virginia coast in those predawn hours of October 24, 1781, but it is likely that the events of the previous three months were still vividly impressed upon them. Robinson, Rider, and Moyse were witnesses to one of the most important chapters in American military history: the Siege of Yorktown, Virginia.

It had all begun for them near the end of July when a massive armada of British ships—transports, victuallers, and commercial merchantmen—had been pressed into Royal Navy service. Their mission had been to carry an army of nearly seven thousand men commanded by General Charles Cornwallis from a temporary base at Portsmouth, Virginia, to the little village of Yorktown on the banks of the muddy York River.

Cornwallis had been directed sometime earlier, after months of maneuvering and fighting in the Virginia interior, by the British Commander in Chief in North America, General Henry Clinton, to establish a fortified base on the Chesapeake readily accessible to a large British fleet. It was also to be suitable for the army's defense. Clinton had suggested Old Point Comfort as a likely spot, with Yorktown as an alternative. Upon consultation with the senior naval officer in the Chesapeake, Captain Charles Hudson of H. M. S. *Richmond*, Cornwallis selected the alternative, noting that Old Point Comfort would be an untenable position in case of enemy attack. Both Cornwallis and Hudson were of the opinion that the army should be removed to Yorktown and her sister village of Gloucester, on the north side of the York, "where we apprehend a better Port can be established for the Protection of the King's troops."[3]

On July 30 the massive evacuation of Portsmouth began. Twenty-three transports, nine victuallers and a mélange of private and commercial ships sailed under the protection of H. M. S. *Charon*, 44, *Guadeloupe*, 28, *Loyalist*, 26, *Bonetta*, 14, and *Swift*, 14. The first shipment of more than forty-five hundred soldiers was embarked when the fleet sailed on the short trip to the York. Two ships, H. M. S. *Fowey*, 20, and the fireship *Vulcan*, were left behind to guard the remainder of the forces at Portsmouth. On August 1 the vanguard of the fleet arrived at the York, and on the following day began landing operations at Yorktown and Gloucester. *Guadeloupe, Loyalist*, and *Swift*, with a flotilla of transports, were soon on their way back to Portsmouth to complete the evacuation and assist in the destruction of the temporary fortification there. Within a few more days, the entire army had been brought up and the majority of the ships belonging to the flotilla came to anchor between the two towns.[4]

The ships composing this large fleet were, for the most part, tired veterans of from four to six years' service in the American theater. The sixth-rate ship *Fowey*, for instance, and a great portion of her 160-man crew saw practically unbroken service from the opening shots in the tidewater in 1775, when the last royal governor of Virginia, Lord Dunmore, had fled aboard her in mortal fear.[5] The 380-ton victualler *Nancy* was among those vessels which carried arms and ammunition from England to General Howe's besieged troops in Boston during the initial days of the conflict. Another victualler, the 298-ton ship *Diana*, threaded the cordon of rebel privateers to reach Barbados to secure armaments, salt, peas, oatmeal, and oil for Howe. The victualler *Betsey*, 266 tons burthen, kept the British garrison in East Florida supplied with powder. And the transport *Elizabeth* managed to get arms through to Governor Guy Carleton, just before the vigorous American attack on Quebec; arms which had meant the difference between British victory or defeat in Canada. There were many other ships with similar services to boast about.

Robert, 254 tons, *Houston*, 258 tons, and *Favorite*, 221 tons, were with Admiral Gambier in New York in 1779. The troop ships *Bellona*, 308 tons, and *Two Brothers*, 336 tons, saw service at Pensacola, while *Lord Howe*, 240 tons, and *Neptune*, 216 tons, served with Admiral Parker during the Savannah Campaign in that year.[6]

For the most part, the rest of the ships lying moored in York River had similar wartime pedigrees, often unglamorous but nonetheless important to the British war effort. These vessels included the transports *Shipwright*, Thomas Kay, *Andrew*, Francis Todridge, *Lord Mulgrave*, Andrew Casterby, *Harmony*, John Duffield, *Providence*, Benjamin Huntley, *Emerald*, Robert Tindall, *Selma*, John Crosskill, *Sally*, Arthur Elliott, *Horsington*, Christopher Jolson, *Race Horse*, Christopher Chesman, *Oldborough*, Lionel Bradstreet, *Present Succession*, William Chapman, *Success Increase*, John Sanderson, *Concord*, Andrew Monk, *Fidelity*, Robert Pilmour, *Mackrell*, William Fraser, and the victuallers *Mercury*, Andrew Ryburn, *Ocean*, John Walker, *Providence Increase*, Thomas Berriman, *Rover*, John Beveon, and *Harlequin*, Thomas Skinner.[7]

In addition to the regular warships, transports, victuallers, and assorted smaller craft belonging to the Royal Navy, there was a sizable contingent of privateers, merchantmen, and private vessels of every description which tagged along with the fleet when it left Portsmouth.

Cornwallis was confident that he had done the right thing by moving to the York. Though he felt the position was not entirely suitable, he believed himself secure in his chosen post on the white marly bluffs overlooking the river. His army was numerically superior to the ragged Continentals under Lafayette, and he was daily in expectation of a strong fleet. Thus, the work of fortifying Yorktown was carried on at a somewhat less-than-hurried pace. The general had begun to feel cocky, a fact which became more apparent to friend and foe alike with every passing day. He was, he explained to Clinton, only going on the defensive to hold the port open for the fleet until the hot weather passed.

The first indication that all would not be going as planned came on August 29. It was a shimmering, hot day, and *Loyalist* was on picket duty near the mouth of the main channel at the entrance to the Virginia Capes with little in the way of diversion from the tedium of such duty. At about midday, the lookout spied the familiar form of the frigate *Guadeloupe* bearing down from the York under full sail. She was carrying dispatches and had been assigned to take a look into the Atlantic to see if the grand fleet expected by Cornwallis was yet near. *Guadeloupe* passed her sister ship with barely a sign of recognition as she headed into the open sea. Suddenly, she was seen abruptly to tack and come about as if the devil himself were in her wake. Several large ships now became visible in the distance. Their signals were unrecognizable, and it was apparent that their intentions were not friendly. *Guadeloupe* was a fast ship and easily outran her pursuers. *Loyalist* was not as fortunate, and soon found herself helplessly swept up in the onslaught of the vanguard of an enormous fleet of French warships. After a brief exchange of artillery fire, she was dismasted and captured by the French 74-gun ship-of-the-line *Glorieux*.[8]

The following day *Guadeloupe* returned to Yorktown with the terrible news. An enemy fleet, believed to be thirty or forty ships strong, and of all classes, had arrived. The Capes were blockaded, and Cornwallis was shut off from the sea.[9]

The French fleet now off the Capes was commanded by Rear Admiral de Grasse, and consisted of no less than thirty-six ships-of-the-line, including the monstrous 110-gun flagship *Ville de Paris*, ten frigates, two sloops-of-war, and an armed ship.[10] De Grasse proceeded to institute his blockade of the Chesapeake with businesslike thoroughness, insuring that Cornwallis was not only shut off from the sea, but from escape to the Carolinas as well. Three ships, *Experiment*, 50, *Andromaque*, 32, and *Diligente*, 26, were immediately sent into the James to prohibit a British move to the south.[11] The warships *Triton*, 64, and *Glorieux* and the frigate *Vaillant* were dispatched to seal off the mouth of the York.[12] The remainder of the fleet came to anchor in a gigantic semicircle off the mouth of the Capes themselves.[13]

Cornwallis, indeed upset over the turn of events, was not one to panic. Efforts were made to notify Clinton in New York of the situation by sending out row galleys, whaleboats, and small schooners, with messages in cipher, often written on the backs of American bank notes, requesting relief. It was hoped that at least one or two of the vessels might elude the French blockade. On August 31, the schooner *Mary* managed to penetrate the French cordon. She carried the last news to reach New York for more than a week.[14]

With the arrival of the French, Cornwallis increased the tempo of his fortifying work at Yorktown. Captain Thomas Symonds, commander of the frigate *Charon* and senior naval commander on the York, busied himself preparing water batteries ashore for the defense of the river. Most of the artillery and ammunition from his ship had already been landed, and the greatest portion of his crew was lodged in tents on the beach at Yorktown and employed in battery construction. The sailors seemed to be constantly digging, though there was a serious shortage of tools. Fewer than four hundred of the army's supply of axes, spades, and wheelbarrows could be found for use in the construction of the water batteries. Both *Charon* and *Guadeloupe* were moored head and stern opposite a small creek above the town to enfilade a gulley across which an attack on the British works might be made.[15]

Within the next few days, Cornwallis learned that the French had not only arrived with a fleet, but had also deposited a 3,100-man army under the command of the Marquis de Saint-Simon on Jamestown Island. Cornwallis nervously assured his officers that Saint-Simon's corps were little more than "raw and sickly troops . . . undisciplined vagabonds, collected in the West Indies," who would quickly fall victim to the first winter chills of the Virginia Tidewater. The landing was carried out uncontested. Cornwallis was now hemmed in by land and sea, but he was confident that the blockade could not last for long.[16]

On September 5 the sounds of a naval battle were heard by the British at Yorktown, coming from somewhere in the vicinity of the Capes. No one could pin it down exactly, and it was at first dismissed as "some slight skirmish" in which a small British naval force had encountered the French squadron and been forced to withdraw. Three days later Cornwallis discovered these astonishing facts: a major fleet engagement between a 27-ship squadron under Admiral Thomas Graves, bent on the relief of Yorktown, and de Grasse's fleet had been enjoined off the Capes; the British had been driven back to New York in a shattered condition after losing the 74-gun ship of the line *Terrible* and the frigates *Isis* and *Richmond*; and the blockade had been maintained.[17]

Soon afterward came even more distressing news from Clinton, in dispatches written on September 2 and 6: Washington was on the march toward Yorktown with at least six thousand American and French troops to close the trap. Cornwallis was beginning to feel the noose tighten. Now the British had little alternative but to redouble their efforts to fortify their position.

For days after the Battle of the Virginia Capes, the French fleet presented a disturbing affront to the army at Yorktown. Frigates and ships-of-the-line alike daily ventured into the river, without the slightest fear. By September 21 the bulk of de Grasse's fleet lay anchored between York Spit and Horseshoe Shoals. The position de Grasse assumed cut off the last of Cornwallis's communication with New York and the Eastern Shore. It was up to the Royal Navy at Yorktown to reopen that line. Captain Symonds directed Captain Palmer of the *Vulcan* to take his four-ship squadron of fire ships to "proceed in the Night, whenever the Wind offered to endeavour to destroy the Enemy, or drive them from the Post they had taken." Palmer seized the first opportunity, at midnight, September 22. The fire ships were heavily laden with tar, sulphur, and other combustibles when they dropped quietly down the river. Manned by skeleton crews and carried by a stiff breeze, they reached the lumbering French warships in two hours. Suddenly, prematurely, one of the fire ships was ignited by her master, a privateersman who had volunteered for the duty. Only at the last minute did the frigate *Vaillant* save herself by cutting her cable and drifting out of the way. She was soon being imitated by others. Two of the ships-of-the-line were run ashore and another damaged in the scene that ensued. The fire ships were totally destroyed, but Cornwallis's lines of communication were reopened.[18]

Six days later the combined armies of Generals Washington and Rochambeau, which had finally reached Williamsburg, took up the march on Yorktown. By October 6 the main allied force had surrounded the British fortification and begun the erection of batteries. At 3:00 P.M. on October 9, the batteries were ready to be opened.[19]

The first barrage, delivered by a French unit under Saint-Simon, succeeded in driving *Guadeloupe* from her post near the creek and across the York to the Gloucester side. By early the next morning, four allied batteries were in operation, totaling forty-six cannon, and were firing with telling effect. A truce was called at noon, and the uncle of Virginia's Governor Thomas Nelson, who had been held in the town, was released. He brought news that Cornwallis was informed that Clinton would be there with help in five days. The attack was renewed with astonishing ferocity.[20]

With the encirclement of his forces, Cornwallis became aware of yet another danger—the possibility of French naval assault on his exposed riverside. Thus, on the first day of the allied bombardment, he sought to deny the French access to the Yorktown beach by scuttling more than a dozen of his transports and victuallers in a semicircle near the shore.[21]

On the evening of October 10 the French batteries began to throw red-hot shot amid the crowded British ships anchored in the river. This was somewhat like shooting fish in a barrel. One shot, which smashed into H. M. S. *Charon*, caused a spectacular blaze which lit the midnight sky.[22] Dr. James Thacher, serving in the American Army, left an eyewitness description of the last moments of the frigate and several nearby transports.

"The ships," he recorded in his journal,

> were enwrapped in a torrent of fire, which spread with vivid brightness among the combustible rigging, and running with amazing rapidity to the tops of several masts, while all around was thunder and lightning from our numerous cannon and mortars, and in the darkness of night, presented one of the most sublime and magnificent spectacles which can be imagined. Some of our shells, overreaching the town, are seen to fall in the river, and bursting, throw up columns of water like the spouting of the monsters of the deep.[23]

Charon's mooring lines were soon broken, probably burned through, and the big frigate promptly swung around with the current and slammed into the anchored transport *Shipwright*, locking her in an unbreakable death grip. Soon the two ships drifted across the black waters to the Gloucester shore, where their incineration was completed. They were not alone, as still another transport fell victim to the same end.[24]

Cornwallis, beset by heavy losses and the approaching trenchworks of the allies, was rightfully despondent. He wrote Clinton on the evening of following the loss of *Charon*, "that nothing but a direct move [by Clinton] to York River which includes a Successful Naval Action can save us." Two hours after the completion of his letter, the allies had begun digging trenches to approach important redoubts, Nos. 9 and 10, on his left flank. Three days later the works were carried and despite a feeble British sortie and temporary capture, remained in allied hands.[25]

Cornwallis was now certain that he could not expect help from Clinton or Admiral Graves in New York. On the night of

October 16 he resolved to make one last desperate attempt to save his army. He would ferry his men across to the Gloucester side and break out through the weaker allied positions there. With a skeleton force of Germans left behind, and Navy gunners keeping up a steady fire to fool the allies, the first wave of troops, a thousand strong, was carried across the York in small boats. But before a second wave could be ferried, a vicious squall blew down from the northwest, scattering the boats necessary for the operation and making the evacuation impossible.[26]

There was no alternative but to surrender. As flags passed between the allies and the British, Cornwallis was determined to see that nothing of use would fall into the enemy's hands. The frigate *Guadeloupe* was scuttled, and *Fowey* was hauled into shallow water where carpenters bored holes in her hull to sink her. All of the transports and victuallers, with the exception of *Bellona* and *Andrew*, were scuttled, along with a number of commercial merchantmen.[27]

Like most of Yorktown's defenders, James Robinson, Jonas Rider, and Robert Moyse were not informed of the high-level decisions, but were aware of the impending surrender. There were many obvious indications: the firing had miraculously ceased and continual communications were being carried on between opposing forces; the town's merchants were desperately attempting to get their property ashore from the merchantmen in the river, as it was said the vessels would all be given up to the French; and, finally, there was the obvious fact that the British could no longer withstand the allied attacks.[28]

Moyse had even heard rumored the exact hour and day the army was to capitulate. Thus, like many in the besieged town, the three men had resolved that escape was far preferable to surrender and possible imprisonment. On October 18, in company with several crewmen belonging to the sloop *Tarlton*, the trio quietly sailed down the York in a four-oared boat in hopes of slipping through the French lines and reaching New York. Twice they fell into enemy hands, and twice they escaped. After six harrowing days at sea, they finally fell in with a powerful armada of British warships commanded by Admiral Thomas Graves, aboard which were Clinton and a relief force for Cornwallis.[29]

When Robinson, Rider, and Moyse boarded Graves's enormous 90-gun flagship *London*, the three men could not know how significant the events of which they had been a part were to world history. They had, perhaps unfortunately, missed the final act. On the afternoon of October 20, the army of General Charles Cornwallis marched in dignity onto the fields of Yorktown to the tune of "The World Turned Upside Down" and surrendered. The American Revolution would officially drag on for another two years, yet most of the fighting was over. Clinton was too late. At the bottom of the York River lay the mute testimony of British defeat. American independence had been assured.

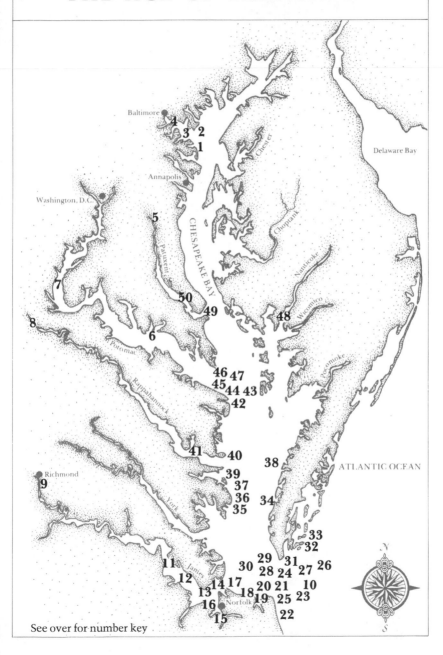

Baltimore

4
3 2
1

Delaware Bay

Annapolis

Washington, D.C.

5

CHESAPEAKE BAY

Chester

Choptank

Patuxent

Nanticoke

7

50

49

Wicomico

48

8

6

Potomac

Pocomoke

Rappahannock

46 47
45
44 43
42

41

40

38

ATLANTIC OCEAN

Richmond

9

39
37
36 35

34

York

33
32

29
31 27 26
30 28 24
11

James

14 17

20 21 10
18
19 25 23

12

13
16 Norfolk

15

22

N

S

See over for number key

MAP KEY: AGE OF TRANSITION

1. Unidentified (1806)
2. *Eagle* (1824)
3. *Mary* (1808)
4. *Union* (1785), *Medora* (1842), *Paul Jones* (1843)
5. U. S. Chesapeake Flotilla (1814)
6. *Ousatonic* (1833)
7. *Union* (1837)
8. *Fredericksburg* (1845)
9. *James Gibbon* (1840)
10. Unidentified (1785)
11. Three unidentifieds (1784)
12. *Hero* (1785)
13. *Favorite* (1788), *Nantz* (1791), *Martin* (1797), *Revanche du Cerf* (1811), Three unidentifieds (1807)
14. *New York* (1805), *Two Friends* (1806), *Ceres* (1806)
15. *Patriot* (1788), *Security* (1788), Three unidentifieds (1791)
16. *Betsey* (1807), *Powhatan* (1823), *Bladen* (1854)
17. Unidentified (1807)
18. Unidentified (1785)
19. *Nestor* (1806), Two unidentifieds (1806)
20. Unidentified (1784)
21. *Warrington* (1806)
22. *Maryland Packet* (1786)
23. *Lucy* (1810)
24. *Robert* (1809)
25. *Nancy* (1785)
26. Unidentified (1785)
27. Unidentified (1785)
28. *Nancy* (1791)
29. Unidentified (1800)
30. *Nonsuch* (1787)
31. *William Murdock* (1808)
32. *Anthony Mangin* (1799)
33. *Joseph and Peggy* (1787)
34. *York* (1785)
35. Unidentified (1784)
36. *London Packet* (1806)
37. *Monmouth* (1856)
38. *Betsy* (1798)
39. Unidentified (1800)
40. *Ocean* (1784)
41. *Cambridge* (1853)
42. Two unidentifieds (1807)
43. *North Carolina* (1859)
44. Unidentified (1787)
45. *Stapleton* (1806)
46. *Carmelite* (1805)
47. *Columbus* (1850)
48. *Lord Charlemont* (1785)
49. Two unidentifieds (1807)
50. U. S. Gunboats *No. 137* and *No. 138*

Chapter Ten

A DISASTER LOG CONTINUED

THE YEARS following the conclusion of the American Revolution in the tidewater region, despite a nationwide postwar depression, saw an enormous increase in maritime commerce. The port of Baltimore was growing by leaps and bounds, outstripping even the Maryland state capital at Annapolis. The new federal city of Washington, just below the fall line on the Potomac, was born and, together with the port of Georgetown, was expected to give the port of Alexandria, just downriver on the Virginia shore, a run for its money. There were other towns and cities on the rise as well—such as Norfolk, Fredericksburg, and Richmond—all hoping to share in the wealth promised by the nation's hard-won independence and the growing tidewater commerce.

But with the incredible growth of maritime activity came an inevitable increase in maritime disasters. The year 1784 proved to be particularly costly. In January, during a frigid cold snap, the James River was suddenly frozen over, imprisoning numerous vessels. The losses were many. At Burwell's Ferry, for instance, one large ship was hulled by the ice and sank at its anchorage. Two other smaller vessels bound for Portsmouth also were hulled and sank.[1]

On February 3 six more vessels were lost in the James as a result of a violent storm which wrought havoc throughout the tidewater. One of its victims, the passenger ship *Ocean*, Captain Beass commanding, bound from Rotterdam with a load of German emigrants was driven aground on a shoal off Windmill

Point, above the mouth of the Rappahannock while working up the Bay, and was totally lost. The storm also resulted in the stranding and loss in the Bay of another vessel above New Point Comfort. This ship, commanded by Captain Ireland, was apparently the scene of a murder as well. It was reported that when the ship ran aground, "some of her passengers, with part of the crew perished, and that her captain had been assassinated by one of the sailors."[2]

Another loss attributable to the February 3 gale was an unidentified brigantine in Lynnhaven Bay. The vessel, en route from London to the tidewater, encountered foul weather and was run aground. Though part of her cargo was saved, the ship was entirely lost.[3]

The following year "the most tremendous gale of wind known in this country," a dreaded "nor'easter," struck the tidewater in late September. The storm raged for three solid days, between the 22nd and the 24th, driving more than thirty vessels ashore. It was later reported that most of the vessels got off, although several victims could not be saved.[4] One brig, sunk in Lynnhaven Bay, had been en route from Dumfries, Virginia, to London with a cargo of tobacco when lost, and was unsalvageable. A Dutch ship, bound from Philadelphia for Norfolk to take on a load of tobacco for France, hit just off the Capes and was totally lost. A third ship, inward-bound from Antigua to Norfolk with a cargo of rum, struck while entering the Capes, and was also lost. The brig *Nancy*, Captain Eastwood commanding, incoming from Madeira with a cargo of wine, was dashed to pieces on the Virginia Capes. The only survivors of the disaster were the captain and a boy.[5]

Having survived the storms of September, the packet ship *York* succumbed to another which followed soon after, at the beginning of October. The storm reportedly "drove [her] from her moorings at Cherrystones [Virginia,] opposite colonel Savage's, and carried [her] into the bay, where she sunk. Captain Walters and the crew saved themselves by swimming." The same gale also drove John Straton's merchant sloop from its moorings in King's Creek, Virginia, "into a cornfield of Colonel Robin's." Though the sloop was high and dry, Straton and his entire crew perished in the storm.[6]

In November the French merchant ship *Union,* while en route from Port-au-Prince to Bordeaux under the command of Captain Sebastian Neau, began taking on water and turned into the Chesapeake to make repairs. Discovering that most of the repair facilities were booked solid in the Virginia ports as a result of the recent storms, Neau decided to try the port of Baltimore. There his ship began undergoing repairs, but accidentally caught fire and was entirely destroyed along with its cargo.[7]

Two other merchantmen were also reported lost at about this time. The first was the ship *Lord Charlemont,* Captain Mackey, bound from Dublin for Maryland, and inexplicably disappeared while in the Nanticoke River.[8] The second was the ship *Hero,* Captain McCarty, bound from London for the James, where she was stranded and, finally, bilged.[9] During the summer of 1786 the ship *Maryland Packet,* Captain Brown, was noted as lost on Cape Henry while en route from London to Maryland.[10]

In May 1787 an unidentified schooner, bound from the island of St. Bartholomew in the West Indies for Maryland, was reported cast away on Smith Point, at the mouth of the Potomac, and became a total loss. One of the few survivors, a young boy, made his way alone from the Potomac to Norfolk. There he informed the press that he believed himself to be the only survivor of the disaster, and that the vessel had carried only two passengers, besides the crew: a Mr. Connelly of Norfolk and a Captain Brown of Philadelphia. It was later learned that others had indeed survived, separately making their way ashore at various points along the beach after the disaster.[11]

The second loss in this year was that of the ship *Nonsuch,* Captain Wallace, which had been stranded and bilged on Middle Ground soon after entering the Capes from London. Little other data concerning this wreck has been found.[12]

The most notable wreck to occur in 1787 was that of the packet ship *Joseph and Peggy.* Owned and commanded by Captain Joseph White, the ship was bound from New York to Portsmouth and Norfolk, Virginia, with a small cargo of rum, when lost. While en route, in early May, she encountered gale force winds and hazy weather which prevented White from taking observations. He thus determined, when he reckoned to be off the Virginia Capes, to steer on a westerly course until a landfall was spotted. Upon sighting land, he ordered soundings to be taken. The water was between three and four fathoms deep, but his position was still uncertain. Suddenly, the ship struck bottom, and appeared to be grinding against a reef. Within a very short time, it was obvious that the ship was doomed as waves began to break over her. Captain White, his crew, and a single female passenger climbed into the shrouds, where they remained until the following morning, May 10. With no assistance in sight, and the ship in imminent danger of breaking up, there seemed no alternative but to attempt to reach the nearest land. Undoubtedly with considerable difficulty, the haggard party managed to reach the shore of Smith Island, near the entrance to the Virginia Capes. Here, however, instead of receiving aid they were plundered by a number of "ruffians in the form of men." The thieves not only took advantage of the shipwreck victims but seized everything of value from the wreck that washed up on the beach, including barrels of rum. "The boors of Cornwall," it was noted later in the *Maryland Gazette*, "would have blushed of such behaviour." Eventually, the survivors made their way to civilization and safety. Most of *Joseph and Peggy* had gone to pieces barely minutes after its abandonment by the passengers and crew. Part of her hull, however, drifted free and was driven into Lynnhaven Bay where it went ashore, and was taken up by Lemuel Cornick and his slaves in behalf of the survivors.[13]

On Wednesday, July 23, 1788, another in a devastating series of hurricanes ripped its way across the lower Chesapeake. A letter printed in the *Times* of London several months later detailing the gale noted, in a classic bit of understatement; "we had a most violent storm of wind and rain, which increased during the night. . . ." Among the losses was the schooner *Patriot* stranded and bilged near Portsmouth, Virginia. Another schooner, Captain White's *Sincerity*, driven aground near the Portsmouth distillery, was a total loss. A third vessel, an unidentified brig, newly constructed, was actually lifted from her moorings and deposited in the main street of the town. Captain John Hughes's ship *Favorite*, trying to ride out the storm in

Hampton Roads, was completely destroyed, while Captain Hunter's ship *Mermaid*, anchored nearby, was run ashore. *Mermaid*'s cargo was later saved, and the vessel refloated with great effort, though she did lose her masts. Captain Wallace's brig *Neptune*, driven ashore and at first thought unsalvageable, suffered only the loss of her bowsprit and foremast and was later refloated.[14]

The next major shipping loss came more than three years later. On April 16, 1791, another severe storm accompanied by extremely high tides inflicted costly damage to Portsmouth, Virginia. Many vessels were driven ashore, destroyed, sunk, or damaged. Among the vessels lost were several schooners, two of them commanded by Captains Brown and Cowper. An unidentified Baltimore schooner and the cargo she carried were also entirely lost.[15]

On December 2, 1791, the merchant ship *Nancy*, Captain Sharp commanding, left Virginia for Europe with a cargo of tobacco. "The vessel," it was reported, "in coming down the Chesapeake, got on the Middle Ground and was so much damaged that she sank on her way to Norfolk." Another vessel, *Nantz*, Captain Forster, also bound from Virginia to London, was lost at about the same time in Hampton Roads. Since the two incidents were only reported in the British press well after the fact, it is possible that the two losses may be a garbled account of the same sinking.[16]

The next years saw relatively few losses, most of which were small coasting sloops and schooners. The only notable loss occurred in 1797, when the ship *Martin* bound from Virginia to London was driven ashore and lost in Hampton Roads during a gale.[17]

In 1799 the ship *Anthony Mangin* came to grief on Cape Charles. The ship had set sail from Hamburg on November 28, 1798, under the command of Captain Edward Sanford with a cargo of dry goods bound for Baltimore. It had been a miserable voyage for Sanford and his crew of seventeen, for the entire trip had been one of continuous foul weather and heavy gales. On February 10 the captain managed to get an observation and found himself in the latitude of the Virginia Capes. But try as he might, the freezing winds kept driving him back out to sea, and it was not until February 20 that he was finally close enough to try a run in. Once he could get into the Bay, Sanford fully expected to be met by a pilot boat which might assist his battered ship. At 6:00 P.M. the weather worsened. No lights from the shore or a lighthouse were to be seen. The captain, believing himself to be to the south of the Capes, laid the ship on a course to the north under a close-reefed topsail and mizzen. It was a dangerous calculation, sailing by dead reckoning, but he was confident and figured to be in the Bay by midnight.

At 10:00 P.M. the extent of Sanford's miscalculation struck home when the ship was driven onto a shoal a little to the north of the tip of Cape Charles. Within less than ten minutes *Anthony Mangin* had completely filled with water and lay a victim to the pounding seas. Several of the crew "immediately cut loose their longlines, in order to try to save their lives; but the sea broke over them so heavy, that the boat was beat to pieces on the deck. . . ." Eight of their number were lost. In desperation, the crew attempted to climb the rigging to get into the tops to prevent being washed overboard. They remained there until noon of the following day as their ship was being beaten to pieces beneath them.

The weather finally cleared at noon on the 21st. Captain Sanford, at last able to see land, resolved to construct a raft and try for shore to secure assistance. With two crewmen and a passenger named Williams, the captain diligently set his plan into action. A raft was constructed from the debris of the ship and bravely launched by the four men. No sooner had they shoved off, however, than their conveyance capsized, and all aboard perished.

The remainder of the crew, now suffering from frostbite, were slowly freezing to death in the shrouds, and most certainly would have died had help not come. Several were already near death. The wreck was reported to be "much frosted" over with ice when the rescuers finally arrived. Eventually, part of the cargo was salvaged by Nathaniel Wilkins, Customs Collector for Northampton County, Virginia, and a Mr. Savage, County Comissioner of Wrecks.[18]

One of the more touchingly tragic accounts of a loss in the post-Revolutionary period concerned the foundering of the schooner *Betsy* on April 22, 1798. Under a reefed foresail the vessel was scudding along down the Bay before a strong west wind, making excellent time even though deeply laden with a cargo of wheat and flour. Her master, Captain Duncan, had recently lost his wife and was taking the opportunity of this voyage to remove his family (a younger brother, his own two infant children, a sister, and a niece) to a new home.

As the ship sailed on, Captain Duncan became concerned when the seas broke over his bow with every swell although there had not been a change in the wind or weather in hours. He had had the ship pumped dry half an hour before but decided to check below again, and was astonished to find three feet of water in her hold. Now, for some reason, pumping failed to keep the level down, and so the crew quickly ripped up the cabin floor to expedite bailing. But, all efforts proved to be in vain. *Betsy* was approximately five miles off Cradock, Virginia, on the Eastern Shore, when Captain Duncan spotted a vessel at anchor off his starboard bow. In desperation, he turned his own craft toward her, but the water was now rushing in too fast. The schooner began to sink. One of his crewmen, a mulatto, tried to cut the schooner's small boat loose but bungled the job and scampered up the mast in abject fear. "When all hopes of saving the vessel were over," it was later reported, "[Duncan] held his two children one in each arm, at the risk, and certainly the cause, of his not saving himself." His body was later found with one of his children clasped tightly to his breast. His vessel had gone to pieces in eighteen feet of water. The only survivor was the mulatto.[19]

Occasionally, there was no one left to tell the tale. In December 1800 the merchantman *William*, en route from Elbe to Virginia, took on a pilot off Smith Island, one of Virginia's barrier islands at the mouth of the Bay, to guide the ship through the Virginia Capes. The pilot informed the master of *William* that the region had just been subjected to a severe gale, and that in coming out he had fallen in with a ship's longboat and yawl while passing Middle Ground. He had stopped to inspect the yawl, which had a compass and three oars in her, he said, but the longboat was sinking and had a "great many beds and buckets floating around her." On December 15, when *Wil-*

liam passed Middle Ground, her master spotted the mizzen topmast of a ship sticking up out of the water from a depth of six fathoms and supposed it to be the ship from which the longboat and yawl had come. The following day, December 16, *William* was sailing up the Bay. Passing the mouth of the Piankatank River, again in six fathoms of water, the master spied the tops of a large schooner which had sunk. "Her mainmast [was] on end but all her rigging gone but her shrouds. . . ." *William's* master took her to be a recently built vessel as the shrouds and boom appeared new. Neither of the two sunken ships was ever identified, for both of them had apparently been lost with all hands.[20]

Though shipping losses in Maryland were not as great as in Virginia, they still occurred with regularity owing to the shoaly nature of much of the Maryland tidewater. In January 1805, for instance, the brig *Carmelite,* from Bordeaux, France, after experiencing fierce gales and foul weather, managed to enter the Bay and drop anchor near the Tail of the Horseshoe Shoals to ride out the storm. When both her anchors parted, the master, Captain Hunt, had little choice but to take her before the wind up the Bay. Unfortunately for him, the wind shifted to the northwest. He found it impossible to get further up, and the ship was driven ashore and lost on Point Lookout. Her crew and cargo, fortunately, were saved.[21]

At about this time, the schooner *New York,* Captain Smith commanding, twelve days out of New York City and bound for Virginia, entered the Capes and was injured in her stern by an ice floe. She was forced to run aground on Sewell's Point, Virginia, where she bilged and was lost.[22]

One of the worst years on record for shipping in the tidewater was 1806. On January 8 the entire Bay area was blinded by a terrible snowstorm. In Lynnhaven Bay, Captain Dirreck's ship *Nestor,* sailing under Trinidad registry and bound from Cuba to Baltimore with a cargo of logwood and fustic, was driven ashore. Another vessel, an unidentified merchant sloop bound from Rhode Island to Norfolk, was also driven ashore there and lost.[23]

Four months later, on the night of April 12, the ship *Stapleton,* of Baltimore, Captain Hays commanding, bound from the city of Santo Domingo to Baltimore with a cargo of mahogany, became stranded on Smith Point. The ship was first spotted the day after her grounding by the schooner *Federal George*, Captain Fields, which was en route from Boston to Baltimore. A signal of distress was fired from *Stapleton* along with a request for a derrick to help get her off. Apparently *Federal George* found it impossible to get in to assist, although an unidentified pilot boat had managed to come close enough to find out who she was. Though it was at first expected that the ship might be gotten off, subsequent records are silent on the point.[24]

In the same month another ship, *London Packet*, was lost in the Virginia tidewater. This particular vessel, commanded by a Captain Spafford, was bound from Baltimore for the Mediterranean with stores for the U. S. Navy squadron there when she was cast away and lost on Wolf Trap Shoals during a storm.[25]

Two gales in the month of December wrought considerable damage to shipping in the Bay. The first occurred on the third and fourth of the month. The ship *Two Friends*, Captain Williams, en route from Baltimore to Havana, Cuba, and the brig *Ceres*, bound from Baltimore for New York, were both driven ashore and lost on Sewell's Point, in Hampton Roads. A number of smaller Bay craft were also reported lost there during the storm.[26]

On December 15 a blizzard swept across the entire tidewater. In the upper Bay an unidentified schooner was driven aground and lost on Bodkin Point at the mouth of the Patapsco River. Another vessel, described as "a Northern built schooner," was stranded and bilged in Lynnhaven Bay. Also driven ashore and bilged during the storm was the ship *Warrington*, en route from Boston to Norfolk and Baltimore with a cargo of rum and beef. The ship had fortunately been driven ashore at the lighthouse on Cape Henry, and part of her cargo was saved. The wreck of *Warrington* was spotted soon after her loss by the Baltimore-bound schooner *Mary*, Captain Almeda commanding, eighteen days out of Havana with a cargo of sugar.[27]

During the first week of February 1807 an unidentified merchant brig belonging to the firm of Redmond and Frith, commanded by Captain Tudor Frith, is noted as having stranded above Willoughby Point.[28] On March 31 of that year, the Bay was struck by strong gales, driving an Alexandria schooner and another vessel bound to Baltimore hard aground from their moorings in the Patuxent River. The latter, a Bay boat, was reported entirely bilged. During the same storm, an unidentified brig, schooner, and sloop were driven ashore in Hampton Roads and lost.[29] On Monday, September 28, the schooner *James*, Captain Beard commanding, en route from Cuba to Baltimore, passed a large two-topsail schooner stranded on Smith Point.[30] Again, about November 27, two more schooners were spotted stranded on Smith Point, this time by the schooner *Fame*, twenty-five days out of Guadeloupe with sugar and coffee. Though one of the stranded vessels reportedly got off, the other remained hard aground and was probably lost.[31] Sometime during the year, the American merchantman *Betsey*, commanded by Captain Tredwell, was burnt while at anchor near Norfolk, and totally lost.[32]

In January 1808 the British merchantman *William Murdock*, en route from Rotterdam to the Potomac, in ballast and under the command of Captain Brooks, came to grief on the shoals of Cape Charles, fortunately without the loss of lives.[33] On September 12 the ship *Mary*, Captain Hunt commanding, was destroyed during a gale, while at anchor near Baltimore.[34]

The ship *Robert*, Captain Stocking commanding, while en route from Jamaica to Philadelphia, was wrecked on the shoals of Cape Henry on August 31, 1809.[35] The following year the Capes claimed still another victim. This time it was Captain Pickman's ship *Lucy*, bound from Madeira to Baltimore with a cargo of wine. Though the vessel was entirely lost on Cape Henry, her crew and a portion of her cargo were saved.[36]

On April 16, 1811, the citizens of Norfolk witnessed the destruction of the privateer *Revanche du Cerf*, which had been captured earlier in the year by American naval vessels, and hauled into Hampton Roads. Off Norfolk, the ship was stripped and put to the torch by her captors.[37]

The billows of black smoke which arose from the ship spread across Hampton Roads like a pall. Perhaps it was an omen. Perhaps it was nothing at all, but the smell of a burning vessel undoubtedly caused more than a few old-timers to shudder. The memories of the destruction of Portsmouth during the last war were readily evoked as the acrid smoke wound its way into the nostrils of the old salts. Talk of war was again on everyone's lips. Soon it would be more than talk.

On June 1, 1812 the President of the United States requested Congress to issue a declaration of war against Great Britain. And once again the Chesapeake tidewater became the focal point of military contention, a conflict in which large quantities of commerce and shipping would unwillingly suffer.

Chapter Eleven

THE MUCH VAUNTED FLOTILLA

BARELY eight months after President James Madison announced the opening of hostilities between the United States and Great Britain, a contest which history would record as the War of 1812, Chesapeake Bay had virtually become a British lake. The waterfront towns and plantations of the tidewater region succumbed with startling regularity to Royal Navy depredations. Plantation establishments on islands in the Bay and in its many tributaries (such as Sharps, Pooles, Tilghmans, Poplar, Blackistone, St. Clement's, and St. Catherine), were regularly attacked and plundered. Frenchtown, Maryland, was burned to the ground, and Havre de Grace fell with little resistance. Hampton, Virginia, was captured and pillaged, and many of its residents cruelly brutalized. From their fortified base on Tangier Island, the British maintained a wooden wall of ships which efficiently throttled maritime commerce in the tidewater. The British awaited only a large infusion of land troops to carry out a major attack on urban centers such as Norfolk, Baltimore, Annapolis, and Washington. With only a few frigates available for the defense of the Chesapeake—and these already blockaded in—Secretary of the Navy William Jones appeared incapable of coping with the crisis. He needed money, men, and ships, all in critically short supply. But, most of all, the navy secretary needed a comprehensive plan of action which could stand a modest chance of success and a man capable and determined enough to carry it out.

On July 4, 1813, Joshua Barney, a native Marylander, Revolutionary War hero, and privateersman of great renown,

penned for Jones an unsolicited plan for the defense of the
Chesapeake. Barney recognized that the enemy awaited only
the arrival of land forces before an attack could be made on the
major cities of the tidewater area.

> I am therefore of [the] opinion the only defence we have in our
> power, is a kind of barge or row-galley, so constructed, as to draw
> a small draft of water, to carry oars, light sails, and one heavy
> gun. . . . Let as many of these barges be built as can be manned,
> form them into a flying squadron, let them be continually watch-
> ing and annoying the enemy in our waters, where we have the
> advantage of shoal water and flats in abundance throughout the
> Chesapeake Bay.

The flotilla could hover about the enemy constantly, preventing the nuisance attacks that had hitherto been unopposed.

> Should the enemy land all their forces with a design on any of our
> cities, they must be met in the field, but unless their heavy ships
> can cover the landing, and receive them on board again, the barge
> squadron might, and could cut off a retreat by acting in concert
> with our troops on shore.

One barge would cost less than $3,000. Fifty such vessels would
cost less than half the price of a conventional frigate, provide
the same firepower, and go where a frigate would not dare to
go.[1]

Barney's plan was accepted by a grateful Secretary of the
Navy on August 20, 1813, and in early September Barney was in
Baltimore attending to the birth of his little squadron. The first
vessels of the flotilla were purchased and included the tiny row
galley *Vigilant*, and barges *No. 5* and *No. 6*, all acquired from
Baltimore's own flotilla defense force. The row galley *Black
Snake* and the 3-gun schooner *Asp* were dispatched from Washington, along with the flagship-to-be, the topsail sloop *Scorpion*, which formerly belonged to the Potomac Flotilla. Two
antiquated Baltimore-built gunboats, *No. 137* and *No. 138*,
were also added. The backbone of the squadron, however, was
to be two newly designed classes of barges, one seventy-five feet
long and the other fifty feet long. Each of these was armed with
a single carronade forward and a long gun aft, and each was to be
constructed under contract at both Baltimore and St. Michaels,
Maryland.[2]

By the spring of 1814, Commodore Barney's construction program was on schedule, but recruitment was going slowly. Nevertheless, enemy depredations having again resumed, Barney sallied forth with eighteen vessels to attack the main enemy base on Tangier Island. His force included the *Scorpion, Vigilant, No. 137, No. 138,* six 50-foot-class barges, seven 75-foot barges, a lookout boat, and a small flotilla of merchantmen bent on running the blockade.[3]

On June 1, 1814, the Chesapeake Flotilla encountered superior British forces led by H. M. S. *Dragon,* 74, and *St. Lawrence,* 18, off St. Jerome Creek, St. Mary's County. After a brief skirmish off Cedar Point, the American squadron was obliged to retreat into the Patuxent River. With the arrival of a strong reinforcement of frigates, the British imposed a blockade of the river and prepared to attack the flotilla. Barney, outgunned nearly seven to one, retired into the shallow fastness of St. Leonard's Creek, a narrow tributary a few miles up the river which was shouldered on both sides by steep highlands.[4] The British immediately pursued. On June 8, 9, and 10, a nearly continuous series of naval battles, the first major flotilla engagements ever fought in Maryland waters, were carried out on the creek's waters as the British sent wave upon wave of their own barge forces in against the Americans. Unable to enter the creek with their large warships, the British were met by a stout resistance and routed after each encounter.[5]

Assured that Barney could not be defeated in his lair, the British commander, Captain Robert Barrie, sought to lure the flotilla into the open by forcing it to come to the defense of the towns and plantations of the Patuxent. The British soon instituted a campaign of terror, laying waste to town and farm alike in an effort to force Barney's hand. Calverton, Huntingtown, Prince Frederick, Benedict, and Lower Marlboro were among the towns either burned to the ground or totally plundered.[6]

On June 26, his spirit fortified by the arrival of reinforcements from the U. S. Army under Colonel Decius Wadsworth, and U. S. Marines under Captain Samuel Miller, Barney resolved on a breakout. A stunningly successful predawn attack by land and sea on the blockading frigates at the mouth of St.

Leonard's sent the British reeling and permitted the flotilla to move upriver to Benedict. Gunboats *137* and *138*, however, too sluggish for speedy escape, were scuttled in the creek to prevent capture after the flotilla's departure. To avenge their defeat, a strong British force ascended the abandoned creek, captured and burned the ancient (1683) town of St. Leonard's at its head, and vandalized the sunken gunboats. The Royal Navy, however, was not inclined to reengage Barney.[7]

In mid-August, with a British invasion force of nearly four thousand hardened veterans of the Napoleonic Wars aboard, the largest armada of warships ever to visit Maryland waters came to anchor off the Patuxent. Under the overall command of Admiral Sir Alexander Cochrane and tactical control of Admiral Sir George Cockburn, this force had as its objective nothing less than the capture and destruction of Washington, D. C. However, instead of the obvious route of advance—up the Potomac—Admiral Cockburn suggested an ascent up the Patuxent and a landing at Benedict. From there the army, under the command of General Robert Ross, and a strong barge force, three times as large as Barney's, might ascend in tandem, using the Chesapeake Flotilla as a pretext for the advance. The flotilla, which had retired above Pig Point (modern-day Bristol) could then be destroyed. Once the army gained Upper Marlboro, it might then swing west and, after a forced march, capture Washington by surprise.[8]

Realizing the possibility of the flotilla's falling into enemy hands, Secretary of the Navy Jones ordered Barney to take the squadron as high up as possible, even to the old river port of Queen Anne's. Should the enemy appear, he was to destroy the entire American squadron. On August 21 Barney, having come to anchor above Pig Point, left the squadron with the majority of his men to join an American Army under General William Henry Winder which had been gathering at Woodyard, Maryland. A skeleton crew commanded by Lieutenant Solomon Frazier was left behind to destroy the American squadron if necessary.[9]

Admiral Cockburn's own words perhaps best describe the last moments of the Chesapeake Flotilla. Shortly before 11:00

A.M. on August 22, 1814, the admiral began to focus his attention on the capture of Barney's squadron. "I then proceeded on with the boats," he noted in his final report of the affair,

> and as we opened the reach above Pig Point, I plainly discovered Commodore Barney's broad pendant in the headmost vessel, a large sloop, and the remainder of the flotilla extending in a long line astern of her. Our boats now advanced towards them as rapidly as possible, but on nearing them we observed the sloop bearing the broad pendant to be on fire, and she very soon afterwards blew up. I now saw clearly that they were all abandoned and on fire with trains to their magazines, and out of the seventeen vessels which composed this formidable and so much vaunted flotilla sixteen were in quick succession blown to atoms, and the seventeenth, in which the fire had not taken, were captured. The commodore's sloop was a large armed vessel, the others were gun boats all having a long gun in the bow and a carronade in the stern, but the calibre of the guns and the number of the crew of each differed in proportion to the size of the boat, varying from 32 pdrs. and 60 men, to 18 pdrs. and 40 men. I found here laying above the flotilla under its protection thirteen merchant schooners, some of which not being worth bringing away I caused to be burnt such as were in good condition, I directed to be moved to Pig Point. Whilst employed taking these vessels a few shots were fired at us by some of the men of the flotilla from the bushes on the shore near us, but Lieutenant Scott whom I had landed for that purpose, soon got hold of them and made them prisoners. Some horsemen likewise shewed themselves on the neighbouring heights, but a rocket or two depended them without resistance. Now spreading his men through the country, the enemy retreated to a distance and left us in quiet possession of the town, the neighbourhood, and our prizes.[10]

Within several days of the flotilla's destruction, Washington, D. C., was in ruins. When the British withdrew from the Patuxent, the flotilla remains became the target of considerable scavenging. Finally, John Weems of Anne Arundel County was appointed to attend to the salvage of the wrecks. From a base of operations established at Mount Pleasant Landing, he proceeded to recover more than twenty-five pieces of artillery, tons of munitions, most of the squadron's anchors, and a large amount of miscellaneous arms and materials lost with the fleet. Several

A contemporary British portrayal of the destruction of the U. S. Chesapeake Flotilla. (Below) the British, with Admiral Cockburn in the lead, close with the already burning flotilla. (Upper right) the British army led by General Robert Ross marches on Washington. (Center and left) Washington, D. C., the president's mansion, the Capitol Building, and the Washington Navy Yard are burned. The Greenwich Hospital Collection, Royal Maritime Museum, Greenwich, England. Courtesy: Library of Congress.

vessels were raised. Though the *Scorpion* and a large privately owned merchant ship belonging to Georgetown, which had been hired to carry ordnance, received considerable attention, it seemed that their resurrection, even with the aid of the *Asp* sent down from Baltimore, would prove impossible.[11]

Resting in the upper Patuxent River, the hulks which had once been the United States Chesapeake Flotilla were gradually forgotten. They were derelicts of a costly war Americans preferred to forget, except as curiosities noted in a few local histories. Nevertheless, in 1907 the hulks were mentioned in official U. S. Army Corps of Engineers reports.[12] Elderly residents of the region recall that several of the vessels were still to be seen as late as the 1930s; and more than a few watermen grudgingly remember the loss of their nets on the sunken obstructions.[13]

In 1978, with the initiation of the Patuxent River Submerged Cultural Resource Survey, the first comprehensive underwater archaeological survey in the state of Maryland, the United States Chesapeake Flotilla became a focal point of investigation. Carried out by the Calvert Marine Museum of Solomons and Nautical Archaeological Associates of Upper Marlboro, Maryland, under the direction of Dr. Ralph Eshelman and me, an intensive effort was launched to locate the flotilla and to conduct comprehensive archaeological examination of one of its ships.

In 1979 utilizing a proton precession magnetometer, we carried out a remote sensing survey of the upper Patuxent River. The fleet was soon located. The following year, one of the vessels affectionately dubbed the *Turtle Shell Wreck* (because the first item recovered was a turtle shell) became the subject of an intensive survey. Discovered lying in the main river channel near Wayson's Corner and covered by five feet of silt, we found the ship to be in an excellent state of preservation, though her bow section had been torn apart by an obvious explosion. Artifacts of a unique nature, including a complete surgical kit, military accoutrements, and numerous domestic shipboard items were recovered in a remarkable state of preservation, almost as if they had been recently taken down from a store shelf. Unfortunately, with limited funds, the investigation was concluded before the entire ship could be examined, and the ship's hold, into which we had been excavating, was ordered filled in with sediments to assure the site's continued preservation.[14] Our survey team, however, was permitted to leave a memento of their own, a plastic milk jug, tightly sealed, containing the names of the last persons to visit "the much vaunted flotilla."

Chapter Twelve

A GOLGOTHA OF HORROR

GENERAL Horatio Gates, Revolutionary War hero, victor of Saratoga, and the greatest celebrity who ever graced the environs of the village of Shepherdstown, Virginia (now West Virginia), watched with jaundiced eye as the diminutive-looking watercraft was boarded by a number of ladies in their best go-to-meeting finery, each carrying a colorful parasol. With Captain Charles Morrow at the helm, the vessel's inventor and constructor, James Rumsey, a onetime innkeeper, painter of miniature portraits, and many-talented artisan from Bohemia River, Maryland, began to attend to the odd-looking machinery and boilers below. Suddenly, the engines were started, and the vessel slowly moved into the middle of the Potomac, pausing ever so slightly as it met the current, and began chugging up the river against the flow—on its own power. This event which General Gates witnessed on October 3, 1787, was one of the first successful demonstrations of a new era—the Age of the Steamboat.[1]

Robert Fulton has generally been credited as the inventor of the steamer. But his vessel, *The North River Steamboat of Clermont,* did not make its first successful voyage until 1807. By that time at least sixteen steam-powered vessels had been constructed and launched in America;[2] several were in the Chesapeake Bay region. In 1795 a tiny steam-driven packet boat was plying the Potomac between Georgetown and Alexandria, and by 1810, the new Federal City of Washington was being serviced by a packet running from Barry's Wharf on the Eastern

Branch to Alexandria.[3] On June 13, 1813, Captain Edward
Trippe sailed out of Baltimore Harbor in command of the 130-
foot-long Baltimore-built ship *Chesapeake*, the first steamer to
commercially ply the Chesapeake.[4] The new age had finally
begun to bloom, and within a few years commercial freight and
passenger transportation in the tidewater would be dominated
by this revolutionary form of water travel. The cost in lives,
merchandise, and shipping would unfortunately be high, for
with this new era an unfamiliar but devastating new form of
marine disaster was ushered in—the boiler explosion.

On a clear June day in 1816, three years after the opening of
steamer commerce on the Bay and its tributaries, the first
steamboat explosion in America occurred below Marietta,
Ohio, when the boilers of Henry Miller Shreve's stern-wheeler
Washington blew up, killing nine and injuring twenty.[5] The
news caused scarcely a ripple in the far-off tidewater. Soon,
however, such occurrences would be noted in the local Chesapeake press with often sensational but dreary repetitiveness.

On September 20, 1823, the first steamboat explosion in
the tidewater occurred when the boiler of the four-year-old
181-ton steamer *Powhatan*, Captain Coffin commanding, blew
up at Norfolk, Virginia. It is not known if any lives were lost.[6]
The first steamer explosion which is definitely known to have
resulted in loss of life in the Chesapeake occurred on April 18,
1824, less than a year after the *Powhatan* disaster. The 110-
foot-long *Eagle*, constructed in Philadelphia in 1813 and owned
by the Briscoe and Partridge Line, saw her initial service on the
Delaware and in 1814 began the first recorded regular steamboat operations between Philadelphia and Wilmington. In 1815
she was transferred by her owners to the Chesapeake. Brought
around under the command of Captain Moses Rogers via the
Virginia Capes, *Eagle* thus gained the distinction of being the
first steamboat to appear below Cape Henlopen and the first to
traverse the lower Bay. Steaming up to Baltimore, she was also
the first to navigate the entire Chesapeake. Under the banner of
the Elkton Line, *Eagle* made her maiden commercial trip in the
Bay on July 24, 1815, departing from Bowley's Wharf, Baltimore
to Elkton, Maryland. Regular runs were made to Elkton three
times a week, although several excursions down the Chesa-

peake to the James River and Richmond were also undertaken. In 1819 the Elkton Line failed, and *Eagle* was sold to Captain George Weems, who promptly opened up service between Baltimore, Annapolis, and the Patuxent River. Weems operated *Eagle* with little difficulty until that fatal day in 1824. While steaming off North Point at the mouth of the Patapsco, *Eagle*'s boiler erupted in a massive explosion, killing one passenger, Henry M. Murray, and scalding Captain Weems so badly that he would never fully recover. The vessel itself was irreparably damaged and finally scrapped in 1827.[7]

At Leonardtown, Maryland, the tiny 81-ton screw steamer, *Ousatonic*, built at New York in 1825, provided the next casualty. On September 3, 1833 the ship was burned and totally destroyed, though fortunately no lives were lost.[8]

In 1837 the new side-wheel steamer *Union*, owned by Thomas Berry of Oxon Creek, Maryland, was serving as a ferry boat between Alexandria and Fox's Wharf, Prince Georges County, Maryland. On July 13, the ferry master, Joseph Fox, for some unexplained reason, ran a free service all day long, and passenger traffic was heavy. At about 3:00 P.M., as the 71-foot-long boat put out into the Potomac, her boiler suddenly ripped apart in a violent explosion. An eighteen-inch section of the boiler plate and forty bolts were hurled into the massed passengers. Three persons were killed on the spot and their bodies terribly mangled, including the chief engineer's wife and a black couple. Fifteen others were badly scalded and injured, three of them seriously. Later investigation revealed the cause of the explosion.[9]

Though the boiler which had burst was not lacking in bolts or braces, it was discovered that a large quantity of horse dung had been put inside the tube to stop some small leakage. Along with other sediments, the dung had collected and clogged a small space several inches below the furnace, "and prevented the water from preserving the iron, and at the same time the iron became exposed to a hot fire, became heated, and yielded to the pressure."[10]

Another tragedy occurred three years later, on August 28, 1840, when the ten-year-old steamer *James Gibbon*, of 116-tons burthen, succumbed to a boiler explosion while at Richmond, Virginia. Three persons were lost.[11]

In terms of loss of life the worst disaster to occur prior to the Civil War was the destruction of the Baltimore and Norfolk Steam Packet Company's wooden side-wheel steamer *Medora*. Built at Baltimore by the firm of Brown and Collyer, *Medora* measured 180 feet in length, 23 feet 6 inches abeam, and 9 feet 6 inches depth in hold. Construction specifications were strict and directed that the ship be fitted with a lever-beam engine and boilers manufactured from the finest Pennsylvania iron.[12]

On the morning of April 14, 1842, *Medora* lay at her moorings in Baltimore Harbor at the wharf of John Watchman, the man responsible for manufacturing her engine. Watchman was undoubtedly anxious, for his engines were going to get their first workout when *Medora* sailed on her initial sea trial later that day. A large crowd had gathered to watch, and many officials of the Baltimore and Norfolk Steam Packet Company, besides the vessel's regular crew and an assortment of yard workers, boarded for the historic voyage. Expectations were high as the lines were cast off and the ship began to back away from the wharf.[13]

Suddenly, as the giant paddle wheel began its second revolution, an enormous explosion tore through the bow as the boiler blew up. The giant iron boiler itself was hurled into the air, splintering the forward section of the ship into pieces, then falling back and landing crosswise on the deck. Gigantic oak beams became slivers of frayed wood, and massive iron bars were broken or wrenched into grotesque shapes. Instantly, a cloud of steam enveloped the ship, scalding anyone it touched. There was no time to escape, for within moments, *Medora* slipped to the bottom of the Patapsco only a few feet from her wharf and a few seconds into her first voyage.[14] "The lately calm, tranquil and beautiful Patapsco, " one newspaper reported of the event, "in one awful moment has been converted to a Golgotha of horror and desolation."[15]

The crowds who gathered on the shores to view what was expected to be a pleasant, memorable scene were stunned. Then wives and children of workmen and company officials who had boarded began to moan and sob in a growing crescendo of grief. One woman rushed to the water's edge and, looking down, cried out, "What is that?" She stooped and picked up an object floating on the water. It was a human hand. Horrified, she noted the ring upon its finger. On it she read her husband's name: "a love plight" given years before.[16]

"A settled pall of gloom" enveloped the city of Baltimore after the *Medora* disaster. Mayor Soloman Hillen personally directed the recovery of the dead while consoling the families of the deceased. Throughout the day, the booming of cannon could be heard across the waters, for it was the belief of the time that the concussion would make a dead body lying beneath the water rise. The final tabulation counted twenty-six persons killed, thirty-eight injured, and only fifteen unhurt.[17] Despite her tragic beginnings, *Medora* was eventually raised, rebuilt, and taken into service as the steamboat *Herald*, and operated under that name until 1885, when she was abandoned in the Hudson River.[18]

By comparison with the disaster of *Medora*, the loss of Captain Russell's Talbot Line steamer *Paul Jones* two months later seemed insignificant. Built in 1837, this 120-foot-long 157-ton steamer, which had served on the Washington-Baltimore run, suffered a boiler explosion on June 3, 1843, while at Baltimore.[19] Though four lives were lost, only slight notice was given in the press.

The first steamboat reported lost in the Bay due to foundering was the side-wheeler *Fredericksburg*. This 199-ton ship, 112 feet in length, was built in 1827 for service between Baltimore and the Potomac River. In 1842 her owners placed her on a trial service between Baltimore and the Sassafras River and Worton Creek. She was later in service on the Rappahannock River run when she foundered near Fredericksburg, Virginia, on December 29, 1845.[20]

On November 27, 1850, the venerable wooden side-wheel steamer *Columbus* came to her end while steaming off Point Lookout, Maryland. Built in 1829 and operated initially by the Maryland and Virginia Steamboat Company and, later, at the time of her loss, by the Powhatan Line, *Columbus* was 416 tons gross, 137 feet in length, 30 feet abeam, and 11 feet in hold. She carried a conventional "square" or "crosshead" steeple engine with a single 50-inch cylinder and a 6½-inch stroke. While off the mouth of the Potomac, the ship caught fire, burned, and sank, a terrible disaster which occasioned the loss of at least nine lives. Eventually, several days after the tragedy, portions of her gutted hull and machinery were located and partially salvaged.[21]

The next major vessel lost was *Cambridge*, a steamer of 462 tons built in 1846, which sailed under the command of Captain John Griffith. In 1850 from her wharf at Light and Conway Street, Baltimore, she is known to have sailed on alternating days on runs to the Rappahannock River, Annapolis, West River, Choptank River, and to the Chester River, on alternating days. On September 16, 1853, on a normal run to landings on the Rappahannock, *Cambridge* was burned while in Carter's Creek. No lives were lost, and an immediate effort was launched to salvage her machinery. By October 14 her engines were finally removed, loaded aboard a schooner, and towed to Baltimore by the steamboat *Martha Washington*. The burnt-out hulk remained.[22]

The details of the loss of the little 63-ton side-wheel steamer *Bladen* are sketchy. Built in 1853 at Baltimore, the vessel apparently enjoyed a short life, for she appears only once in the records and that as lost at Norfolk, Virginia, in 1854.[23]

Two years later, the side-wheel steamer *Monmouth* became the first steamboat in the tidewater lost as a result of a collision. Built at Baltimore in 1836, *Monmouth* was 184 tons burthen. Though first home-ported at Perth Amboy, New Jersey, she came to Maryland about 1850 and operated as an independent. She is known to have been running between 1850 and the time of her loss between Baltimore and Walkerton, Virginia, at the junction of the York and Mattaponi rivers, with regular stops at Pungoteague, on the Eastern Shore, and in the East River, Mathews County, Virginia. On October 14, 1856, while traversing the lower Bay, she collided with the merchant brig *Windward* off Wolf Trap Light and sank. With the loss of seven lives, *Monmouth* became the last major steamboat casualty with a sizable cost in human life before the Civil War.[24] Many more, however, would follow.

Chapter Thirteen

PEACEMAKER

O N OCTOBER 20, 1842, the first screw steam warship of the United States Navy was laid down at the Philadelphia Navy Yard under the supervision of Captain Robert F. Stockton. Stockton had taken every care in the construction of this most innovative step for the navy, and within a year the U. S. S. *Princeton,* named after the captain's birthplace and the scene of a famous battle of the American War for Independence, was launched and commissioned. Her engines had been built by the firm of Merrick and Towne of Philadelphia, and her three tubular boilers designed by John Ericsson, a man later destined to earn fame for the revolutionary ironclad ship of war *Monitor.*[1]

Stockton was excited about the potentials of his warship.

> She has an auxiliary power of steam and can make a greater speed than any seagoing . . . vessel heretofore built. Her engines lie snug in the bottom . . . out of reach of enemy shot and do not interfere with the use of her sails. . . . Making no noise, smoke or agitation of the water, and if she chooses, showing no sail, she can surprise the enemy.[2]

With a displacement of 954 tons, the ship was 164 feet in length, 30 feet 6 inches abeam, and had a draft of 17 feet. Besides twelve 42-pounder carronades, she was armed with two long 12-inch guns, of Stockton's own design, which tossed enormous shells weighing 225 pounds each. One of the guns, dubbed "Oregon," had been manufactured in England to the design specifications of Ericsson, but the other, "Peacemaker," weighing in at 27,000 pounds, was manufactured in New York and was said to be "by far the better piece of workmanship of the two."[3]

Stockton experienced some difficulty in obtaining manufacturers willing to produce the two wrought-iron guns to the size and design he wanted. When he applied to the New York firm of Hogg and Delameter, which ultimately produced Peacemaker, he was first told the job was impossible. The use of wrought iron in artillery construction had been attempted with regularity for some years, but with frustratingly little success, except in the production of small caliber weapons. The difficulty lay in the welding of the larger parts together, particularly around the breech. Bronze was usually used but was costly, and subsequent overheating of the piece often resulted in inaccuracy when firing. Stockton had run into additional problems when expenditures allocated for the manufacture of the two guns were not sufficient to cover the costs of the expensive trial testing. Thus it was not until the captain promised the New York manufacturer that he would pay all expenses for testing out of his own pocket that the firm consented.[4]

The final trials were stunningly successful, and the jubilant captain reported: "As a gun, it is quite perfect, and I do not think that any charge of powder can injure it; and as a piece of forged work, it is certainly the greatest achievement up to this time."[5]

Having undergone successful sea trials, Princeton sailed from Philadelphia for New York, where she received her two massive guns on January 1, 1844. She was then ordered to Washington, D. C., arriving there on February 13.[6] Both Stockton and the Secretary of the Navy were aware of the interest Princeton had aroused. She was, after all, the most revolutionary, if untried, ship in the navy. In an effort that would make a modern public relations firm envious, Stockton extended invitations to the chief executive, members of the Senate and the House of Representatives, and the upper crust of Washington society to visit the ship. He was not disappointed by the response. On February 16, the public as well as members of the government came aboard and were treated to a voyage down the Potomac. The trip was topped off by the firing of Peacemaker. On the 18th and 20th, trips were made down the river and the guns were again successfully demonstrated. Everyone was thoroughly impressed.[7]

The artillery demonstrations soon became routine for Stockton. Usually, when but a few miles below Alexandria, the gun was loaded with thirty pounds of powder and one enormous cannonball. Stationed in the bow of the ship on a revolving carriage, the piece had such precision that the captain boasted it could hit an object the size of a hogshead in the water nine times out of ten from a distance of half a mile.[8]

All of the preparations for firing, with the exception of loading the powder and ball, were made by Captain Stockton. Visitors were intrigued by the tackle assembly fixed to the breech of the weapon by which a motion was given simulating that of a heavy swell at sea and a "secret" device "known only to the Navy Department and the inventor" which permitted the trigger device to fire at the precise moment the target was in sight.[9]

On February 20, with a large contingent of congressmen aboard, *Princeton* traveled as far south as Mount Vernon, and Peacemaker was fired no less than five times. On the fourth firing, the ball struck land and was lost sight of by the visitors. Stockton was requested to fire the gun a fifth and final time.[10]

"All those in favor of another fire will say, Aye," he shouted. The air resounded with a chorus of "Ayes." "All those opposed to another fire will say, No." Not a solitary voice was heard.

"The Ayes have it," said the captain. "I have the assent of Congress, and I'll go ahead."[11]

This time nearly fifty pounds of powder, an unheard-of amount for a wrought-iron gun, were poured into Peacemaker. As before, the gun was to be fired by Stockton. The ball went nearly four miles, rebounding more than fifteen times off the ice on one side of the river, before it stopped.[12] Stockton's illustrious visitors were awestruck.

On February 28, President Tyler consented to visit *Princeton*. And with him came, it seemed, practically half of the federal government, cabinet members, military officers, statesmen, and diplomats, as well as prominent citizens from the Federal City, and their ladies. Even Dolley Madison, the former

First Lady, was in attendance. The president and his entourage of more than three hundred fifty boarded the steamboat *Joseph Johnson* at Washington for passage to Alexandria. There they were to embark aboard *Princeton* for the final gala excursion to Mount Vernon and back.[13]

"The day was most favorable and the company was large and brilliant," recorded one local newspaper. There could scarcely have been a greater or more colorful assemblage of the political authority of a single nation in such a small, compact place as was aboard *Princeton* on that fatal day in February 1844.[14]

"Never," wrote President Tyler later,

did the eye gaze on a brighter or more animated scene than that which the beautiful river exhibited during the forenoon on that fateful day. There floated the ship whereon had been concentrated so many hopes and anticipated joys. . . . The decks were soon crowded with a host of happy visitors. . . . A cloudless sky added to the brilliancy of the scene.[15]

With her full complement of 178 officers and crew, *Princeton* got underway at 1 P.M., on schedule, and steamed slowly downriver toward Mount Vernon. As usual, Captain Stockton was urged to fire Peacemaker, and with the usual appropriate ceremony he did so. As always, the crowd was enthralled by the near deafening report, the dense black smoke, and the enormous geyser of water kicked up miles away.[16]

At 3:10 PM. *Princeton* neared Mount Vernon and was brought about for the return trip to Alexandria. Ten minutes later, a second firing of the gun was ordered, climaxing, Stockton hoped, the demonstrations for the day. Again the crowd roared its approval, and then adjourned below decks to continue a sumptuous repast which had been underway. Owing to the inordinate number of people aboard, the feast was being carried out in shifts, the men dining first, and then the ladies. Many of the men remained below for a jovial round of song, while others returned topside to the crisp winter daylight and animated discussions of the new weapon.[17]

At 4:00 P.M. word came down to Captain Stockton that several gentlemen requested to see one more shot fired from the great gun. Peacemaker was still heated from its earlier firing and Stockton may have been reluctant but, urged by Secretary of the Navy Thomas Walker Gilmer, had little choice other than to acquiesce.[18]

One of the eager observers, Charles Augustus Davis, of New York, was unable to see over the tightly packed crowd gathered to watch the firing and clambered up the inner rigging of the ship along with a young woman, Mrs. Wethered, from Baltimore. There, suspended but a few feet above the deck, they had a perfect view of the proceedings.[19]

The captain was methodical in his preparations, calibrating range and elevation, even as the gun was being loaded. The crowd closed around into an even tighter knot, vying to catch every detail. Lieutenant Hunt, ordnance officer in charge, fed the great gun a charge of twenty-five pounds of powder, and then directed the loading of one of the big cannonballs.[20]

The crowd, composed mostly of dignitaries and statesmen, pressed closer. Below, President Tyler, his family, and a twenty-three-year-old socialite, Julia Gardiner, daughter of New York Senator David Gardiner, were summoned to witness the firing. But as the president and his party were about to go on deck, a gentleman remarked that one of the ladies would give a toast, and that they must wait for it, which they conceded to do. Mayor Seaton of Washington was more interested in the toast, but urged by the Secretary of the Navy, decided to witness the firing. He was delayed in going topside. Both his and the president's delays saved their lives.[21]

It was exactly 4:30 P.M. and *Princeton* was two miles below Alexandria when Peacemaker was fired by Captain Stockton for the last time. The roar was ferocious, and the smoke blanketed the ship in a pall difficult to penetrate. When it cleared, it had become painfully apparent that a disaster of enormous consequence had occurred. The giant gun had burst apart three feet from the breech, scattering death and destruction indiscriminately among both the illustrious and the lowly.[22]

"The scene upon the deck," it was later reported, "may more easily be imagined than described. Nor can the imagination picture to itself the half of the horrors." Bodies were mangled beyond description by the shrapnel which splattered everything and everyone near the gun. Lying dead and wounded

The tragic explosion of the Peacemaker, February 28, 1844, aboard the U. S. steam frigate *Princeton* while in Potomac River. Original lithograph by N. Currier in the Naval Collection of Franklin Delano Roosevelt. Official U. S. Navy Photograph.

were more than two dozen people, among them United States Secretary of State Abel Upshur, Secretary of the Navy Gilmer, Chargé d'Affaires to the Hague Virgil Maxcy, Commodore Beverly Kennon, Chief of the Navy Bureau of Construction, and Senator David Gardiner of New York, all of whom had been standing to the immediate left of the gun. Incredibly, Captain Stockton, though stunned, escaped injury with the exception of having all his hair singed from his head. Lieutenant Hunt suffered a concussion, but an aide, William Strickland, who had been standing behind the captain and lieutenant, was untouched. Seventeen seamen and a black servant to the president lay battered or dead about them.[23]

Charles Davis and Mrs. Wethered, positioned well above the crowd, lost only their hats, but were spattered with the blood and gore of those immediately below them. Davis later recalled: "I saw Stockton fire the gun, and then for a few seconds all was darkness to me—and then the scene presented was this devastation in the group directly under me."

One man, slightly dazed, rushed below shouting, "The Secretary of State is dead." For a moment the crowd of celebrants below sat in stunned silence. Then the young New York socialite, Miss Julia Gardiner, jumped up and screamed, "Let me go to my father." She struggled to get through the crowd to go topside, but was restrained by a friend. Then came the tragic news that Peacemaker had exploded. The young woman grew frantic. Within moments even more tragic news arrived: her father was among the dead. Trying to console her, one woman said, "My dear child, you can do no good. Your father is in heaven."[24] Julia Gardiner fainted and did not revive until the ship had returned to Alexandria where she was carried off the boat. She awakened in the arms of President Tyler.[25]

The news of the disaster swept Washington and the nation. The shredded bodies of the deceased were transferred from Princeton to Joseph Johnson and landed in Washington the day after the tragedy and carried to the White House in hearses. Orders went out to all military posts and ships that guns would be fired at half hour intervals throughout March 1 to honor the dead. Captain Stockton was in a deep state of shock, continually expressing his desire that he should have been the only victim.[26]

An investigation of the Peacemaker incident was immediately launched, called for by Stockton himself. Despite the
testimony of the ship's chief gunner, Mr. King, formerly a
blacksmith, that the gun was made of iron of an inferior quality,
and of the Ordnance Department that Captain Stockton had
not secured the department's final approval of the weapon, the
investigating committee failed to place blame on the captain or
his officers. Commodore W. Binford Shubrick, chairman of the
committee, concluded the investigation by stating:

> The Committee, as well from the foregoing testimony, as from
> their personal observation and examination before and after the
> accident, have no hesitation in exonerating Captain Stockton
> and every officer and man under his command, from the slightest
> imputation of rashness and carelessness, and are unanimously of
> the opinion that this melancholy event rests upon causes over
> which they could have no control.[27]

As a result of the disaster, a series of ordnance tests were
carried out and the development of a gun capable of producing
the same power and accuracy as Peacemaker was developed,
ultimately culminating in John A. Dahlgren's famed bottle-
shaped cannon which was deployed so successfully during the
Civil War.[28] Captain Stockton eventually went on to achieve
fame, gaining national prominence for his role in the conquest
of California during the Mexican War, and then as a U. S.
Senator.[29] Julia Gardiner, the bereaved daughter of the New
York Senator killed by Peacemaker, married President Tyler
four months after the disaster.[30]

Chapter Fourteen

A COMFORTABLE NIGHT'S REST

THE BRAZEN headlines of the advertisement, set in bold, black type were both exciting and inviting to the traveler of 1858. "THE SOUTH! Direct from New York, Philadelphia and Baltimore, via the 'BAY LINE,' To Norfolk, Weldon, Raleigh, Wilmington, Charleston, Augusta, Atlanta, Montgomery, and New Orleans."[1]

Here, for the first time, was easy access to the metropolitan centers of a part of America which had hitherto been accessible only with great difficulty. The route was conveniently linked by a series of rail and steamboat companies, including the Seaboard and Roanoke Railroad and the Baltimore Steam Packet Company, affectionately known as the "Old Bay Line." The steamboat line provided the key middle link in the route with runs departing from the company's Union Dock wharf at the foot of Concord Street in Baltimore at 5:00 P.M. daily, except Sundays.[2]

Passage was provided by sister ships *North Carolina* and *Louisiana*, two enormous steamers, which were the pride of the Old Bay Line and reputedly the finest, most luxurious ever to float on the Chesapeake. Passengers and baggage, arriving from Philadelphia by train, were conveyed without charge to the depot where they boarded ship. "Passengers by this Line," were assured, "enjoy a comfortable Night's Rest on the Bay Steamers, and are privileged to Lay Over at Night at any Point, and resume their Trip by Daylight." A ticket for the Baltimore-Norfolk leg of the journey, including accommodations in the "unsurpassed state rooms and berths," was a mere $5.00.[3]

Built in 1852 for the Baltimore Steam Packet Company for the then-astronomical price of $111,272.03, *North Carolina*, elder of the sisters, had proved her worth to the company quite early and many times over.[4] She had been cited as a model boat in every respect, reflecting infinite credit upon her proprietors and the artisans employed in her construction. Her record-breaking thirteen-hour-long maiden voyage to Norfolk would have by any other standard been considered excellent time, but it was prophesied that when she was fully broken in she would do even better. She did. Her initial success was so great that within two years of construction her owners ordered to be built her equally superb sister, *Louisiana*.[5]

The most luxurious ships of their day on the Chesapeake, both vessels were lavishly fitted and superbly gilded according to the tastes of the times. One writer for the *American Beacon* noted that *North Carolina* "would attract attention even among the splendid palaces that float upon the North River," in New York. Her main saloon was eighty feet in length and twenty feet wide and "fitted with an elegance of taste and liberality which will compare favorably with any of the steamers in the country." There were imported Brussels carpets, elegantly carved and velveted chairs and sofas, marble-topped tables, enormous Gothic mirrors, and decorated lamps and furniture richly enhanced by white wall panels, gilded and carved mouldings, and the finest in interior decor. The ship itself was nearly two hundred forty feet in length and eight hundred sixty-one tons net and was powered by a vertical beam engine, fifty-four inches in diameter with a stroke of 11 feet. She boasted two tubular boilers suited for the use of either wood or coal, which had been especially constructed at a cost of nearly thirty thousand dollars.[6] *North Carolina*'s master, Captain James Cannon, indeed had every reason to be proud of his charge, the first undisputed "Queen of the Chesapeake."[7]

On Friday evening, January 28, 1859, *North Carolina* departed the Union Dock at her usual time, bound for Norfolk with a much smaller-than-usual passenger list, just twenty-six persons, and a crew of forty. No one could foretell that it was to be her final voyage.[8]

The trip down the Chesapeake, at least as far as the Potomac River, proved uneventful. The day had been rainy, and an extremely dense fog blanketed the water. At 1:00 A.M., off the Potomac, Captain Cannon was alerted to the approach of another vessel by the sounding of a ship's bell. That had to be Captain Pearson in the steamer *Georgia*, bound for Baltimore. "Right on schedule," Cannon told himself, though he could not see more than a few yards ahead.[9]

At 2:45 A.M. *North Carolina* approached the Smith Point Lightship, permanently anchored five miles below Smith Point and the mouth of the Potomac. Captain Cannon was on lookout in the wheelhouse, exhibiting his usual caution as his ship picked its way carefully through the dense fog. Suddenly, a steward burst into the wheelhouse informing the captain that there was a fire in one of the staterooms in the upper saloon, forward of the engine. Cannon immediately gave the signal to his engineer, Noah Bratt, to stop the engine, and he promptly rushed to the scene of the fire. The blaze had started in a linen storage room in the passenger section, and by the time the captain arrived it was already spreading to the staterooms. Quickly, he ordered a section of hose attached to the first-class Worthington pump and another to the donkey engine. A steady stream of water was soon playing on the flames. It was Cannon's intent to douse the fire before awakening the passengers, but the flames were soon reaching the gallows frame of the lower walking beam. Thus, even as the captain and several of his men fought on, others raced along the saloon passageway, bursting open doors and rousing the sleeping passengers. Within minutes, the fire hose itself had been burned through, and the attempt to fight the blaze was given up.[10]

The ship carried four large "Frances" lifeboats aft the main deck, with a large supply of "life buoys." There was also an abundant supply of material suitable for the rapid construction of life rafts. "It was evident, therefore, that with courage and discipline," noted an editor of the *Baltimore American* some days later, "in the quiet state of the weather, all might be saved." Cannon and his crew acted with coolness and dispatch in the face of the crisis by directing the passengers to the lower deck.[11]

The flames spread rapidly through the upper saloon which, in the space of but a few minutes, was entirely consumed. Few who had been blissfully asleep only moments before managed to save even the slightest remnants of their belongings. Women rushed out in their nightclothes. A lucky few were shielded from the January cold by blankets which someone had thought to take with him from a stateroom. Though most passengers were able to descend stairways, several cut off from escape by the fire were forced to climb from the upper deck to the lower by the stanchions. Several lives were very nearly lost in this manner of escape.[12]

Mr. and Mrs. Crayton and their infant child, of Beaufort, North Carolina, unable to escape from their stateroom through the door, succeeded in getting through a window. Like many, Mr. Crayton decided that they must shinny down a stanchion. Reluctantly, Mrs. Crayton followed with her child in arms, assisted by her husband below. By the time they reached the lower rail, panic gripped them. Quickly, the husband snatched the infant from his wife's arms, wrapped it in a large blanket, and tossed it into the water. He then jumped overboard himself and, holding the child up, treaded water, urging his wife to follow. Again reluctantly, she did, but unfortunately fell on her husband, knocking him temporarily senseless. Brought back to consciousness by the frigid water, however, Mr. Crayton, a strong and determined swimmer, succeeded in keeping himself and his family afloat until rescued by one of the lifeboats. "There was," noted the *Baltimore American*, "scarcely any need of such an adventure, for the officers had made provision for their safe rescue."[13]

Many aboard *North Carolina* would experience a similar "adventure." Captain Henry Fitzgerald, a well-known Norfolk oyster exporter, was among them. Fitzgerald had turned in at his usual hour in a stateroom on the hurricane deck. He was a sound sleeper. When finally aroused, he discovered he was cut off and in danger of perishing. Thinking quickly, he located a length of rope and was in the act of lowering himself in order to reach one of the lifeboats when, halfway between the sea and the deck, the fastening of the rope gave way, and he was plummeted into the waters of the Chesapeake. Unfortunately, Fitzgerald had never learned how to swim. Yet somehow he managed to keep his head above water for a time until saved by a boat.[14]

Even as many of the officers and crew were arousing the passengers, others were engaged in getting the remaining lifeboats into the water. This effort was not accomplished without extreme difficulty and exposure to the heat. In one instance, the tackle of a boat was burning by the time it hit the water. Passengers quickly filled two of the boats manned by two crewmen each. Despite the captain's orders that all the boats remain together since visual contact would quickly be lost in the fog, one of the boats shoved off on its own.[15]

The rapid, incessant advance of the flames which had now descended to the lower deck drove the remaining passengers toward the bow. The last two empty lifeboats were brought forward to be loaded. Once all of the passengers who could be accounted for were safely embarked, the boats were lashed together. In the meantime, the deck hands constructed and launched a makeshift raft which was secured along with the lifeboats. Thirteen crewmen soon crowded aboard.[16]

Cannon and a few officers remained aboard the burning luxury steamer to survey quickly those portions of the ship to which the flames permitted access. Musing over the dictates of fate, the captain secured a small pocket compass from one of the ship's rooms while purser Lloyd B. Parkes penetrated the smoke-filled lower saloon in search of any persons who might have slept through the alarm or been overcome by smoke. None were to be found.[17]

Having done all that was possible, at 3:20 A.M., less than an hour after the fire had been discovered, the lifeboats pushed off from the sides of the doomed ship. As they did so, the men continually cried out so as to alarm any persons possibly left behind. With Cannon's boat in the lead, the little flotilla set off into the fog in a line, linked together by a single rope. The raft was towed behind at the end of the line, but before leaving the dim arc of light formed by the burning ship in the fog, the men on the raft were distributed aboard the lifeboats and their own makeshift craft set adrift.

Cannon resolved to make for the Smith Point Lightship, the bell of which could be distinctly heard across the water, though the light itself could not be seen. They proceeded only a short distance when the boat which first left the steamer was heard, hailed, and secured to the others.[18]

The water was now perfectly calm. An eerie stillness blanketed the bay, punctuated by the doleful fog bell. Guided by the bell's rhythmic clanging, the lifeboats proceeded without difficulty and at 5:00 A.M. reached the lightship. Captain Heyden, master of the lightship, had seen nothing of the fire, but perceiving of the disaster by the approach of the boats, responded with great compassion.[19]

Because of the fog, the passengers and crew were obliged to remain aboard the lightship until Saturday afternoon, when the steamship *Locust Point* was finally hailed and passage for the survivors to Norfolk secured. In the interim, however, a careful check of the purser's book and a roll call among the passengers and crew revealed that a Reverend Doctor Thomas Curtis of Camden, South Carolina, and a black steward, Isaac Watters, were not among the rescued. Though neither of the men had been seen, it was believed that Curtis had jumped overboard and drowned, and that Watters, an extremely heavy sleeper who went off watch only an hour or so before the fire, had burned to death in his bunk.[20]

The survivors were deeply grateful to the officers and crew of *North Carolina*, and while aboard *Locust Point* they drafted several resolves commending Captain Cannon, purser Parkes, first mate James Marshall, second mate Thomas J. B. Walker, first engineer Noah Bratt, and second engineer James Brownley for their "courage, good judgement, resolute firmness and indomitable preseverance, that enforced discipline among the passengers and crew," which permitted their survival.[21]

Within five days of the disaster, the Baltimore Steam Packet Company gave notice that it would accept sealed proposals to raise the ship. Richard W. Crosset, the successful bidder, proposed to lift the ship from her grave by using four canal barges. He would receive seventy percent of the value of whatever might be recovered. Crosset's efforts unfortunately resulted in failure, his own bankruptcy, and what was probably a case of decompression sickness, or "the bends." A second attempt was launched the following fall by Isaiah Gifford. Gifford attempted to remove the ship's valuable machinery, but the water being "as thick as tar, and the tide running as much as five knots," he too was obliged to give up the attempt.[22] Gifford's failed salvage attempts ended the tale of *North Carolina*, and her remains rest, to this day, in the depths of the Chesapeake, still marked on modern charts as "wreck."

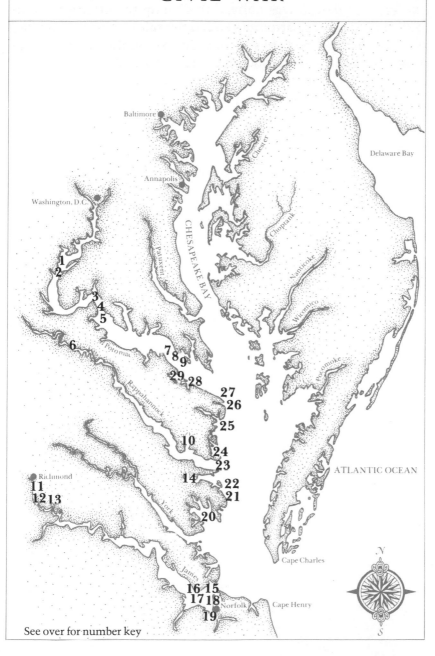

PART FOUR
CIVIL WAR

Baltimore

Delaware Bay

Chester

Annapolis

Washington, D.C.

CHESAPEAKE BAY

Patuxent

Choptank

Nanticoke

1
2

3
4
5

6

Potomac

Wicomico

7
8
9

29
28

Rappahannock

27
26

Pocomoke

25

10

24
23

ATLANTIC OCEAN

Richmond

14

22
21

11
12 13

York

20

Cape Charles

James

N

16 15
17 18
19

Norfolk   Cape Henry

S

See over for number key

MAP KEY: THE CIVIL WAR

1. *Martha Washington* (1861)
2. C. S. S. *George Page* (1862)
3. *Passenger* (1861)
4. *Frances Elmore* (1862)
5. *Christiana Keen* (1861)
6. U. S. S. *Satellite*, U. S. S. *Reliance*, *Two Brothers*, *Coquette* (1860)
7. U. S. S. *Tulip* (1864)
8. *Somerset* (1861)
9. *Favorite* (1861)
10. *Ada* (1861)
11. C. S. S. *Patrick Henry*, C. S. S. *Shrapnel*, C. S. S. *Nansemond*, C. S. S. *Torpedo*, C. S. S. *Hampton*, C. S. S. *Roanoke* (1865)
12. C. S. S. *Virginia No. 2*, C. S. S. *Richmond*, C. S. S. *Richmond*
13. U. S. S. *Commodore Jones*
14. U. S. S. *Titan* (1864)
15. *Julia Baker* (1862)
16. U. S. S. *Cumberland* (1862)
17. U. S. S. *Congress* (1862)
18. C. S. S. *Virginia* (1862)
19. U. S. Atlantic Squadron (1861)
20. *Elma* (1862)
21. Unidentified (1862)
22. *Alleghanian* (1862)
23. *Golden Rod* (1862)
24. *Harriet DeFord* (1865)
25. *Arctic* (1862)
26. *Knickerbocker* (1862)
27. *Jane Wright* (1861)
28. *Sarah Margaret*, *Odd Fellow* (1862)
29. *Charity*, *Flight*, *Gazelle* (1862)

Chapter Fifteen

THE STUFF OF WAR

WITH THE outbreak of the Civil War, the United States government found itself hopelessly attempting to cope with insurrection on every front. Events moved with heady swiftness after the opening attacks on Fort Sumter in Charleston Harbor, South Carolina, and everywhere in the South, federal property became the target for secessionist assaults. Nowhere on the Atlantic seaboard, however, was there a more exposed or a more strategically important base to the infant Confederacy than Hampton Roads. And, nowhere was there a greater arsenal of warlike materiel than at Norfolk.

At the Norfolk Navy Yard, a powerful, though dormant, segment of the United States Navy lay out of commission. Here the largest ship of the line ever built for the Navy, the 120-gun *Pennsylvania*, lay in ordinary near two of her sisters, *Columbus* and *Delaware*, both of 74 guns. Then there were the three 50-gun frigates *United States*, *Columbia*, and *Raritan*, also in ordinary. Two sloops of war, *Plymouth* and *Germantown*, each of 28 guns, and the brig *Dolphin*, 4 guns, lay at anchor and ready for sea but without crews. One 74-gun frigate, *New York*, sat on the stocks awaiting further work. Off the yard in the Elizabeth River lay Flag Officer Garrett J. Pendergast's flagship *Cumberland*, 28 guns, awaiting sailing orders for Veracruz. But of great importance to the events which were to ensue was the recent arrival of the powerful 275-foot-long steam frigate *Merrimack*, 40 guns, which had been sent in for repairs.[1]

The commandant of the navy yard was a crusty veteran of fifty years naval service, Captain Charles S. McCauley. The commandant's situation was certainly an unenviable one. Many of his mechanics and workmen, and even a number of his own officers, were openly in sympathy with the South and of questionable loyalty. Manpower was in short supply. Besides the seamen manning *Cumberland* and a detachment from *New York* assigned to the yard, there were precious few military men at his disposal for defense.

It was clear the federal government was as concerned with McCauley's position as the commandant himself was. As early as April 10, two days before the firing on Fort Sumter, McCauley received orders from Secretary of the Navy Gideon Welles to exercise great vigilance in guarding the property committed to his charge. Welles expressed concern for the safety of *Merrimack* and suggested that she be sent to Philadelphia, or any other yard, if the disintegrating military and political situation warranted it. Hours later, McCauley received an order from the Chief of the Bureau of Construction directing him to prepare *Merrimack* for temporary service under steam alone. Having been subjected to weeks of pressure, personal threats from local elements about Norfolk, and misleading advice from some of his less than loyal officers, the commandant irately responded that it would take at least a month to prepare the ship's engines for the service contemplated.[2]

Welles was not a man to be put off, and on April 12, 1861, the day the Civil War began, he directly ordered *Merrimack* removed from Norfolk to Philadelphia with utmost dispatch. Commander James Alden was ordered down to take command of her. Four engineers under B. F. Isherwood were also sent to do the work which McCauley had said would take a month in less than a week. Isherwood reported to McCauley at Norfolk on April 14 and began surveying the steamship's engines and hull which were in a wretched state. Isherwood's title of Chief of Engineers had not been lightly bestowed. He immediately established an around-the-clock schedule and work proceeded without respite.[3]

As Isherwood labored through his first night aboard *Merrimack, Cumberland* lay at anchor off the naval hospital at Norfolk. At 11:30 P.M., the officer of the watch, Lieutenant Thomas O. Selfridge, observed a small tug cautiously, almost surreptitiously, steaming past his ship. As it went by the hospital lights, he could see she had two lightships in tow. Something, he sensed, was amiss. He decided to remain on deck, even after being relieved at midnight. Half an hour later he observed another tug with another lightship in tow. He immediately sought and received permission from Captain John Marston to follow the tugs in an armed boat.[4]

The night was unusually dark and rainy, and so thick, in fact, that he was unable to see more than the length of his boat. After pulling down as far as Craney Island without discovering anything, he returned to the ship about 4:00 A.M., thoroughly wet and disgusted with his failure. Four hours later the tugs returned—without the lightships. With the first gray swash of morning it was noticed that three lightships which had been lying at anchor at Norfolk were gone. Later it was discovered that they had been captured by an armed body of men, carried down to a position in the narrowest part of the channel off Sewell's Point, and there scuttled and sunk to block the entrance to the navy yard. *Cumberland* was immediately moved from her anchorage off the hospital to a position off the yard and moored head and stern.[5]

Selfridge quickly offered to take the brig *Dolphin* down to Craney Island and prevent further attempts to obstruct the channel. Commodore Hiram Paulding, a senior to McCauley, then on a brief inspection visit to the navy yard, cordially approved. McCauley too gave his consent, but after Paulding's departure for Washington, withdrew permission. The continued threats on his life and the bad advice of his subordinates were being felt in his every decision. During the next several days, several schooners, lighters, and other watercraft were towed unopposed down from Norfolk and sunk in the channel. It was soon openly boasted among Southerners that *Cumberland* would never leave the harbor.[6]

On April 16 McCauley received new orders from Secretary Welles. *Plymouth* and *Dolphin* were to be placed beyond danger of immediate assault, and *Germantown* was to receive on board all the stores and armaments in the navy yard. Should the yard be threatened with attack, the giant warship was to be taken in tow by *Merrimack* and hauled to a place of safety (assuming *Merrimack* was herself capable of moving). The crew of *New York* was to assist in moving the vessels. *Cumberland* was both to protect and assist the operation. But again, Mc-Cauley delayed in carrying out his orders.[7]

Despite McCauley's recalcitrance, Commander Alden proceeded to make every preparation for the departure of *Merrimack*, praying all the while that Isherwood would have her ready before the Southerners completely obstructed the channel. He procured a pilot; the coal and engineer stores were taken aboard; and forty-four firemen and coal heavers were engaged for the trip. The hull repairs had been completed on Tuesday, April 16, but the more critical engine repairs were still underway. Finally, at 4:00 P.M. on April 17, a tired, dirty chief engineer called on Commodore McCauley and reported that *Merrimack* was ready for steam.

"Should I fire up at once?" Isherwood asked hopefully.

"Not this afternoon," replied the commodore. "If you have steam up tomorrow morning it will be time enough."[8]

As Isherwood and the commodore spoke, the state of Virginia formally seceded from the Union. It would now be a race between the Union and the Confederacy, with the Norfolk Navy Yard and all that lay within it as first prize. Within hours of the Virginia secession, the Virginia State Navy was reborn. The first mission of its senior officer, Captain Robert B. Pegram, was to wrest control of the Norfolk Navy Yard from the North. Pegram set off immediately with two companies of volunteers to take and hold his objective.[9]

On April 18 Secretary Welles ordered Commodore Paulding to do likewise.

> You are directed to proceed forthwith to Norfolk and take command of all the naval forces there afloat . . . On no account should the arms and munitions be permitted to fall into the hands of the insurrectionists, or those who would wrest them from the custody of the Government; and should it finally become necessary, you will, in order to prevent that result, destroy the property.[10]

At Norfolk Engineer Isherwood called upon McCauley that same morning, and reported *Merrimack*'s engineer department ready for departure. The ship's chief engineer, a Mr.

Danby, his assistant, firemen, and coal heavers were all aboard, with steam up and engines working at the wharf. The only thing lacking was the commandant's orders to cast off.[11] McCauley said nothing, then turned his back on the engineer and stared blankly at the ceiling. "I have not yet decided to send the vessel," he said. "I will inform you further in the course of a few hours."[12]

The engineer was incredulous. He called the commandant's attention to the navy department's orders and then expressed his opinion that the ship could easily pass any of the obstructions the enemy had placed in the channel. A few more hours' delay would mean the loss of another day, and possibly even the ability to pass the growing barrier of obstructions. "I will inform you further in the course of the day," the commandant reiterated.[13]

Isherwood stormed out of the office and proceeded directly to Commander Alden. Boarding *Merrimack* with the officer, he pointed out that all of the required personnel were aboard, the engines repaired and ready, and a full head of steam raised. There was simply no excuse for *Merrimack* to remain. Alden concurred, but it was still up to McCauley.[14]

At 2:00 P.M. the engineer called on McCauley for the last time. The commandant informed him in no uncertain terms that the ship would be retained at Norfolk, and that her fires must be drawn. Despite the engineer's pleas, *Merrimack* and *Germantown* would not be moved.[15]

The following morning, April 19, began auspiciously enough. President Lincoln issued a proclamation declaring a blockade on Southern ports from South Carolina to Texas. It seemed a somewhat inappropriate gesture, for Washington itself had been cut off by rail from the North and troops had to be brought in by steamboat. In Texas, the southern terminus of the blockade, Confederates had seized the U. S. steamer *Star of the West*. At Norfolk a southern-born navy captain, David Glasgow Farragut, left his home to take up residence in New York and to serve the Union.[16]

Outside of the Norfolk Navy Yard Captain Pegram and his two companies of Virginia State Navy volunteers, bolstered by a body of local militia called the Norfolk Grays, under General

J. B. Taliaferro, had arrived the preceding evening. Pegram and Taliaferro were undoubtedly aware that with the still inadequate forces in hand that there would be little hope in carrying out a direct attack on the navy yard. They thus fell upon a scheme to trick McCauley into believing that a much larger force menaced him. Trains of railroad cars were sent out empty from the nearby station, in full view of the navy yard. At a short distance away, they were filled with troops which had gone out for that purpose, to be brought back and landed in plain sight of the ships. Men were then marched back toward the city and reloaded in the cars. The whole process was repeated many times, conveying the impression that fresh troops were constantly arriving.[17]

McCauley was taken in, hook, line, and sinker. He was soon given to believe that large numbers of Southern troops were arriving at Portsmouth and Norfolk from as far away as Richmond and Petersburg as well as those mustered in the immediate neighborhood. Despondently, he observed the rebels to be apparently throwing up batteries immediately in front of the navy yard. Seeking to buy time, he dispatched Lieutenant Selfridge under a flag of truce to speak to General Taliaferro. The message the lieutenant carried bordered on the ridiculous: should the Virginians continue to menace the navy yard by placing batteries opposite the yard, it would be considered an act of war and would warrant retaliation by gunfire. The lieutenant returned a short time later, accompanied by a Colonel Heath, with what seemed to McCauley an equally preposterous reply. There were, according to Heath, no batteries.[18]

It was now that most of the commandant's officers, who had made their Southern sympathies known, proceeded to choose sides. By noon, nearly all of the officers and the majority of the workers at the navy yard resigned or deserted to the Confederacy. Even the night watchman left, taking the keys to the front gate with him.[19]

With an inadequate force of men to handle the shipping, the way out blocked by obstructions, and strong enemy forces apparently confronting him, Commandant McCauley was at a loss. He decided on the only course of action open: destroy the navy yard and the shipping thereabout. He was entirely unaware that Commodore Paulding, aboard the steam sloop of war *Pawnee*, was at the same time departing Washington, D. C., to come to his aid with a strong force of marines.

That very night a party of officers from *Cumberland*, assisted by Lieutenant A. A. Semmes of *Dolphin* and a handful of men, began spiking the guns stored throughout the different parts of the navy yard. Unfortunately, the only materials at hand to spike so great a number of cannons were wrought nails, which formed only a temporary obstruction, and did not permanently injure the ordnance. At the same time a large quantity of ordnance stores was carried aboard *Cumberland*. The big ship was thus converted into a veritable floating bomb.[20]

The following morning, McCauley commenced scuttling *Germantown*, *Plymouth*, *Dolphin*, and *Merrimack*, destroying the same engine and machinery of the latter which Engineer Isherwood had worked so diligently to repair. The guns aboard the ships lying in ordinary were spiked, including those aboard the monstrous *Pennsylvania*. A large number of small arms could not be carried aboard *Cumberland* and were thrown into the water. By 6:00 P.M. McCauley considered the job completed.[21]

Less than two hours later *Pawnee* appeared in sight. Commodore Paulding had reached Fortress Monroe, barely twenty miles away, only hours before, secured the services of a regiment of Massachusetts volunteers, and embarked with them aboard. At 6:45 P.M., Paulding turned *Pawnee* toward Norfolk.[22]

At Norfolk, *Cumberland* lay moored in the main channel off the navy yard and *Pennsylvania* just out of the channel and some distance below. Unaware of the character of the approaching ship, both vessels sounded general quarters. *Pawnee* was immediately hailed by *Cumberland*, but the wind blowing fresh downstream prevented the reply from being heard aboard the flagship. The hail was repeated, but without success. At that moment the officer commanding the forward 11-inch pivot gun on *Cumberland* loudly requested permission to fire. Aboard *Pennsylvania*, which had in fact heard the reply, it was immediately apparent that *Pawnee* might soon be the recipient of an unwelcome gift. At that moment Lieutenant W. N. Allen, comprehending the danger of a mistaken identity, sang out to his commanding officer, "Donaldson, let us give her three cheers."[23] "Good," said Donaldson, and in a few minutes three rousing cheers rang out across the water and was then taken up by *Cumberland* as well. From the approaching *Pawnee* came a hearty response and jubilant cheering.[24]

Within a short time after reaching the wharf, Commodore Paulding was chagrined to learn that the vessels he had come to tow away had been scuttled only two hours before. An examination was made to see if the leaks might be arrested. But it was already too late. There was no alternative but to complete the destruction which McCauley already considered finished.[25]

Paulding acted with dispatch. One hundred officers and men from *Cumberland* were sent to destroy or render unserviceable all of the 2,000 guns in the yard, 300 of which were of the latest Dahlgren pattern. Though most had already been spiked once, it had been a temporary expedient. Paulding thus decided to knock off their trunnions with sledge hammers. However, the tenacity of the iron was such that, try as they might, the wreckers failed to break a single trunnion.[26]

Commander Rogers and Captain Wright were dispatched to blow up the dry dock, while Commander Alden was sent to prepare the storehouses, workshops, and other buildings for destruction. Officers and men alike were ordered to distribute combustibles on board the various ships in ordinary and prepare them for burning. Speed was essential, for should the insurrectionists discover the Yankees' intentions, outright assault was a strong probability.

While these proceedings were underway, a flag of truce came in from General Taliaferro with a message: "That to save the effusion of blood, the general would permit the *Cumberland* to leave the port unmolested, if the destruction of public property should be discontinued." Paulding replied that the consequences of any act of violence on the Southerners' part would devolve upon them.[27]

At 1:45 P.M. on Sunday, April 21, all was in readiness. Trains of powder had been laid on board *Plymouth, Merrimack, Germantown, Raritan, Columbia, Dolphin, Columbus,* and *Pennsylvania* in the order in which they lay moored. *Delaware* was left out on account of her distant position; and the elderly *United States* was considered to be in such an advanced state of decay as to be worthless.

Orders were given to embark all personnel except those required to ignite the powder trains. A rocket fired from *Pawnee* by order of Paulding himself would be the final signal. As the last boats were shoving off, McCauley's young son came to the landing with tears in his eyes. His father, he said, refused to leave his post. Commander Alden was immediately directed to convince the old man that the yard had to be fired at once and that his life would undoubtedly be lost if he remained. After some cajolery, Alden managed to persuade the commandant to abandon the post, and with great reluctance the two boarded *Cumberland*.[28]

The shore parties having been withdrawn, only two boats remained tied up along the quay. One of these was under the command of lieutenants Wise and Phelps. Her party was charged with firing the ships. The second boat, under Captain Wilkes and Lieutenant Russel, was to bring off the remainder of the officers and men that had been left ashore to set charges. There were three shore parties, totaling eight men, assigned to destroy the Norfolk Navy Yard.

At 2:25 A.M. *Pawnee* left the wharf and passed hawsers to *Cumberland*. At 4:00 A.M. the two vessels, assisted by the tug *Yankee* and a favorable tide, started down the river. Twenty minutes later the signal rocket was fired. Waiting torches were applied to shipping and buildings alike. In a very few minutes, the entire navy yard was a sea of flames. Those aboard *Pawnee* could make out the ship houses and *Merrimack* burning briskly in the predawn breezes.[29]

Within moments two of the three shore parties, under Commander Alden and Captain Wilkes, had rendezvoused with their boats, but the third party was nowhere to be seen. Minutes passed and the conflagration was growing in intensity. The searing heat and smoke were overpowering as the two parties waited patiently at the boats for their mates. The third party, under Commander Rogers, however, failed to appear. Surely, they thought, Rogers had either perished or been cut off from the rendezvous by the fire. Reluctantly, the two boats pulled away.[30]

After picking up their boats, *Pawnee* and *Cumberland* passed unopposed downriver en route to Fortress Monroe. Despite Taliaferro's threats, and a brief delay caused by the obstructions in the river, Paulding's force was soon out of harm's way. From the vantage of the open river, the view of the Norfolk Navy Yard ablaze in the night was to the loyal Union men a sight of unforgettable grandeur and sadness. Not only had the navy's most important yard on the mid-Atlantic seaboard been destroyed, along with an enormously powerful segment of the Union Navy itself, but one of its finest officers was believed to have died as a consequence.

Or, so everyone thought. Rogers and his men had, in fact, experienced great difficulty in placing and lighting their fuses, all of which had gone out without communicating fire to the powder trains. Frustrated in their designs, the three men decided at the last second to abandon the project and ran as hard as they could across the entire length of the yard, through a veritable inferno, to reach the rendezvous point, only to discover that the boats had departed. The question now was how to escape from the yard and the Confederates that lay beyond. The only exit they knew of was through the main gate, which they expected had been locked as usual. Passing up the yard near the flagstaff, they encountered three men trying to hoist a small rebel flag. Commander Rogers, concluding that where there was ingress there was egress, immediately went up to the men and demanded to know how they had entered the yard. Shocked at seeing an officer in what they had expected to be an abandoned yard, the men answered respectfully that they had come in through the front gate. Rogers restrained his joy at the news and bellowed out to no one in particular, "Who left that gate open?"[31]

The party had soon passed through the gate and down to the water's edge, where they knew a small boat lay berthed. By this time the fire was so intense, night had become day, denying the party the mask of darkness. A small boatload of men hailed them from the river. "Who are you and where are you going?" In less than polite terms the questioner was informed that it was none of his business. It was certainly a most inappropriate reply. Shots rang out as the Yankees shoved off, and it was soon apparent that escape was out of the question. Sensible to the danger, Rogers ordered the boat back to shore and surrendered his party to a detachment of gray-clad Virginia riflemen, even as

Destruction of the Norfolk (Gosport) Navy Yard and ships of the U. S. Navy,
April 21, 1861. Official U. S. Navy Photograph.

the Norfolk Navy Yard and nine of its ships went up in smoke.[32]

Despite the desperate efforts to deny the rebels the fruits of Norfolk, the South was able to utilize more than 1,200 heavy guns, 2,800 barrels of powder, tons of shells, cannonballs, and thousands of side arms and rifles which could not be destroyed. Steam engines, tools, machinery, and a wide assortment of miscellaneous equipment were ultimately salvaged from the ruins. And there were, of course, the ships. *Germantown* would eventually be raised, taken into the Confederate Navy and refitted as a floating battery to serve near Craney Island. *Plymouth* was also raised as was *Merrimack*, which was refitted as an ironclad, and ultimately participated in the first battle between ironclad ships in history. Even the decrepit *United States* was refitted and taken into active service.[33]

Had Commodore Paulding been two hours earlier, who knows what might have happened. Without the stuff of war captured at Norfolk, the great rebellion may even have died aborning.

Chapter Sixteen

IRON AGAINST WOOD

WHEN THE Confederate government was moved from Montgomery, Alabama, to Richmond, Virginia, in the opening days of the Civil War, it quickly became apparent to both the North and the South that Hampton Roads, key to the strategic James River, would inevitably become a focal point of contention. A Union blockade and control of Hampton Roads, and later, naval penetration into the river, could threaten the very heart of the rebellion. The South lacked even a rudimentary navy to defend the waterway at the outset, but it was not long in beginning one—and a revolutionary one at that!

On May 10, 1861, less than a month after the opening shots of war at Fort Sumter, the capable new Confederate Secretary of the Navy, Stephen R. Mallory, penned a momentous letter to the Confederate House Committee on Naval Affairs, a letter which would set in motion a chain of events destined to alter the course of naval history. He wrote,

> I regard the possession of an iron-armored ship as a matter of the first necessity. Such a vessel at this time could traverse the entire coast of the United States, prevent all blockades, and encounter, with a fair prospect of success, their entire Navy. If to cope with them upon the sea we follow their example and build wooden ships, we shall have to construct several at one time; for one or two ships would fall an easy prey to her comparatively numerous steam frigates. But inequality of numbers may be compensated for by invulnerability; and thus not only does economy but naval success dictate the wisdom and expediency of fighting with iron against wood. . . .[1]

Significantly, on May 30, 1861, the hulk of the U. S. S. *Merrimack* was resurrected from its watery grave.[2] Mallory soon had Lieutenant John M. Brooke draw up plans for the first Confederate ironclad warship. After a survey of *Merrimack*'s hull, found to be in good shape, and of her saltwater-soaked engines, thought to be salvageable, Mallory directed Brooke to adapt his plans for an ironclad to the remains of the former U. S. steam frigate. Once deployed, she would, it was hoped, be the invincible equalizer on which Mallory was counting.[3]

On February 17, 1862, the ex-U. S. S. *Merrimack*, though still unfinished, was officially commissioned as the ironclad ram C. S. S. *Virginia*.[4] She was awkward-looking, appearing more like a floating rooftop of iron than a ship. Her decks, upon which the roof rested, were usually awash, and her unarmored wooden hull, drawing twenty-two feet of water, lay well below the aproned armor line, quite secure from shot and shell. Her engines were somewhat balky, barely capable of five knots, and her steering was slow, taking half an hour or more to complete a full turn. As one of her officers later wrote, "She was as unmanageable as a water-logged vessel," and "as unwieldy as Noah's Ark."[5] But from all outward appearances, *Virginia* was awesome indeed. Her armor, manufactured by the Tredegar Works in Richmond, consisted of plates of iron two inches thick and eight inches wide. Her battery was of ten guns, two 7-inch reinforced Dahlgren rifles, two 6-inch reinforced Dahlgrens, and six 9-inch smooth bores.[6]

As the month of March approached, laborers worked at fever pitch to complete this revolutionary warship, for word had just arrived that the Union Navy was also building an ironclad. That the two should clash seemed inevitable. One rumor indicated that the Yankee ironclad was on the way to the Chesapeake. Ignoring this rumor, *Virginia*'s commander, Commodore Franklin Buchanan, nevertheless devoted every waking moment to getting his ship to sea. Only seventeen years before, in 1845, he had been responsible for locating the site and organizing the U. S. Naval Academy at Annapolis, Maryland, where he served as its first superintendent. And now, he would be sailing out to do battle with many of its graduates.

On the morning of March 8, 1862, *Virginia* was ready to sally forth. The federal blockading squadron lay barely six and a half miles off Old Point Comfort and a dozen miles from Norfolk. Lying at anchor off Fortress Monroe were *Virginia*'s sister ships before the war, the 47-gun steam-frigate *Minnesota* and 44-gun *Roanoke*, with over twelve hundred men between them. There was also the 52-gun sailing frigate *St. Lawrence*, as well as several gunboats and storeships. Off Newport News, several miles above, and well out in the stream, swinging lazily at anchor lay the 50-gun frigate *Congress* and the 24-gun sloop of war *Cumberland*. The day was clear and calm. Washed clothing hung from the rigging, and boats were hanging to the lower booms of the latter two vessels. No one in the federal squadron expected an attack.

The tide reached its height at 1:40 P.M., and Commodore Buchanan was aware that he would have to take advantage of it if he were to launch his surprise assault on the Union blockaders with any effect. As the lumbering ironclad, with a plucky little consort of gunboats, *Beaufort* and *Raleigh*, steamed into the deep channels of Hampton Roads, a new era in warfare was about to begin.

Immediately sighting the ironclad's smoke, the Yankee men-of-war struggled to strip for battle, even as the strange-looking warship approached. Wash was ripped from the rigging, the boats hanging to the lower booms were dropped astern, and the booms themselves brought alongside.

Shortly after 2:00 P.M., as the little Confederate squadron moved up, the tiny gunboat *Beaufort* fired the opening shots. Signals were hoisted up *Virginia*'s flagstaff giving the order for close action.

Both *Cumberland*, under the command of Acting Lieutenant Commander George W. Morris, and *Congress*, under Lieutenant Commander Joseph B. Smith, served their guns with remarkable speed, despite their initial surprise. Before the ironclad was three-quarters of a mile off, *Cumberland* had opened a deafening fire with her heavy pivot guns, an effort which was soon being duplicated by *Congress*, the gunboats, and the adjacent shore batteries.

In their haste to join the fight, *Minnesota, Roanoke,* and *St. Lawrence* hurriedly got underway, and just as promptly ran aground in rapid succession on the nearby mud flats. Though they managed to get off a few shots, the three ships were for the most part helpless and too far from the battle to be of value.[7]

Virginia held her fire until within easy range of her prey. She then blasted away with her forward pivot gun, decimating the after pivot gun and gun crew of *Cumberland.* As the ironclad passed close by *Congress,* obviously intent on attacking *Cumberland,* she received a broadside which normally would have severely crippled or sunk a wooden ship. The shots merely bounced harmlessly from her sloping thick-skinned side. A deadly point-blank broadside was issued in reply. *Congress* reeled from its impact. Resolute in her objective, *Virginia* plodded ominously forward, leaving *Beaufort* and *Raleigh* behind to do battle with the injured frigate.[8]

Undismayed by the powerful enemy broadsides offered by *Cumberland,* which lay ahead, the ironclad charged, firing her bow gun as she came on, intent on goring the Yankee with her massive iron bow ram. It seemed at that moment that every Union gun within range was concentrating its fire on her, but shot and shell merely ricocheted or exploded harmlessly against her armor. On she came, slowly, 3,200 tons of death and destruction. Then, with a mighty crunching sound, her 1,500-pound cast-iron ram mortally pierced the wooden *Cumberland* under the fore rigging of her starboard side. Aboard *Virginia* the shock was instantaneous. Pandemonium reigned in the engine room as engineers ran about examining boilers and machinery to see if anything had been wrenched loose. Quickly, Commodore Buchanan ordered her engines thrown into reverse. It was only with great difficulty that the ironclad was able to extract herself because her beak had lodged fast in the hull of her victim. The foundering Yankee vessel was trying to take her assailant with her. Suddenly, the ironclad broke free, backing clear of the doomed ship but leaving her ram stuck within the fatal wound it had caused, a wound described by Lieutenant John Taylor Wood, one of *Virginia*'s officers, as "wide enough to drive in a horse and cart."[9]

The giant wooden ship began listing badly, but her gallant crew failed to cease their firing. A crewman from *Virginia*, momentarily appearing outside of the iron roof of his ship, was instantly cut in half by the blaze. But *Cumberland*'s minutes were few. The crew was soon being driven from the gun deck to the spar deck by the mounting waters as she listed further and further to port. Suddenly, a pivot gun broke loose, rampaged wildly across the tilted deck, and crushed one sailor to death. Within forty minutes after the battle had been enjoined, *Cumberland*'s mighty keel rested on the river bottom in fifty-four feet of water. Her colors were still flying from her three masts, pointing heavenward at a forty-five-degree angle. Then she rolled on her side and the flags disappeared.[10]

Virginia now turned her attention to *Congress*, which had slipped her cables, set her fore-topsail, and, with the aid of the tug *Zouave*, retreated into shoal water to beach herself beneath the protection of the nearby shore batteries. Suddenly *Congress* found herself under attack not only by *Virginia*, *Raleigh*, and *Beaufort*, but also by three more Confederate vessels which had entered the fray: the 2-gun *Jamestown*, 12-gun *Patrick Henry*, and 1-gun *Teaser*. Though injured and taking on water through leaks caused by the loss of her beak, *Virginia* attempted to close on the stranded frigate. After dragging her keel through the muddy bottom, the ironclad halted 200 yards away and opened a deadly broadside, knocking out one after another the guns and the crews of the ill-fated *Congress*. The Yankee ship was soon afire in her wardroom, sickroom, and main hold. Finally, only two guns in her stern remained, until a shot blew the muzzle off one, and the other was blown from its carriage. The carnage was terrible, and the decks of *Congress* literally ran red with blood. With absolutely no hope of salvation and her captain dead, she ran up the white flag of surrender—but not before *Beaufort* got in a final shot.[11]

Commodore Buchanan quickly ordered *Beaufort* and *Raleigh* to steam alongside the frigate and take off her crew. The ship was surrendered to Lieutenant Commander W. H. Parker of *Beaufort*, by Lieutenant Austin Pendergast, who had succeeded her mortally wounded master, Commander Smith.[12]

The sinking of the U. S. S. *Cumberland* off Newport News, Virginia, by the Confederate ironclad ram *Virginia*, March 8, 1862. Official U. S. Navy Photograph.

Despite the flag of surrender, Union riflemen and artillery ashore resumed firing at the first sight of the rebel seamen on *Congress*'s decks, killing a number who had been assisting Union wounded from the frigate, as well as several of the *Congress*'s own crew. The fire soon became so intense that the gunboats were forced to withdraw.[13]

Not able to take possession of his prize and violently incensed that the Yankees would continue to fire even under a white flag, Buchanan summoned his men back from *Congress* and ordered hot shot prepared to burn the enemy ship. While Buchanan directed this operation, a Union bullet ripped through his thigh, and command was assumed by Lieutenant Catesby ap R. Jones. Within a short time thereafter, the U. S. frigate *Congress* was fatally wrapped in flames.[14]

Momentarily, the ironclad's new commander toyed with the idea of attacking the stranded *Minnesota* (the other two ships having in the interim floated free), but with night coming on and the tide falling, he decided to await the morning, when the entire blockade might be lifted. Reluctant but jubilant, the Confederate squadron steamed back into its lair in the Elizabeth River.[15] The end of the age of the wooden fighting ship had arrived.

Word of the Confederate victory spread across the North and South by telegraph. The Union was mortified, but a heady air reigned in Dixie. The Yankees had lost two major warships and nearly four hundred men at the cost of hardly sixty casualties to the Confederacy.[16] The blockade would, in all probability, be lifted the next day. There were prophesies that Washington, New York, and even Boston might soon be subjected to the shelling of the ironclad's big guns.[17]

At daybreak, the Confederates were astonished to find a diminutive craft lying between themselves and the stranded *Minnesota*. It was quickly ascertained that the innocuous-looking vessel was nothing less than the Union's answer to *Virginia*, John Ericsson's single-turreted ironclad ship *Monitor*.

The historic engagement which followed, the first battle in history between iron ships of war, need not be recounted here in full, for it is a tale familiar to every schoolchild. Suffice it to say that the battle, though hotly fought, resulted in a standoff. The Union blockade of Hampton Roads and the James would be maintained. *Virginia*'s end came, not as a result of battle, nor even of the elements, as would be the fate of her nemesis *Monitor*, but because of her own massive size and design.

During the following month, the tide of war shifted dramatically in the Virginia theater of operations. Confederate land forces under General Joseph E. Johnston had retired up the peninsula formed by the James and York rivers to meet an expected onslaught by an enormous Union army under General George B. McClellan. Rumors of the impending evacuation of Norfolk increased each day. On May 9, while at anchor off Sewell's Point, the commander of *Virginia*, having sallied out to meet the enemy, noticed that the Confederate flag was no longer flying over the batteries there. The site had been abandoned. When an officer from the ship was dispatched to Norfolk to inquire why the battery had been abandoned, he was astonished to discover the entire town deserted of troops and the navy yard on fire.[18]

"This precipitate retreat was entirely unnecessary," one of *Virginia*'s officers later asserted,

> for while *Virginia* remained afloat, Norfolk was safe, or, at all events, was not tenable by the enemy, and James River was partly safe, for we could have retired behind the obstructions in the channel at Craney Island, and, with the batteries at that point, could have held the place, certainly until all the valuable stores and machinery had been removed from the navy yard.[19]

Two courses of action lay open to the ironclad. She could run the blockade of the Union-held forts and ships. In which case, because of her slow speed and great draft, she would probably cause little damage to Yankee shipping, and would inevitably have to cross swords again with *Monitor* and other powerful warships, and in the end face defeat. The alternative was to lighten ship and go up the James to Harrison's Landing or City Point to assist in the defense of Richmond. *Virginia*'s third, and destined to be her last, commander, Commodore Josiah Tattnall, decided on the latter course of action.[20]

Tattnall summoned all hands and informed them that they were going up the James but must first lighten the ship by no less than five feet. They would then be obliged to fight their way past strong Union batteries at Newport News and a great many Yankee warships lying in Hampton Roads.[21]

With three rousing cheers, his men went to work, throwing over ballast, spare stores, water, and practically anything that was not bolted down. By midnight the ship had been lightened by three feet. Only two more feet and she would be ready. Yet by decreasing her draft, the ship was made entirely unfit for the action she would inevitably face. Two feet of her wooden hull below her iron-plated shield had become fully exposed. Two more feet, and she would be fatally vulnerable to enemy fire. But she could not be returned to her former draft by the necessary expedient of letting in water without putting out her furnace fires and possibly even flooding her magazine. And to make matters worse, her pilots informed Tattnall that with the westerly wind then blowing, the tides would be cut down so much that the ship would never even make it upriver to Jamestown Flats. They refused, in fact, to assume any responsibility at all for taking her out. The latter news provoked one of the ship's officers to remark sarcastically, "All officers . . . should learn to do their own piloting."[22]

There seemed no other course for Tattnall but to give the order to destroy the ship. Coolly, he had her run aground on a shoal near Crancy Island and landed her 300-man crew with their arms and several days' provisions. With only two small boats at his disposal, the landing took more than three hours. Lieutenants Catesby Jones and John Taylor Wood, after setting the ship afire fore and aft, were the last to leave. Pulling for shore, and guided by the light of the blazing ship, Jones and Wood reached safety at daybreak.[23] "Thus," Tattnall later wrote, "perished the *Virginia*, and with her many highflown hopes of naval supremacy and success."[24]

Chapter Seventeen

THE PRESIDENT
DEEMED IT ADVISABLE

JUST FIVE days after the Union evacuation of Fort Sumter,
President Abraham Lincoln declared six southern states
which had seceded from the Union (South Carolina, Georgia,
Alabama, Florida, Mississippi, and Texas) to be in a state of
insurrection. This momentous proclamation stated that "the
President deemed it advisable to set on foot a blockade of the
ports within the States aforesaid." And to insure the success of
this objective, he directed that

> a competent force will be posted so as to prevent the entrance and
> exit of the vessels from the ports aforesaid. . . . If, therefore, with
> a view to violate such blockades any vessel shall attempt to leave
> any of said ports, the vessel will be duly warned . . . and if the
> same vessel shall again attempt to enter or leave the blockaded
> port, she will be captured and sent to the nearest commercial
> port, for such proceedings against her and her cargo as may be
> deemed advisable.

On April 27 the blockade was extended to include North Carolina and Virginia.[1]

Many are the tales of the sleek, fast, blockade-running
steamers which regularly plied the waters between Nassau and
the Carolinas, surreptitiously threading through the thick cordon of Yankee cruisers which surrounded every Confederate
Atlantic and Gulf port, under the blanket of night or fog. Yet
today, few realize that, at the outset of the war, a fairly large
rebel commerce was carried on in the Chesapeake. Not only
supplies, but men, recruits for the Confederate army from oc-

cupied southern Maryland, slipped with shocking regularity across the Potomac River to Virginia, despite the strong measures imposed by the U. S. Navy. To meet the crisis and to prevent a successful blockade of the river by Confederate forces, U. S. Secretary of the Navy Gideon Welles ordered a strict patrol to be maintained by the small, and at first, undermanned Potomac Flotilla. As the war dragged on, the flotilla increased in strength, usually through the addition of ferry boats or small steamers outfitted with a few guns. The flotilla's sphere of control was also enlarged, and patrols were carried out as far south as the Rappahannock and Piankatank rivers. The southern half of the Bay, with the exception of the rebel-held James, York, and Elizabeth rivers, was managed by naval forces based in Hampton Roads off Fortress Monroe, and later, after the recapture of Norfolk, the Norfolk Navy Yard.

On May 4, 1861, Flag Officer Pendergast, in the frigate *Cumberland*, then lying off Fortress Monroe, seized the first of literally dozens of blockade runners which would eventually be apprehended in the tidewater area. The two vessels proved to be the schooners *Mary and Virginia* and *Theresa C.*, laden with coal and cotton.[2] Ten days later Flag Officer Silas H. Stringham, in the U. S. S. *Minnesota*, captured the schooners *Mary Willis*, *Delaware Farmer*, and *Emily Ann*, all laden with tobacco, in Hampton Roads. The ship *Argo*, bound from Richmond for Bremen, was taken soon after.[3] By the end of May the bark *Star*, bound from Richmond to Bremen, the steamboats *James Guy* and *Thomas Colyer*, and the bark *Winifred* were captured also.[4] Yet, it was estimated that for every vessel taken five slipped through. And, for every three captured intact, one was burned or sunk.

On June 8 the U. S. S. *Resolute*, a tiny commercial steamer which had been purchased by the Navy for service in the Potomac Flotilla just one month earlier, while serving under the command of Acting Master William Budd, captured what would turn out to be the first casualty, the blockade-running schooner *Somerset*, in Breton Bay. The prize was towed close to the Virginia shore and burned by her captors.[5]

Almost as if in response to the insult of capture, on June 15, Confederates seized the large Yankee schooner *Christiana*

Keen, aground in five feet of water on the Potomac opposite Cedar Point. The schooner had boldly ventured down the river unescorted by a single Federal warship and had struck a shoulder of the wide mud flats which extended from the Virginia shore well into the river off Upper Machodoc Creek. It was not long after her stranding that a party of thirty or forty rebels boarded the ship and set her afire. "The wreck," one Yankee naval officer reported, "is now a good mark, one not easily removed."[6]

Two weeks later, on June 30, while on patrol, the U. S. S. *Reliance,* Lieutenant J. P. K. Mygatt commanding, encountered the Baltimore sloop *Passenger* capsized and barely afloat in the Potomac. Close investigation revealed someone attempting to conceal himself behind the vessel's centerboard. It was later ascertained that the fellow, named Kerr, though claiming he was escaping from the rebel shore, was indeed a Confederate probably attempting to run the blockade.[7]

Occasionally, Yankee naval reconnaissance patrols got lucky. On Monday, July 18, one such patrol, which included the U. S. S. *Yankee, Resolute,* and boats from the steam sloop *Pawnee,* penetrated into the Yeocomico River and discovered several large rebel schooners with sails unbent. One of the vessels, *Favorite,* was preparing to run the blockade. Taken in tow, she was hauled to an anchorage off Piney Point, near the Maryland shore. Potomac Flotilla Flag Officer Tunis A. M. Craven later reported that the vessel was sunk on July 18 "either by being carelessly run into by another vessel or from the neglect on [my] part to leave men on board to watch and keep her pumped out."[8]

During the early days of the war, especially after the Union defeat at the First Battle of Manassas on July 21, Confederate invasion across the Potomac seemed a distinct probability to federal authorities in Washington. Flotilla Commander Craven was thus directed to destroy all vessels on the Maryland and Virginia shores if invasion seemed imminent. In early August, the merchant sloop *Jane Wright,* Captain John Lawrence, commander and owner, was seized while at anchor off Hallowing Point, Virginia, in the upper Potomac. Lawrence managed to persuade his captor, Master's Mate A. G. Harris of the U. S. S. *Scout,* that he was a loyal citizen bound downriver on bona fide business not inimical to the best interests of the Union. Harris provided the captain with a pass, and the sloop was released. Unfortunately for Lawrence, he again met up with Yankee blockaders off Smith Point, and his vessel was seized on August 16. This time she was sunk by her captors. Lawrence protested to Secretary of the Navy Gideon Welles, who queried Craven on the reason for the action. Craven replied that he had been informed by the Assistant Secretary of the Navy of an imminent invasion and was simply following orders.[9]

Four days after the sinking of *Jane Wright*, the sloop *T. W. Riley*, a commercial vessel belonging to James W. Gessford, was ordered by Craven seized and sunk. A protest was raised by the owner; Craven was queried; and again the whole matter, much to Gessford's chagrin, was buried.[10]

In early October Union authorities learned that the rebels were fitting out a large schooner called *Martha Washington* in Quantico Creek, off the Potomac. The danger of invasion still loomed large in the minds of Union military authorities, and it was feared that the schooner, in conjunction with the sole rebel gunboat on the river, the C. S. S. *George Page*, would be used to ferry troops across to the Maryland shore in the assault. Thus, an expedition was fitted out under the command of Lieutenant Abraham D. Harrell. With a handful of men in a gig and two launches, Harrell entered the mouth of the creek at about 2:30 A.M. on October 11. Searching in pitch darkness and within pistol shot from shore, the party discovered the schooner tied up close to land and guarded by a single sentry. The sentry immediately detected the approach of the Yankees and fled to alarm the nearby camp. Without wasting a moment, the Yankees boarded the schooner, heaped up her furniture, and watched nervously as she was put to the torch by Acting Master Amos P. Foster of the U. S. S. *Resolute*. Guided by the light of the burning ship, Harrell and his men had to dodge a vicious hail of Confederate bullets before reaching the open Potomac. Their gallant mission, however, had been a success for which Harrell received a commendation and promise of a better command from the Secretary of the Navy.[11]

Not long afterward, on November 6, the big rebel schooner *Ada* was discovered at anchor five miles up Corrotoman Creek, off the Rappahannock River, by a party from the U. S. S. *Cam-*

bridge. This vessel, which was hard aground, was discovered to be of Baltimore registry and the property of a certain Captain Pritchard. Unable to remove the stranded ship from the shoal, another boat party from the U. S. S. *Rescue* boarded her and set her afire.[12]

In his annual report to the President, issued on December 2, 1861, Secretary of the Navy Welles noted that since the institution of the blockade in April, a total of 153 rebel vessels had been captured.[13] Of these, nearly thirty, or one-fifth, had been taken in the Chesapeake tidewater, nine of which had been destroyed. The effects of the growing strength of the blockaders were being felt by the Confederacy, particularly in the realm of the Potomac Flotilla. Rebel strongpoints all along the Virginia shore of the Potomac had been tested and silenced. On January 12, 1862, the U. S. S. *Pensacola* successfully ran past once-strong rebel batteries at Cockpit and Shipping points in an open demonstration that the Southerners' use of the river was coming to an end.[14]

In early March 1862, major rebel contention for the river did come to an end with the destruction of the single Confederate gunboat which had operated on its waters. The 410-ton side-wheel steamer *George Page* had been built as a transport in 1853 at Washington and was attached to the U. S. Army Quartermaster's Department when captured by Confederate forces at Aquia Creek on the Potomac in May 1861. Though armed with only two 32-pounders, forward and aft, and a single pivot gun amidships, the gunboat had served as a continual threat to Union control over the Potomac. She had a full complement of 150 men, but her commander, Lieutenant Charles Carroll Simms, had rarely been able to take her out beyond the Quantico-Chopawamsic Creek area, owing to the presence of strong Union batteries across the river at Budds Ferry and to vigilant patrols by the Potomac Flotilla.[15]

By the beginning of 1862, Abraham Lincoln had become increasingly aggravated over the continued presence of rebel batteries commanding the upper Potomac below Washington, and several expeditions to silence them were planned by General George B. McClellan, commander in chief of the Army.

Capture and destruction of the Confederate blockade-running schooner *Martha Washington* in Quantico Creek, Virginia. From *Frank Leslie's Illustrated News*. Courtesy: U. S. Naval History Division, Department of the Navy.

The only Confederate gunboat to operate on the Potomac River, *George Page* was blown up in Quantico Creek, Virginia, to prevent capture. From *Harper's Weekly*. Official U. S. Navy Photograph.

None, however, materialized. In the end, it was on the orders of Confederate General Joseph E. Johnston, commander of Confederate forces in Northern Virginia, that the batteries were abandoned and rebel naval forces on the Potomac destroyed to prevent capture.

On the morning of March 9, 1862, the U. S. S. *Anacostia* and *Yankee*, on patrol in the upper Potomac, observed a number of unusual fires at the rebel battery posts on either side of the entrance to Quantico Creek on Cockpit Point and Shipping Point. Massive explosions were heard which reverberated down the river. When Union batteries opened fire on the rebel positions, there was no reply. The sites had been abandoned and destroyed. Among the last rebel holdings to blow up was the C. S. S. *George Page*.[16]

Full control of the Potomac River had been returned to the Union, but rebel efforts to run the blockade, though now infrequent, continued elsewhere in the tidewater.

On September 15, 1862, the Confederate blockade-running schooner *Arctic* was captured in the Great Wicomico River by the U. S. S. *Thomas Freeborn*, Lieutenant Commander Samuel Magaw commanding, and burned to the waterline by her captors.[17]

Frequently, the rebels used forged or captured papers to get through the blockade. On February 18, 1863, the schooner *Elma* was boarded in Mobjack Bay, Virginia, by Acting Master Thomas Andrews of the U. S. S. *Crusader*. Andrews was informed by the schooner's master that the vessel was bound from New York to Baltimore. After reviewing his pass, the Yankee permitted *Elma* to remain near his station that evening. Later that night, the schooner quietly hoisted anchor and proceeded under the stern of the U. S. schooner *Samuel Rotan* and was promptly stopped and examined by Acting Volunteer Lieutenant William W. Kennison, the schooner's master. It took some convincing, but Kennison finally released *Elma*. Two days later the supposed merchantman was discovered burned to the waterline in the East River, Virginia. Federal authorities surmised that she had been a Confederate runner trying to slip through the blockade, but upon being stopped while coming in, and then stopped again while attempting to run back out, found further efforts to be in vain and was burned to prevent her inevitable capture.[18]

On March 13, another blockade-running schooner ran into Milford Haven, the quiet little sound between Gwynn's Island and the Virginia shore below the Piankatank River. The following evening, alerted to the approach of boat parties sent out from the U. S. S. *Crusader*, the vessel's cargo was quickly removed by the rebels. Not able to get her out, they burned the 50-ton vessel to prevent capture.[19]

Three schooners, *Charity*, *Flight*, and *Gazelle*, found themselves cornered in the Yeocomico River on May 27, 1863, by the U. S. S. *Coeur de Lion*, Acting Master William G. Morris commanding.[20] All three were put to the torch. Two weeks later, Morris discovered two more runners, the schooners *Odd Fellow* and *Sarah Margaret*, at anchor in Coan River and dispatched boat crews to take and burn them.[21]

Despite the overwhelming Union naval superiority, the Confederates occasionally struck back. On March 11, 1864, for instance, the merchant schooner *Julia Baker* was boarded near Newport News, Virginia, by a band of rebel guerrillas and captured. After more than $2,500 was removed from her master and crew, the ship was put to the torch.[22]

On July 24, 1864, the steamship *Kingston* ran aground in shallow water between Smith Point and Windmill Point in Chesapeake Bay. The ship was boarded by a band of local guerrillas and burned.[23] A similar fate was in store for the 858-ton steamboat *Knickerbocker*, which unfortunately ran aground in ten feet of water off Smith Point. By February 13, 1865, her situation had been discovered by rebel units and an attempt was made to board and destroy her. The rebels were driven off by the timely arrival of the U. S. gunboat *Mercury*, Acting Master Thomas Nelson commanding. A second attempt was made by the rebels on the 15th. This time the ship was taken and burned to the waterline.[24]

On April 15, 1865, the steamer *Harriet DeFord* was boarded in the Bay barely thirty miles below Annapolis by a party of twenty-seven Confederates led by Captain Thaddeus Fitzhugh. A Federal naval detachment was immediately dispatched to recapture the steamer. The ship soon became the focal point of a large naval search. It was ultimately learned from a rebel prisoner that Fitzhugh had taken the ship into Dimer's Creek above the Rappahannock River and had run aground numerous times in the process. Much of her cargo had to be thrown overboard to lighten her, and the remainder was removed with the assistance of local farmers. Once relieved of her freight, Fitzhugh had her put to the torch, the last vessel destroyed in the Chesapeake tidewater during the Civil War.[25]

Chapter Eighteen

A PRIZE TO THE
SOUTHERN CONFEDERACY

B Y THE autumn of 1862, the Chesapeake Bay north of the
James and York rivers was firmly in Union hands. Tran-
quility on this backwater of the war was credited to the Potomac Flotilla of the United States Navy, a force composed primarily of overaged, lightly-armed tugs, ferryboats, and steamers which had been hastily inducted into service during the
early days of the conflict. Yet despite the flotilla's weaknesses,
few in the Confederate States Navy, blockaded within the
confines of the James by an enormously powerful Federal
squadron, held much hope that the Union could ever be seriously injured in the waters of the upper Bay region. There was
simply no way that any force could be maneuvered to hurt the
weakly-manned flotilla.

One man, however—Lieutenant John Taylor Wood of the
Confederate States Navy—had other ideas. Wood was a re-
sourceful naval officer who had been assigned to the Richmond
Station at the outbreak of war. He served aboard the ironclad C.
S. S. *Virginia* during her historic engagement with the "cheese-
box on a raft," the U. S. S. *Monitor*, and acquitted himself
admirably. With the fall of Norfolk and the destruction of his
ship in May 1862, he was retired up the James with the ragtag
remains of the Confederate Navy.

Unlike most Confederate naval officers in Richmond,
whose attentions had been riveted to the blockaders at Hampton Roads, Wood was intrigued by the opportunities which the
weakened rear of the Union naval forces in the upper Bay

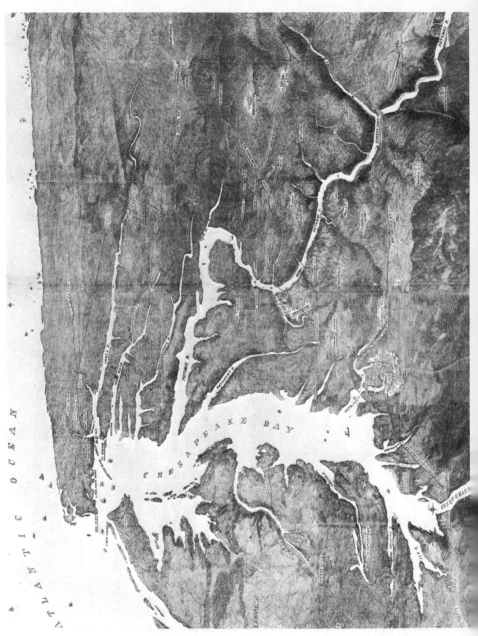

A pictorial map of the seat of war, including the Chesapeake Bay and its tributaries. From *Harper's Weekly*, 1861. Courtesy: U. S. Naval History Division, Department of the Navy.

presented. They may have seized control of the waters, but they had yet to hold the shores. Might not a serious blow to Federal naval supremacy be struck by a well-organized guerrilla force operating from those very shores? A daring nighttime boarding and capture of some unsuspecting, lightly-armed Yankee warship held infinite possibilities for wreaking havoc in the tidewater shipping lanes. A surprise attack on one or more of the Potomac Flotilla steamers which regularly patrolled the waters of the Potomac, Rappahannock, or Piankatank rivers offered the best possibilities, for all were operating in Confederate territory, and all were usually undermanned and lightly armed.

Carefully, Wood laid out his plan to the Confederate naval command. The scheme was accepted. Wood and his second, Lieutenant Francis Hoge, were permitted to handpick a crew from the Confederate school ship *Patrick Henry*, anchored off Richmond, and by the first of October he was ready to depart.

The project was undertaken in the utmost secrecy, for Yankee spies were everywhere, and the element of surprise was imperative for success. Wood's small band of volunteers were armed only with cutlasses, French revolvers, shotguns, and muskets.[1] They would, therefore, have to rely on stealth, surprise, and mobility rather than firepower, and would carry with them overland four small boats saved from C. S. S. *Virginia*. Only at the last minute were the volunteers informed of their destination. They were to proceed to Mathews County, on the Piankatank River. There they were to link up with a certain Lewis Hudgins, an acting master in the Confederate navy and a knowledgeable resident of the area. Hudgins and his men called their band "The Arabs" of Mathews County and were prepared to provide whatever assistance was necessary.[2]

Within a few days Wood and his men had reached their destination and after a brief consultation decided to proceed further north to test the waters of the Potomac. On October 7, after a period of patient vigil in concealment, the Southerners spied the schooner *Frances Elmore* at anchor in mid-channel below Popes Creek, Maryland. Without the least opposition, they boarded the vessel. They were disappointed, however, to find her laden only with hay. *Elmore*'s crew was quickly taken prisoner, but while looting the ship, the Southerners spotted a flotilla steamer bearing down on them. Quickly, Wood ordered the *Elmore* put to the torch, even as he and his men shoved off for the Virginia shore. By the time the U. S. S. *Yankee* arrived, the schooner was a raging inferno.[3]

Wood and his band retired south to Gwynn's Island, frustrated at their failure to waylay a warship on the Potomac. Perhaps here, they hoped, they might have better luck. A blockade had been thrown up across the Piankatank and Rappahannock rivers, and naval patrols regularly penetrated into them on reconnaissance missions. The rebels awaited the right moment—that precise instant when one of the Federal warships let its guard down. Days passed without incident—then a week. The initial zeal which had permeated the band gradually dissipated as a second week passed without action. Finally, an opportunity (of sorts) presented itself. An unprotected ship was sighted at anchor off the Rappahannock. She was not a warship, but she *was* big and she *was* a Yankee!

Alleghanian was a 1,400-ton merchantman of New York registry, heavily laden with a cargo of guano. She was en route from Baltimore to London with a pilot and a complement of twenty-two officers and crew. Twenty miles off the mouth of the Rappahannock she met a strong head wind and was obliged to come to anchor.[4]

At 9:45 P.M., October 28, seaman James L. Jackson and another crewman were at the watch when they spied several boats loaded with men rowing up alongside the ship. Almost instantly, she was boarded by more than two dozen rebel seamen vigorously brandishing sabers and revolvers. Resistance was not offered, for there were few, if any, arms aboard, and the U. S. Navy (usually present in these waters) was nowhere to be seen.[5]

The rebels immediately proceeded to tie up the crew and sack the ship. Personal belongings, chests, and trunks were ransacked. The crew was then untied, one by one, and passed over the side of the ship into a small boat, though the captain, the chief mate, and the pilot were held prisoner. Hours later, the crew was picked up adrift by the steamer *Daniel Webster;* they spilled out their tale of woe. Because several were well dressed and had managed to carry a few of their bags with them, however, they were immediately packed off to Washington and incarcerated under suspicion of mutiny. By the time their story was verified, it was too late. The Confederates had set *Alleghanian* ablaze near Milford Haven during the night and escaped to Gwynn's Island, guided by the lights of bonfires ashore.[6]

At 2 A.M. on October 29, the U. S. mortar schooner *T. A. Ward*, Acting Master W. L. Babcock, arrived on the scene, attracted by the glow of the burning ship. There she found the U. S. S. *Crusader*, recently arrived, with its newly-appointed captain, Thomas I. Andrews. Daylight revealed the extent of the rebel arson. "The vessel now lies at anchor," Andrews reported, "with her mizzenmast gone, together with the cabin, leaving the after part of the hull a mere shell to within 6 feet of the waterline." The Yankees were unable to save a thing from the blazing ship.[7]

Though Wood and his men had caused the destruction of two Northern ships, they had not achieved their intended objective, the capture of a Union warship. The important element of surprise had been lost, and the rebels returned to Richmond. Wood's avowed intentions to return, however, did not go unobserved, especially by Northern spies operating near Richmond. On November 17, slightly more than two weeks after the destruction of *Alleghanian*, Commodore A. A. Harwood, commander of the Potomac Flotilla, received information from the Secretary of the Navy that the rebels were again planning to capture a U. S. steamer in Virginia waters. Concern had grown so great by this time that strong orders were issued for officers to guard against surprise attack, and instructional pamphlets were printed telling how to repel boarders.[8]

Time did not lessen the flotilla commander's concern. On July 24, 1863, an urgent dispatch from a Federal spy in rebel territory reached the War Department. Five hundred men, the message noted, had been spotted at Old Church, Virginia, on July 16 with six boats on wagons going to surprise a Yankee gunboat on the Rappahannock.[9] Commodore Harwood immediately dispatched the intelligence to Lieutenant Commander Magaw, senior officer afloat with the flotilla, along with directions that those vessels on patrol at the mouth of the Rappahannock were to keep within support distance of each other at all

times. They were not to ascend the river under any circumstances without specific orders.[10] Though Harwood could not
have known it, the spy's information was only partly correct.
For obvious reasons the Confederate operation was recalled to
Richmond to await a more propitious moment.[11]

In August Wood was ready to give it another try. On the
12th, with eleven officers, seventy-one men, and four boats, he
departed Richmond for the Piankatank. Late on August 16, he
arrived at his destination, twenty-five miles up from the river's
mouth. The boats were launched without delay and that night
were rowed down to the Bay in search of Federal warships.
Upon reaching the Chesapeake they spotted two gunboats
which were underway. Wood ordered the party to retire back up
the river two miles to seek concealment.[12]

Soon after daylight on August 17, a gunboat was observed
coming up the river. Upon anchoring off the creek in which the
rebels lay, the gunboat dispatched five small boats to investigate. Still seeking to keep his force concealed, Wood ordered his
own boats further up the creek. Should the Yankees attack,
Lieutenant Hoge was ordered to defend the boats vigorously.[13]

Quietly the rebels withdrew although Wood and ten men
maintained an advanced position at the mouth of the little
waterway. The Yankee probing operation, however, failed to
penetrate the creek. As they rowed back downriver, one of
Wood's men at the creek entrance was seen, and the Union
seamen opened fire. The skirmish was brief but intense, and the
Northerners were driven off with losses.

His position now known, Wood decided that a move down
the Piankatank would be out of the question. Without hesita-
tion, he decided that the boats should cross the river and be
hauled overland to the Rappahannock where the Federals were
less likely to suspect an attack. On the 19th he reached Urbanna. Twice he sallied forth downriver in quest of Yankee
blockaders, only to return empty-handed.[14] The third time, he
vowed, would be different.

The evening of August 23 was sultry on the Chesapeake.
The last thing the officers of the U. S. Navy gunboats *Satellite*
and *Reliance* expected was a rebel attack. The two ships lay
quietly at anchor in five to seven fathoms of water at Butler's

Hole, one and a quarter miles from the nearest shore.[15] *Satellite,* a 217-ton side-wheeler armed with a 30-pounder Parrott gun and an 8-inch naval gun, dwarfed her companion, the 90-ton screw steamer *Reliance,* anchored 200 yards away. Though *Reliance* was armed with two guns, a 12-pounder howitzer and a 24-pounder howitzer, only the latter was serviceable.[16] Both vessels were extremely shorthanded, and by midnight their crews, exhausted by constant patrol duty, had turned in.

By 12:20 A.M. most of the crew of *Reliance* was asleep. Several lay in hammocks rigged across the quarterdeck adjacent to the howitzer, while others were in cabins or below. Most of *Satellite*'s crew was similarly disposed.[17]

Nearby, four rebel boats quietly probed the darkness in search of the sleeping Yankee prey. When Wood discovered the two gunboats, he was momentarily stunned. He had hoped to catch one gunboat unawares—but two at once was more than he had counted on. Yet there was extreme danger. The warships were anchored so close together that he would be obliged to divide his forces and board them simultaneously. He refused to pass up such an opportunity. Within minutes, his orders were being passed from one boat to the next in whispers. "Put in line ahead until within hailing distance, then form a line abreast. Board them on each bow." Thereby, the Yankees would not be given a chance to slip their lines. The cable bitts had to be secured at all costs. Lieutenant Hoge and Midshipman Cooke would lead two boats against *Reliance;* Wood would lead the attack on *Satellite.*[18]

On board *Satellite,* the watch on the hurricane deck, an ex-slave, Nelson Frazier, was the first to sight the approaching boats in the dark. He immediately called for identification.[19]

"Second cutters," came the reply.

"Come alongside," the lookout ordered, and then requested a more informative answer. "Identify yourself."

"Privateers," the rebel boat defiantly answered as she bumped the steamer's side.

On the opposite side of the ship, the second boat approached simultaneously. Acting Master's Mate William H. Fogg, the officer of the deck, called out for identification.

"Commodore Morris," came the reply, even as rebels began to board on the port side of the ship. Instantly, Fogg wheeled about and ran along the deck, lustily yelling out, "Boarders. Boarders."[20]

Awakened by the noise, Ensign Rudolph Sommers came forward, ordered Fogg to rouse the crew, and seized his own cutlass and pistol. Stepping onto the deck, his attention was drawn to a noise aft. Thinking he would see his own men there, he approached the quarterdeck and was struck in the neck by a bullet from above and immediately accosted by three or four rebels wielding cutlasses. Pressed closely, the officer retreated. Unfortunately, as his weapon was not capped, he later noted, "I freely used my pistol as a sling shot." Seeing Sommers' predicament, Boatswain's Mate Jack Tye rushed to help fend off the rebels, but was fatally shot through the shoulder from the upper deck. Having now lost his own cutlass and slashed repeatedly on the arm, Sommers was overpowered.[21]

By this time the Yankees aboard were entirely roused, but it was too late. Rebels were everywhere: on the hurricane deck, forward, and at the entry gangway.

Acting Master John F. D. Robinson had been in his cabin. When notified of the boarding attempt, he ordered his men to drive off the enemy, then promptly locked himself in his room.[22]

Master-at-Arms William Bingham, when awakened, ran to the armory and distributed three pistols, but they too were not capped. He then ran for the hurricane deck to get a boarding pike, but when he raised his head above the awning he was slashed by a cutlass and driven back. Gunner's Mate William R. Northrup was captured when he tried to arm himself with a pike from the same place.[23]

Many cringed in terror as the rebels methodically secured the ship. Assistant Engineer Isaac Johnson, emerging from his cabin, saw the ship's black cabin boy sliced across the face with a sword, and retreated horrified into his room.[24]

Upon securing the greatest portion of the ship, the rebels surrounded the captain's cabin and demanded capitulation. Robinson meekly cried out through the door, "I surrender." Immediately, the rebels forced the door open and told Robinson that if he did not come out, stand on a gun carriage, and cry out loudly that he surrendered, they would blow his brains out. Quaking with fear, the captain emerged, went to the quarter-deck, and yelled out that the ship was given up. All resistance ceased.[25]

The contest for the *Reliance,* simultaneously underway, was not as easily or cheaply won. Lieutenant Hoge's boats were spotted in the dark by the alert watch aboard *Reliance* while still seventy-five yards distant. The lookout, one Mr. Hand, hailed them. No answer. Again he hailed them. This time he received the cryptic reply, "Putnam." Alerted by the shouting, the lookout aft, Anthony Spisenger, came forward and hailed the approaching boat. No answer. With the boat barely ten yards away, Spisenger opened fire.[26]

Unimpeded by the Yankees' guns, the rebels came along-side and began clambering over the sides, which were no higher than a cutter's gunwales, and slashed their way through the boarding nets with cutlasses. Spisenger, Hand, a seaman, and a rebel deserter stationed at the cable bitts contested the board-ing with rifle fire, seriously wounding both Hoge and Cooke, but were soon overwhelmed. The rebels' first objective was to prevent the cable from being slipped, although the deserter stationed there was fatally wounded, even as the three remain-ing defenders retreated. Desperately, Hand fled aft to rouse the crew and officers as the remainder of Hoge's men came aboard.[27]

Hearing gunfire and assuming resistance was forming aboard *Reliance,* Lieutenant Wood, having only moments be-fore completed the capture of *Satellite,* dispatched a boatload of his men to assist in the assault. Also awakened by the firing, Acting Master Henry Walters, commander of *Reliance,* jumped from his hammock on the quarterdeck and ran forward. Un-aware that the man at the cable bitts had been shot, or even that the ship had been boarded, he sang out loudly, "Slip the cable." A flash of fire blinked in front of him and a bullet passed close by. Still, he rushed forward. Suddenly, as he reached the pilot-house steps, dark forms appeared ahead. At the same instant that he realized that there was no one at the cable, a cutlass slashed his hand open and a bullet smashed into his stomach.

Dazed, he collapsed on the steps. Unaware that the *Satellite* had also been attacked, he reached for the lanyard in a desperate attempt to blow the ship's whistle for assistance, and then fell into a bloody heap.[28]

By now the third rebel boat was bumping along the port side of *Reliance*, but it was met by the stout resistance of a small cluster of defenders led by Spisenger. Two more rebels were wounded; yet Spisenger's defense, though gallant, was doomed. As the rebels forward moved aft, they captured or wounded the disorganized defenders one by one. Among them was Acting Master's Mate and ship's Executive Officer Thomas Brown. Awakened by the battle, Brown had emerged from his cabin and rushed forward unarmed. Reaching the engine room door, he encountered the rebels and immediately cried out his surrender. He was instantly bound and placed in the engine room, even as the battle swirled about him. Within minutes of Brown's capture, however, resistance collapsed. *Reliance* was now in rebel hands and her crew in irons.[29]

Wood now had two gunboats at his disposal behind Union lines—and for the moment the Yankees did not know it. From the captured crews, he soon learned that a third gunboat, U. S. S. *Currituck*, was due back at the anchorage with a supply of coal in the morning. Perhaps, he reasoned, that vessel might also be captured, and with his mini-armada, he could blaze a path of destruction in the upper tidewater before the Yankees could organize a defense. Unfortunately, he discovered, neither *Reliance* nor *Satellite* had a sufficient supply of coal aboard to conduct such an operation. He thus decided to take the ships up the Rappahannock to Urbanna to take on coal, and descend in the morning to the river's mouth to attack the unsuspecting *Currituck*.[30]

On the morning of August 24, the two gunboats arrived at Urbanna. Wood went ashore to obtain additional men for his expedition and prevailed upon Colonel Rosser, commander of the Fifth Virginia Cavalry, to provide thirty sharpshooters, a request which the colonel was only too glad to fulfill. The coal, however, always in short supply in the Confederacy, could not be procured. Boldly Wood decided to conduct his foray with the stock in hand; he divided the stores equally between the two warships and stood down the river. With her engines beginning to act up, however, *Reliance* was ordered back up to the town of Port Royal. Wood nevertheless proceeded on alone in *Satellite* but was hindered in the Bay by a fresh breeze and rough waters. Furthermore, no federal warships were to be seen. Undismayed, Wood returned to a concealed position upriver to await the dawn and, he hoped, better hunting. He was not disappointed.[31]

Before dawn on the morning of August 25, *Satellite*, still flying United States colors, hailed the schooner *Golden Rod*, bound from Baltimore to Maine with coal. The ship was taken without contest. Since she drew too much water to reach Port Royal or Urbanna, Wood ordered her stripped, burned on the spot, and scuttled.[32]

Within a short time, two more schooners were spotted lying off the mouth of the river. As *Satellite* approached the two unsuspecting merchantmen, Wood hailed them and asked where they were bound and what cargo they carried.

"Anchors and chains, and bound for New York."

"You are my prisoners," Wood informed them, "and the vessel's a prize to the Southern Confederacy."[33]

The two ships, wisely giving up without a fight, proved to be *Two Brothers*, William Boozby, master, and *Coquette*, William Wible, master, with 43,000 weight of anchors and chain. Prize crews were placed aboard, and the vessels taken up the river in tow.[34]

Word of Wood's coup on the Rappahannock did not reach federal authorities until August 28. A single Yankee witness, William Spillman, a member of the crew of *Satellite*, had jumped overboard just before the ship was carried and had managed to swim ashore with another crewman named Clarke. Clarke had been captured by rebel cavalry, but Spillman managed to elude patrols until he was picked up by a friendly boat off Windmill Point.[35]

Yankee authorities were stunned and outraged. Lieutenant Commander Samuel Magaw, U. S. S. *Dragon*, called the capture "the most disgraceful neglect of duty I have ever heard of" and passed the report on to Commodore Harwood.[36]

Harwood acted immediately and ordered Magaw down to the Rappahannock with five gunboats to recapture *Satellite*

and *Reliance* and was soon on the Bay to join them in command
of the new ironclad monitor U. S. S. *Sangamon*. Acting in
concert with the Navy, the U. S. Army dispatched Brigadier
General Kilpatrick with 2,000 cavalry and two batteries of
artillery to Port Conway, Virginia, to assist in the recapture of
the gunboats—or to assure their destruction. To protect Kilpatrick's flank, Brigadier General Buford was ordered down with a
brigade of cavalry and a battery to hold Falmouth Crossing on
the upper Rappahannock, and Major General Warren with
5,000 infantrymen to hold the crossings at Banks and United
States Fords.[37] All to stop less than one hundred thirty
Confederates.

Commodore Harwood, incensed by the rebels' boldness,
strained his flotilla to the limits to reach Port Royal before the
army. His force, composed of the gunboats *Commodore Jones*,
Commodore Morris, *Currituck*, *Jacob Bell*, and *Dragon*, and
the ironclad *Sangamon*, reached Windmill Point at 5:30 A.M. on
August 31. With *Dragon*, *Morris*, and *Bell* in company, Harwood, in *Sangamon*, immediately set off up the Rappahannock
and by 2:15 P.M. had dropped anchor off the town of Tappahannock. *Dragon* was sent ahead to take soundings, and *Sangamon*
was lightened so that she could go further upriver. The following morning, however, after running aground several times, she
found penetration further than Tappahannock impossible. Harwood could not reach Port Royal, and refused to send his gunboats up without the ironclad.[38]

John Taylor Wood and his small band, with the Yankee
navy in hot pursuit, could only go as high as Port Royal. Once
there, he stripped all of the vessels of their arms and machinery
and scuttled them in the shallows. Everything that could be
saved was saved (the anchors and a 30-pounder lost overboard
were abandoned) and moved to the railroad at Milford for shipment to Richmond.[39]

His completion of the task came none too soon. On Tuesday night, September 1, General Kilpatrick and three regiments
of Union cavalry and a 4-gun battery arrived at Port Conway.
The following morning, the guns were opened on the four ships
lying awash off Port Royal. The bombardment lasted four

hours. Taylor and his men were perfectly content to let the Yankees finish off their ships, which were soon little more than smouldering rubbish heaps in the river.[40]

Wood's notoriety spread after the Rappahannock episode, but his ambitions were insatiable. In February 1864, he led another small-boat expedition against a Federal warship, this time in the Neuse River, North Carolina, and succeeded in capturing and destroying the U. S. S. *Underwriter* in the same manner in which he had taken *Satellite* and *Reliance*. The Chesapeake, however, would see more of John Taylor Wood.

In a little more than a month after the destruction of *Underwriter*, Wood returned to his favorite stamping grounds, the domain of the Potomac Flotilla. This time, his target was to be the Federal telegraph station at Cherrystone Point on the Eastern Shore and several army steamers employed in cable operations there. On the evening of March 4, 1864, Wood set off across the Chesapeake with forty or fifty men in open barges. The rebels landed quietly near the unprotected station at 4:00 A.M. The last thing the dozing station operator, a Mr. Dunn, expected was half a hundred yelling Confederates swooping down on him. Dunn and the station, along with a number of horses, were quickly taken, with only the exchange of a few gunshots. Before capture, however, the operator threw his telegraphic instruments into the Bay.[41]

The rebels methodically set about burning the guardhouse and commissary stores. The horses were slaughtered to prevent word of the Confederate's raid getting out too soon after their departure. Fortunately for the Yankees, Dunn had destroyed a number of important messages which had been sent just before the attack, and Wood was denied critical intelligence about Federal naval operations on the Bay.[42]

While the rebels were ransacking the Cherrystone station, the U. S. Army dispatch steamer *Titan* arrived, unaware of the proceedings ashore. Within minutes she was taken and swarming with rebels. Wood soon learned that another steamer, a cable boat called the *Aeolus*, which was armed with a 24-pounder, was out laying cables and he resolved to take her. But *Titan* was unarmed, except for a large quantity of rifles aboard,

and Wood, changing his mind, decided to make a run for the
Rappahannock across the Bay. He failed to consider the dili-
gence of Mr. Dunn, whom he paroled before casting off.[43]

Quickly Dunn made his way to the town of Eastville,
where he sent an urgent telegraph to the War Department in
Washington, informing them of the raid.[44] Secretary of the
Navy Gideon Welles was immediately notified and sent a communication to Commander F. A. Parker,new chief of the Potomac Flotilla, to send two or three of his best gunboats to fan out
on the Bay and track down the raiders.

Acting promptly, Parker threw up a naval screen of gunboats which he hoped would snare Wood once and for all.
Commodore Read, Acting Master Smith, and *Fuchsia*, Acting
Master Street, were dispatched at once to Cherrystone Inlet.
After securing the site, *Commodore Read* was to begin a cruise
in search of *Titan*, informing every Federal warship she encountered of the Southern raiding party. Parker also sent a
dispatch to Lieutenant Commander Hooker, in charge of the
flotilla's First Division, then cruising off the Rappahannock, to
send one of his best gunboats out in search of the marauders and
to make every effort to seal off the myriad creeks lying between
the Rappahannock and Smith Point. A tug and two heavily
armed schooners were ordered to maintain patrol off the prisoner of war camp at Point Lookout. A brig and two schooners
would maintain station at Piney Point. The remainder of the
flotilla, with the exception of two tugs in Nanjemoy Creek,
were to spread out over the reach between the Piankatank River
and Smith Point. Parker did not think it likely that even the
indomitable Lieutenant Wood could manage to penetrate such
a blockade.[45]

The one thing Parker failed to consider was the weather.
The afternoon of March 5 was unusually hazy when Commander Hooker, aboard U. S. S. *Yankee*, was notified that an unidentified steamer had been sighted off the mouth of the Piankatank. He immediately dispatched the gunboat *Tulip* to investigate. Ghostlike, the steamer disappeared into the haze
with *Tulip* in pursuit. Within a short time, Hooker dispatched
the gunboat *Currituck* to join the search.[46]

Hours later, *Tulip* returned to the squadron anchorage and
informed the commander that she had indeed pursued the

mystery ship, a lead-colored vessel, but had lost her in the haze. When last seen, however, she was under a full head of steam heading up the river. Unfortunately, *Tulip*'s captain noted, without a pilot who was knowledgeable about the river, he dared not enter under present weather conditions.[47]

Cursing his luck, Hooker dispatched the steamer *Thomas Freeborn* to find and inform the *Currituck* to take up pursuit. At 7:00 P.M. *Freeborn* returned with word that *Currituck* had penetrated the river more than eight miles but had found nothing. The strange vessel was further upriver than anyone had guessed.[48]

The following morning at daylight, leaving the gunboats *Teaser, Yankee,* and *Tulip* to guard the mouth of the Rappahannock, Hooker proceeded into the Piankatank with *Freeborn, Commodore Read, Jacob Bell, Currituck,* and *Fuchsia.* With *Bell* and *Fuchsia* in the advance, the squadron moved slowly up the river, firing continuously into the woods that lined both shores to drive off possible ambushers. By 10:30 A.M. the squadron had reached Piankatank Muds, beyond which only the lighter-draft vessels could go. *Freeborn, Bell,* and several armed cutters and barges were sent on ahead, toward the town of Freeport.[49]

Again, Wood denied his enemies their prize, for even as Hooker's flotilla was ascending the river, the Southerners were busily dismantling *Titan.* She was then set afire and burned to the waterline. Again, the Yankees came up empty-handed.[50]

The capture and destruction of *Titan* was to be the last of John Taylor Wood's daring raids on the Chesapeake. Yet his performance did not go unnoticed by the Confederate Navy, and in August 1864 he was given command of the C. S. S. *Tallahassee,* in which he promptly proceeded to run the blockade at Wilmington, North Carolina.[51] Wood's short but brilliant raid on Yankee shipping, as far north as Nova Scotia, resulted in the destruction of twenty-six ships and the ransoming of seven others. By the war's end, John Taylor Wood had thus personally accounted for the loss of thirty-four Union military and commercial vessels, a score the United States Navy wished only to forget.

Chapter Nineteen

TULIP

C*HIH KIANG* was not very large, only 93 feet 3 inches in length and 183 tons burthen. The little screw steamer was built before the war for Mandarin Henry G. Ward, of China, specifically for service as a lighthouse tender, but had never been delivered. Upon Ward's death, in June 1863, the U. S. Navy offered to buy her for $30,000, along with another of Ward's ships, *Fuschia*.[1]

With its usual vigor, the Navy spruced up the ship, made the necessary repairs, and armed her with two 24-pounders and a 20-pounder Parrott gun. She was soon assigned to the Potomac Flotilla. The name *Chih Kiang*, however, simply had to go. On June 24, 1864, her new name, U. S. S. *Tulip*, was entered on the Navy lists.[2]

Tulip acquitted herself well, considering her diminutive size. She was just right for the shallow-draft squadron in which she served, and quite suitable for the service required of her by the shoaly Chesapeake tidewater. Operating from the Navy's coaling station in St. Mary's River, Maryland, she had participated in a number of minor actions and patrols, primarily aimed at keeping rebel guerrilla operations along the Potomac, Rappahannock, and Piankatank rivers in check. In January 1864, for instance, she engaged in an operation against rebel forces in Westmoreland County, Virginia, and only two months later was involved in the search for the U. S. Army steamer *Titan*, captured by John Taylor Wood and his band of guerrillas. In April, she joined in an expedition that resulted in an engagement with Southern cavalry units and the destruction of their camp on Carter's Creek, Virginia.[3]

After nearly a year and a half of continuous duty, she badly needed repairs, and her engines were beginning to show signs of stress. In July 1864, two engineers assigned to her reported that her boilers were unseaworthy, and they refused to run the boat. They were promptly suspended and demoted. By November, however, the ship's starboard boiler was obviously defective, and it was promptly condemned as unsafe.[4] After calling at her base on St. Inigoes Creek in the St. Mary's and taking on a load of coal, *Tulip* was ordered to proceed to the Washington Navy Yard for repairs.[5]

Tulip's commander, Captain William H. Smith, was upset over the orders of his superior, Potomac Flotilla Commander Foxhall A. Parker, not to employ the defective boiler on the trip up the Potomac. He informed Parker that without the ability to use both boilers he would be obliged to travel at a severely retarded speed, making his ship a perfect target for the Confederate mobile batteries and snipers on the Virginia shore of the river. He was perfectly willing to risk the danger of explosion in return for greater speed. The order, however, was sternly reiterated. Smith grudgingly agreed to comply—at least for the moment.[6]

At 3:00 P.M., November 11, 1864, *Tulip* departed the St. Inigoes coaling station with 59 officers and crew aboard. Within a short time she had passed the guard schooner *William Bacon*, stationed at the mouth of the St. Mary's, and was on her way up the Potomac. Few aboard even considered it might be their last voyage.

Captain Smith apparently had no intention of complying with Parker's orders. Soon after departing St. Inigoes he queried his senior engineer, George H. Parks, whether or not steam could be raised in the idle boiler. Parks informed the captain, while in the presence of the ship's executive officer, Ensign R. M. Wagstaff, that if a two hour layover at Piney Point could be made, it would be possible to work up a full head of steam in the defective boiler. Undoubtedly delighted, the captain promptly directed the pilot, James Jackson, to bring the ship into Piney Point.[7]

Third Assistant Engineer John Gordon, apparently eager to impress his superiors, didn't wait for the layover to begin building steam in the boiler. As the ship neared its new destination, Acting Master's Mate John Davis, unaware of the layover order, was queried by the pilot why the ship was altering course. Engineer Parks, then in the pilot house with Davis and the pilot, volunteered the information that the ship would soon be running under both boilers. Gleefully, Engineer Gordon, then on watch, informed the trio that "there was no use of stopping at Piney Point, for he had already steam[ed] up." Thus, the ship continued on her way up the Potomac and passed the point.[8]

At approximately 6:00 P.M. Davis was relieved of duty and went forward for a stretch. Ensign Wagstaff and Engineer Parks had already gone below to the wardroom. Captain Smith was on the bridge with Pilot Jackson, Master's Mate John Hammond, and the ship's quartermaster.

It was exactly 6:20 P.M. when *Tulip* commenced passing Ragged Point. Suddenly there was a commotion near the engine room door, and Engineer Gordon was heard calling loudly, "Haul your fires." Engineer Parks, hearing the shouts, bolted from the wardroom onto the deck, followed closely by Ensign Wagstaff. Mate Davis, on the forward deck, also raced aft to see what was going on. Upon reaching the midship, he saw billows of steam pouring out of the engine and fire room hatchways. Seeing the danger, he continued on toward the aft deck, a move that ultimately saved his life. Parks, however, bravely charged into the scalding, steam-filled room, even as Gordon bellowed out, "For God's sake, somebody raise the safety-valve."[9]

But it was already too late. The explosion which ripped U. S. S. *Tulip* apart was tremendous. The blast noise resounded up and down the Potomac for miles. Even rebel prisoners at the Point Lookout prison camp nearly twelve miles away heard the explosion. The upper portion of the ship and all those upon it, including Smith and his officers on the bridge, were instantly pulverized. Those less fortunate were scalded to death or hurled like rag dolls in every direction.[10]

A few men, miraculously surviving the explosion, desperately attempted to lower the gig, but before they could even get it down, *Tulip* slipped beneath the waters, sucking most of those still aboard down with her.[11]

The lucky few cast into the water and still alive seized whatever debris they could to stay afloat. At dusk, the little U. S. Army tug *Hudson*, Captain James Allen commanding, arrived on the scene. Only ten men could be found amid the fragmented, floating wreckage, and those more dead than alive. Despite hours of diligent searching, no more survivors could be located in the twilight of that November evening. Eight bodies and the sole remains of Captain Smith—his hat—were all that were recovered. The following morning the ship's purser, having been missed by the searchers and obliged to tread water all night, reached Piney Point. Of the ten survivors brought aboard the rescue tug, and transferred to the U. S. Navy Storeship *Wyandank* at the St. Mary's Naval Station, two died within hours, and three more were not expected to live.[12]

On the day following the disaster, the U. S. S. *Juniper*, Acting Ensign Philip Sheridan commanding, was dispatched to Ragged Point to search for the bodies of the crew and the remains of *Tulip*. Sheridan's report was succinct.

> I sent out two boats and landed on the beach, where I found large fragments of her remains. I found a trunk belonging to Acting Master's Mate Reynolds, of that vessel, a valise belonging to the pilot, a coat, bag and several blue shirts and a number of officers' caps. I also found two sponges, a lot of letters marked U. S. steamer *Tulip*, large portions of her deck, the top of her pilot house, and her first cutter [which] lay on the beach, but up to the present time I have not been able to find any bodies.[13]

Though initial reports of the disaster and the loss of nearly fifty seamen managed to filter back to the press in Washington, after a few days, news of the incident was quietly muffled. Gradually, the *Tulip* incident was forgotten, until 1940, when a small monument to the victims of the disaster was erected at Cross Manor, near the burial site of the eight dead seamen recovered by the tug *Hudson*. On the centennial anniversary of the little gunboat's loss, November 11, 1964, a small but dignified ceremony was held to commemorate the memory of the men of the U. S. S. *Tulip*[14]

Chapter Twenty

THE INFERNAL MACHINE

THE YEAR 1864 began inauspiciously enough for the North Atlantic squadron blockading Hampton Roads. Despite its massive efforts in the two preceding years, the Union failed to maintain a strong foothold on the James River, and the Confederates had characteristically put the time to good use building a singularly powerful though small flotilla of ironclads. Federal activity was at first minimal. Early in the year, two joint army-navy expeditions were made into the neighborhood of the Nansemond River, but both ended in miserable failure.

Finally, in May, an order came to ascend the James in force. Five ironclads were to be towed up the river by ten small steamers. The advance would be led by a force of seven gunboats which were to protect a large flotilla of troop transports scheduled to land at City Point.[1]

The ascent and landing were carried out on May 5 without the slightest opposition. Orders then directed several gunboats to drag the river above City Point for Confederate torpedoes, or mines.[2] The South had, from the very beginning of the war, been freely deploying these new "infernal machines," first in the Potomac River barely two weeks before the First Battle of Manassas.[3] Charleston and Mobile harbors had also been mined with similar devices, as were sections of the Mississippi, Yazoo, Ogeechee, St. Johns, Roanoke, and Cape Fear rivers.[4] In December 1862 the Union ironclad river gunboat *Cairo* was sunk by one in the Yazoo River, Mississippi,[5] and in July of the following year the U. S. S. *Baron DeKalb* suffered a similar fate.[6] A Confederate Torpedo Bureau was established to train crews and advance the development of the weapon. And the advances were remarkable.

The early torpedoes employed by the Confederates were primitive, but experimentation brought improvement. By the summer of 1863 an electronically detonated torpedo, which could be triggered from afar, was developed and deployed in the James. In August of that year, the little Union gunboat *Commodore Barney* narrowly missed total destruction by one of the mysterious new devices while conducting a reconnaissance of the river near Cox's Farm, six miles above the rebel works at Fort Darling. The device was fired prematurely, but nevertheless lifted the ship's front half into the air a full ten feet. Twenty men had been thrown into the water; two of them drowned.[7]

It was indeed a fiendish device which the U. S. Navy did not wish to encounter unwittingly again. Thus, when runaway slaves informed federal authorities that electric galvanic torpedoes had again been deployed in numbers in the James prior to their ascent in the spring of 1864, every precaution was taken to locate and remove them. On May 6 three Union gunboats, the side-wheelers *Mackinaw, Commodore Morris,* and *Commodore Jones,* were dispatched to take on this task.[8]

Acting on the information of the runaway slaves, the little flotilla, under the overall command of Commander J. C. Beaumont of *Mackinaw,* proceeded cautiously up the river to the vicinity of Four Mile Creek.[9] Here, maintained the runaways, was where the rebel mines were placed. Boat parties were sent out ahead of the three ships to drag the river and investigate the shoreline as the flotilla came to a halt 500 yards from the danger zone. Beaumont was concerned that even though the boat parties were screening the area ahead, they might miss something. He thus ordered the commanders of *Commodore Morris* and *Commodore Jones* not to approach the drag boats. Despite the fact that the order was repeated several times, Acting Lieutenant Thomas Wade, master of *Commodore Jones* permitted his ship to drift forward.[10]

At 2:00 P.M. he had just passed Four Mile Creek and was barely 250 feet from the muddy western shore of the river when the hull of his 542-ton converted ferryboat was lifted completely out of the water as if by the hands of some unseen giant. A huge, 2,000-pound electric torpedo, in Wade's own words, "was exploded directly under the ship with terrible effect, causing her destruction instantly, absolutely blowing the vessel to splinters." *Commodore Jones* sank immediately. Sixty-nine of her crew were casualties, including forty dead. Wade, although seriously injured, was saved, along with several others, by an extraordinary act of heroism by his executive officer, Ensign George W. Adams.[11]

Acting Master's Mate J. F. Blanchard was on the eastern shore of the James River searching several houses for wires and galvanic batteries when the explosion took place. Rushing to his boat, he pushed off and began hauling in the wounded and drowning crew. Someone pointed at a man running along the opposite shore. Several shots were fired, and the man collapsed in a heap. Blanchard promptly landed there and discovered two hidden batteries. He immediately returned to *Mackinaw* and reported his discovery to Commander Beaumont.[12]

Beaumont was concerned, not only about the terrible loss of *Commodore Jones*, but also that other batteries and torpedoes might still be undiscovered. He thus directed Blanchard to return to the western shore and search for additional batteries. Blanchard soon spotted several wires running from the water's edge. Following the wires, he came upon a small box, four feet square, buried in the ground. In the box two Confederates were hiding.[13]

"On close examination," he reported, "I found in two corners of the box a plug, with a wire in each of them. By these wires the torpedoes were exploded." The role of the two captured rebels was immediately apparent. They were preparing to explode another torpedo should one of Beaumont's other vessels venture over it.[14]

The two captives, Master's Mate P. W. Smith and his assistant, Jeffries Johnson, belonged to the Confederate Submarine Battery Service. They were immediately hauled off to be interrogated by Fleet Captain John S. Barnes. Smith informed Barnes that there were more torpedoes in the river, but refused to divulge their locations. Johnson quickly revealed

Destruction of the U. S. Navy gunboat *Commodore Jones* on the James River by a Confederate galvanic torpedo. From *Harper's Weekly*. Courtesy: U. S. Naval History Division, Department of the Navy.

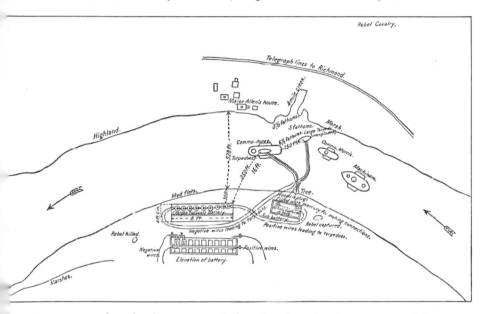

Contemporary sketch plan prepared shortly after the destruction of the gunboat *Commodore Jones* showing the positions of the rebel galvanic torpedos and the Union reconnaissance squadron off Four Mile Creek, James River, Virginia. Official Records of Union and Confederate Navies in the War of the Rebellion. Courtesy: U. S. Naval History Division, Department of the Navy.

that he had been conscripted into the Confederate Army, unwillingly, and had jumped at the chance to transfer to the Submarine Battery Service when he found he would be stationed near his home at Deep Bottom.[15]

Johnson was the less communicative of the two prisoners, neither of whom was willing to provide information on the actual locations of torpedoes remaining in the river. However, when Barnes ordered Johnson placed on the bow of the forwardmost gunboat employed in dragging for torpedoes and "given to understand that he would share the fate of the boat, [Johnson] signified his willingness to tell all he knew about them."[16]

From Jeffries Johnson, the United States Navy learned more about rebel torpedoes in ten minutes than they had in four years. As a consequence, not again would a federal ship be lost in the tidewater because of the "infernal machines."

Chapter Twenty-One

CHAINED BULLDOGS

P RESIDENT Lincoln slept fitfully the evening of April 1, 1865. The war weighed heavily upon him, and he had been obliged to spend the entire night with his legs bent because his bunk aboard Rear Admiral David D. Porter's flagship *Malvern*, anchored in the James River off City Point, was far too short to accommodate his lanky frame. Yet he was more ebullient the following morning than he had been in months, for he knew that America's great tragedy, the Civil War, was drawing to a close. General Grant's powerful army was on the move and, at that moment, was preparing the sledgehammer blows which would culminate in a final grand assault on the rebel works around Petersburg, key to Richmond and the Confederacy.[1]

Admiral Porter, aware of Lincoln's short bunk, had quietly ordered *Malvern*'s carpenters quietly to remodel the President's cabin on the sly during the day. The next morning the chief executive appeared at breakfast completely refreshed, jesting that he had apparently shrunk during the night "six inches in length and about a foot sideways." Throughout April 2, as Grant's troops battled for every scrap of ground at Petersburg, Lincoln and Porter sat on the upper deck of the flagship listening attentively to the thunder of artillery duels ashore.[2]

With the end of the war at hand, Lincoln felt a twinge of irritation at the apparent idleness of the naval forces about him. "Can't the Navy do something at this particular moment to make history?" he queried Porter.[3]

"The Navy," Porter replied with perfect aplomb, "is doing its best just now, holding the enemy's four heavy iron-clads in utter uselesness."[4]

Porter's words were not lightly spoken. The James River Squadron of the Confederacy was the most potent rebel naval force in the South. If it was allowed to break through to City Point, the Union's strategic and logistical fulcrum on the river, there was no end to the havoc that might follow. Perhaps Grant's final grand offensive might be aborted, and the course of the war changed!

A few miles to the north lay the Confederate squadron and its capable commander, Rear Admiral Raphael Semmes. The admiral had been appointed to command on February 10, replacing an old and valued friend, Commodore J. K. Mitchell, who had been responsible for organizing and moulding the squadron into the dangerous fighting machine that it was. Yet Semmes was an officer of great merit. For the better part of three years he had commanded the famed Confederate commerce raiders *Sumter* and *Alabama* and personally carried out the capture and destruction of more than six dozen Yankee merchant and military vessels while eluding the best of the Union Navy on the high seas.[5]

At 4:00 P.M. on April 2, even as Porter and Lincoln sat aboard *Malvern* listening to the battles ashore upriver, Raphael Semmes was sitting down to a late lunch in the wardroom of his flagship, C. S. S. *Virginia No. 2*, lying off Chaffins Bluff. While eating, he reviewed the critical situation into which he had been thrust and the forces at his disposal.[6]

Arrayed against him were no less than 64 ships, mounting 276 guns. Of these, many were Porter's front-line ironclad monitors, practically invincible in battle and excellent fighting ships in the shallow, placid confines of the James. His own forces seemed minuscule by comparison; yet operating in conjunction with the considerable maze of fortifications on the river banks, and protected from surprise attack by an obstacle course of scuttled vessels below Drewry's Bluff, the squadron was a nearly impervious link in the chain of Confederate defenses of Richmond.[7]

Backbone of his squadron, and all veterans of clashes with Union naval forces, were three giant ironclads, each carrying four enormous guns and armored with four to six inches of iron which was backed by nearly two feet of yellow pine. Oldest of the lot was the ram *Richmond,* a 172-foot 6-inch long monster built at the Norfolk Navy Yard with money and scrap iron collected by the citizens of Virginia. *Richmond* had been launched, unfinished, on May 6, 1862, just before the recapture of the navy yard by Federal forces, and it had caused unending worry to the Yankees. Next to *Richmond* was the 188-foot-long *Fredericksburg,* which had been laid down at the Richmond Navy Yard between 1862 and 1863. Largest of the ironclads was Semmes' own flagship, the ram *Virginia No. 2,* a 197-foot behemoth laid down at Richmond in 1863. A fourth ironclad ram, *Texas,* lay uncompleted on the stocks at the yards in Richmond awaiting parts and an engine.[8]

A number of smaller craft, primarily gunboats, completed the squadron. Principal among these were the two shallow-draft "Maury Gunboats," *Hampton* and *Nansemond,* designed by the brilliant Confederate scientist and naval officer Matthew Fontaine Maury. These wooden-hulled vessels had been designed early in the war to conduct lightning raids on Federal naval forces in Hampton Roads, but after the fielding of C. S. S. *Virginia,* the Southern love affair with the ironclad ship blossomed, and many such boats were deemed obsolete before they could be proven. Another gunboat in the squadron, C. S. S. *Roanoke,* was an iron-hulled steamer which had served before the war on the Chesapeake and Albemarle Canal. Inducted into the Confederate Navy in May 1861, she was armed with a single gun and had served in numerous campaigns, from Cape Hatteras to Hampton Roads, where she operated as tender to the famed *Virginia.*[9]

The squadron also possessed two service boats, *Shrapnel* and *Torpedo,* and the armed tug *Beaufort. Shrapnel* was a small craft which had been actively employed on the James towing fire craft, delivering mail and torpedoes, and conducting picket duty. *Torpedo,* a 150-ton screw steamer armed with a single gun, had served in a variety of capacities, ranging from flag of

The Confederate ironclad *Richmond*, backbone of the James River Squadron. Official Records of Union and Confederate Navies in the War of the Rebellion. Official U. S. Navy Photograph.

The C. S. S. *Patrick Henry*, veteran of numerous engagements in the Virginia Theater of Operations, ended her career while serving as a Confederate school ship. From the photographic collection of the U. S. Naval History Division, Department of the Navy. Official U. S. Navy Photograph.

truce boat to a boat in charge of the James River submarine batteries. *Beaufort,* barely 85 tons burthen, carried but a single gun, yet had served with distinction throughout the war, engaging in several battles, including those at Roanoke Island and Elizabeth City, and in the numerous clashes on the James.[10]

The last major vessel in the squadron was the school ship *Patrick Henry,* the giant 1,300-ton 250-foot-long side-wheeler built before the war as the oceangoing passenger and freight steamer *Yorktown.* In April 1861 she had been serving the run between New York and Richmond when she was seized by the Confederacy. Although too big for service on the upper James, she was lightly armed with four guns and actively employed throughout the war at Hampton Roads and on the river. Remodeled in 1863, she became the training ship for the Confederate States Naval Academy, in which capacity she continued to serve.[11]

Semmes reviewed the events of the past few days, and in particular the bombardment the evening before. Unknown to him, Admiral Porter had directed his flotilla of monitors and gunboats to turn its attentions to Confederate shore batteries at Howletts, just downriver from the rebel fleet, letting go with everything they had, from rockets to bombs. "The object," Porter had informed his officers, "is merely to make the rebels think that we are about to make an attack. They are prepared to sink their gunboats at the first sign of one."[12]

Though the attack was made, Semmes was not about to sink his gunboats just yet. Or so he thought. As the admiral finished his lunch, a messenger entered the wardroom and handed him a sealed dispatch from Confederate Secretary of the Navy Stephen R. Mallory in Richmond.

Sir: General Lee advises the Government to withdraw from this city, and the officers will leave this evening, accordingly. I presume that General Lee has advised you of this, and of his movements, and made suggestions as to the disposition to be made of the squadron. He withdraws upon his lines toward Danville, this night; and unless otherwise directed by General Lee, upon you is devolved the duty of destroying your ships, this night and with all the forces under your command, joining Lee. Confer with him, if practicable, before destroying them. . . .[13]

To say that Semmes was stunned, especially by such short notice, is an understatement. Yet the order had been as difficult for Mallory, father of the Confederate States Navy, to give as it was for the admiral to accept. "The James River Squadron," he later wrote, "with its ironclads, which had lain like chained bulldogs under the command of Rear Admiral Raphael Semmes to prevent ascent of the enemy's ships, would, in the classic flash of the times, 'go up' before morning . . . and the naval operations of the Confederacy east of the Mississippi would cease."[14]

Despite his personal feelings, Semmes dutifully notified his captains and prepared for the hectic evening ahead. Though he probably could have carried out the flotilla's destruction during the day, he preferred to await evening to avoid unduly alarming the civilian population. A message was sent from the signal tower high above Drewry's Bluff to inform Lee, but, though the signalman continued sending for more than an hour, there was no reply. Semmes had resolved to sink his ships in deep water rather than to blow them up, but as darkness fell, he observed many fires ashore as Lee's decimated army burned its stores before abandoning its position. It was then that he decided that the James River Squadron would be blown up.[15]

Hour after hour his men labored, placing charges, removing provisions from the ships, and drawing arms. Then the fires were set. At 3:00 A.M. on April 3, 1865, Admiral Raphael Semmes withdrew his 400 men to the gunboats from the burning ironclads.[16]

"My little squadron of wooden boats," he later recorded in his memoirs,

> now moved off up the river [to Richmond] by the glare of the burning iron-clads. They had not proceeded far before an explosion, like the shock of an earthquake, took place, and the air was filled with missiles. It was the blowing up of the *Virginia* [*No. 2*], my late flagship. The spectacle was grand beyond description. Her shell-rooms had been full of loaded shells. The explosion of the magazine threw all these shells, with their fuses lighted, into the air. The fuses were of different lengths, and as the shells exploded by twos and threes, and by the dozen, the pyrotechnic effect was very fine. The explosion shook the houses in Richmond, and must have waked the echoes of the night for forty miles around.[17]

Semmes and his men brought the little gunboats of the James River Squadron up to Richmond. Here public pandemonium reigned supreme. Yet with quiet resolve, Semmes and his sailors put *Shrapnel, Nansemond,* and *Patrick Henry* to the torch. Then came the steamers *Torpedo, Hampton,* and *Roanoke.* The explosions which resulted from the burning ships were not as grand as those from the ironclads, but for the admiral and his men, they were just as sad. In their haste to evacuate the city, however, they overlooked *Beaufort* and *Texas.* It didn't matter, for now the Confederates' James River Squadron ceased to be.[18]

April 4 was a mild spring day. Birds were singing, and trees were in full bloom, as a small boat party pulled up the James River toward a city afire. Richmond, capital of the Confederacy for four years, was in flames, the fire set off by the evacuating Confederate army. The small boat party, commanded by Admiral Porter, carried President Lincoln, and had been preceded only a short time before by Admiral David Glasgow Farragut, who had four years earlier fled Norfolk and the dreadful scene of destruction there. The party landed a block above the infamous Libby Prison, and the President was received "with the strongest demonstrations of joy."[19]

"Thank God," remarked Farragut, "it is about over."[20]

PART FIVE
THE MODERN ERA

Baltimore

Chester

Delaware Bay

Annapolis

Washington, D.C.

1

CHESAPEAKE BAY

Patuxent

Choptank

2

3

Nanticoke

7

Wicomico

Potomac

Pocomoke

4

Rappahannock

5
6

Richmond

ATLANTIC OCEAN

York

Cape Charles

James

N

Norfolk

Cape Henry

S

See over for number key

MAP KEY: THE MODERN ERA

1. *Levin J. Marvel* (1955)
2. *New Jersey* (1870)
3. *Three Rivers* (1924)
4. *Express* (1878)

5. U. S. C. G. Cutter *Cuyahoga* (1978)
6. *Louisiana* (1874)
7. *Wawaset* (1873)

Chapter Twenty-Two

THE PITCHER WRECK

HERE WERE six of us aboard Captain Varice Henry's little
fishing boat, *Bammy II,* when she put out from Chesapeake Beach on the morning of October 4, 1975. Our objective, as divers, was to identify a shipwreck which Captain Henry had located on his fathometer nearly a year before. The site, he said, lay at a depth of approximately eighty feet and was roughly eight miles from the western shoreline of the upper Bay. It would be a somewhat dangerous dive, not only because of the depth, swift currents, and poor visibility, but also because the wreck lay uncomfortably close to the main shipping lanes, over which the big tankers and freighters bound to and from Baltimore passed. Even though cramped aboard *Bammy,* we were excited. Captain Henry had unerringly put us on numerous other "virgin" wrecksites, and this one was unmarked on the nautical charts.

Close examination of a fathometer record of the site suggested a definite U-shape configuration, possibly indicating an open hull with a charactcristic mudbank buildup on either side. The record indicated that the wreck was fifty-five feet deep at one point—almost twenty-five feet above the bottom. She was big, and there was a reasonably good chance she was intact.

With uncanny accuracy, Captain Henry piloted the boat to what seemed a random spot smack in the middle of the Chesapeake and nonchalantly announced that we had arrived. We were directly adjacent to the site, claimed the good captain. Marker buoys were dropped and then an anchor. Inner tubes,

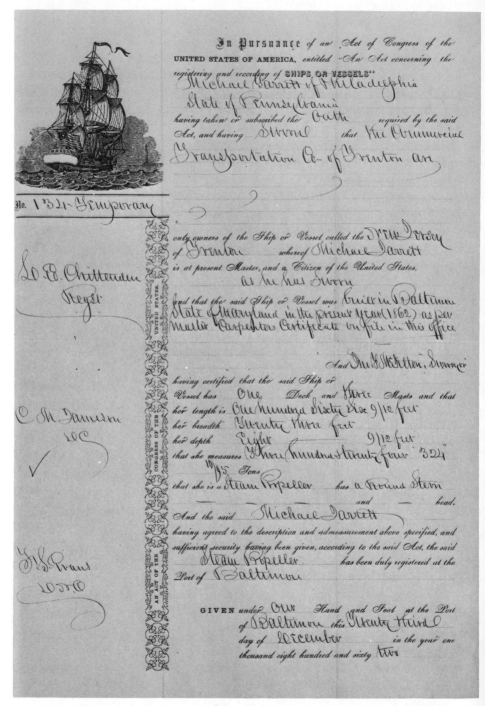

In Pursuance of an Act of Congress of the UNITED STATES OF AMERICA, entitled "An Act concerning the registering and recording of SHIPS OR VESSELS" Michael Garrett of Philadelphia State of Pennsylvania having taken or subscribed the Oath required by the said Act, and having Sworn that the Commercial Transportation Co. of Trenton are

No. 1321 Temporary

L. E. Chittenden Regst

C. M. Damon sC

✓

Y. S. Evans sC

only owners of the Ship or Vessel called the New Jersey of Trenton whereof Michael Garrett is at present Master, and a Citizen of the United States, as he has Sworn and that the said Ship or Vessel was Built in Baltimore State of Maryland in the present year (1862) as per Master Carpenters Certificate on file in this office

And Thos S McFelton, Surveyor having certified that the said Ship or Vessel has One Deck and Three Masts and that her length is One Hundred Sixty Six 9/12 feet her breadth Twenty three feet her depth Eight 9/12 feet that she measures Three Hundred Twenty four 324 Tons that she is a Steam Propeller has a Round Stern and — head. And the said Michael Garrett having agreed to the description and admeasurement above specified, and sufficient security having been given, according to the said Act, the said Steam Propeller has been duly registered at the Port of Baltimore

GIVEN under Our Hand and Seal at the Port of Baltimore this Twenty third day of December in the year one thousand eight hundred and sixty two

Registry papers for the steamboat *New Jersey*. Courtesy: National Archives.

attached to the boat by 300-foot lines, were set afloat in case of emergencies when the divers surfaced. Diving could only be undertaken at slack tide because of the unusually strong currents of the channel, and all safety precautions were meticulously checked by the team's dive master, Eldon Volkmer, a satellite communications engineer from the National Aeronautics and Space Administration's (NASA) Goddard Space Flight Center at Greenbelt, Maryland.

As we suited up, Captain Henry, in a casual, off-the-cuff manner, informed us exactly how to locate the wreck, even though he had never donned a wet suit in his life. "Just go down the anchor line, boys, and head due west. Turn right at the first mudbank and you can't miss her." Small consolation, we grumbled, for diving in water with less than one foot visibility.

"Heck," remarked one diver, "you could swim within a yard of a wreck in this stuff and never know it was there!"

Straws were drawn to see who would descend first; I drew the shortest. As a veteran of more than ten years of black-water diving, I chose as my buddy a novice mud diver, Dr. Jay Cook of the National Institutes of Health. Cook was eager to get into the water and even remembered to turn his air on before splashing down. I joined him, and though it was just turning slack tide, noticed a strong tug on my body from the water flow. At a depth of ten feet, darkness set in, and our underwater dive lamps went on. At twenty feet, visibility dropped to six inches. As we slid gently down the anchor line, I sensed Cook begin to tense up the deeper and darker it became.

Before realizing it, we reached the bottom and were actually swimming headlong into the extremely soft mud. After unmucking ourselves we followed Captain Henry's instructions, headed west and encountered the predicted steep mudbank. The impact of the slightest touch upon the mudbank was phenomenal. Billowing clouds of silt erupted, completing obliterating all visibility and the last shreds of light. Cautiously, we turned slightly toward our right and crept up the incline, hand over hand and practically blind.

Suddenly, Cook tugged hard on the short buddy line, almost wrenching my arm from its socket. I could make out a joyous, if muted, noise, which I later swore was escaping from the novice's bubbles. Cook had run directly into upright timbers, mask first. We had found the wreck. Captain Henry was, as usual, absolutely correct.

Allowing the silt to settle, we began to inspect our find closely. Eighteen-inch-thick framing ribs projected five or six feet above the mudbank, sweeping ominously out over our heads. After backing up, ascending these obstacles, and attaching an underwater cave reel line to one of the more sturdy members, we clambered over and began a slow ten-foot descent into the bowels of the hulk.

Visibility inside the hull had increased to approximately a foot, and we both felt more at ease now that we could "see." As we inched downward, I could feel giant iron bolts protruding from the rotten wood disintegrating at the merest touch. This wreck was obviously old, and we would have to proceed with utmost caution.

As we gently touched down on the "deck," I could feel something smooth, possibly glass, under my open heel. Groping around on hands and knees, I discovered that we were apparently in what was left of a cargo hold. I was pawing over nothing less than broken crates of intact cargo! Gingerly, I picked up some of the loose contents. Pitchers. A cargo of milk-glass molasses pitchers. And hobnail syrup pitchers! Dozens of them, perhaps hundreds.

Excitedly, we picked up several select examples and stowed them in our collection bags. Torn between exploring further and admiring our treasure trove, we opted for the former. There was simply no room left in our bags to carry more glassware in reasonable safety, and our time, at this depth, was extremely limited. Climbing over the remains of several bulkheads, we continued our exploration, never losing physical touch with the wreck.

Debris was everywhere; we soon encountered a tangle of machinery, copper pipes, and giant lumps of coal. A huge fallen cylinder blocked our way, apparently one of the ship's smokestacks. We retreated at an angle and found ourselves hugging an immense boiler, still upright and intact, a giant beam lying askew and against one side. It was becoming readily apparent that we had discovered an ancient, forgotten Chesapeake Bay steamboat.

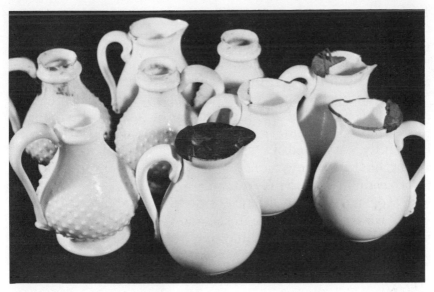

Several molasses pitchers, hobnail and plain pattern, recovered from the wreck of the Old Bay Line steam packet *New Jersey*. The pitchers had been manufactured by the J. H. Hobbs Company, Wheeling, West Virginia, and bore a patent date of May 11, 1869. Photograph by the author.

Author Donald Shomette (left) and associate Eldon Volkmer examine molasses pitchers and the ship's whistle recovered during archaeological investigations of the wreck of the Old Bay Line steam packet *New Jersey*, lost in the Chesapeake in 1870. Courtesy of the author.

But time was running out. Inadvertently, Cook leaned against a huge timber which swayed and collapsed—fortunately, away from him—again immersing us in total darkness. It was definitely not a place for the claustrophobic. The message was clear: we had already pushed our luck in the black maze, our air was low, and a return to the surface was in order. Carefully, we picked our way out, rewinding the cave line as we went, liberated a few more pitchers for later study, and headed up the anchor line to the surface.

Topside, in the brilliance of daylight, we fingered the treasures we could barely see in the water, looking for some sign, some identification, anything that might furnish a clue to the ship's identity or date of loss. Sure enough, on one pitcher's pewter lid was engraved "J. H. Hobbs & Co., Pat. May 11, 1869."

Subsequent dives on the site revealed two gigantic iron anchors, an enormous iron drum from which oozed a black, sticky substance, and a collection of unidentifiable corroded iron conglomerates. Most of the ship's hold was filled with silt, and there was no telling what artifacts lay buried.

Weeks later, after numerous visits to the site, extensive research, and many trips to the National Archives, the Library of Congress, and the Smithsonian Institution, the identity of the wreck, the date, and cause of loss were gradually pieced together. The vessel had obviously gone down after 1869. That she was a steamboat was apparent. But how many steamers had been lost in that vicinity over the ensuing 106 years? At least one—the Baltimore Steam Packet Company's round sterned wooden propeller steam packet *New Jersey*.

She was constructed in 1862 by Fardy Brothers at Baltimore, Maryland. Her engines were produced by the foundry concern of Reamy and Archibald of Chester, Pennsylvania.[1] The vessel was employed primarily as a freighter and was of 494 tons burthen and powered by a simple reciprocating engine. The vessel was 166.5 feet in length, 22.6 feet across the beam, and 9 feet deep in the hold.[2]

Acquired by the Baltimore Steam Packet Company in 1867 in trade for the *Thomas A. Morgan* and $2,000, the *New Jersey* became the Old Bay Line's first steamboat to be propelled by a propeller instead of paddle wheels.[3] One of her first crewmen, Assistant Engineer John R. Sherwood, was destined to become a captain for the line and eventually president of the entire company, serving a term eleven years in duration.[4]

The *New Jersey* had been regularly employed on the Baltimore-Norfolk run, for her a trip of seventeen to twenty hours in duration, hauling merchandise and produce. On February 25, 1870, while under the command of Captain A. K. Cralle, a longtime employee of the Old Bay Line, she set out on her final voyage. On board were approximately 750 tons of freight—primarily flour, corn, bacon, and petroleum (in large iron drums)—consigned to Norfolk merchants and valued at $40,000. There were no passengers.[5]

At about midnight, or shortly thereafter, as the ship steamed along in the upper Chesapeake Bay, fire was reported midway between decks. Every effort was made to extinguish the flames, but the wooden ship proved too much fuel for the blaze. Captain Cralle and his crew had no alternative but to take to the lifeboats. Hoping against hope that the light of the conflagration would draw the attention of rescuers, the desperate seamen remained near the burning vessel for several hours. Slowly, *New Jersey* drifted southward.[6]

At 4:00 A.M., Saturday, February 26, an oyster pungy hove in sight and rescued the crew. Another vessel, the steamship *Pacific*, was soon on the scene, and Captain Cralle and his men transferred aboard and immediately attempted to tow the burning ship onto a shoal in order to save whatever possible of the ship and cargo. The effort, however, was in vain, and by daybreak, only two miles distant from the shallows near a small island, the stricken ship sank in eleven fathoms of water.[7]

Rumors reached Baltimore all day Saturday. It was first claimed that the stricken vessel was the steamboat *Matilda*, belonging to the Baltimore and Fredericksburg Line, a ship which, like *New Jersey*, was employed in hauling heavy freight and produce. Other stories had the correct identification, but verification was not forthcoming until Sunday morning, when *Pacific* returned to the city with Cralle and his men.[8]

New Jersey, a vessel valued at $30,000 at the time of her destruction, was among the first few vessels to be lost by the

Baltimore Steam Packet Company since its inception in 1840. Fortunately, no lives had been lost. Captain Cralle could only claim that "the fire occurred from some accident unknown."[9]

Operations of *New Jersey* had been quite profitable for the Old Bay Line, and it was only logical to replace her with a similarly designed screw steamer—built of iron. In June 1870, barely four months after *New Jersey*'s destruction, an agreement was drawn up with Harlan and Hollingsworth Company of Wilmington, Delaware, for the construction of a vessel of similar type and size. The new ship, *Roanoke*, was completed in 1871 and was the first of many iron steamers expressly built for the Old Bay Line by Harlan and Hollingsworth. *New Jersey* was, in fact, one of the last all wooden steam packets to serve the Old Bay Line.[10] As for Captain Cralle, his service was continued aboard the steam freighter *Seaboard*, after an inquiry on the loss, from which he was entirely exonerated from guilt.[11]

With time and tide, the memory of *New Jersey*, with but a line or two in the history books to recall her life, sinks ever deeper into the silt of the Chesapeake, a curious memento of the past, accessible now to only a few.

Chapter Twenty-Three

LOOK AFTER YOUR LIFE

AUGUST was an especially unhealthy month in Washington, D. C., and the sultry heat made it even more unpleasant. For those who could afford it, the riverboats that lined the wharves of the waterfront provided some escape; a daylong trip down the Potomac aboard an excursion steamer offered the general public one of the best bargains available. The finest excursion ship making the run to Coan River, Virginia, and back was the Potomac Ferry Company's big side-wheeler *Wawaset*.

Built during the height of the Civil War, in 1863, at Wilmington, Delaware by Pusey and Jones, *Wawaset* had originally been intended as a river freighter. Due to the exigencies of war, she had been quickly snapped up by the U. S. Army for service as a troop transport. In 1864, however, she was purchased back from the government by the Potomac Ferry Company for service on the river.[1]

Wawaset was 129 feet long, 26 feet abeam, 9 feet in the hold, and 258 tons burthen. In the spring of 1873 she was completely overhauled and newly furnished and upholstered. The finishing touch to her remodeling was the addition of a luxurious new saloon to her upper aft deck. She was soon reputed to be the finest steamer in service on the Potomac.[2]

Legally, the ship was permitted to carry a total of fifty passengers—thirty cabin and twenty steerage—besides her fifteen-man crew. It was not uncommon, however, during the peak of the summer season for upwards of one hundred fifty passengers to be taken aboard for the weekend excursion cruise.[3] After all, she had been outfitted with the latest fire extinguishers, besides her regular "double-acting fire pump" and two dozen or more leather fire buckets. The company, in fact, had even exceeded the 75 life jackets required by law by stuffing an additional 425 into the overheads. Each of her officers and crew averaged nine to ten years of steamboat experience on the river, most of which had been with the Potomac Ferry Company. And finally, the vessel had been insured by no less than six of the most reputable agencies available for more than $25,000. Her owners felt she was more than ready to cope with even the slightest trouble.[4]

By 5:00 A.M., on August 8, 1873, a Friday, the temperature in Washington had already begun to rise. Aboard *Wawaset,* tied up as usual at her Seventh Street dock, Captain John Wood, her master, joked quietly with Pilot John W. L. Boswell as passengers began boarding. The steamer was ready to depart for her regular excursion run to Currioman and Coan River, with a return scheduled for midday Saturday. She would, of course, make the normal stops at various landings along the way. Wood casually observed without comment the abnormally large number of passengers boarding. There had been serious sickness in Washington during the preceding weeks, especially among the children, and many mothers were taking advantage of the excursions simply to get away with their offspring. Since the trip was scheduled for Friday and Saturday, however, there were fewer working-class men booked for the excursion. By 5:15 A.M. the tally of passengers included 117 adults and 20 children. But additional passengers were boarding right up to departure time.[5]

At 5:30 A.M. sharp, *Wawaset* sounded her whistle, pulled in her boarding ramp, and cast off her lines.[6]

As was usual practice, many of the black passengers, allotted the hot, exposed bow deck section, were obliged to find seats amidst the cattle, peach boxes, and chicken coops being carried as freight. The white passengers, generally working-class folk, were provided the more comfortable, sheltered accommodations of the aft deck, saloon, and cabins below.[7]

By midmorning the steamer had already called at several landings, including Liverpool Point, Glymont, and Smith's, taking on passengers. Near noon, the vessel passed Thom's Gut, completed her call at Riverside, Maryland, and was making for her next stop, Chatterton's Landing, on the Virginia shore. There were no passengers below or in the stifling cabins. Most were on the aft deck or in the saloon attempting to escape the intense midday heat.[8]

Chatterton's was a minor pickup and delivery stop five miles below Aquia Creek and opposite Maryland Point. It consisted of little more than a crude landing and a small shelter box. There was no wharf there and the transferral of passengers and freight had to be made by small boat. *Wawaset* was equipped with two boats for such purposes, one of metal and the other, a lesser craft, of wood.

At 11:45 A.M. with a full head of steam the ship was approximately a third of a mile from shore, having just left Riverside Wharf. She was not more than five minutes from Chatterton's Landing, where a number of relatives and friends of passengers, as well as a few awaiting passage, lined the shore.[9]

As Chatterton's loomed ahead, ship's fireman John Forman went below after a pair of overalls. It would be his turn at the watch in less than half an hour, and he wanted to be ready. On opening the door to the fireman's room, however, he was confronted by a wall of smoke. Excitedly, he rushed off to report his discovery to the mate, Robert W. Gravatt. As he emerged from the stairwell into the hall, he encountered Gravatt who immediately ordered up a fire hose to fight the blaze. Chief Engineer Robert Nash had been standing less than six feet from the engine room, in full view of the steam and water gauges, when the first word of the fire came. At Gravatt's order he ran to the forward deck to secure the hose. At the same time, fireman Lorenzo Brown started down the fireman's steps to determine just how bad the situation below actually was. Driven back by a sheet of flames, he tried vainly to reach the donkey engine to pump the water.[10]

By now, Forman had reached the pilothouse and informed pilot Boswell of the situation. "Captain," Boswell said calmly to Wood, who had come up only moments before, "the best thing we can do is to run her ashore [at] the nearest place,

Chatterton's Landing."[11] "Keep cool; don't raise any excitement," responded the captain. Perhaps the situation wasn't serious. He hoped to get down into the hold and put out the fire without raising passenger concern. Incredibly, the flames had already started running up the ship's big walking beams and the captain was driven back. Quickly, he attempted to ring the engineer's department, but there was no answer.[12]

There seemed little choice but to follow Boswell's advice and run *Wawaset* ashore. Wood would remain in the pilothouse to direct her beaching. He immediately ordered the deck hands below to close all amidships doors to prevent the drafts from feeding the flames.[13]

Passenger William E. Emerson, sitting on the starboard side of the upper deck, his back against the framework of the smokestack, was reading the *Alexandria Gazette,* when he smelled something burning. Looking down the aperture where the beam works were, he was stunned to see smoke. Quietly, so as not to cause a panic, he informed a gentleman at his side, "The boat is on fire," and then went aft to look for his small niece. The general alarm had yet to be given as he stepped into a passageway to get life preservers. "These I found stowed in the frames of the ceiling in the passageway between the wheelhouse and the engine," he later testified. "They were packed so tight it was about three minutes before I got one loose." During that small interval of time the fire had burst up from the engine-room hole alongside. Persevering amidst the flames, Emerson finally retrieved two life jackets and attempted to crawl aft to the saloon in search of his niece. There he encountered a scene of complete pandemonium.[14]

Peter McKenny, *Wawaset*'s barkeeper, was on the upper deck in the bar when the alarm was given. He immediately rushed to the lower deck and found the fire running up the walking beams. Breathlessly, he too ran into the crowded saloon and attempted to calm the largely female group assembled there. With great restraint, he advised the women to go forward. At the same time, the steamer's clerk, J. W. Wheeler, who had been sitting on the promenade deck, also entered the saloon to try and calm the crowd and saw them try to rush to the forward deck as McKenny had advised, only to be driven back by a wall of flame. Crazed by fear, many nevertheless continued to dare the fire. Horrified, Wheeler screamed at them, "For God's sake don't go there."[15] It was no use. An indescribable panic gripped the passengers.

Wheeler attempted to assist several passengers aft, including A. J. McGuiggan, a printer for the Chronicle Printing Office. But when McGuiggan handed Wheeler a carpet sack, the clerk yelled at him, "For God's sake, don't look after your baggage—look after your life."[16]

John W. Reed, resident of northwest Washington, was standing at the forward port gangway on the main deck when he heard someone cry out "Fire!" Looking around, he noticed smoke issuing from the boiler house and rushed to the forward deck. The flames immediately spread to the hurricane deck. Though his brother-in-law's family, an aunt, and several cousins were on the aft deck, he knew it would be impossible to penetrate the barrier of flame. Ahead, he could see Chatterton's Landing looming ever larger as the ship rushed to her destiny. In extreme panic, many about him attempted to jump overboard, but Reed persuaded them to wait until the ship had stopped.[17]

The situation grew from bad to worse for Wood. There was no possibility for him or his officers to get aft to show the passengers how to use the life jackets, or even where they were. Nor were there any officers in attendance at the small boats there. And then he discovered that the fire was burning the tiller rope connections. Desperately, he began to pour buckets of water on the ropes to fend off the flames. He knew that the situation would be hopeless should he lose steering control.[18] Suddenly, the engine stopped. The shaft had been bent by the intense heat. For a brief, agonizing moment, *Wawaset* glided forward on her own momentum, the roaring flames fanned by the breeze of her motion. Chatterton's grew nearer and nearer. Five hundred yards. Four hundred yards. Three hundred yards.[19]

Whipped up by the breeze, the flames literally rushed from the midships section aft. The crazed panic of those trapped at the stern was immediately transformed to one of sheer terror. The long dresses of the women caught fire and children screamed as their mothers were wrapped in flames. There was an immediate stampede to the stern rail. Rapidly, the deck took fire in the footsteps of the mob. Passengers too slow to respond were crushed to death underfoot. Somewhere, a bull bellowed in fierce agony as it was roasted alive.[20]

A yawl which had been partially lowered earlier to carry passengers to Chatterton's was immediately seized by the mob. A deckhand attempted to direct the passengers in its use, but his instructions went unheeded in the blind frenzy. Crowded with a number of blacks and five or six children, the boat hung over the side by the davits. No one aboard knew how to handle the lines to lower the craft. In a complete panic, one man pulled out a penknife from his jacket and cut one of the ropes. The small boat instantly spilled its passengers into the water like so many peas from a pod. Only the man who had cut the rope survived.[21]

In the wheelhouse, Captain Wood and Pilot Boswell had done what they could to get the ship as close as possible to the shore. Unfortunately, with the loss of power and steerage she had grounded on a lump barely four and a half to five feet deep more than one hundred fifty yards from shore. Her stern end, on which most of the passengers were trapped, lay in nine feet of water and began to swing to port, and deeper water, immediately after the grounding.[22]

On the forward deck John Reed and another passenger, John H. Wise, were among the few men aboard who attempted to save others. Immediately upon hearing the alarm, they threw planks and peach boxes overboard to the people floundering in the water.[23] Finally, Wise, finding himself practically alone on the burning deck, cast the last available peach box in for himself. It was snatched up by another man. Though he could not swim, Wise took the plunge. Miraculously, he managed to stay afloat and reach the shore.[24]

John Reed was equally fortunate, though the rest of his family were not. Bessie Reed, a niece, had been aft when the fire started. Panic-stricken, she had run directly through the blaze and had collapsed near the pilothouse, her lungs filled with smoke. With great difficulty, Captain Wood had passed her limp body down to the forward deck where she was revived, still in a frenzied state. Just before the ship struck, she jumped over the bow and was crushed between the hull and the bottom. John Reed's sister and her three children remained aft and were among those who were burned to death or drowned.[25]

When *Wawaset* ran aground, one of her paddles continued to turn, a giant flaming pinwheel which drove those unfortunate enough to be near it beneath the water. To the astonished spectators ashore, the burning ship and its struggling, terrified passengers presented a nightmarish panorama. At one moment they saw three small children, sobbing as they clung to the ship's rudder chain, frozen in place by fear. One by one the children were seared to death. And then in another instant they spotted a man sliding down the rudder to the water. There he held on until the flames reached him. Twice he sank and reappeared. A third time his body went under, but was snatched up at the last minute by several men in a small boat from shore. A number of life jackets, thrown into the water by the crew, floated unused nearby.[26]

Engineer Robert Nash could not swim, but he jumped in anyway, grabbing a floating peach box, and did his best to stay away from the burning ship. His son, an assistant engineer, jumped in beside him and towed the elderly man to shore.[27]

Passenger William Emerson had reached the aft saloon where his niece had been with friends. He had made the little girl sit patiently beside him as he methodically took off his coat, shoes, socks, cuffs, and other encumbrances. He paid scant attention to the panic following the loosing of the yawl. As he put a life preserver on his niece, he ignored the screaming, flame-wrapped women, whose long dresses doomed them. When another man attempted to wrest the remaining life preserver from his hands, he resisted successfully, and put it on. He took his niece in his arms and slid down a rope to the freight deck, where he remained at the rail until the heat became unbearable. Then he slid into the water with the child and pushed off from the boat which, at that time, was still moving. He watched in horror from a half mile out in the Potomac as she grounded and burned. His last glimpse of the ship's stern rail revealed two children afire.[28]

Mrs. Overton Taylor of Alexandria, Virginia had been among those aft when the fire broke out. In the ensuing rush to the stern rail, she was obliged to clear away the dismembered limbs of a number of passengers crushed in the onslaught. Taking her sister's boy in hand, she jumped headlong into the river. With the child clinging to her neck, she was kept afloat by the air bubble under her long skirt, and reached shore safely.[29]

Sixteen-year-old Virginia Marbury of Glymont, Maryland, a clerk with the Treasury Department, was not as fortunate as Taylor. She had boarded the steamer at Glymont with her cousin, Kate McPherson, to visit relatives at Eagle's Nest, an estate adjoining Chatterton's. The two companions had been driven down the gangway by the smoke, but in the crush that followed they became separated. Young Kate was forced to jump overboard. She sank, rose, and sank again. Her next recollection was of a boat rocking softly beneath her. Her companion, "a young lady of eminent piety and amiability," however, was burned and lost.[30]

Charles Jones, a deckhand aboard the ship, was preparing to land a passenger at Chatterton's when the alarm sounded. He helped Wood pour water on the tiller rope, but saw his life in danger and jumped overboard and swam ashore. There, he found a batteau and went back to the burning ship and saved three drowning women from the water.[31]

Captain Wood and Pilot Boswell were the last to abandon the ship and live. Seeing that nothing more could be done, the two men jumped into the water from the hurricane deck. As they swam toward the shore, Boswell managed to grab two floundering women and tow them along with him. Once ashore, he, too, secured a small boat and went back out to help whomever he could. The pilot eventually managed to save more than half a dozen people as well as one of the ship's boats, which he bailed out and towed behind to hold the rescued.[32]

There had been only one local vessel in sight when the fire broke out, but now, drawn from both sides of the river by the screams of the dying, boats were as thick as waterbugs. There was now, however, little that anyone could do but to wait for the ship to burn down completely and recover the bodies.

Peter "Doc" McKenny, the barkeeper on *Wawaset*, brought the first news of the disaster to Washington. He had commandeered a small boat at Chatterton's in an effort to get to the city as soon as possible and obtain help. En route up the Potomac with a few of the survivors, he was picked up by the steamer *Express* which had been coming up from Point Lookout and Piney Point with an excursion party of men belonging to the Washington Painter's Union.[33]

McKenny told a bleak story upon his arrival at 1:15 A.M., August 9. The citizens of Chatterton's, though well intentioned for the most part, were incapable of providing the aid most needed by the burned and injured victims. Bodies of the black passengers had, in most cases, simply been dragged ashore and ignored. Plundering of some of the dead, in fact, took place on the spot, even as the ship burned. Some of the bodies were brought ashore at Steuart's Wharf in King George's County, where a magistrate of the county, C. G. McClelland, took charge of the valuables of the deceased and their temporary interment.[34]

The efforts to bring the survivors and dead back to Washington filled the Washington, D. C., Alexandria, and Fredericksburg, Virginia newspapers for days afterwards. The steamer *Georgianna,* out of Baltimore, was the first to reach Steuart's Wharf the morning after the disaster. Chatterton's and Steuart's Wharf were soon cluttered with vessels of every description offering to help in the search for bodies or in taking the dead to Washington.

The steamer *National* was among the first to reach the Washington docks with the dead and living of the *Wawaset* disaster. She arrived at 5:30 P.M., August 9, with twenty-five survivors and ten bodies aboard.[35] Half an hour later the tug *Gedney,* belonging to the Potomac Ferry Company, left the city with grappling hooks and long poles to fish for additional bodies. The steamer *Charlotte Vanderbilt,* under the command of Captain Hollingshead, was also dispatched to the scene. Aboard were several reporters and artists from the *New York Daily Graphic.* At 7:40 P.M. the *Georgianna* arrived at the Seventh Street Mailboat Wharf with Captain Wood, Engineer Nash, and several of *Wawaset*'s crew aboard. The steamer was instantly stormed by hundreds of citizens seeking word of their families and friends. Within days, the disaster would be national news.[36]

The hulking charred remains of *Wawaset* sat like an eerie monument to the dead 250 yards below Chatterton's Landing and less than 150 yards from the shore. All that remained was her smokestack, walking beam, and paddlewheel frames. Her shaft was bent in the middle, and the wheels careened on either side. The first boatman on the site after the fire, W. H. Lee, reported that bodies could be seen in the hull which was, at low tide, barely knee-deep.[37]

For days thereafter, bodies of disaster victims were found up and down the river. On the Sunday morning following the fire, one woman's body, clad in calico, bobbed up to the surface 150 yards from shore, and then sank immediately only to surface again and begin to float off with the tide. When a boat was sent to recover the corpse, terribly disfigured by the crabs, she was found to have hair nearly a yard long and $8.66 in her purse.[38]

The shoreline between Chatterton's Landing and Boyd's Hole was littered with the detritus of destruction. Peach boxes, hen coops, and personal belongings of every kind cluttered the beach. Most obscene of all were the bodies washed ashore after several days in the water. Several consisted of little more than skeletons in clothing. On August 11 two bodies were recovered "their faces and ears completely eaten off . . . leaving the teeth and bones of the face clean." The crabs were not discriminating. The body of Virginia Marbury was found late on Sunday evening floating off Boyd's Hole. She was identified only by a description of her dress provided by Kate McPherson.[39]

Within a short time the nearly ten-mile-long shoreline was lined with hastily dug graves. Near Chatterton's, approximately thirty unidentified bodies were interred together in a temporary burial site (dubbed the *Wawaset* Cemetery) until they could be shipped back to Washington. In the days following the disaster, the death toll climbed until the final tally reached seventy-six. Only forty-one of the dead were identified.[40]

A local inquest was held at Steuart's Wharf the day after the fire, even as bodies were still being pulled from the river. The officers of the ship were exonerated of all blame. However, on August 15 a public investigation was opened in the offices of the Supervisor Inspecting General of Steamboats, and was con-

On the spot drawing made by an artist from the *New York Daily Graphic* showing the remains of the steamboat *Wawaset* and dredging for the dead at Chatterton's Landing, Virginia. Courtesy: Library of Congress.

ducted by Commodore William Rose, Inspector of Hulls at
Savannah, and John E. Edgar, Inspector of Boilers at Norfolk.[41]
During the investigation, it was determined that the fire had
started in an overheated partition between the decks and near
the ship's boiler, about the time *Wawaset* passed Liverpool
Point. A number of violations of steamer regulations were also
discovered. Captain Wood and Mate Gravatt had both failed to
renew their licenses as officers. Members of the crew, in violation of the law, were involved in huckstering at various points
along the river.[42]

As a consequence of the hearing, the investigators recom-
mended that the Potomac Ferry Company be prosecuted for
employing officers known to be operating without licenses;
and that Wood and Gravatt be prosecuted for knowingly serving without licenses in violation of steamer regulations. The
District Attorney to whom the case was referred, however,
refused to institute requested criminal proceedings, stating
that he believed there was insufficient evidence to warrant a
charge of manslaughter against any officer or inspector involved in the *Wawaset* disaster. Clearly, none of the officers
were guilty of misconduct or inattention to duty. They had
acted with professional aplomb during the fire, and in some
instances heroically. As for their failure to renew their licenses,
however, they were both fined $100.[43]

Within two months of the *Wawaset* disaster, a fine new
steamer, *Palisade,* began making the Coan River run for the
Potomac Ferry Company. The same Friday morning depar-
tures, the same overcrowded decks, and the same landings were
made. All was as it had been before, with the exception of
several dozen new bodies interred in Congressional Cemetery
on Capitol Hill.[44]

Chapter Twenty-Four

A HORSE AND A CANARY

THE WAR had been over nearly a decade when Captain
Wyndham R. Mayo on the afternoon of Friday, November
13, 1874, watched seven U. S. Navy officers—two commo-
dores, four captains, and a lieutenant—board his ship. The
officers, having recently served on a board of inquiry investigating the stranding of the U. S. S. *Brooklyn*, were en route from
Portsmouth Navy Yard to Baltimore, entirely unaware that the
captain of the ship upon which they were embarking had once
been their sworn enemy.[1]

Captain Mayo had not long been in his present position as
master of the Baltimore Steam Packet Company's mammoth
side-wheel steamer *Louisiana*, but he was certainly as experienced as any of the company's veteran captains. He began his
career as a cadet at the U. S. Naval Academy during the beginning days of the Civil War. Unlike many Southerners who had
resigned their commissions at the outset of the conflict, young
Mayo had wrestled with his conscience until 1862. Finally, he
too resigned his commission and slipped into Virginia to join
the Confederate Navy. By the end of the war he had served
aboard at least three Confederate warships, including C. S. S.
Patrick Henry, in the James River, the ironclad steam sloop
North Carolina, in the Cape Fear River, and the little wooden
gunboat *Yadkin*.[2]

The presence of the U. S. naval officers, and snatches of
their conversations regarding the recent stranding of the big
warship *Brooklyn* must have stirred in Mayo vivid memories of

the late war. He had been assigned to *Yadkin* in the Cape Fear in January 1864 when an enormous Yankee fleet appeared off Fort Fisher at the mouth of the river. The massive bombardment of the fort, led by U. S. S. *Brooklyn*, was among the most devastating of the war, and Federal control of the river became, as a result, a foregone conclusion. The destruction of *Yadkin* soon afterward was not unexpected.[3]

Though he said nothing to the seven naval officers, Wyndham Mayo may have secretly enjoyed the fact that *Brooklyn* had fallen on hard times. Still, the war was over, and the years which had followed had not been nearly as bad for him as they had been for many Southerners. He had found little difficulty in securing work on Potomac River steamers, and he had risen rapidly to command one of them. Only recently he secured command of the finest vessel on the Chesapeake Bay.

Without question his ship was the largest commercial vessel of her day to regularly ply the Bay. She was more than 266 feet long, 36 feet abeam, and 12 feet 2 inches deep in hold. Her capacity was 1,126 tons gross, and her powerful engines, manufactured by Charles Reeder & Sons, were capable of producing a thrust of 2,037 horsepower. Built in 1854 at Baltimore as a sister ship to the highly touted, though ill-fated, side-wheeler *North Carolina*, she was considered to be one of the most elegant ships on the water. Her white oak and cedar hull, which was fastened with both copper and iron, had been built by the noted firm of Cooper & Butler of Baltimore. Her sleek appearance more closely resembled the imperial-looking side-wheelers of Long Island Sound than the somewhat stunted steamers of the Chesapeake. She was quite recognizable from a distance, primarily because she carried a distinctive-looking pair of hog bracing frames—a strong set of wooden bridge trusses running parallel to each other fore and aft. The frames were necessary to prevent hogging, or sagging, amidships, caused by the enormous weight of her engines and structural weaknesses resulting from a grounding on Hatteras Inlet while in Union service during the Civil War. Yet, her design was superb, and she was often cited as the best example of the advanced marine technology of her age; and, like her late sister, she was one of the most luxurious.[4]

"The *Louisiana*," it was reported during her construction, "is doubtless one of the most substantial, commodious, and elegant boats of the day, but exceeding in expenditure in money. . . ." At a cost of nearly a quarter of a million dollars, she was indeed "exceeding." Yet she was also extremely successful; so successful that after seventeen years of continuous service, her owners decided rather than to scrap or sell her, to rebuild her completely, whatever the cost. Safety had been one of their prime considerations, and during reconstruction, her boilers were removed from their exposed positions near her sides to a more protected location deep within the hold.[5]

"Her staterooms," one newspaper of the day noted, "were finely furnished, and able to accommodate two hundred passengers, and by reason of improved machinery she was a very rapid sailer." In fact she was reputed to be the fastest steamer ever to run out of the port of Baltimore.

It was an interesting group of travelers who boarded the ship in Virginia. Besides the sixty-four regular officers and crew and two chambermaids, there were fifty-seven passengers, a horse belonging to Daniel Steever of Baltimore, and a pet canary. Among the passengers was Detective Robert Steele of Norfolk, who had charge of a young woman whom he was bringing to Baltimore to be placed in the House of the Good Shepherd, no doubt to help her see the error of her ways. There was an oyster merchant from Norfolk, and a doctor and his family from North Carolina, and the regular assortment of faces which had, over the years, become familiar to the crew.[6]

After a brief stop at Old Point Comfort, the trip to Baltimore would, as usual, be nonstop. Arrival time was set at 7:00 A.M. the next day. And, as always, *Louisiana*'s departure from Norfolk went off without a hitch.[7]

It was a brisk, starlit night, with visibility nearly five miles, when Captain Mayo decided to turn in at 11:00 P.M. First Mate Jacob Kirwin, the officer on duty, and Henry Williams, the wheelman, were in the pilothouse. George W. Wheeler was on lookout and two black crewmen were on watch. Like Mayo, most of the passengers had turned in for the evening.[8]

At about 1:05 A.M., as *Louisiana* approached Smith Point, lookout Wheeler spotted the red light of an approaching vessel and matter-of-factly reported to the pilot that a steamer was off the quarter bow. Nothing to worry about, he assured himself. All of *Louisiana*'s lights were glowing brightly, and Wheeler assured himself that his own ship would easily be seen. There was no alteration in the approaching ship's course. Within a mile and a half to two miles of the approaching vessel, *Louisiana* blew her whistle. There was no reply. After a few minutes had passed, a second whistle was blown, signifying her intention to pass to the east of the oncoming ship.[9]

Mayo slept fitfully and had been easily aroused by the first whistles. Dressing quickly, he came topside in time to hear the other steamer blow two sharp, shrill blasts on her own whistle, indicating that she too intended to pass on the east. The time was now 1:25 A.M. As the captain peered across the black sea, the light of the dark, oncoming steamer appeared to be bearing down directly on him. Collision was imminent.

"Hard aport," he told the wheelman.

"It already is turned hard aport," came the reply.

"Then hard astarboard."[10]

Perhaps, Mayo reasoned almost instantaneously, he could steer her stern off and slide by the oncoming ship. But it was already too late. Within seconds of the order, the steamer struck *Louisiana* amidships, six feet forward of the shaft, and then smashed through the port paddle box and into a stateroom behind. The bow of the mysterious steamer had crushed the stout sides of *Louisiana* like an eggshell, causing a flood of water to begin filling her innards. For a brief moment the two vessels were locked as if in mortal combat. Within seconds, the assaulting steamer swung around, her broadsides meeting those of her victim. Then the two vessels were separated by wind and tide.[11]

The shock of collision instantly awakened everyone aboard *Louisiana*, including the two navy officers in the stateroom behind the paddle box, who were now trapped by a buckled doorway. Only after rescuers bashed the doorway apart could the men be removed. Desperately, Mayo and his men sought to get the main engine, which had ceased working, to start again, but to no avail.[12]

Passengers in their nightclothes were now rushing out into the cold night air to see what had happened, even as the mysterious steamer sheered away. There was, fortunately, no panic, and *Louisiana*'s officers and crew went immediately to their emergency posts, exhibiting exemplary discipline and courage in a most hazardous situation. The passengers, too, conducted themselves with exceptional restraint, many of them following the example of the wife of Dr. W. J. Hawkins of North Carolina, who, with her husband and two children, "behaved as cooly as though nothing of great importance had transpired." The only instance of panic was exhibited by a blind Civil War veteran who, amid the sounds of chaos, feared he would be left behind and constantly screamed out, begging not to be forgotten.[13]

The officers of *Louisiana* exuded confidence in their ability to handle the situation, and served as an inspiration to the passengers, who were told to dress and "prepare themselves for the worst." Alarm bells were sounding throughout the ship, arousing the few still sleeping. Several crewmen directed passengers to assemble in the saloon, while others of the crew were seeing to their duties. Quickly, they cleared away and began lowering the lifeboats, even as Captain Mayo went below to inspect the damage.[14]

There were already six to seven feet of water in the hold, but it was possible that a shift of the cotton cargo might elevate the wound to such a degree that the flow would not be as rapid. After setting several crew members to the task, Mayo immediately returned topside and hailed the other vessel. She proved to be the steamer *Falcon* of the Baltimore and Charleston Line, Captain John F. Haynie commanding, en route from Baltimore to Charleston. Fortunately, *Falcon* had herself only suffered minor damage to her bow and was still watertight. Mayo requested she stand by, and had a hawser passed to her. He then went to the saloon to address the passengers. His words were brief and well chosen, "and in a few sentences [he] inspired the timid with some of his own courage." The passengers were told to keep quiet and orderly. They were instructed to provide themselves with life preservers, and were assured that everything would be done to protect their lives and property. But, as they were all going to be transferred to *Falcon*, speed was of the essence.[15]

Falcon rested much lower in the water than *Louisiana*, and gangplanks were run over to her with ease. Mayo again went below to inspect the progress of the water and found nine feet in the hold. His crew's desperate attempt to shift part of the ship's cargo to the starboard side had obviously failed. The end was near, and Mayo decided to make every attempt to save whatever he could. Since the hold was filling rapidly, he resolved to remove as much of the ship's expensive furniture as possible. All personal baggage and even the ship's iron safe, filled with valuables belonging to the Adams Express Company, were efficiently transferred to *Falcon*.[16]

Mayo was pleased at the orderly exodus, in part facilitated by the fact that the U. S. Navy officers were of great assistance, and that they and a number of the commercial travelers were quite familiar with emergency procedures.[17]

By 1:50 A.M., *Louisiana* had sunk so low that the gangplanks leading from her upper deck to the *Falcon* were almost perpendicular, and the hawsers were creaking and threatening to break at any moment. Everyone had left her except Captain Mayo, who stood upon the upper deck of his fast-sinking steamer and watched with deep concern as her bow gradually dipped and lowered. It was a dramatic spectacle, that of the dark hulled *Falcon*, her deck rail lined with human freight which had been miraculously spared a watery grave, anxiously watching the movements of the solitary figure on the half-sunken steamer below. The captain, after looking below and satisfying himself that the horse, which had been pathetically prancing and snorting on the lower deck, could not be saved, left his ship and was hoisted up to the *Falcon*. The only living creatures left aboard the doomed vessel were the horse and the canary, which no one had thought to carry off.[18]

Quickly, the ship dipped even deeper, and then, in a sudden motion, sank, less than ten minutes after Mayo's transfer. As she settled on the bottom, her stacks and glowing beacon light remained visible above the surface. *Falcon* hesitated for a few minutes, swimming amid the floating debris, and then began her slow crawl back to Baltimore.[19]

Two days later, the local board of steamboat inspectors, W. O. Saville and James D. Lowry, began their examination of the disaster. Several board members of the Old Bay Line, Captain Smith and Mr. Shoemaker, and David Mordecai, superintendent of the Baltimore and Charleston Line, were summoned to closed-door sessions and the investigation commenced. Eventually, despite counterclaims by the *Falcon*'s owners and crew, the Baltimore and Charleston Line was held at fault.[20]

Wrecking operations were immediately begun to salvage the sunken ship. The firm of B. & J. Baker of Norfolk was immediately brought up with its boats and salvage gear and set to work. Much of the ship's cotton cargo floated off but was recovered. It was initially thought that the gash in *Louisiana*'s side might be repaired and the ship refloated and towed to Baltimore in less than two weeks' time. Divers, however, quickly discovered that the upper saloon and the upper works of the ship had already gone to pieces and were swept away by the stiff currents.[21]

Despite such bad news, the wrecking steamer *Resolute* remained on the job. Divers were eventually able to recover most of her cargo of cotton, and *Resolute*'s decks were soon lined with the large bales. The Old Bay Line steamer *Roanoke* was engaged to pick up the salvaged goods, and several floating bales were recovered by the steamer *Highland Light*. But the Chesapeake tenaciously held her victim in her grip. Though her engines were eventually recovered, refurbished, and placed in another steamer, *Louisiana*'s body remained unmoved, a silent tomb for a horse and a canary.[22]

Chapter Twenty-Five

THE *EXPRESS* DISASTER

CAPTAIN James T. Barker, master of the Potomac Trans-portation Line steamer *Express*, usually made a point of greeting personally each of his passengers as they boarded ship. The afternoon of Tuesday, October 22, 1878, was different; Barker's concern with normal protocol was interrupted by the latest news of the storm warnings coming in from the lower Bay. The ship, tied up at her Light Street dock on the Baltimore waterfront, was scheduled to depart at 4:00 P.M. with freight and passengers for Washington, D. C., and other points along the Potomac River. And, Barker was under orders to sail as usual.[1]

Preoccupied as he was, the captain could not help noting the beautiful, twenty-five-year-old woman, handsomely dressed and wearing an old-fashioned gold watch and chain, glide grace-fully up the gangplank. Yet he failed to pay much attention to the fortyish-looking woman who followed. Behind the two women sauntered a tall, spare, gray-haired fellow with a full beard, and another man, about twenty-five years of age, wearing a brown overcoat and a blue sack coat underneath. The purser noted that the two women were Mrs. Randolph Jones and Mrs. M. A. Bacon (wife of the late Doctor James Bacon of Bacon's Wharf in St. Mary's County). The bearded gentleman was Hen-ry B. Ullman, a well-to-do Baltimore cattle dealer. The young man with him was Mr. Levalrine, a traveling salesman. Dr. Burch, a well-known physician from St. Mary's County, board-ed soon afterward, followed by Mrs. Tarleton of St. Inigoes, with her six-year-old child. Then the black passengers were permitted to board. There were only two on this trip, Chloe Dyson and Mrs. Thomas.[2]

The passenger list for the freighter was small on this day, many potential sojourners having been frightened away by the weather reports. If Barker was concerned, he failed to show it, other than with a few more than usual anxious glances skyward. *Express* cast off on schedule and steamed out of the harbor and down the Bay with a crew of twenty-one, nine passengers, and a fair-sized cargo. Her first stop was at St. Inigoes, in St. Mary's River, where she was to disembark Mrs. Jones, the wife of Captain Randolph Jones.[3]

Though *Express* was an old ship, built in 1841, she was as reliable as any on the Bay, and had seen service during the Civil War at Hampton Roads as a Union express boat. After the war she had resumed commercial service without missing a beat. In 1872 Reuben Foster, her owner, had her original length of 160 feet enlarged to 200 feet, and a few sparse amenities of a passenger carrier added.[4]

The trip down the Bay was uneventful, the weather holding off quite well. At midnight, however, the wind began to freshen, increasing steadily until 2:00 A.M., when it veered from east to southeast and reached gale force. The storm labored heavily, generating immense waves which began to break over the ship's upper deck with frightening power. By 4:00 A.M. the winds reached vicious hurricane proportions.[5]

Barker was in a quandary. To the west of his ship was the unbroken wall of the Cliffs of Calvert County; to the east were the treacherous shoals of Taylors Island. The next safe harbor of refuge was Patuxent River, on the western shore, but to turn in there would bring her broadside against the winds until she could round Drum Point and actually enter the river. No, he thought, he would run for the next sanctuary, Hooper's Straits, on the Eastern Shore.[6]

But sanctuary was a long way off, and the hurricane had now become so furious that it was almost impossible to stand against it. The rolling of the gigantic waves prevented the engines from working fast enough to maintain adequate steerage. With each violent battering, the ship's joiner work screeched as

if it were tearing apart. It was evident to Barker that the upper
deck would soon give way unless something was done, for
Express could no longer maintain her head to the wind. He
ordered the anchors let go. Perhaps they could ride out the
storm, or at least survive until it subsided. No sooner were the
anchors thrown over than their chains snapped. There was now
little alternative but to struggle onward.[7]

At 5:00 A.M. the ship was directly in the middle of the Bay,
between Point No Point on the western shore and Barren Island
on the Eastern Shore. Despite the danger, every man of the crew
bravely stood at his post without a sign of panic. Many of the
officers and men stayed below, throwing over cargo to lighten
the ship, which, with her hold full of water, was now wallowing
heavily. Several of the passengers soon assisted in the desperate
struggle.[8]

A driving rain, Barker noted with some glimmer of hope,
was helping to beat down the sea somewhat, but the swells
were still enormous, towering well above the upper deck of the
ship. *Express* bobbed about with only limited control until a
single, gigantic wave smashed over her, filling her hold and
drowning her fires. She was now entirely without control, a
slave to the winds and sea.[9]

The women passengers seemed calm and resigned, assisting one another with their life preservers. Ship's purser F. J.
Stone later noted of their bravery:

> These preparations were silently made for the fight for life which
> all saw was inevitable. An audibly uttered prayer here and there,
> a moan of suppressed emotion from one or another of the passen-
> gers in the saloon were all the outward evidences given of the
> intense feeling which possessed the breasts of all on board.[10]

Suddenly, the wind veered to the southwest. The ship was
now off Hooper's Straits, captive to the bidding of the storm.
Shortly after 5:00 A.M. the sea struck a stunning blow. With a
single, earsplitting crash, the joiner work was ripped from its
stanchions, and before either passengers or crew realized what
was happening, a second wave tore away the saloon deck "like
so much paper work." The entire ship was flipped on her side in
an instant, and lay in a trough of the sea awaiting final burial.

Almost everyone on the upper deck had been cast into the water, floating off in various directions with whatever piece of flotsam they could grasp.[11]

Then *Express* rolled completely over, her keel facing skyward. As she rolled, several persons who had managed to cling to her clambered up the sides to her bottom, but failed to retain their perches against the wind and seas for long. Ullman, the two black female passengers, Mrs. Tarleton and her child, and four crewmen were trapped inside the ship.[12] Only one of the black ladies managed to escape.

Most of those more fortunate individuals who had been swept from the hull found temporary shelter from the gale under the protection offered by the lee side of the wreck. Respite, however, and time to do whatever could be done for self and fellow man, was only momentary. Ship's purser F. J. Stone had stripped to his underwear before the capsize, but was caught with his overcoat on, "the climax having come so quickly that he had not time to throw it aside." In the water, one of the officers assisted him in freeing himself of the encumbrance.[13]

For barely two minutes, the survivors gathered together whatever timbers and planks they could. Quartermaster James Douglas secured a sturdy piece of wood. In the pitch darkness, he could barely make out Captain Barker and others doing likewise. Several men attempted to help Mrs. Jones and Mrs. Bacon into a small yawl which had bobbed up, but the tiny craft could not withstand the vicious seas, and sank. Both women were drowned in an instant.[14]

When the makeshift life rafts of random timbers drifted from the lee of the wreck, the waves struck them brutally, segmenting the frail cluster of human life even more. Dr. Burch clung to a broken railing, but was weakened by the battering seas. Three times he lost his grip, and three times he was saved by others. The fourth time proved fatal. A chambermaid, Matilda Isaacs, was last seen clinging to a mattress floating from the wreck.[15]

Purser Stone managed to take hold of a timber with several other crewmen, among whom was the ship's fireman Robert Hawkins. Hawkins had valiantly stood at his post, in waist-deep water, before the ship sank. Aboard the raft, he was equally cool and courageous, constantly inspiring those about him not to give up hope. On another raft, Willie Barker, the captain's son, had become entirely demoralized and would have drowned had not another crewman taken care of the lad.[16]

Gradually, the few survivors lost sight of each other. Quartermaster James Douglas, alone on a shredded plank from the saloon, was certain that his brother, wheelman John Douglas, had perished. At daybreak he attempted to sort out, in the still-turbulent seas, the flotsam of the wreck from what might be the remnants of human life. But it was an impossible task, for what at one moment appeared to be a man or woman in the next instant turned out to be a piece of furniture or cargo. Douglas drifted for hours, his body gradually becoming numb from exposure. His grip weakened on the slender piece of wood which was going to pieces in his hands.[17]

By late morning, the quartermaster found himself adrift in a sea of debris. Out of nowhere, suddenly appeared a schooner. It was apparent that he had been spotted, but no effort was made to save him. Instead, the valuable barrels of oil and other freight belonging to the wreck were picked up and the schooner then disappeared.[18]

At noon on Wednesday, almost totally exhausted, and with only a small sliver of wood keeping him afloat, Douglas was finally saved nearly twenty miles from the wrecksite by the schooner *Samuel H. Watte.* Aboard the boat, Douglas learned, to his great joy, that others had been picked up as well, most of them by boats from the steamboat *Shirley,* which had herself been driven ashore on Barren Island. Purser Stone, four blacks, and, incredibly, his brother, had been saved and were on their way to Baltimore.[19]

Captain Barker, the ship's wheelman, and a black passenger had fared in the same way, having remained for some hours afloat on a contrived raft of planks. They were taken to Crisfield and transferred to the steamer *Maggie* going to Baltimore. Two other crewmen were picked up by a three-masted schooner and transferred to a tugboat which arrived at Baltimore soon afterward. On October 25 the steamer *Louise* arrived at Baltimore bringing the rest of the survivors.[20]

When the final statistics were computed, fifteen persons survived; sixteen were lost. The storm which destroyed the steamer *Express* did not ignore other vessels unfortunate or foolish enough to be on the Bay during its peak. The steamer *Massachusetts* was driven ashore in the Patuxent River, and the steamer *Theodore Weems*, having lost a rudder and sustained serious damage to her joiner work, had to be towed into Crisfield by the steamer *Tangier*. *Tangier* herself lost an anchor and chain and some of her own joiner work. *Louise,* of the York River Line, after barely riding out the storm, was fortunate enough to limp back to Baltimore. *Shirley* was believed to be hopelessly grounded on Barren Island. Only two steamers in the upper Bay, *Highland Light* and *Georgianna*, both running out of the Choptank, survived the hurricane without injury.[21]

About the time *Georgianna* steamed into Baltimore Harbor, the bloated body of a once beautiful, handsomely dressed young woman, approximately twenty-five years of age, wearing an old-fashioned gold watch and chain, washed ashore on a small, sandy island south of Hooper's Straits, a mute witness to the terrible *Express* disaster.

Chapter Twenty-Six

CAPTAIN HALL'S PREMONITION

S PENCER D. HALL, Spence, as his friends called him, was a
man whose smile was both wide and easy. Wire-rimmed
glasses, perched astride a rather full nose gave him an absent-
minded-professor look. Yet when he wore his captain's hat and
uniform, he looked what he was—one of the most experienced
steamboat captains on the Chesapeake. To the legions of Wash-
ingtonians and Baltimoreans who regularly enjoyed his numerous excursion runs from Baltimore to Crisfield and back, he had
become something of a fixture.[1] To the watermen of the Bay,
men who often held steamboaters in low regard, he was well-
known and respected.

He was a no-nonsense man, not easily given to emotional-
ism, always the perfect officer. At fifty-four years of age, he had
been employed in the Baltimore, Chesapeake and Atlantic Rail-
way Company's steamboat branch for nearly thirty years. Having started his career as a quartermaster, he rose rapidly to the
rank of Captain. In 1921 he was given command of one of the
company's finest ships, the 1,110-ton 180-foot-long prop steamer *Three Rivers*, a command which he hoped to maintain until
his retirement.[2]

Built in 1910 at Sparrows Point, Maryland, by the Maryland Steel Company for $125,000, *Three Rivers* was designed
specifically for service on the Potomac River. She quickly became one of the line's most popular ships on that run, even
though her main role was that of a freight hauler, possibly
because of her top deck staterooms, an innovation which she

was among the first on the line to feature. In 1920 she was shifted to the lucrative Baltimore-Crisfield run, a route with which Hall was happy.[3] It was shorter than the Potomac run and permitted him a bit more time with his wife, a luxury denied him by his earlier commands.

On the morning of July 3, 1924, Captain Hall prepared to leave home for the two-day run down the Bay and back. But he had not slept at all well the previous night. Before kissing his wife goodbye, he told her of a disturbing premonition he had had. Though he could not put his finger on it, he felt that something disastrous was about to happen. He was certain of it, and informed her that he dreaded this trip more than any other in his entire life. He had experienced many close calls during his career, but this voyage, he knew, would be tragically different.[4] But Hall was a seasoned skipper, stoic and duty-bound to both his company and his passengers. He refused to let what was possibly just a bad dream mar his respectable reputation for on-time efficiency.

Three Rivers took aboard nearly ninety passengers at Baltimore that morning. Most were bound for Crisfield to watch the Chesapeake Bay Workboat Championship Races, an annual event sponsored by the *Baltimore Evening Sun* newspaper in observance of Independence Day. That year the newspaper was sending fifty-nine members of the *Sun* Newsboy's Band to participate in the festivities.[5]

Embarkation went without a hitch, and the trip down the Bay was both pleasant and uneventful. The celebration and festivities were enjoyed by all. By midnight, the steamer was off Cove Point, steaming north on her return with a shipload of weary passengers. Captain Hall was in the pilothouse when the first word of trouble was brought to him by a frantic passenger. There was a fire in the saloon deck, and it was gaining rapidly.

For a split second, Hall experienced a sense of *déjà vu*. But then he swung into action. The fire, he immediately learned, was already out of control, and billows of suffocating black smoke were spewing forth. Instantly the alarm was given, but many of the passengers, already asleep, had to be awakened and warned. Grabbing several axes, the captain and his first officer scurried about the ship bashing in windows of locked cabins in which there was no reply, and waking passengers. "Get out of your room and onto the deck!" he told them.[6]

Within minutes, the entire saloon deck, pulsating with flames, was impassable. Many of the passengers had already secured life preservers and jumped overboard. Others had lowered several lifeboats and escaped. Two lifeboats remained swinging from the davits amidships, but they could not be reached through the heavy smoke. Hall reacted quickly by ordering the forty or fifty passengers still on the upper deck to go to the lower deck which, for the moment, was still free of flames. To fight the fire at this stage would only prove futile. It was best to concentrate efforts on saving as many lives as possible.[7]

Once on the lower deck, Hall ordered a crewman to rip off the slats which held the life preservers in place, and then directed the passengers to put them on and jump into the water immediately. A few hung back, hesitating for a moment. A glance at the roaring furnace above and behind them soon decided the issue. Individually and in groups they plunged into the Bay. Some swam and some dog-paddled, but all wisely attempted to put as much distance as possible between themselves and the burning ship.[8]

Six miles away, the 200-foot-long side-wheeler *Middlesex,* also belonging to the Baltimore, Chesapeake and Atlantic Line, spotted the glow of the burning ship in the midnight sky and made for her. Within a short time, many other vessels in the vicinity, including the steamship *Alleghany,* did likewise. Within half an hour after the beginning of the fire, *Middlesex* had arrived on the scene and commenced picking up survivors floating in the water.[9]

Weeping, hysterical persons, some clad only in makeshift clothing, were lifted aboard. By dawn, all who could be found had been taken up. A cursory head count revealed that five of the band members were missing. The bodies of two drowned passengers were taken up, and one crewman, a pantryman who had been picked up, died soon after the rescue. Within two days, two more bodies were recovered, one of which had drowned even though wearing a life jacket.[10]

An immediate effort was made to tow the carcass of *Three Rivers* back to Baltimore. It was then that the charred remains of the five *Baltimore Sun* newsboy's band members were discovered amid the burnt-out hulk of the ship.[11]

Captain Hall's premonition had indeed proven agonizingly correct.

Chapter Twenty-Seven

THE LAST CRUISE
OF *LEVIN J. MARVEL*

B UILT in 1891 on the Nanticoke River at Bethel, Delaware, *Levin J. Marvel* was one of the last of a dying breed of sailing ships, the Chesapeake Bay ram. She and her kind were ungainly in appearance, more like barges than ships. Their flat bottoms, wall sides, baldheaded three-masted schooner rigs, and stubby bows were a sharp contrast to the smaller, more graceful skipjacks and pungys of the Bay. Yet the rams had been built to perform a specific service: hauling lumber brought up from the Carolinas through the narrow Chesapeake and Delaware Canal to Philadelphia.[1]

Levin J. Marvel, over 125 feet long, but only 24 feet abeam (to permit passage through the narrow C&D Canal locks), and 183 tons gross, had done her job well for more than six decades but by 1954 was ready for retirement. Her seams were weakened by years of heavy-duty service carrying fertilizer, lumber, and merchandise up and down the Bay. Now, with competition from the large, powered commercial carriers, railroad, and trucking operations, she was no longer profitable to operate. *Marvel*'s freight hauling days were over and her last owner, J. A. Kunst of Fairfax, Virginia, knew it. She had to be sold. Kunst was not long in finding a buyer.[2]

At thirty-eight years of age, John Meckling had had his fill of the white-collar life of a certified public accountant. Ever since he built his first sailboat from a do-it-yourself magazine article, he yearned for the life of the sea. Gary, Indiana, his hometown, was certainly not the place to realize *that* dream. But fate already laid the groundwork for him, and he was drawn to the Eastern Shore of the Maryland tidewater by another magazine article, this one on skipjacks. There he promptly bought the first skipjack offered for sale. Yet he was still tied to the land. The climax of his love affair with sailing would not come until he saw the "For Sale" sign on *Levin J. Marvel*. The "perfect life" loomed large before Meckling's eyes, and he quickly purchased the ship for $18,000. He would refit her as a Chesapeake Bay windjammer vacation cruiser and captain her himself.[3]

There were other sailing vessels carrying "landlubbers" on week-long tours of the Bay, but Meckling's ship was certainly the largest, and he knew that, with a little repair, she would be one of the best. By 1955 the ship, boasting seventeen state-rooms with running water in each, sailed from her home port of Annapolis on regular five-day cruises to historic points on the Bay, carrying as many as forty-one persons, including crew.[4]

But she did have her troubles. Twice during the early summer season of 1954 she rubbed bottom and had to be repaired. Once, in July of that year, while en route from Salisbury to Baltimore for overhauling, her aged planks leaked so badly that she sank on a Wicomico River mudbank. Not long afterwards, back in service, she promptly ran aground south of Choptank River and had to be freed by a Coast Guard tender. Two days later, with fifteen passengers aboard, her radio went dead and she was late in arriving at Annapolis. She had quickly become the embarrassing object of an extensive marine search. The life of a windjammer cruise captain and owner was perhaps not quite what Meckling had expected. This year, he had assured himself, would have to be better.[5]

Marvel and her four-man crew waited quietly at her Annapolis dock on Monday, August 8, 1955, as a group of generally well-to-do passengers boarded for a five-day cruise. Most of the twenty-three passengers were from New York, although there were also some visitors from New Jersey, Connecticut, and North Carolina.[6]

Typical among them was Deborah Killip of Rochester, New York, who had been urged to take the trip by a friend from her hometown. Perhaps, like many other passengers, she had been dismayed on first seeing the hulking ram tied up at the Annapolis waterfront, but concluded that since she had come this far for a vacation, she might as well see it through. Besides, she loved to sail, and the beautiful Chesapeake was beckoning. Once underway, she was relieved to discover the meals were good, the company excellent, and the Bay, as she had expected, a genuine delight.[7]

But, far to the southeast, off Puerto Rico, Mother Nature was giving birth to Hurricane Connie. By Monday morning, when the ram sailed from Annapolis Harbor, Connie was off the Bahamas and crawling northwest, picking up speed and strength as she moved. By Thursday evening, she was off the Carolinas. At 6:00 P.M. she swerved from a westerly track and headed north. Hurricane warnings were soon displayed from Myrtle Beach to as far north as the Delaware Breakwater. Tides along the Atlantic side of the Eastern Shore of Maryland and Virginia, the U. S. Weather Bureau warned, were likely to be four to five feet above normal, but the Bay itself was expected to remain relatively calm.[8]

The storm struck the Carolinas with incredible impact, destroying waterfront communities and watercraft alike; it threatened to do equal damage to the Virginia Capes. At Norfolk, the Red Cross mobilized more than a thousand standby volunteers. Eleven schools were prepared as shelters if needed. First aid stations and fifty mobile communications units were fielded for use in the area. Peak winds up to 130 miles per hour and 50- to 75-mile-per-hour gales were reported spreading across the storm area, which was 120 miles long and 60 miles wide.[9]

Though the principal topic of discussion aboard *Levin J. Marvel*, the storm was not expected to hit the upper Chesapeake. Half-joking, half-serious conversations about having to leave the ship and being stranded at Cambridge, where she had come to berth temporarily, were forgotten when the hurricane warnings were lifted on Thursday.[10]

On Thursday morning, Meckling prepared to bring his ship across the Bay on the final leg of her cruise. It was a beautiful day, and he permitted his passengers an invigorating swim party before the ship weighed anchor. Then the big ram proceeded out into the Choptank, steering a course for Sharps Island Light in the Bay. A northeast breeze blowing at ten to twelve miles an hour filled her sails, and the ugly duckling glided gracefully over the water like a swan. Once off Sharps Island, Meckling turned his ship up the Bay on a course for Annapolis. The day was pleasant but uneventful.[11]

Although the sky by evening was still clear and starlit, the velocity of the wind was increasing. On deck, Deborah Killip was fascinated by the grandeur of the open Bay and the heady breeze stirring its water into a black frenzy. There was something exciting about it which kept her up until nearly 4:00 A.M. Then the wind velocity picked up sharply.[12]

Meckling was not worried about the increased wind. His ship's sails had been filled all night, and he fully intended to make Annapolis, or at least a safe anchorage in South or West River, before the expected fringes of the hurricane hit.

By daylight the wind was beginning to blow at gale force. It was now becoming obvious that the upper Bay would get more than the fringes of Connie. Hopes of reaching the western shore before the brunt of the storm hit now seemed slim. Meckling thus ordered a change of tack to run the ship into the lee behind Poplar Island where he might secure a safe anchorage. The ship's yawl, normally used to assist *Marvel* in berthing, was soon pressed into service to push her along, but the tiny craft's pumps clogged and her motor failed. Off Poplar, the seas coming out of Eastern Bay into the Chesapeake were even worse than those in the open Bay itself. The wind, laced with rain, was now thrashing about in violent gusts, and an anchorage anywhere between Poplar Island and Bloody Point Light to the north would be dangerous.[13]

Despite the increasing turbulence, ship's cook Elry Pinkney, a retired veteran of thirty-five years in the U. S. Navy, prepared breakfast as usual. Most of the passengers had been awake for some time. Suddenly, the ship was struck by a fifty-mile-an-hour gust which instantly shredded or ripped away all of her canvas. Not a single sail remained aloft, and *Marvel* turned broadside to the sea. The yawl line was also snapped, and the little craft disappeared into the storm. Meckling acted quickly and ordered the forward staysail raised. He now had no alternative to the sea's incessant battering but to run the ship westward before the wind.[14]

The captain resolved to make a direct run for West River from Bloody Point Light, a distance of somewhat less than six nautical miles, but the wind decided against him. He could, he hoped, still make Herring Bay if he were lucky and instantly determined to take what then seemed the only course of action.[15]

By 10:00 A.M. the wind and rain had whipped up a mist off the sea, dropping visibility to less than three hundred yards. The ship was sailing blindly through this mist. Yet morale among the passengers was high. Everyone appeared calm.[16]

Finally, after what seemed like endless hours of blind sailing, the ship entered Herring Bay and prepared to anchor in a local fish trap area off Holland Point. The first anchor was dropped but did not take hold immediately. Then it grabbed, and the ship's bow was brought very nicely into the wind. Everyone breathed a sigh of relief, but only temporarily.[17]

The seas were now fostering swells of twenty to twenty-five feet. The wind was still increasing when suddenly the anchor was ripped from the bottom by a particularly vicious swell, and *Marvel* was thrown a second time broadside to the sea. The auxiliary anchor was quickly dropped and took hold with wrenching force. Though *Marvel*'s bow was again into the wind, her weary seams had given way in some places. Except for a few porthole leaks, she had hitherto remained dry below, but now she was taking on water fast. The forward electrical bilge pumps were able to carry the load for awhile. Then, nature had her way. "The moisture in the air and on deck," Meckling later noted, "whipped up into foam, and the rain . . . drowned out the forward bilge pump." With the forward pump inoperative, every man aboard was put to work at the hand-operated emergency pumps, two men at a time. A gasoline-powered pump was started up aft. The situation was still under control.[18]

When the auxiliary anchor had wrenched the ship's seams apart, the force had also been enough to tear loose her bottled gas installation in the galley as the cook was preparing the noon meal. Undaunted, he proceeded to produce a light lunch of fruit juice and cookies in the lounge.[19]

At Captain Meckling's behest, the passengers had all assembled there. The captain was not about to chance losing a passenger overboard without a life jacket. He knew by then it was impossible to keep the ship from eventually filling. The pumps were far behind or useless, having been clogged with paper and other debris which was now floating in the bilge. An effort was made to radio for help, but no contact could be raised.[20]

With commendable restraint, Meckling addressed his passengers. It was possible that they would have to abandon ship, though for the moment not likely. There were fifty-three life preservers aboard. He directed them to put them on, and explained in detail how to abandon ship should the occasion arise. His presentation caused no panic among the passengers. In fact, they were in excellent spirits. It was bound to be a vacation, noted one, that they would not soon forget.[21]

The captain stepped onto the fantail. As each passenger came through the hatch, a line was attached joining him or her to the preceding passenger. Nearly a third of the passengers had come onto the fantail when suddenly, without warning, the ship's bow was nosed in under a large incoming sea. "Apparently," Meckling later recalled, "when [the ship] rose out of the water it must have lifted the anchor and dropped broadside to the sea." Then she rolled twice and capsized on her starboard side.[22]

Below, in the lounge when the wave struck, Charles Greenwald, a Brooklyn, New York, electrical engineer, was trying desperately to get the rope passed to him through his life preserver. When the ship suddenly heeled over sharply, he and the passengers with him were thrown back. A veritable deluge rushed in upon them as *Marvel* began to capsize.[23]

Deborah Killip was also below and had futilely attempted to stuff a pillow into a porthole to help stem the surging water. Suddenly there was no light, and the cabin roof came crashing in on her. Someone wearing a raincoat was thrashing wildly about her in the darkness. Someone else was grasping her leg in a viselike grip. She kicked free and somehow, choking, made it through the hatch, only to be thrown by another wave into the sea.[24]

The surge of water which carried Deborah Killip out also washed Charles Greenwald through a porthole where his foot stuck. For what seemed endless seconds, he struggled to free himself as the water rose about him at an incredible rate. Suddenly, he was loose and grasping for a hold on the floating timbers torn from the cabin.

It was 2:40 P.M. and the *Levin J. Marvel* lay wallowing ignominiously in the heavy seas, ready to die.[25] There were perhaps half a dozen people on the upper fantail when the ship capsized, and chaos reigned. Captain Meckling was shoved down beneath the shredded remains of the after sail, and by the time he had fought his way clear of the shreds of encumbering canvas, there were five or six more passengers struggling through the lounge hatch. Instantly the seas grabbed him, washing him clear of the ship. With a surge of energy, he pulled himself back onto the sinking craft and freed a young woman, Nancy Madden of Washington, D. C., from a potentially fatal entanglement in the sails and boom.[26]

Meckling and several others struggled futilely to climb to the upper side of the ship. Thrashing bodies swept by them. Reaching out, the captain managed to snag Frances Roberts of Orange, Connecticut, and pulled her up. Then he, Roberts, and Madden managed to pull in another passenger, Meryle Hutchinson. A member of the crew swept by on the opposite side of Roberts but was snagged by her at the last second. There were now five or six persons clinging to the ship in the water and perhaps an equal number on the top of the hull.[27]

Again the surge struck, washing over the struggling group for more than a full minute, throwing them helter-skelter into the sea. Upon surfacing, they discovered that they had been torn free of the vessel and were afloat. "We grabbed at each other in the excitement," said Meckling later. "We clutched in a group and held hands in a group of five." Yards away *Levin J. Marvel* porpoised, finally going down by her bow. "Whatever you do," Meckling said to the tiny cluster of humanity about him, "don't ever let go and we'll be all right."[28]

After each sea passed over the quintet, temporarily inundating them, Meckling made a check to see if they were still all right. "We were doing fine. We kept our legs in motion as much as we could to keep up circulation and the seas and the wind swept us shoreward."[29]

A hundred yards from the shore the group could see the surf breaking violently against the beach. There seemed no chance of swimming through the turbulence, for the enormous force of the pounding waves would drive them under, breaking every bone in their bodies. Undecided about what to do, they huddled together while nature selected their destiny for them. They were soon being swept back out beyond Holland Point toward the open Bay. Visibility closed in again, and the shoreline disappeared. Suddenly, a dark object loomed ahead of them, and the five struggling survivors expended their last bit of collective strength to reach it.[30]

It was 6:10 P.M. when the quintet reached the object, a dilapidated duck blind. Grasping the bottom of the structure, they heard a voice hail them from above. It was Perry Schwartz, another passenger, who had reached the blind barely five minutes before them. Assisting each other as best they could, the bedraggled survivors climbed into the refuge. The inside of the blind was covered with loose tar paper, and the survivors, nearly frozen from the constant exposure, promptly stripped the paper from the walls and wrapped themselves in it to keep warm.[31]

It was apparent that the duck blind offered but a temporary sanctuary. With every crashing wave the structure wavered a bit more than before. It was only a matter of time before it would succumb totally to the force of the hurricane. From their vantage point above the waves, the weary passengers could see the lights from the shore, and several mumbled quiet prayers.[32]

In the meantime, Deborah Killip and a 17-year-old lad from Bloomfield, New Jersey, John Ferguson, having been hurled from the ship into the brine almost simultaneously, grabbed the same large timber. Several people floated by shouting at Killip, but she did not answer, preferring to keep quiet and save her strength for the ordeal ahead. Not knowing which way the shore lay, the two drifted with the surge. Killip plucked an orange which had floated by, with the intention of keeping it as a source of nourishment should they drift out into the Bay. Hours passed.[33]

Ashore with his brother Bob, Arthur Kvale stood in front of his mother-in-law's cottage and watched in awe as the brunt of the hurricane collided with the beach. Then he spied two shapes floundering in the surge. The Kvale brothers rushed to the beach. Bob Kvale tore off his shoes and plunged into the surf. Within minutes he reached Killip and Ferguson and towed them toward the beach. "My God, am I glad to see you," cried the girl. When Kvale asked what had happened, she gasped, "I am one of twenty-seven. We were shipwrecked."[34]

The two were taken to the cottage where Killip, in a state of shock, became hysterical. Kvale's mother-in-law, Mrs. Edwin N. Fox, immediately notified the Coast Guard in Baltimore as well as the North Beach Volunteer Fire Department of the disaster. By then, survivors were being washed up all along the beach. And so were the dead.[35]

The only thing that Elry Pinkney, the cook, could recall was seeing his galley float by, yet, somehow, he managed to survive. Charles Greenwald had snagged a floating piece of debris and was washed ashore. William Balle staggered ashore after drifting for hours on a contrived raft of timbers from floating ship debris. Others were not so fortunate. Hilliard R. Nevins, his wife, and two children were drowned, along with Dr. Walter Goldstone, his sister Florence, and Dr. B. H. Roberts, an assistant professor of psychiatry at the Yale Medical School. And there were more.[36]

William McWilliam, twenty-eight, a North Beach volunteer fireman who, with his friend George Kellum, a construction worker, were among the first people to hear of the disaster drove to the beach to see if they could lend a hand. When they arrived they saw a number of people wading in water up to their waists, daring the breakers, in search of bodies. It was getting dark, and the collapsing duck blind on which Captain Meckling and his five fellow survivors were stranded could barely be seen. Though only six hundred yards from the beach, it might as well have been a thousand miles, but not to McWilliam and Kellum. McWilliam began an immediate search for some craft capable of reaching the survivors. Finally, he encountered a woman who owned a small johnboat and asked if he could borrow it. "To hell with the boat," she said. "You can take it if you're game enough."[37]

It wasn't much, barely fourteen feet in length and powered by a small outboard engine. But, it was all there was. Both men bravely pushed her off through the breakers, somehow managing to avoid being swallowed. On reaching the blind, Kellum, 6 feet 2 inches tall and 240 pounds of muscle, grabbed a piling and held the boat to it with one hand while helping the stranded survivors off with the other. Two people were taken aboard and carried to the shore at a time. Finally, after three harrowing trips, all six survivors were safe.

Within minutes of the final rescue trip, the duck blind, sanctuary of the last survivors of *Levin J. Marvel*, collapsed into the sea and was smashed to bits.[38]

Chapter Twenty-Eight

CUYAHOGA

THE Chesapeake Bay was at her matronly best on that October night in 1978 as the 125-foot Coast Guard Cutter *Cuyahoga* scudded quietly along her surface at nearly twelve knots. Yet on the bridge of this 320-ton ship, Chief Warrant Officer Donald K. Robinson, her commander, had little time to muse over the beauty of the clear, starlit evening. His ship, at fifty-one years of age the oldest commissioned vessel in Coast Guard service, was rapidly approaching Smith Point Light and preparing to cross the turbulent conflux of Potomac River and Chesapeake Bay.[1]

The skipper was not thinking about his twenty-seven-year career in the service at that moment, nor of his recent promotion to the command of *Cuyahoga*. Thoughts of his wife and six children or of his late bout with an asthmatic lung infection were out of his mind as he paced the tiny ship's bridge. He was tired, but no more so than usual since his illness four months earlier. He had experienced sleeping problems since September and in recent days had been unable to relax, except for occasional catnaps. He was worrying more, and the responsibility of command must have seemed at times a heavy burden.[2]

Robinson's judgment had rarely been questioned until recently. In the previous spring his ship lost her radar antenna when the closing of a drawbridge over Curtis Creek near Baltimore was misjudged. Several weeks later under his command *Cuyahoga* collided with a granite seawall while mooring. But Robinson was a stoic individual who preferred to meet each day head on. A deeply religious man, his creed was simple: "God is my strength to face each day. He will help me through."[3]

He rose to command through the ranks, learning seamanship from practical experience, having little faith in sailing learned by the book. He had served in a variety of positions on eight different vessels during his career, though prior to taking the bridge of *Cuyahoga*, it had been more than six years since he had seen sea duty. Despite the lapse of time, however, he had politely chosen to ignore official recommendations that he attend refresher classes on practical navigation and seaman's rules of the road.[4]

Upon assuming his position in June 1977, Robinson discovered numerous shortcomings with his ship and plagued his superiors to patch up or replace a number of faulty items aboard. He was worried about the shipboard electrical system, the wiring of which was rated from poor to outright inoperative. He soon gave up, however, his quest to have a qualified electrician assigned to the crew. And he tired of repeatedly reminding his superiors that *Cuyahoga* was the only cutter in the Coast Guard without a wheelhouse radar display—and the radar that it did have had failed no less than a dozen times in the last nine months. The ventilation system was so inadequate that hatchways frequently had to be left open to allow the below decks to be livable. Even the vessel's magnetic compass was off the mark and the deviation card, which displays such errors, had not been updated since June 1978.[5]

Cuyahoga was indeed a far cry from the ship she had been in her early days. She had enjoyed a spirited youth, pursuing rum runners during the prohibition years. In World War II she had patrolled the East Coast in search of German U-boats and had once even served as a high seas escort to Franklin D. Roosevelt. But those days were gone. Now she was relegated to finish out her allotted time as a floating classroom, running training missions for officer candidates, most of whom had yet to gain their sea legs.[6]

There were twenty-nine persons aboard *Cuyahoga*, nearly two-thirds of whom were officer candidates fresh from four weeks of dry land school at the big Coast Guard base at Yorktown, Virginia. The skipper, despite his own ascendancy through the ranks, maintained a fatherly attitude toward his crew, most of whom were only slightly older than his own kids. He tried hard to overlook their weaknesses and embrace their virtues.[7]

There was much to be said for the practical experiences gained during training cruises on vessels such as *Cuyahoga*, voyages that could take a seventeen-year-old apprentice or officer candidate and turn him into a worthy, knowledgeable seaman or officer. Seaman Kevin Henderson was an example of what a bit of practical experience and rigorous Coast Guard training could do. Henderson had served aboard *Cuyahoga* for ten months as a deckhand. Though little more than a mess cook at the Yorktown Reserve Training Base, he had developed into a jack-of-all-trades at sea; the skipper had frequently come to rely on him. He could handle almost everything well, from the crisp log book entries, to checking the radar system, to instructing the officer candidates.[8]

Ensigns Peter Eident, the cadet officer of the watch, and Frederick Rienier, the cadet at the helm, were among those candidates the regular ten-man crew of the ship were supposed to ease into their jobs. There were also two Indonesian Navy officers participating in an exchange training program in the group. One of these men, Lieutenant Jonathan Arisasmita, though he had had little radar training and experienced considerable difficulty with the English language, was at that moment manning the radar.[9]

Twenty-two-year-old Quartermaster Second Class Randy Rose had only been aboard since October 2. Yet among his duties were the training of four of the officer candidates, the monitoring of the Indonesian at the radar set, and the navigation of the ship. Though he too had never undergone formal radar training, he had been able to pick up enough information and experience here and there to get by. In fact, through no fault of his own, he had never even taken the examination necessary to win his quartermaster rank. The tests had been discontinued as a result of a service-wide manpower shortage. Rose's familiarity with the Chesapeake was only cursory, and that had been acquired during his limited service aboard the cutter *Reliance*. As for his knowledge of the Smith Point entry into the Potomac, or of the sometimes heavy marine traffic plying its waters, he knew nothing. But then the navigator he had just relieved, Yeoman William Carter, had not been any better equipped, having previously served as a secretary at the Yorktown base![10]

At approximately 8:45 P.M. that night, October 20, Officer Candidate Officer of the Deck Earl Fairchild was diligently scanning the horizon, as was the lookout, Seaman's Apprentice Michael Myers. Despite the clarity of the evening, Myers, a young recruit had difficulty differentiating lights on land from those at sea. Fairchild had no such problems and managed to pick out a faint flicker on the northern horizon of the Bay and dutifully reported the observation to the skipper. Both Robinson and Fairchild then observed the flickers through binoculars and soon determined them to be from a masthead light and a red sidelight of another vessel. The skipper promptly went to the chart room where the radar display was located and determined the range to be 15,700 yards. The seemingly insignificant size of the radar contact and his own perception of the white light seemed to suggest a vessel of minimal size, probably a small fishing boat, turning into the Potomac River. It was certainly nothing to worry about.[11]

North of Cuyahoga, the source of the flickering light, a giant, dark, torpedo-shaped form, heaped mountainous piles of water before it as it cut a wide swath through the Chesapeake. Santa Cruz II, Captain Abelardo Albonoz commanding, was a 521-foot Argentinian bulk freighter, fully laden with a 19,000-ton cargo of coal, bound from Baltimore on an 18-day voyage to San Nicolas, Argentina. Little more than a year old, the ship was the pride of the Argentinean government's E. L. M. Line and carried a crew of thirty-seven men. Her pilot was twenty-nine-year-old John P. Hamill of Baltimore, a veteran of more than seven hundred piloting trips down the Chesapeake.[12]

Hamill, too, had maintained a close watch of the horizon, on radar and visually, and readily spotted the approaching lights of Cuyahoga. His radar display, in fact, indicated two vessels on the horizon, one on a southbound course and the other on a northerly approach. The nearest, Cuyahoga, appeared to be presenting a port-to-port passing situation and caused neither Hamill no Captain Albornoz much concern.[13]

Aboard *Cuyahoga*, Seaman Kevin Henderson hovered impolitely over the shoulder of the Indonesian officer manning the radar and attempted to get his own fix on the blips appearing on the screen. Quartermaster Rose was more concerned with the locations of Smith Point and Point Lookout and the treacherous shoals about them than with the seemingly remote chance of a collision.[14]

Minutes ticked by as the two ships rapidly closed. *Cuyahoga* was approaching her turning point into Potomac River approximately four miles north-northeast of Smith Point Light. Aboard *Santa Cruz*, plowing along at well over fourteen knots, pilot Hamill still viewed the approach of the cutter with little concern. Suddenly, he noted the oncoming vessel turning west, toward the path of the freighter. Reacting instantly, he checked his radar to get another range on the vessel. Incredibly, the spectre of collision emerged as a distinct possibility. Again he looked down the starlit Bay. The cutter's navigation lights were clearly visible, and it was apparent she had turned her bow even further west and would definitely cross the *Santa Cruz II*. The distance between the two ships had narrowed to 1,200 yards. Instantly the pilot sounded the whistle, signaling that his ship would maintain course and speed. It was up to the cutter to turn off and avoid collision. Thirty seconds passed with no apparent response. As the two vessels closed, he sounded a danger warning of five short blasts.[15]

Aboard *Cuyahoga*, Seaman Henderson finally got a fix on the approaching ship when she was 4,700 yards off. The skipper, he assured himself, must know what he was doing, but it certainly looked dangerous. On the bridge, Robinson had heard the whistle of the oncoming freighter, "still believing that the other vessel was proceeding on a near parallel course that would take it into the Potomac River." He ordered a whistle of acknowledgment, and altered course even further west, still blindly believing that he was overtaking a small fishing boat.[16]

Below, Randy Rose was aroused by a distinct feeling of impending danger. Perhaps it was something astir topside. Perhaps it was only intuition. Looking out to sea he was stunned to see the running lights of *Santa Cruz II* thirty to forty degrees off his starboard bow and less than 2,000 yards distant. He was among the first to discern that the oncoming behemoth was more than a simple fishing boat.[17]

When the second blast of *Santa Cruz*'s whistle pierced the night air, Robinson was taking bearings on the freighter. He too, now finally aware of an impending collision, stepped quickly into the wheelhouse to order the engines all stop, and then back onto the bridge. From below Boatswains Mate Roger Wild, *Cuyahoga*'s second in command, came bounding up from below shouting, "Oh my God, Captain, he's going to hit us." Instantly Robinson ordered the engines into full reverse.[18]

Pilot Hamill, on *Santa Cruz II*, was stunned by the realization that he was on a direct collision course. Less than 200 yards separated the two ships as he desperately ordered the engines stopped and began sounding the whistle again, five times, but to no avail. Barely yards from the cutter he attempted to divert the momentum of the huge coal freighter hard aport in a last ditch effort to avoid the crash, even as the whistle screamed its fatal warning. It was to be the last sound many aboard *Cuyahoga* would ever hear.[19]

At exactly 9:07 P.M. the bulbous ramlike underbow of *Santa Cruz II* ripped through *Cuyahoga*'s starboard midship, goring the ancient cutter fatally forty feet from her stern and tipping her over bodily at a fifty degree angle. By ordering her engines reversed, Robinson had succeeded in literally backing into a collision.[20]

Chaos was instantaneous in the cutter crewmen, equipment, and personal effects were thrown about brutally by the severe concussion. With her starboard side hung up on the bow of the freighter, *Cuyahoga*'s port side was plowed underwater by the giant's sheer momentum, and the sea rapidly flooded her innards.[21]

Some men reacted instinctively. Roger Wild immediately started pulling people up over the bridge and into the water as the ship was shoved aside by *Santa Cruz* and began to sink. Some crawled and some climbed up to the starboard side, perched on the deckhouse, and then jumped into the water as the cutter went down. The suction caused by the foundering ship pulled some under as they struggled in the darkness to grasp whatever flotsam came to hand for support. It was over quickly, for within two minutes of the collision, *Cuyahoga* had disappeared beneath the waves, and with her many of the Coast Guardsmen aboard.[22]

Miraculously, the cutter's 14-foot utility boat had come free and, with an air pocket trapped by a tarpaulin over it, bobbed to the surface as the survivors pitched about in search of salvation. Captain Robinson was among them, in a complete state of shock, unable to breathe freely or swim, and kept afloat only through the diligent efforts of Quartermaster Rose. When the utility boat broke the surface, Roger Wild swam directly to it and immediately took charge of the situation in an effort to make the tiny craft a platform for survival. Unable to carry all of the eighteen survivors that had, through the efforts of one of the officer candidates, begun to cluster together, he permitted only the injured aboard. The remainder were directed to maintain positions around the periphery to avoid swamping the boat.[23]

Within a short time the searchlights of *Santa Cruz II*, which had come about, began to play on the waters and soon discovered the little craft. The big 12,000-ton freighter herself had sustained serious damage below her waterline in the bulbous under-bow section, where a three-foot wide hole had been split. Yet she was kept afloat by the watertight bulkheads forward of her cargo compartment and was soon able to dispatch her own motor lifeboat to help the floundering men and search for other possible survivors.[24]

Santa Cruz had soon come to anchor a few hundred yards from the sunken wreck and quickly marked the site with a buoy, even as Wild gathered up the survivors in the freighter's boat. Wild was concerned over the condition of the dazed, pale, and drawn captain beside him in the lifeboat, worried whether he would even live through the ordeal. Finally, the eighteen men were brought aboard the freighter. "I wasn't cold until we got on the *Santa Cruz*," Wild later recalled, "then I realized how many people were missing."[25]

The Coast Guard was immediately notified. Within hours, its Atlantic Strike Team, an elite ten-man unit headed by Commander Barry Chambers, had arrived on the scene in a small boat. Eleven of *Cuyahoga*'s men were missing, but it was initially thought that some may have been trapped alive inside the ship, possibly surviving in an air pocket. Though the strike team was primarily a pollution control unit whose principal function was to isolate large oil spills from tankers or shipwrecks, it was also a group of experts in undersea rescue.[26]

The commander's first objective was to locate the wreck. It was at first believed that all that would be necessary would be to descend the buoy line laid out by *Santa Cruz*. Chambers was among the first in the water and was soon hauling himself down the line. He immediately discovered that the line was drifting—and with it the slender hopes for the eleven men who may have been trapped.[27]

Believing the drift to be minimal, the team began an exhaustive series of bounce dives and then a crisscrossing underwater search. The results, in the coal-black waters, were negative. By 4:00 A.M. the weary team had all but given up hope.[28]

Chambers had one more idea. The sophisticated locational gear needed to find the wreck was en route but still hours away, and might arrive too late to be of use. Why not use the CB (citizens band) radio aboard their small boat to ask any vessels equipped with depth sounders to lend a hand? Perhaps they could pick up the wreck's superstructure with a standard Fathometer or fish-finder.[29]

Within a short time, a fishing boat, *Bay King*, responded. At first light Chambers and the fishing boat began canvassing the area, looking for the telltale sign of an oil slick emanating from *Cuyahoga*'s punctured hull. If they could locate the characteristic oil "blips" of a damaged wreck, then it would be possible to run a systematic search pattern over the area using the depth-sounder to find the hull itself.[30]

For a commander in the Coast Guard, Chambers did not appear to be a standard by-the-book officer. He was fond of wearing cowboy boots, and his favorite belt buckle was emblazoned with nine bronze dolphins. Yet he was said to be one of the best commanders in the service. His most recent challenge, a thankless task, had been confining the oil spill from the giant tanker *Argo Merchant*, wrecked on Nantucket Shoals. He thrived on diving, often simply for the thrill of it. He had been down on the wreck of the *Andrea Doria*, the Mount Everest of the diving world, not once, but four times.[31]

Soon an oil slick was spotted by *Bay King*, and after a few runs with the Fathometer switched on, the wreck was located. Taking the fishing boat's small anchor in hand, Chambers tossed it like a fishing line into the water and dragged backwards, snagging it on the wreck. Donning his gear, he was soon in the water, going hand over hand down the line. Finally, at a depth of fifty-eight feet, he encountered the dead ship, heeled over on her side, her white hull now a dirty pale gray in the turbid water.[32]

From the gaping 15-foot-long hole in her side and the demolished condition of her aft cabin and deck, it was immediately apparent to Chambers that all hope of anyone surviving within had to be given up. "We could at least make the motions," he later stated, "to see if there were any survivors." He hammered on the hull, but there was no response. He removed the hatchway cover over the crew's sleeping quarters, but there were no bubbles. Inside the hatchway, in a water-filled cell, he found two bodies. Two other crewmen in the wardroom had been killed by the impact itself and floated against the ceiling. Others would soon be found in similar situations.[33]

At first light of dawn, looking more like pallid ghosts than anything else, the *Cuyahoga* survivors were ferried to the Coast Guard Station on St. Inigoes Creek. Grimly, led by several officers, they stepped onto the dock to be taken to the Patuxent River Naval Air Station Hospital.

The lawsuits, court martials, and Congressional investigations that were certain to follow were the last things on Captain Robinson's troubled mind. With the shock of the disaster now crushing down upon him, he could only think of the loss. "I feel hurt and I feel pain," he mumbled. "Some of those eleven boys were no older than my own children." He looked at the ground as he shuffled toward the car waiting at the end of the dock. "It was like losing eleven sons. We were like a big family."[34]

Salvage operations to recover *Cuyahoga* began late on Sunday evening, October 29. Two U. S. Navy floating cranes were anchored over the site, as several Coast Guard strike team divers maneuvered lift cables through the sand and under the wreck. Before surfacing, the divers lowered *Cuyahoga*'s flag to

half-mast in honor of their dead mates. With the cranes strain-
ing, the 320-ton craft inched slowly upward. The first section to
break the surface was the tip of her mast, upon which her ensign
was half-raised, followed by the flying bridge.[35]

The vessel's white hull now glistened, though it appeared
to be a total wreck. Life jackets were still attached to her
railways, axes mounted on the cabin walls, and the gangway
was still lashed to the bridge deck. The cabin aft had been badly
injured, her deckhouse destroyed, and fifteen feet of her teak-
wood deck had been grotesquely peeled back. There was a hole
in her side large enough to drive a car through. Water gushed in
torrents through her various wounds as Navy tugs maneuvered
a barge beside her, on which she was to be placed and hauled to
Baltimore.[36]

The General Services Administration refused to accept the
Cuyahoga wreck, and the Maritime Administration wanted
only a few portions of it. She was ignominiously stripped of her
mast, wheel, screws, anchors, and anything else worth saving,
painted over, and the massive hole in her side patched at Portsmouth, Virginia. On November 26, 1978, it was decided to
scuttle the ship off the Virginia Capes.

At the request of the Virginia Natural Resources Administration, she was towed fifteen miles out from the coast and
sunk, joining a number of hulks which form an artificial off-
shore fishing reef. And ex-Captain Donald K. Robinson would
find it more difficult than ever to sleep at night.

Appendix

CHRONOLOGICAL INDEX
TO DOCUMENTED VESSEL LOSSES
IN THE CHESAPEAKE

EXPLANATION

The following table is an index of over 1,800 vessels lost in and about the Chesapeake tidewater between the years 1608 and 1978. As with any such listing, it is undoubtedly incomplete. Each listing included has been fully documented as far as possible from original source material or, when not available, from reputable secondary sources. All vessels included, with the possible exception of several colonial vessels, are of five tons or greater burthen. Those who may wish to investigate further one or more of the listings are directed to the bibliography where the documentary sources examined are fully listed.

The list is presented in chronological sequence, by year, month, and day. Whenever multiple vessel losses occur on a single date, the vessels are listed in alphabetical order. Often, a national, state, or service designation will precede the name of a vessel. These designations are as follows:

C.N.	Continental Navy	U.S.C.G	United States Coast
C.S.N.	Confederate States		Guard
	Navy	U.S.S.	United States Navy
H.M.S.	Royal Navy	V.S.N.	Virginia State
M.S.N.	Maryland State		Navy
	Navy		

Multiple listings of unidentified vessels for which the number of vessels lost is known appear with the specific number, e.g., (4). When the exact number lost is unknown, but is a verifiable multiple loss, (+) will appear.

The following is a key to vessels by type:

Bat	Batteaux	RmSch	Ram schooner
Bgt	Brig or brigantine	S	Submarine
Bkt	Barkentine	Sch	Schooner
Brg	Barge	Sch(BR)	Schooner (Blockade runner)
Brk	Bark		
BS	Battleship	SchBrg	Schooner barge
BSch	Bugeye schooner	SchF	Schooner ferry
Bt	Boat (type unknown)	SchY	Schooner yacht
		ScS	Steam screw
CB	Canal boat	ScSGb	Steam screw gunboat
CBrg	Canal barge		
CSch	Canal schooner	ScStb	Steam screw torpedo boat
Drg	Dredge		
FB	Ferryboat	Scw	Scow
Fgt	Frigate	Sh	Ship
Ft	Freighter	Shl	Shallop
Gal	Galley	Sk	Skiff
GB	Gunboat	Skj	Skipjack
GSc	Gas screw	SlOW	Sloop of War
GScSch	Gas screw schooner	Slp	Sloop
GScY	Gas screw yacht	Sn	Snow
IR	Ironclad ram	SOL	Ship of the Line
K	Ketch	SOW	Ship of War
LB	Lookout boat	St	Steamboat (type unknown)
LS	Lightship		
M	Merchantman (type unknown)	StScw	Steam scow
		StT	Steam tug
MS	Mail ship	StY	Steam yacht
MSch	Mail schooner	SWS	Side wheel steamboat
OSc	Oil screw		
OScT	Oil screw tug	SWSF	Side wheel steam ferry
OScY	Oil screw yacht		
PB	Pilot boat	T	Tug
Pgy	Pungy	Tsp	Transport (military)
Pnk	Pink	U	Unidentified vessel type
Pr	Privateer		
PS	Packet ship	V	Victualler (military)
PSch	Pilot schooner		

Vessels were lost in the Chesapeake tidewater in many ways. The following is a key to the circumstances that occasioned each loss. Where loss was caused by collision, the name of the vessel or the object with which it collided appears in the notes. Vessels lost as a result of combat or military related causes are listed as war losses (WL). Frequently, the vessels so listed will be accompanied by an additional listing in parentheses documenting the specific circumstances in which the vessel came to an end.

A	Abandoned	I	Ice
B	Burned	NL	Noted only as "lost"
BU	Blown up (intentionally)	S	Stranded
C	Collision	Sc	Scuttled
CA	Noted only as "cast away"	T	Torpedo or Mine
Cap	Capsized	W	Wrecked
E	Boiler or other explosion	WL	War loss
F	Foundered	U	Manner of loss unknown

Space limitations preclude identifying the exact location of every vessel listed, although many sites are actually well known. Nor has it been possible to relate the ultimate fate of vessels that were salvaged, removed, or rehabilitated after wreckage.

CHRONOLOGICAL INDEX TO DOCUMENTED VESSEL LOSSES IN THE CHESAPEAKE TIDEWATER

DATE	VESSEL	TYPE	MANNER	LOCATION
1608	Unidentified	Sk	F	Hog Island, near Jamestown, Va.
1642	Unidentified	Sh	I	Off Piscataway Creek, in Potomac River
1657 Feb	Seahorse of London	Sh	S	Near Mattox Creek, Va.
1667	H.M.S. Elizabeth	Sh	WL(B)	Virginia
1697 Oct 12	H.M.S. Roe	K	W	York River, Va.
1699	Roanoke Merchant	Slp	S	Elizabeth River, Va.
1700 Apr 22	George	Slp	B	Virginia Capes
Apr 26	Pennsylvania Merchant	U	B	Off Cape Henry, Va.
	Unidentified	U	Sc	Off Virginia Capes
1706	Unidentified(14)	M	NL	North coast of Cape Charles, Va.
1707	Richard and Mary	Pnk	U	Patuxent River, Md.
1721 Nov 13	Unidentified	Pnk	CA	Middle Ground, Chesapeake Bay, Va.
Nov 22	Content	Slp	CA	Cape Charles, Va.
Nov 25	Unidentified	Sh	S	Cape Henry, Va.
1723 Feb 23	Unidentified	Bt	NL	Between Wicomico and Annapolis, Md.
1724 Jun	Unidentified	Sh	B	Annapolis, Md.
Aug 12	Unidentified (+)	Sh	W	James River, Va.
1728 Dec	Unidentified	Slp	U	In the vicinity of Pocomoke Sound, Va.
1729 Feb	Unidentified	Sh	F	Off the James River, in Chesapeake Bay, Va.
1736 Dec	Unidentified	U	I	James River, Va.
1738 Feb 21	Needham	Sh	B	West Point, Va.
Apr 4	Richmond	Sh	S	Middle Ground, Chesapeake Bay, Va.
Apr 16	Rose	Sh	B	Littlepage's Wharf, Pamunkey River, Va.
1739 Jan 3	Unidentified	Sh	S	Lynnhaven Bay, Va.
Sep 18	Unidentified	Bt	Cap	James River, Va.
1745 Mar 27	Unidentified	Sch	F	Fleets Bay, Va.
Nov 12	Unidentified	U	Cap	Chesapeake Bay
Dec 31	Success	Sh	F	Middle Ground, Chesapeake Bay, Va.
1746 Apr	Unidentified	Sh	F	Mouth of Chesapeake Bay, Va.
Oct 7	Unidentified	SchF	S	Bodkin Point, Md.
	Glasgow	M	WL(B)	Near Cape Charles, Va.
	Prince George	U	WL(B)	Near Cape Charles, Va.

Date	Name	Rig		Location
Mar	Unidentified	Slp	CA	Virginia Capes
Sep 3	Unidentified	Sh	C	In Rappahannock River, at Urbanna, Va.
1748 Mar 20	Unidentified	Sch	S	Severn Point, Md.
Apr 13	Unidentified	PB	Cap	Choptank River, Md.
Jun 2	Unidentified	PB	Cap	Off Kent Island, Md.
1749 Jan	Susanna	Sh	I	Nanjemoy Creek, Md.
Oct 7	Unidentified	Slp	S	Worcester County, Md.
Oct 7	Unidentified	Sh	F	Near mouth of Chesapeake Bay, Va.
Oct 7	Unidentified (2)	U	S	Cape Henry, Va.
Oct 7	Unidentified (+)	Sh	S	Norfolk, Va.
Oct 27	Unidentified	U	U	Thomas Point, Md.
Oct 28	Unidentified	Slp	S	Chesapeake Bay
Nov	Unidentified	Slp	S	Eastern Neck Island, Md.
Nov	Unidentified	Sch	S	Eastern Neck Island, Md.
Dec	Unidentified	Slp	F	Thomas Point, Md.
1750 Jan	Brothers	Sh	S	Pongoteague Shoals
Aug 19	Unidentified	Sch	S	Virginia Capes
Aug 19	Unidentified	Slp(3)	NL	Virginia Capes
Aug 19	Unidentified	U	NL	Virginia Capes
Nov 23	Unidentified	U	Cap	Chester River, Md.
Dec 19	Unidentified	U	S	Herring Bay, Md.
Dec	Unidentified	U	S	Calvert Cliffs, Md.
Dec	Unidentified	U	S	Craney Island, Va.
1751 Mar 19	Unidentified	FB	Cap	Between Kent Island and Annapolis, Md.
Aug 23	Unidentified	Sh	S	Poplar Island, Md.
1752 May 1	Speedwell	U	Cap	Kent Island, Md.
Oct 1	Unidentified	FB	F	Kent Island, Md.
Oct 22	Peggy and Nancy	Sh	S	Willoughby Point, Va.
Nov 30	Unidentified	Sch	Cap	Near Patuxent River, Md.
Nov	Unidentified	Bt	Cap	Between Norfolk and Hampton Roads, Va.
Dec	Unidentified	Bt	Cap	Below Annapolis, Md.
1753 Jan 26	Lucy	Sh	S	Northwest Branch, Baltimore, Md.
Jan	Unidentified	Sh	S	Middle Ground, Chesapeake Bay, Va.
Mar	Unidentified	Sch	U	Pooles Island, Md.
Apr 24	Unidentified	U	S	Mouth of Patuxent River, Md.
Jul 21	Swan	Bgt	B	Kent Island, Md.
Nov	Industry	Sh	S	Swan Creek, Md.
				Worton Creek, Md.

DATE	VESSEL	TYPE	MANNER	LOCATION
1754 Jan	Unidentified	U	S	Middle Ground, Chesapeake Bay, Va.
Nov 5	Beaumont	Sn	F	Off Virginia Capes
Nov 12	Unidentified	Sch	S	Thomas Point, Md.
1755 Dec 25	Pearl	Sh	BU	Cape Charles, VA.
Dec	Penguin	Slp	F	Lynnhaven Bay, Va.
	Patowmack	Sch	F	Lynnhaven Bay, Va.
1757 Jan 13	Sea-Flower	Slp	S	Thomas Point, Md.
	Lydia	M	F	Near Cape Henry, Va.
1758 May 5	Unity	Sh	B	Northwest Branch, Patapsco River, Md.
1759 May 5	Sophia	Sh	B	Chestertown, Md.
Sep	Unidentified	U	F	Chester River, Md.
Oct	Adventure	Sn	F	Off Virginia Capes
1760 Apr 10	Unidentified	F	Cap	Mouth of Choptank River, Md.
Nov 1	King of Prussia	Bgt	F	Off Virginia Capes
1761 April	Unidentified	Bgt	S	Smith Point, Va.
	Russel	M	NL	Near Cape Henry, Va.
	Sally	M	NL	Near Cape Charles, Va.
1762	Unidentifieds (2)	Sh	NL	Near Cape Charles, Va.
1764 Nov 25	Friendship	Sch	W	South of Cape Henry, Va.
	Brothers	Sh	W	Near Cape Henry, Va.
	Rogers	M	W	Middle Ground, Chesapeake Bay, Va.
1766 Jul	Unidentified	Sch	Cap	Greenbury Point, Md.
Sep	Ranger	Sh	S	Cape Henry, Va.
Oct	Dunlop	Sn	S	Willoughby Point, Va.
Dec	Hawke	M	F	Upper Chesapeake Bay, Md.
1767 Jan	Liverpool	Sh	S	Five miles south of Cape Henry, Va.
Feb	Lockhart	U	CA	South of Cape Henry, Va.
Apr	Baltimore Packet	U	Cap	Horn Point, Md.
Oct 16	Unidentified	Slp	CA	Lynnhaven Bay, Va.
Oct 16	Unidentified	Slp	CA	Off Virginia Capes
Oct	Unidentified	Sch	F	Off Virginia Capes
	Mercury	K	F	Off Virginia Capes
	Norfolk	Sh	S	Cape Henry, Va.
	Tartar	U	F	Off Virginia Capes

Date	Vessel	Rig	Cause	Location
				… Point, Va.
Dec	Unidentified	U	S	Outside of Virginia Capes
1769 Aug	Unidentified	U	CA	Eastern Shore
Aug	Unidentified (+)	U	CA	Virginia Capes
Sep 7	Unidentified (4)	M	W	York River, Va.
Sep 7	Unidentified (2)	M	W	James River, Va.
Sep 21	Fortune	Sn	S	North of New Point Comfort, Va.
Oct 19	Unidentified	Slp	W	Cove Point, Md.
Nov	Randolph	Sh	S	Cape Henry, Va.
	Earl of Chatham	Sn	U	Near Cambridge, Md.
1770 Apr 17	Gorrell	Bgt	S	North of Cape Charles, Va.
1771 Apr 25	Boyne	Bgt	W	Near Baltimore, in Chesapeake Bay, Md.
	Unidentified	PB	Cap	Below Jordans Point, James River, Va.
1772 Jan	Kitty	M	F	Off Cape Charles, Va.
	Henry	Sh	I	Four miles below Sassafrass River, Md.
Dec 24	Jane Pierre	M	F	Near Cape Henry, Va.
1773 Jan	Margaret	Sh	CA	Just south of Cape Henry, Va.
	Unidentified	Bgt	S	Mouth of York River, Va.
Mar	Unidentified	U	U	York Spit, Va.
Jul 28	Unidentified	Bt	WS	Mouth of Chester River, Md.
	Donald	Sh	S	Near Cape Charles, Va.
1774 Oct 19	Peggy Stewart	Bgt	B	Windmill Point, Severn River, Md.
	Unidentified	U	CA	Chesapeake Bay
1775 Jul 9	Totness	Sh	B	Three Sisters Islands, Md.
Sep 2	Hibernia	M	W	South of Cape Henry, Va.
Sep 2	Liberty	Slp	WL(B)	Back River, Va.
Sep 2	Unidentified (25)	U	CA	Norfolk, Va.
Sep 4	Minerva	M	W	Cape Charles, Va.
1776 Mar 1	Unidentified	Sch	WL(B)	Below Jamestown, Va.
Mar 7	Unidentified (3)	Shl	WL(B)	Near mouth of Severn River, Md.
May 22	Unidentified (3)	Sch	WL(Sc)	Norfolk Flats, Norfolk, Va.
May 25	Unidentified (3)	Slp	WL(B)	Sewell's Point, Va.
Jul 9	Unidentified (3)	U	WL(B)	Milford Haven, Va.
Jul 10	Unidentified	Slp	F	Milford Haven, Va.
Jul 11	Unidentified	Sh	S	Mouth of Rappahannock River, Va.
Jul 11	Unidentified (2)	Sh	S	Eastern Shore, Va.
Jul 11	Unidentified	U	WL(Sc)	St. Marys County, Md.
Jul 31	Unidentified	Bgt		Off St. George's Island, Md.

DATE	VESSEL	TYPE	MANNER	LOCATION
Aug 1	Unidentified (20)	U	WL(S & B)	St. George's Island, Md.
Aug	Susannah	Slp	WL(Sc)	In mouth of Chesapeake Bay, Va.
Aug	Unidentified (2)	Sh	WL(B & Sc)	Three miles from Cape Henry, Va.
Nov	Patience	Sch	CA	South of Cape Henry, Va.
1777 Feb	Molly	M	B	Norfolk, Va.
Feb	Lydia	Sh	WL(Sc)	Potomac River
Mar 2	Ninety-Two	Sch	WL(Sc)	Off Cape Henry, Va.
Mar 5	Hannah	Slp	WL(Sc)	Off Cape Henry, Va.
Mar 8	Betsey	Slp	WL(B)	Off Cape Henry, Va.
Mar 14	Dolphin	Slp	WL(B)	Off Cape Henry, Va.
May	Betsey	Slp	S	South of Cape Henry, Va.
May 6	Unidentified	Bgt	S	Virginia Capes
May 6	Unidentified	Slp	S	Virginia Capes
Jun 19	Unidentified	Bgt	S	South of Cape Henry, Va.
Sep	Unidentified	Bt	St	Eastern Shore of Va.
1778 May 28	V.S.N. Norfolk Revenge	Gal	F	Nansemond River, Va.
Aug 14	Unidentified	U	CA	Old Point Comfort, Va.
Aug 14	Unidentified (+)	U	S	Hampton Creek, Va.
Aug	Unidentified	Slp	Ca	Near Chesapeake Bay
Nov	H.M.S. Swift	SOW	WL(W & B)	Cape Henry, Va.
Nov	V.S.N. Lewis	Gal	WL(B)	Carter's Creek, Rappahannock River, Va.
	Unidentified	Brg	WL(BU)	Maryland
1779 May 5	V.S.N. Virginia	Fgt	WL(B)	Portsmouth, Va.
May 5	Unidentified (137)	U	WL(B & Sc)	Elizabeth River, Va.
	V.S.N. Polly	Sch	S	Eastern Shore, Va.
1780 Jan 29	C.N. Baltimore	Btg	S	Cape Henry, Va.
Jan	V.S.N. Jefferson	Bgt	F	James River at Jamestown, Va.
Jan	Unidentified	Bgt	S & I	In James River below Martins Hundred, Va.
Jan	Unidentified	Sn	S & I	In James River below Martins Hundred, Va.
Sep 29	Unidentified (2)	Bgt	WL(B)	Vienna, Md.
Sep 29	Unidentified (2)	Sh	WL(B)	Vienna, Md.
1781 Jan 22	M.S.N. Cato	Bgt	WL(S&BU)	Near St. Jeromes Creek, Md.
Jan 22	Hawk	Sch	WL(S & B)	Near St. Jeromes Creek, Md.
Apr 24	Unidentified (+)	U	WL(B)	In Appomattox River, at Petersburg, Va.

Date	Vessel	Rig	Cause	Location
Apr	…	…	WL(B)	On Osborne's, in James River, Va.
Apr	V.S.N. Jefferson	Brg	WL(B)	Off Osborne's, in James River, Va.
Apr	Unidentified (2)	Sh	WL(B)	Off Osborne's, in James River, Va.
Apr	Unidentified (4)	Brg	WL(B)	Off Osborne's, in James River, Va.
May	Unidentified (+)	Gal	WL(Sc)	Chickahominy River, Va.
Oct 5	H.M.S. Charon	Fgt	WL(B)	Yorktown, Va.
Oct 5	Shipwright	Tsp	WL(B)	Yorktown, Va.
Oct 5	Unidentified	Sh	WL(B)	Yorktown, Va.
Oct 17	Betsey	Vic	WL(Sc)	Yorktown, Va.
Oct 17	Concord	Tsp	WL(Sc)	Yorktown, Va.
Oct 17	Diana	Vic	WL(Sc)	Yorktown, Va.
Oct 17	Elizabeth	Vic	WL(Sc)	Yorktown, Va.
Oct 17	Emerald	Tsp	WL(Sc)	Yorktown, Va.
Oct 17	Favorite	Tsp	WL(Sc)	Yorktown, Va.
Oct 17	Fidelity	Tsp	WL(Sc)	Yorktown, Va.
Oct 17	H.M.S. Fowey	Fgt	WL(Sc)	Yorktown, Va.
Oct 17	H.M.S. Guadeloupe	Fgt	WL(Sc)	Yorktown, Va.
Oct 17	Harlequin	Vic	WL(Sc)	Yorktown, Va.
Oct 17	Harmony	Tsp	WL(Sc)	Yorktown, Va.
Oct 17	Horsington	Tsp	WL(Sc)	Yorktown, Va.
Oct 17	Houston	Tsp	WL(Sc)	Yorktown, Va.
Oct 17	Lord Howe	Tsp	WL(Sc)	Yorktown, Va.
Oct 17	Lord Mulgrave	Tsp	WL(Sc)	Yorktown, Va.
Oct 17	Mackrell	Tsp	WL(Sc)	Yorktown, Va.
Oct 17	Mercury	Vic	WL(Sc)	Yorktown, Va.
Oct 17	Nancy	Vic	WL(Sc)	Yorktown, Va.
Oct 17	Neptune	Tsp	WL(Sc)	Yorktown, Va.
Oct 17	Ocean	Vic	WL(Sc)	Yorktown, Va.
Oct 17	Oldborough	Tsp	WL(Sc)	Yorktown, Va.
Oct 17	Present Succession	Tsp	WL(Sc)	Yorktown, Va.
Oct 17	Providence	Tsp	WL(Sc)	Yorktown, Va.
Oct 17	Providence Increase	Vic	WL(Sc)	Yorktown, Va.
Oct 17	Race Horse	Tsp	WL(Sc)	Yorktown, Va.
Oct 17	Robert	Tsp	WL(Sc)	Yorktown, Va.
Oct 17	Rover	Vic	WL(Sc)	Yorktown, Va.
Oct 17	Sally	Tsp	WL(Sc)	Yorktown, Va.
Oct 17	Selina	Tsp	WL(Sc)	Yorktown, Va.
Oct 17	Success Increase	Tsp	WL(Sc)	Yorktown, Va.

DATE	VESSEL	TYPE	MANNER	LOCATION
Oct 17	Two Brothers	Tsp	WL(Sc)	Yorktown, Va.
1782 Feb 24	Venus	Sh	Cap	Chesapeake Bay
Feb	Unidentified	Bgt	S	Willoughby Point, Va.
Dec 29	Unidentified	Sh	WL(B)	Cape Charles, Va.
1784 Jan	Unidentified	Sh	I	Burwell's Ferry, James River, Va.
Jan	Unidentified (2)	U	I	James River, Va.
Feb 3	Ocean	Sh	S	Windmill Point, Chesapeake Bay, Va.
Feb 3	Unidentified	Sh	S	New Point Comfort, Va.
Feb 3	Unidentified (6)	U	U	James River, Va.
Mar	Unidentified	Bgt	S	Lynnhaven Bay, Va.
1785 Sep 22	Unidentified	Bgt	S	Lynnhaven Bay, Va.
Sep 22	Unidentified	Bgt	S	Virginia coast
Sep 22	Unidentified (2)	Sh	S	Virginia coast
Oct	York	PS	F	Cherrystone, Va.
Oct	Unidentified	Slp	S	King's Creek, Va.
Nov 4	Union	U	B	Baltimore, Md.
	Grange	Sh	S	Cape Charles, Va.
	Hero	U	S	James River, Va.
	Lord Charlemont	U	U	Nanticoke River, Md.
1786 Sep	Mary	Bgt	F	Virginia Capes
	Maryland	PS	NL	Cape Henry, Va.
1787 May 9	Joseph and Peggy	PS	O	Smith Island, Va.
May	Unidentified	Sch	CA	Smith Point, Va.
Jun 24	Unidentified	Bt	Cap	Mouth of Severn River, Md.
	Nonsuch	M	NL	Middle Ground, Chesapeake Bay, Va.
1788 Jul 23	Favorite	Sh	S	Hampton Roads, Va.
Jul 23	Mermaid	Sh	S	Hampton Roads, Va.
Jul 23	Neptune	Bgt	S	Armand's Point, Va.
Jul 23	Patriot	Sch	S	Portsmouth, Va.
Jul 23	Sincerity	Sch	S	Portsmouth, Va.
Jul 23	Unidentified	Bgt	S	Portsmouth, Va.
1790 Sep 5	Fanny	Bt	Cap	Tolly Point, Md.
	Unidentified	Sh	W	Cape Charles, Va.
	Jane & Dianna	Sh	Nl	Near Cape Henry, Va.

Year	Date	Vessel	Rig	Cause	Location
					Chesapeake Bay, Va.
		Louisa	Sh	S	Near Cape Charles, Va.
		Lovely Ann	Sh	W	On Cape Charles, Va.
		William	Sch	W	Portsmouth, Va.
1791	Apr 16	Unidentified (2)	Sh	F	Portsmouth, Va.
	Apr 16	Unidentified	U	S	Chesapeake Bay, Va.
	Dec 2	Nancy	U	F	Hampton Roads, Va.
		Nantz	M	NL	Near Cape Henry, Va.
		Rainbow	U	NL	Portsmouth, Va.
		Unidentified (+)	U	S	York River, Va.
1792		Rebecca	Fgt	S	Smith Island, Virginia coast
1795	Jan	Unidentified	Sh	F	Off Cape Charles, Va.
	Aug 2	Unidentified (2)	Slp	S	Chesapeake Bay
1796		Martin	M	S	Hampton Roads, Va.
1797		Anthony Mangin	Sh	S	North of Cape Charles, Va.
1798	Feb 20	Betsy	Sch	F	In Chesapeake Bay, five miles off Craddock, Va.
	Apr 22	Greyhound	Slp	F	Off Rappahannock River, Va.
1799	May 16	Sally and Nancy	Bgt	F	Near Cape Henry, Va.
	May 31	Richard	U	WL(B)	Chesapeake Bay
		William	Sch	F	Off Cape Henry, Va.
1800	Jun 16	Unidentified	Bgt	F	Off Cape Charles, Va.
	Dec 11	Betsey	Sh	B	Off Virginia Capes
	Dec 12	Unidentified	Sh	F	Middle Ground, Chesapeake Bay, Va.
	Dec 16	Unidentified	Sch	F	Off Piankatank River, Va.
1801		Suffolk	M	F	Middle Ground, Chesapeake Bay, Va.
1804		President	Slp	NL	Smith Island, Virginia coast
	Dec 20	Unidentified	Sch	CA	Off Virginia Capes
	Dec 25	Samuel Smith	S	Cap	South of Cape Henry, Va.
1805	Jan 1	Aurora	Sh	W	Cape Henry, Va.
	Jan 23	Eliza	Sh	S	Love Point, Kent Island, Md.
	Jan	Carmelite	Bgt	S	Point Lookout, Md.
	Jan	New York	Sch	I & S	Sewell's Point, Va.
	Jan	Unidentified (+	Sh	S	Cape Henry, Va.
		Unidentified (+	U	S	South of Cape Henry, Va.
	Feb 16	London Packet	Sh	S	Greenbury Point, Md.
	May 10	Unidentified	Bt	C	Curtis Creek, Md.
	May 10	Unidentified	PB	S	Norfolk, Va.
	Sep 7	Adventure	Bgt	S	On Cape Henry, Va.

DATE	VESSEL	TYPE	MANNER	LOCATION
1806 Jan 8	Nestor	Sh	S	Lynnhaven Bay, Va.
Jan 8	Unidentified	Slp	S	Lynnhaven Bay, Va.
Apr 12	Stapleton	Sh	S	Smith Point, Va.
Apr	London Packet	Sh	CA	On Wolf Trap Bar, Va.
May	Unidentified	Slp	W	Off Cape Henry, Va.
Aug	Unidentified	Sch	Cap	Point Lookout, Md.
Nov 8	Consolation	Sch	F	In Chesapeake Bay between James and Rappahannock rivers
Dec 3	Ceres	Bgt	S	Sewell's Point, Hampton Roads, Va.
Dec 3	Two Friends	Sh	S	Sewell's Point, Hampton Roads, Va.
Dec 3	Unidentified (+)	U	S	Hampton Roads, Va.
Dec 15	Warrington	SH	S	Cape Henry Lighthouse, Va.
Dec 15	Unidentified	Sch	S	Bodkin Point, Md.
Dec 15	Unidentified	Sch	S	Lynnhaven Bay, Va.
Dec	Unidentified	Sch	S	Below Cape Henry, Va.
	Impetueux	S	WL(S & B)	Near Cape Henry, Va.
	Ruthy	U	W	Near Patapsco River, Md.
	Sheperdess	S	W	Near Cape Henry, Va.
1807 Feb	Unidentified	Brg	S	Willoughby Point, Va.
Mar 31	Unidentified	Sch	S	Patuxent River, Md.
Mar 31	Unidentified	Bt	S	Patuxent River, Md.
Mar 31	Unidentified	Brg	S	Hampton Roads, Va.
Mar 31	Unidentified	Slp	S	Hampton Roads, Va.
Nov	Unidentified (2)	Sch	S	Hampton Roads, Va.
1807	Betsey	M	B & S	Smith Point, Va.
1808 Jan	William Murdock	M	W	Norfolk, Va.
Sep 12	Mary	Sh	NL	Cape Charles Va.
1809 Aug 31	Robert	U	W	Baltimore, Md.
1810 Mar 9	Unidentified	Sch	WL(B)	On Cape Henry, Va.
Mar 14	Unidentified	Pr	S	Cherrystone Harbor, Va.
Mar 24	Unidentified	Sch	WL(B)	Smith Island, Va.
	Lucy	U	W	Nansemond River, Va.
1811 Apr 16	Revanche du Cerf	Pr	WL(B)	On Cape Henry, Va.
1813 Apr 29	Unidentified	U	WL(B)	Norfolk, Va.
	Unidentified	U	WL(B)	Cresswell's Ferry, Md.

Date	Name	Type	Cause	Location
Jun 22	Unidentified(+)	Brg	WL(S)	Craney Island, Va.
Jul 6	Unidentified(2)	U	WL(B)	Four miles up Lawn's Creek, Va.
Jul 7	Unidentified	Sch	WL(B)	Four miles up Lawn's Creek, Va.
Jul 19	Unidentified	Bt	WL(B)	Mattox Creek, Va.
Jul 21	Unidentified (3)	U	WL(B)	Cole Harbor, near Hollis's Marsh, Va.
Dec	Unidentified	U	W	Chesapeake Bay
	Tamerlane	Sh	NL	Cape Henry, Va.
	Unidentified (3)	U	W	Chesapeake Bay
	Unidentified (+)	U	WL(B&S)	Potomac and Patuxent Rivers, Md.
	Unidentified (7)	U	WL(B)	Little Annemessex River, Md.
1814 Apr 8	Unidentified	Sch	WL(B)	Under Cove Point, Md.
Jun 1	Gunboat No. 137	GB	WL(Sc)	St. Leonard's Creek, Md.
Jun 26	Gunboat No. 138	GB	WL(Sc)	St. Leonard's Creek, Md.
Jun 26	Unidentified (+)	Sch	WL(Sc)	St. Leonard's Creek, Md.
Jun	Unidentified	Sch	B	Off Sandy Point, Chesapeake Bay, Md.
Jul 2	Unidentified	Sch	WL(Sc)	South end of Tangier Island Shoals, Va.
Jul 23	Unidentified	Sch	WL(B)	St. Clement Bay, Md.
Jul 25	Shamrock	Bt	F	In Potomac River, below Alexandria, Va.
Jul 25	Unidentified	Sch	Cap	Patuxent River, Md.
Jul 26	Unidentified (6)	Sch	WL(B)	Nomini Creek, Va.
Jul	Unidentified (5)	Sch	WL(B)	Slaughter Creek, Md.
Aug 3	Unidentified (2)	Sch	WL(B)	Kinsale, Yeocomico River, Va.
Aug 22	U.S.S. Scorpion	Slp	WL(SC)	Pig Point, Patuxent River, Md.
Aug 22	U.S.S. Vigilant	Gal	WL(Sc)	Pig Point, Patuxent River, Md.
Aug 22	Unidentified (13)	Brg	WL(Sc)	Pig Point, Patuxent River, Md.
Aug 22	Unidentified (8)	LB	WL(Sc)	Pig Point, Patuxent River, Md.
Aug 22	Unidentified	Sch	WL(Sc)	Pig Point, Patuxent River, Md.
Aug	Unidentified	Bat	WL(B)	St. Inigoes Creek, Md.
1815 Jan 29	Clarissa	Sch	S	Craney Island, Va.
Sep 4	Deborah	Slp	S	Sewell's Point, Va.
Sep 4	Hamilton	Sh	S	On Craney Island, Va.
Sep 4	Harriet	PSch	NL	Near Pig Point, mouth of Nansemond River, Va.
Sep 4	St. Andrew	Sh	S	Off Point No Point, Chesapeake Bay, Md.
Sep 4	Unidentified (7)	Sh	S	In Nansemond River, Va.
Sep 4	Unidentified (3)	U	S	Below Cape Henry, Va.
Sep 4	Unidentified (+)	U	S	Near Pig Point, Nansemond River, Va.
Sep	Unidentified	U	NL	Upper Chesapeake Bay, Md.

DATE	VESSEL	TYPE	MANNER	LOCATION
Nov 23	*Norfolk Packet*	Sh	S	Kent Island, Md.
Nov 23	Unidentified	Sch	S	Sandy Point, Chesapeake Bay, Md.
Nov	*Friendship*	Sch	NL	Willoughby Point, Va.
Nov	*Union*	Sch	S	Willoughby Point, Va.
Dec	*Dispatch*	Bgt	S	Below Cape Henry, Va.
1817 May	*Hannah*	Bgt	W	Mouth of Potomac River, Md.
1818 Mar 5	*Clotilda*	U	W	Cape Henry, Va.
1821 Sep 3	Unidentified (+)	Bgt	S	Norfolk, Va.
Sep 3	Unidentified (+)	Sch	S	Norfolk, Va.
1822 Oct 22	*La Plata*	Sh	NL	Near Cape Charles, Va.
	Janus	Sh	W	On Cape Henry, Va.
	Seaflower	Sh	NL	Near Cape Henry, Va.
1823 Sep 20	*Powhatan*	SWS	E	Norfolk, Va.
1824 Mar 10	*Liverpool*	Sh	NL	Below Cape Henry, Va.
Apr 18	*Eagle*	SWS	E	North Point, Md.
1833 Sep 3	*Ousatonic*[1]	ScS	E	Leonardtown, Md.
1837 Jul 13	*Union*	SWS	E	Fox's Wharf, Potomac River, Md.
1840 Aug 28	*James Gibbon*	SWS	E	Richmond, Va.
1842 Apr 15	*Medora*	SWS	E	Baltimore, Md.
1845 Jun 6	*Paul Jones*	ScS	E	Baltimore, Md.
Dec 29	*Fredericksburg*	SWS	F	Fredericksburg, Va.
1850 Nov 27	*Columbus*	SWS	B	Point Lookout, Md.
1853 Sep 16	*Cambridge*	SWS	B	Rappahannock River, Va.
1854	*Bladen*	SWS	NL	Norfolk, Va.
1855 Jan	*Lafayette*	Sch	I	Selby's Landing, Patuxent River, Md.
1856 Oct 14	*Monmouth*	SWS	C[2]	Off Wolf Trap Light, Va.
1859 Jan 29	*North Carolina*	SWS	B	Off Smith Point, Va.
Mar	*Daniel P. Shenfelder*	SWS	B	Cape Charles City, Va.
1861 Apr 20	U.S.S. *Columbia*	Fgt	WL(B)	Gosport Navy Yard, Norfolk, Va.
Apr 20	U.S.S. *Columbus*	SOL	WL(B)	Gosport Navy Yard, Norfolk, Va.
Apr 20	U.S.S. *Delaware*	SOL	WL(B)	Gosport Navy Yard, Norfolk, Va.
Apr 20	U.S.S. *Dolphin*	Bgt	WL(B)	Gosport Navy Yard, Norfolk, Va.
Apr 20	U.S.S. *Merrimack*	SlOW	WL(B)	Gosport Navy Yard, Norfolk, Va.
Apr 20	U.S.S. *Pennsylvania*	SOL	WL(B)	Gosport Navy Yard, Norfolk, Va.

Date	Vessel	Rig	Code	Location
Apr 20	Kettle Bottom Lightship	LS	WL(B)	Kettle Bottom Shoals, Potomac River, Md.
May 4	Glen Cove	SWS	WL(Sc)	James River, Va.
Jun 8	Somerset	Sch(BR)	WL(B)	Off Breton Bay, in Potomac River, Md.
Jun 15	Christiana Keen	Sch(BR)	WL(B)	Near Upper Machodoc Creek, Va.
Jun 30	Passenger	Slp(BR)	Cap	Potomac River, Md.
Jun	Unidentified	U	WL(Sc)	Warwick Creek, Md.
Jul 18	Favorite	Sch(BR)	WL(Sc)	Off Piney Point, in Potomac River, Md.
Aug 16	Jane Wright	Slp	WL(Sc)	Smith Point, Va.
Aug 20	T. W. Riley	Slp	WL(Sc)	Wades Bay, Potomac River
Oct 11	Martha Washington	Sch	WL(B)	Dumfries, Va.
Nov 6	Ada	Sch	WL(B)	Corrotoman Creek, Va.
1862 Jan 7	Unidentified (2)	Bt	WL(B)	West Point and White House, Va.
Jan 7	Unidentified (+)	Brg	WL(B)	West Point and White House, Va.
Jan 25	Unidentified	U	S	Near Norfolk, Va.
Mar 8	Pendulum	SWS	F	Hampton Roads, Va.
Mar 8	U.S.S. Congress	Fgt	WL(S)	Newport News, Va.
Mar 8	U.S.S. Cumberland	SOW	WL(S)	Hampton Roads, Va.
Mar 9	C.S.S. George Page	SWS	WL(B)	Quantico Creek, Va.
Mar 10	U.S.S. Whitehall	SWS	B	Old Point Comfort, Va.
Apr	C.S.S. Rapahannock	SWS	WL(B)	Fredericksburg, Va.
May 4	Champion	Slp	WL(B)	Above Gloucester Point, York River, Va.
May 4	General Scott	St	WL(B)	York River, Va.
May 5-10	California	Sch	WL(B)	Cumberland, Va.
May 5-10	Caroline Baker	Sch	WL(B)	Cumberland, Va.
May 5-10	Claudio	U	WL(Sc)	White House Landing, Pamunkey River, Va.
May 5-10	David Vaname	Sch	WL(B)	Cookes Island, Pamunkey River, Va.
May 5-10	Diana Hopkins	Sch	WL(B)	Cookes Island, Pamunkey River, Va.
May 5-10	Friendship	Sch	WL(Sc)	Cookes Island, Pamunkey River, Va.
May 5-10	Hannah Ann	Sch	WL(Sc)	Cookes Island, Pamunkey River, Va.
May 5-10	J. & G. Fair	U	WL(Sc)	Cookes Island, Pamunkey River, Va.
May 5-10	J. T. Connor	U	WL(Sc)	Cookes Island, Pamunkey River, Va.
May 5-10	Jenny Lind	St	WL(B)	Garlick's Landing, Va.
May 5-10	Josephine	Sch	WL(Sc)	Cookes Island, Pamunkey River, Va.
May 5-10	King William	Sch	WL(Sc)	Cookes Island, Pamunkey River, Va.
May 5-10	Little Addie	U	WL(Sc)	White House Landing, Pamunkey River, Va.
May 5-10	Mary Elizabeth	U	WL(Sc)	Cookes Island, Pamunkey River, Va.
May 5-10	Mary Luyster	U	WL(Sc)	Cookes Island, Pamunkey River, Va.
May 5-10	Ornament	Slp	WL(Sc)	Cookes Island, Pamunkey River, Va.

DATE	VESSEL	TYPE	MANNER	LOCATION
May 5-10	Palestine	Sch	WL(Sc)	Cookes Island, Pamunkey River, Va.
May 5-10	Princess	Sch	WL(Sc)	Cookes Island, Pamunkey River, Va.
May 5-10	R. P. Waller	Sch	WL(Sc)	Cookes Island, Pamunkey River, Va.
May 5-10	Reliance	U	WL(B)	Indian Town, Va.
May 5-10	Sarah Ann	Sch	WL(Sc)	Cookes Island, Pamunkey River, Va.
May 5-10	Star	U	WL(B)	Garlick's Landing, Va.
May 5-10	Way	Sch	WL(B)	Indian Town, Va.
May 5-10	William Edward	Sch	WL(Sc)	Cookes Island, Pamunkey River, Va.
May 5-10	William Shamberg	Sch	WL(Sc)	Cookes Island, Pamunkey River, Va.
May 6-7	Logan	SWS	WL(B)	Barrett's Landing, Pamunkey River, Va.
May 10	C.S.S. Germantown	SOW	WL(Sc)	Elizabeth River, Norfolk, Va.
May 10	C.S.S. Norfolk	ScS	WL(B)	Gosport Navy Yard, Norfolk, Va.
May 10	C.S.S. United States	SOW	WL(Sc)	Elizabeth River, Norfolk, Va.
May 10	William Selden	SWS	B	Norfolk, Va.
May 11	C.S.S. Virginia	IR	B	Craney Island, Va.
May 15	C.S.S. Jamestown	SWS	WL(Sc)	Drewry's Bluff, James River, Va.
May 17	Ann Bell	U	WL(Sc)	Bassett's Landing, Va.
May 17	Betsey Richards	U	WL(Sc)	Bassett's Landing, Va.
May 17	Francis and Theodore	U	WL(Sc)	Bassett's Landing, Va.
May 17	J. R. Baylis	U	WL(Sc)	Bassett's Landing, Va.
May 17	James Braden	U	WL(Sc)	Bassett's Landing, Va.
May 17	Jefferson	Sch	WL(B)	Newcastle, Va.
May 17	John Allen	Sch	WL(Sc)	Bassett's Landing, Va.
May 17	Little Wave	U	WL(Sc)	Bassett's Landing, Va.
May 17	Margaret Schultz	U	WL(B)	Newcastle, Va.
May 17	Mary Alice	U	WL(Sc)	Bassett's Landing, Va.
May 17	Mary Baxter	U	WL(Sc)	Bassett's Landing, Va.
May 17	Mirage	U	WL(Sc)	Bassett's Landing, Va.
May 17	O. Whitmond	U	WL(B)	Newcastle, Va.
May 17	Oxford	Sch	WL(Sc)	Cookes Island, Pamunkey River, Va.
May 17	Paragon	Slp	WL(Sc)	Bassett's Landing, Va.
May 17	Sarah Washington	Sch	WL(Sc)	Bassett's Landing, Va.
May 17	Sea Witch	U	WL(Sc)	Bassett's Landing, Va.
May 17	Union	Sch	WL(Sc)	Bassett's Landing, Va.

Year	Date	Vessel	Type	Cause	Location
					Newcastle, Va.
	May 17	*Watchman*	U	WL(B)	Newcastle, Va.
	May 17	*Wave*	U	WL(B)	Newcastle, Va.
	May 17	*Wild Pigeon*	Sch	WL(Sc)	Bassett's Landing, Va.
	May 17	*William and Wesley*	Sch	WL(Sc)	Bassett's Landing, Va.
	May 17	*William Francis*	Sch	WL(Sc)	Bassett's Landing, Va.
	May 17	*William Ryland*	U	WL(Sc)	Newcastle, Va.
	Jun 28	*U.S.S. Island Belle*	T	WL(S & B)	Gilliam's Bar, Appomattox River, Va.
	Aug 3	*Unidentified*	Sch	WL(B)	Smithfield Creek, Va.
	Aug 12	*West Point*	SWS	C[3]	Ragged Point, in Potomac River
	Sep 15	*Arctic*	Sch(BR)	WL(B)	Great Wicomico River, Va.
	Sep 23	*Alliance*	Sch	WL(B)	Milford Haven Bar, Va.
	Sep	*C.S.S. Northampton*	SWS	WL(Sc)	Drewry's Bluff, James River, Va.
	Sep	*Curtis Peck*	SWS	WL(Sc)	Drewry's Bluff, James River, Va.
	Sep	*Damascus*	U	WL(Sc)	Drewry's Bluff, James River, Va.
	Oct 29	*Alleghamian*	Sh	WL(B)	In Chesapeake Bay, five miles off York River, Va.
	Nov 4	*Robert Wilbur*	Sch	WL(B)	Nomini Creek, Va.
	Dec 5	*Unidentified (2)*	Slp	WL(B)	Severn River, Md.
	Dec 5	*Unidentified*	Sch	WL(B)	Severn River, Md.
		U.S.S. Tigress	T	C	Indian Head, Md., in Potomac River
1863	Feb 18	*John Roach*	U	WL(Sc)	Drewry's Bluff, James River, Va.
	Feb 24	*Elma*	Sch	WL(B)	East River, Va.
	Feb 24	*Ben Bolt*	Brg	WL(B)	Back Creek, York River, Va.
	Mar 14	*Mary Jane*	Slp	WL(B)	Back Creek, York River, Va.
		Unidentified	Sch	WL(B)	Milford Haven, Va.
	May 27	*Charity*	Sch	WL(B)	Yeocomico River, Va.
	May 27	*Flight*	Sch	WL(B)	Yeocomico River, Va.
	May 27	*Gazelle*	Sch	WL(B)	Yeocomico River, Va.
	May 31	*U.S.S. Alert*	ScS	B	Norfolk Navy Yard, Va.
	Jun 11	*Odd Fellow*	Sch	WL(B)	Coan River, Va.
	Jun 11	*Sarah Margaret*	Sch	WL(B)	Coan River, Va.
	Jun 24	*U.S.S. Sumpter*	ScS	C(B)[4]	8.5 miles SSE of Smith Island Light, Va.
	Aug 25	*Golden Rod*	Sch	WL(B)	Mouth of Rappahannock River
	Aug 31	*Coquette*	Sch	WL(B)	Port Royal, Va.
	Aug 31	*Two Brothers*	Sch	WL(B)	Port Royal, Va.
	Aug 31	*U.S.S. Satellite*	SWS	WL(B)	Port Royal, Va.
	Aug 31	*U.S.S. Reliance*	ScS	WL(B)	Port Royal, Va.
1864	Feb 1	*Smith Briggs*	St	WL	Smithfield, Va.

DATE	VESSEL	TYPE	MANNER	LOCATION
Feb 24	Charles Henry	Sch	WL(B)	Wicomico River, Va.
Feb 24	Gratitude	Sch	WL(B)	Wicomico River, Va.
Mar 5	U.S.S. Titan	St	WL(B)	Piankatank River, Va.
Mar 11	Julia Baker	Sch	WL(B)	Newport News, Va.
Apr 1	Fair Haven	ScS	S	Cape Henry, Va.
May 6	U.S.S. Commodore Jones	SWS	WL(T)	Four Mile Creek, James River, Va.
May 8	U.S.S. Shawsheen	SWS	WL(BU)	Turkey Bend, James River, Va.
Jul 20	Buena Vista	CB	Sc	Trents Reach, James River, Va.
Jul 20	Commodore Stockton	CB	Sc	Trents Reach, James River, Va.
Jul 20	Fort	CB	Sc	Trents Reach, James River, Va.
Jul 20	John McHale	CB	Sc	Trents Reach, James River, Va.
Jul 20	John Mitchell	CB	Sc	Trents Reach, James River, Va.
Jul 20	Margaret and Rebecca	CB	Sc	Trents Reach, James River, Va.
Jul 20	Mary Ann	CB	Sc	Trents Reach, James River, Va.
Jul 20	Mary Linda	CB	Sc	Trents Reach, James River, Va.
Jul 20	Mussadora	CB	Sc	Trents Reach, James River, Va.
Jul 20	Pilgrim	CB	Sc	Trents Reach, James River, Va.
Jul 20	Richard Vaux	CB	Sc	Trents Reach, James River, Va.
Jul 20	Rolling Wave	CB	Sc	Trents Reach, James River, Va.
Jul 24	Kingston	St	WL(B)	Between Smith Point and Windmill Point, Va.
Sep 3	U.S.S. Brandywine	Fgt	B	Norfolk Navy Yard, Va.
Sep 4	Unidentified (4)	Bt	WL(B)	Stutts Creek, Milford Haven, Va.
Sep 9	Fawn	MS	WL(B)	Dismal Swamp Canal, Va.
Oct 18	U.S. Picket Boat No. 2	ScS	WL(B)	Reason Creek, Great Wicomico Bay
Nov 11	U.S.S. Tulip	ScS	E	Off Piney Point, Md., in Potomac River
Nov 27	U.S.S. Greyhound	SWS	WL(B)	Hog Island, James River, Va.
Nov 28	C.S.S. Florida	ScS	C[5]	Newport News, Va.
Dec 15	Unidentified (30)	Bt	WL(B)	Coan River, Va.
1865 Jan 24	C.S.S. Drewry	ScSGb	WL	Trents Reach, James River, Va.
Jan 26	C.S.S. Hornet	ScSTb	C[6]	James River, Va.
Feb 15	Knickerbocker	St	WL(B)	Smith Point, Va.
Feb 19	A. H. Schultz	SWS	WL(BU)	Chaffins Bluff, James River, Va.
Mar 6	Unidentified	Bt	WL(B)	Passpatansy Creek, Va.
Mar 16	Unidentified (3)	Sch	WL(B)	Mattox Creek, Montrose, Va.

Date	Vessel	Type	Fate	Location
Apr 3	C.S.S. Nansemond	ScSGb	WL(BU)	In James River, Richmond, Va.
Apr 3	C.S.S. Patrick Henry	SWS	WL(BU)	In James River, Richmond, Va.
Apr 3	C.S.S. Richmond	IR	WL(BU)	In James River, Drewry's Bluff, Va.
Apr 3	C.S.S. Shrapnel	St	WL(BU)	In James River, Richmond, Va.
Apr 3	C.S.S. Virginia II	IR	WL(BU)	In James River, Drewry's Bluff, Va.
Apr 4	C.S.S. Beaufort	ScSGb	WL(BU)	In James River, Richmond, Va.
Apr 4	C.S.S. Raleigh	ScSGb	WL(BU)	In James River, Richmond, Va.
Apr 7	Harriet DeFord	ScS	WL(B)	Dimers Creek, Va.
Apr 23	Black Diamond	ScS	C[7]	Potomac River
May 10	C.S.S. Plymouth	SOW	WL(Sc)	Norfolk, Va.
Nov 25	Nellie Pentz	SWS	F	Lynnhaven Bay, Va.
1866 Jan 4	Liberty	SWS	B	Cedar Point, Potomac River
Aug 25	Hobomok	ScS	B	Thomas Point, Md.
Nov 12	Richmond	SWS	B	Baltimore, Md.
1867 Aug 9	Wilson Small	SWS	C[8]	Poplar Island, Md.
1868 Mar 22	M. W. Chapin	ScS	B	City Point, Va.
1870 Mar 22	Dolphin	StTb	B	Solomons, Md.
Mar 26	New Jersey	ScS	B	South of Poplar Island, Md.
Jun 1	Wasp	ScS	B	James River, Va.
Sep 8	Triumph	ScS	B	James River, Va.
1871 Jun 10	George Weems	SWS	B	Baltimore, Md.
1873 Aug 8	Wawassett	SWS	B	Chatterton's Landing, Potomac River, Va.
	Bonita	ScS	F	Richmond, Va.
1874 Nov 14	Louisiana	SWS	C[9]	Off Smith Point, Va.
Nov	Louisa Crocket	Sch	C[10]	Off Fortress Monroe, Va.
1875 Oct 9	Northumberland	Sch	S	Potomac River
Oct 30	Beta	Sch	F	Cove Point, Md.
Nov 12	Starlight	U	U	Rock Creek, Md.
Dec 13	Pennsylvania	Sch	F	Pooles Island, Md.
1876 Mar 31	Arrow	U	U	Chesapeake Bay
Mar 31	Atlantic	U	U	Chesapeake Bay
Apr 26	William Kennedy	Sch	F	Chesapeake Bay
Dec 9	Falcon	Sch	S	Queenstown Creek, Chester River, Md.
Dec 29	Port Smith	Sch	E	Baltimore, Md.
1877 Jan 19	Morning Star	Sch	I	Libby's Wharf, Georgetown, D. C.
Mar 28	Belle Haven	ScS	B	Alexandria, Va.
Apr 9	John C. McShain	Sch	S	Point No Point, Md.

DATE	VESSEL	TYPE	MANNER	LOCATION
May 8	Asow	Brk	S	Back River, Chesapeake Bay, Md.
Aug 18	Matthew White	ScS	E	Fort Monroe, Hampton Roads, Va.
Sep 7	Clara	Sch	C[11]	Hampton Roads, Va.
Sep 19	C. P. Smith	SWS	B	Chesapeake Bay
Oct 16	Tennessee	Sch	Cap	Windmill Point, Chesapeake Bay, Va.
Nov 24	Frank Jameson	Brk	S	Smith Island Life Saving Station, Virginia coast
1878 Jan 4	Francisco Bellagomba	Pgy	S	One mile north of Cape Henry Life Saving Station
Oct 22	A. K. Dukes	U	W	Crisfield Harbor, Md.
Oct 22	Alveretia	Slp	S	Cape Charles, Va.
Oct 22	Dora Weeks	SWS	F	Pickets Hole, Va.
Oct 22	Express	Sch	S	Off Point No Point, Md.
Oct 22	M. E. Ellen	Sch	F	Cedar Point, Md.
Oct 22	Mary Morris	Slp	S	James River, Va.
Oct 22	Morgan	U	S	Pickets Hole, Va.
Oct 22	Spray	Sch	F	Fisherman's Inlet, Va.
Oct 22	Unidentified (+)	Pgy	S	Crisfield Harbor, Md.
Oct 22	Unidentified (5)	Pgy	W	Drum Point, Md
Oct 22	Unidentified	Sch	S	Cedar Point, Md.
Oct 22	Unidentified	Sch	S	Little Cove Point, Md.
Oct 22	Unidentified	Slp	F	Sandy Point, Chesapeake Bay, Md.
Oct 22	A. C. Davis	St	F	Herngar's Wharf, Va.
Oct 23	George Twibill	CSch	S	Near Cape Henry, Va.
Oct 23	Samuel D. Wilson	Sch	S	Stowe Point, Piankatank River, Va.
Oct 23	Unidentified (11)	Brg	F	Cedar Point, near Patuxent River, Md.
Dec 1	Matilda	St	F	Chesapeake Bay
1879 Mar 13	Mariner	SWSF	S	Rappahannock River, Va.
Mar 31	Jas. M. Vance	Sch	W	Baltimore, Md.
Apr 3	Mary A. deKnight	Sch	F	Cape Charles, Va.
Aug 18	John C. Henry	Sch	S	Off Annapolis, Md.
Oct 14	Annie	Sch	C	Off Gwynn's Island, Va.
Nov 7	Falcon	St	S	Chesapeake Bay, off Holland Point, Md.
1880 Apr 13	Peytona	Sch	B	Chesapeake Bay
Oct 3	Isaac Bell	ScS		Mouth of Sassafras River, Md.
				Portsmouth, Va.

Year	Date	Vessel	Rig	Cause	Location
1881	Nov 18	*Mamoose*	Slp	F	Cranberry Beach, Va.
	Feb 2	*Carrie*	StY	E	Chase's Wharf, Havre de Grace, Md.
	Feb 25	*David E. Wolf*	Sch	C[12]	York Spit, Chesapeake Bay, Va.
	Jun 29	*J. F. Tull*	Sch	F	Fox Island, Tangier Sound, Chesapeake Bay
	Oct 5	*James F. Hewitt*	Sch	F	Off New Point Comfort, Chesapeake Bay, Va.
	Oct 28	*Alice*	Sch	B	Off Pooles Island, Md.
	Nov 28	*Unidentified*	Brk	B	Canton Wharf, Baltimore, Md.
	Nov 28	*Unidentified (2)*	CB		Canton Wharf, Baltimore, Md.
	Nov 28	*Unidentified (2)*	Y		Canton Wharf, Baltimore, Md.
	Dec 14	*Agostino C.*	Brg	B	Isaac Shoals, Fisherman's Island, Va.
	Dec 26	*West Point (Shirley)*	ScS	S	West Point, York River, Va.
1882	Jan 7	*Albert Daily*	Sch	B	Smith Island, Va.
	Nov 2	*Cascatelie*	Bgt	S	Mouth of Potomac River, in Chesapeake Bay
	Nov 10	*Brooklyn*	Sch	F	Chesapeake Bay
	Dec 2	*Lucy Virginia*	Sch	C[13]	Chesapeake Bay
	Dec 4	*Excelsior*	St	F	Old Point Comfort, Va.
1883	Jan 30	*Grace*	St	C[14]	Chesapeake Bay
	Jul 31	*Octorara*	St	C[15]	Chesapeake City, Md.
	Aug 10	*Sarah Lavinia*	Sch	C[16]	In Chesapeake Bay, off Point Lookout, Md.
	Sep 14	*Kate*	ScS	C[17]	Alexandria, Va.
	Oct 28	*Unidentified*	Sch	B	Near Benona's Light, mouth of Choptank River, Md.
	Nov 12	*James E. Richardson*	BSch	C[18]	Kedges Strait, Chesapeake Bay, Md.
	Nov 12	*Willie F. Thomas*	Sch	Cap	James Point, Chesapeake Bay
	Dec 2	*Three Sons*	Sch	F	Below Cove Point, off Patuxent River, Md.
1884	Jan 15	*L. A. Rommel*	Sch	C[19]	Cape Henry, Va.
	Mar 3	*Edgar*	Sch	S	Potomac River, Md.
	May 4	*B. S. Ford*	St	F	Chestertown, Md.
	Jun 11	*Gazelle*	St	B	Mouth of Magothy River, Md.
	Jul 26	*Oriole*	St	F	Patuxent River, Md.
	Nov 12	*Crocodile*	Sch	F	Off Annemessex River, Chesapeake Bay, Md.
	Nov 27	*Decatur H. Miller*	St	C[20]	Lower Craighill Channel, Chesapeake Bay, Md.
1885	Jan 6	*Alexander Jones*	T	C[21]	Chesapeake Bay
	May 5	*J. H. Gallagher*	Sch	C	Annapolis, Md.
	Sep 20	*Sallie Solomon*	Sch	S	Isaac Shoals, Fisherman's Island, Va.
1886	Jan 5	*Armenia*	SWS	B	Alexandria, Va.
	Jan 8	*Unidentified (+)*	U	F	Chesapeake Bay
	Jan 20	*Raleigh*	St	I	Seven Foot Knoll, Chesapeake Bay, Md.

DATE	VESSEL	TYPE	MANNER	LOCATION
Feb 3	Althea Godfrey	Sch	F	Lynnhaven Bay, Va.
Feb 3	Col. Stafford W. Razee	Sch	S	Seven Pines, Lynnhaven Bay, Va.
Feb 16	B. Oliphant	Sch	F	Above Cove Point Lighthouse, Md.
Mar 15	Jasper Wood	Sch	C[22]	Off Cheseldine, Md.
Apr 26	J. W. Everman	Brg	F	Off Cape Charles, Va.
Aug 2	Samuel R. Sharp	Sch	C[23]	Chesapeake Bay
Nov 25	Rebecca J. Smith	Sch	Cap	Chesapeake Bay, Md.
1887 Jan 24	John and James	ScS	Cap	Potomac River
Feb 27	Monitor	Sch	S	Tolchester, Md.
Mar 21	Penta	St	S	Tolly Point, Chesapeake Bay, Md.
Apr 23	Capt'n Miller	StScw	B	Centreville, Md.
Jul 19	Peter Cooper	St	B	Near Lyons Creek, Patuxent River, Md.
Aug 2	George Law	Sch	F	Petersburg, Va.
Dec 19	Catherine W. May	Sch	F	SE of Cape Henry, Va.
1888 Mar 11	Eastern Light	Sch	F	Tangier Sound, Chesapeake Bay, Va.
Mar 12	Albert Sidney	Sch	S	Bodkins Point, Md.
Mar 12	Galena	Sch	S	Crisfield Harbor, Md.
Mar 12	Joseph T. Camper	Sch	S	Deal Island, Md.
Mar 12	Somerset	Sch	S	Billie's Island, Chesapeake Bay, Md.
Jun 7	Gleason	U	U	Chesapeake Bay
Sep 18	Vineland	ScS	U	Baltimore, Md.
Dec 10	Unidentified (2)	Sch	C[24]	Chester River, Md.
1889 Jan 5	Montana	St	C[25]	Off North Point, Md.
Feb 24	Comet	ScS	B	Alexandria, Va.
Feb 24	William Fisher	ScS	B	Alexandria, Va.
Mar 14	Agnes Barton	Brg	S	Virginia Beach, Va.
Apr 8	Caroline	Sch	S	Cove Point Bar, Md.
Apr 8	Charles P. Sinneckson	Sch	S	Ocean View, Va.
May 20	Johns Hopkins	St	B	Baltimore Harbor, Md.
May 26	Francis Hutchinson	Sch	F	Tangier Sound, Chesapeake Bay, Va.
Jun 23	Jesse W. Knight	Sch	C	Sharps Island, Md.
Oct 23	Henry P. Simmons	Sch	F	False Cape, Va.
Oct 23	Rover	Sch	F	Ocean View, Va.
Oct 26	Welsh	Sch	C[26]	NE of Cape Henry Life Saving Station, Va.

Year	Date	Vessel	Rig	Cause	Location
	Jan 29	Pettiquamscott	Sch	S	Isaac Shoals, Fisherman's Island, Va.
	Feb 8	Golden Rule	Slp	F	Lynnhaven Roads, Va.
	Feb 14	Fairview	Sch	F	Annemessex River, Va.
	Feb 14	Frank Pratt Lee	Sch	C[27]	New Point, Chesapeake Bay, Va.
	Mar 16	Dart	MSch	S	York Spit, Va.
	Apr 10	Adelia Felicia	Sch	F	Five miles NW of Narrow Island, Chesapeake Bay
	Jul 18	Lizzie Jane	Slp	U	Fox Island, Chesapeake Bay
	Oct 13	John E. Tygert	St	B	Baltimore, Md.
	Oct 22	Volunteer	T	C[28]	Chesapeake Bay
	Nov	Bianca	Slp	S	Little Annemessex River, Md.
	Dec 12	Mary Augusta	Sch	S	Near Cambridge, Md.
	Dec 16	Mary Ellen	Sch	F	Below Poplar Island, Md.
	Dec 19	Lucas Brothers	St	C[29]	Baltimore, Md.
		Louise	U	U	Chesapeake Bay
1891	Jan 9	Phoebe	Slp	U	Four miles SW of Smith Island Life Saving Station, Va.
	Feb 29	Hattie Perry	Sch	U	One mile SSE Cape Henry Life Saving Station, Va.
	Mar 27	Dictator	Brk	S	Virginia Beach, Va.
	Apr 25	Lizzie D. Barker	Sch	U	Near Smith Island, Va.
	May 8	Edith	T	C[30]	Chesapeake Bay
	Jun 4	Kate Jones	U	U	Chesapeake Bay
	Jun 14	Emily	Sch	F	Baltimore Harbor, Md.
	Jun 14	Hiram Brown	Sch	F	Baltimore Harbor, Md.
	Sep 3	W. W. Corcoran	St	B	Washington, D. C.
	Oct 22	Mars	CB	F	Near Cove Point, Md.
	Oct 22	Mingo	CB	F	Near Cove Point, Md.
	Oct 22	P. & R. R. No. 27	CB	F	Near Cove Point, Md.
	Oct 22	P. & R. R. No. 66	CB	F	Near Cove Point, Md.
	Oct. 22	P. & R. R. No. 85	CB	B	Near Cove Point, Md.
	Nov 14	Richmond[1]	St	F	Fredericksburg, Va.
1892	Oct 8	Clarence A. Holland	Rm Sch	F	Elizabeth Harbor, Va.
1893	Jan 1	City of Alexandria	SWSF	B	Alexandria, Va.
	Feb 19	Edith Berwind	Sch	B	Six miles south of Smith Island on Middle Ground, Va.
	Jun 30	Grace Van Dusen	Sch	C[31]	Middle Ground, Chesapeake Bay, Va.
	Oct 4	Onward	Sch	A	Annapolis, Md.
	Oct 13	Colter C. Davidson	Sch	S	South of Cape Henry, Va.
	Oct	Edward Ewing	Sch	S	Store Point, south of Piankatank River, Va.
		D. H. Stetson	U	B	Georgetown, D. C.

DATE	VESSEL	TYPE	MANNER	LOCATION
Nov 6	W. W. Coit	SWS	B	Twelfth Street Wharf, Washington, D. C.
	Minnie Estelle	Slp	F	Wainwrights Cove, Md.
1894 Sep 16	Judy	Sch	F	One-half mile below Havre de Grace, Md.
Oct 9	Henry Lippet	U	C[32]	Three-quarters of a mile below Fort Monroe, Va.
Oct 10	Henry G. Ely	Sch	S	Three Sisters Shoals, off West River, Md.
Dec 27	Effie	Sch	C[33]	Hains Point, Potomac River, Washington, D. C.
	Jesse J. Parks	Pgy	F	Canoe Neck Creek, Md.
1895 Feb 13	Edward C. Thomas	Sch	I	Potomac River, Md.
Feb 13	T. R. Creamer	Sch	I	Tolly Point, Chesapeake Bay, Md.
Feb 15	Lady of the Lake	St	B	Seventh Street Dock, Washington, D. C.
Mar 15	Past Grand	Slp	C[34]	Off Stump Neck Point, Potomac River, Md.
Apr 30	Henry Parker	Sch	S	Isaac Shoals, four miles from Smith Island, Va.
May 16	Josephine	Bkt	S	Little Island, Virginia Beach, Va.
Jun 2	Ashland	SchBrg	B	Bermuda Hundred, James River, Va.
1896 Jan 4	Alliance	Brg	F	Off Tolchester Beach, Chesapeake Bay, Md.
Oct 5	Capitol	Pgy	W	Sandy Point, Md.
Nov 29	City of Philadelphia	Sch	S	Little Island, Virginia Beach, Va.
1897 Sep 5	Edward Deane	Sch	B	Monroe's Creek, Va.
Oct 3	Frederick McOwen	T	B	Francis Point, Carter's Creek, Va.
1898 Aug	General Humphreys	Sch	F	Oxford, Md.
Dec 16	Cape Charles	St	B	Port Norfolk, Norfolk Harbor, Va.
1899 Mar 7	G. P. Keagle	Sch	C[35]	Hampton Roads, Va.
Jun 13	George T. Ash	Sch	A	Washington, D. C.
1900 Jul 30	Templar	Sch	E	Baltimore Harbor, Md.
1901 Jan 2	E. C. Thomas	Sch	U	Baltimore Harbor, Md.
Apr 15	Harp	Sch	A	Alexandria, Va.
Dec 4	Lizzie D. Egerton	SWS	A	Crisfield, Md.
	George Leary	St	B	Virginia
1902 Jan 14	John W. Garrett	Sch	I	Baltimore, Md.
Feb 1	John Spedder	Sch	F	Weeks Point, Chesapeake Bay, Md.
1903 Apr 14	Columbia	FB	B	Washington, D. C.
1904 Apr 15	Emma Berry	Pgy	W	Tappahannock, Va.
Nov 24	Wm. Henry	Sch	S	Old Point, Va.
Dec 24	Two Brothers	Sch	C[36]	Claiborne, Md.

1905	Jan 29	*Mary L. Colbourne*	Sch	S	Tangier Island, Chesapeake Bay
	Feb	*Flora Temple*	Slp	S	Gloucester, Va.
	Jul 18	*Reliance*	GSc	B	Cape Charles, Va.
	Jul 22	*Minnivia Miles*	Sch	S	Diamond Marsh, Va.
	Aug 12	*George Lewis*	Sch	F	Magothy River, Md.
	Aug 26	*Minnehaha*	Sch	F	North Point, Chesapeake Bay, Md.
	Oct 5	*Pearl*	Sch	C[37]	Chesapeake Bay
	Oct 11	*Thomas B. Travers*	Sch	S	Tangier Beach, Va.
	Oct 15	*Edward*	Brg	B	3.5 miles SW of Wolf Trap Light, Va.
	Dec 15	*Bath*	Brg	F	Cape Charles, Va.
	Dec 24	*C. H. Moore*	Sch	S	Southern Beach, Va.
1906	Jan 8	*James E. Stansbury*	Sch	S	North of Cedar Point, Chesapeake Bay, Md.
	Jan 8	*Samuel L. Russell*	Sch	F	Chesapeake Bay
	Feb 20	*Rebecca B. Tennis*	Slp	S	Newport News, Va.
	Feb 25	*Mary V. Duncan*	Sch	C[38]	Chesapeake Bay
	Feb 26	*John Howard*	Sch	B	Portsmouth, Va.
	Mar 12	*Sarah J. Elizabeth*	Sch	C[39]	Baltimore, Md.
	Mar 19	*Oak*	Brg	S	Thimble Shoals, Chesapeake Bay, Va.
	Mar 31	*W. H. Van Name*	Sch	C[40]	Thimble Shoals, Chesapeake Bay, Va.
	Apr	*Adeline*	ScS	F	Wheaton, Va.
	Apr	*John Curtin*	Slp	S	Plum Point, Chesapeake Bay, Md.
	Jun 1	*Three Sisters*	Sch	C[41]	Hampton Roads, Va.
	Jul 3	*Hanover*	BSch	S	Point Lookout, Md.
	Jul 3	*Samuel R. Waite*	Sch	S	Cove Point, Va.
	Aug 10	*Cornelia*	Sch	F	Back Creek, Va.
	Aug 19	*Ann Thompson*	Brg	F	Point Lookout, Md.
	Aug 24	*C. B. Rossell*	Brg	F	Off Poplar Island, Chesapeake Bay, Md.
	Sep 27	*Robert E. Lee*	Slp	A	Alexandria, Va.
	Oct 6	*Edward Wright*	Sch	C	Thomas Point, Chesapeake Bay, Md.
	Oct 10	*John R. Rees*	Sch	F	Off Dymers Wharf, Va.
	Oct 20	*George Farwell*	ScS	S	Cape Henry, Va.
	Oct 23	*Frank Butler*	Sch	S	Windmill Point, Va.
	Oct 31	*Silver Star*	Sch	F	York River, Va.
	Nov 14	*Icicle*	GSc	B	Brents Wharf, Md.
	Nov 29	*Florence R. Zimmerman*	CBrg	F	Entrance to Elizabeth River, Va.
	Dec 8	*Charles L. Mitchell*	Sch	A	Cape Henry, Va.
	Dec 11	*J. J. Stewart*	Sch	F	James River, Va.

DATE	VESSEL	TYPE	MANNER	LOCATION
Dec 12	Gen'l J. L. Selfridge	Sch	S	Fisherman's Island, Va.
Dec 24	Casper Heft	Sch	S	Smith Point, Va.
1907 Jan 14	John I. Snow	Sch	S	Portsmouth Beach, Va.
Jan 22	Cohasset	Sch	B	Canton, Baltimore, Md.
Feb 7	John K. Kirkman	Sch	C[42]	Jamestown Island, Va.
Feb 14	President Roosevelt	Brg	C[43]	Hog Island, James River, Va.
Feb 18	Maggie Hastings	Sch	F	Chickahominy River, Va.
Apr 9	Jerome	Sch	S	Mobjack Bay, Va.
Apr 23	American Eagle	Sch	S	York Spit Bar, Va.
May 9	Horn Point	Slp	F	East Lynnhaven Inlet, Va.
Jun 12	Worcester	GSc	B	Crisfield, Md.
Jul 10	Success	Slp	F	Hampton Bar, Va.
Aug 12	Henry A. Littlefield	SchBrg	B	Off Cape Henry, near Virginia Beach, Va.
Aug 29	Allen	Slp	S	York Spit, Va.
Sep 12	Fannie S. Groverman	Sch	C[44]	Elizabeth River, Va.
Sep 15	Lillie Lockett	Slp	F	Watts Creek, Va.
Sep 18	Dauntless	Sch	C[45]	Pinners Point, Va.
Oct 30	Foam	SchY	F	Off Cape Henry, Va.
Nov 10	Dr. W. J. Newbill	ScS	B	Carter's Creek, Va.
Nov 15	Emma K.	ScS	S	Back River Light, Va.
Nov	Wm. A. Steelman	Sch	C[46]	Tilghman Island, Chesapeake Bay, Md.
Dec 4	St. Mary's	SWS	B	Hallowing Point, Patuxent River, Md.
Dec 12	E. G. Irwin	Sch	C[47]	Point No Point, Chesapeake Bay, Md.
1908 Jan 11	Nettie B. Greenwell	Slp	C	Chesapeake Bay, Md.
Jan 17	D. Corson, Jr.	Sch	W	Newport News, Va.
Jan 22	Ada May	Sch	F	Pungoteague Creek, Va.
Jan 26	Custus W. Wright	Sch	F	Hampton Roads, Va.
Jan 26	Mascot	Brg	F	Thimble Shoals, Va.
Feb 11	Kate McNamara	Sch	B	Tilghman Island Wharf, Md.
Feb	Molly	Slp	F	Chesapeake Bay
Mar 3	Thomas B. Hambleton	Sch	F	Hunting Creek, Va.
Apr 20	J. E. Watkins	BSch	C[48]	Seven Foot Knoll, Chesapeake Bay, Md.
Apr 30	Gertrude	Brg	F	Patapsco River, Md.
May 1	Nellie	StBrg	F	Patapsco River, Md.

Date	Vessel	Rig	Cause	Location
		Sch	S	...g Point, Md.
Aug 20	H. P. Barnes	Sch	S	Eastern Bay, Md.
Sep 16	E. F. Keene	Sch	F	Patuxent River, Md.
Sep 29	Dragoon	Y	B	Claiborne, Md.
Nov 7	Mabel W. Gouldman	ScS	B	Chesapeake Bay
Nov 12	Florence Shay	Sch	S	Virginia Beach, Va.
Nov 14	Andrew Bradshaw	Sch	F	Chesapeake Bay
Dec 5	City Belle	ScS	B	Port Deposit, Md.
Dec 31	Spring Garden	ScS	B	Cobhams Wharf, James River, Va.
1909 Jan 6	Eugenia A. Eley	Slp	Cap	Chesapeake Bay
Feb 21	P. Rasmussen	Sch	S	Smith Island Inlet, Va.
Mar 3	Mary Washington	GSc	S	Sewell's Point, Va.
Mar 4	M. Coulbom	Sch	S	Mouth of Nanticoke River, Md.
Mar 11	Love Point	SWS	B	Love Point, Md.
Jul 7	Belle	Sch	S	Norfolk, Va.
Aug 31	J. O. Fitzgerald	Slp	F	Rock Creek, Md.
Sep 15	Owen Dillard	ScS	B	Urbanna, Va.
Sep 26	W. E. Barker	Brg	F	Sharps Island, Chesapeake Bay, Md.
Sep 28	L. McMurray	Sch	S	Baltimore Harbor, Md.
Oct 4	Edith	St	B	Gibson Island, Magothy River, Md.
1910 Jan 5	Mabel	StY	B	Yorktown, Va.
Feb 1	Effie	BSch	F	Chesapeake Bay
Feb 15	Laura and Ella	BSch	C[49]	Plum Point, Chesapeake Bay, Md.
Apr 11	Lillian	BSch	F	Between Howell Point and Betterton, Md.
Apr 20	Lily	Scw	F	Sparrows Point, Md.
Apr 30	William Henry	Sch	S	Alexandria, Va.
May 16	Game Cock	St	B	Baltimore, Md.
May 16	Herbert D. Maxwell	Sch	C[50]	Off Annapolis, Md.
Jun 3	Aerial	Sch	F	Off Cape Henry, Va.
Jun 7	Virginia S. Lawson	RmSch	C[51]	Hills Point, Chesapeake Bay
Jun 15	J. Dallas Marvil	Sch	F	Off Sandy Point, Chesapeake Bay, Md.
Jul 1	Highland Light	Sch	S	Cedar Point, Md.
Sep 10	J. E. Skylight	Sch	C[52]	Holland Point, Md.
Oct 22	Hattie E. Giles	Sch	S	Cove Point, Md.
Nov 1	Rockaway	Sch	F	York Spit, Chesapeake Bay, Va.
1911 Mar 5	Edna A. Pogue	Sch	C[53]	Cedar Point, Md.
Mar 15	Col. J. C. Hill	ScS	S	Pagan Creek, Va.
Mar 22	San Marcos	BS	BU[54]	SW of Tangier Island, Va.

DATE	VESSEL	TYPE	MANNER	LOCATION
Mar 23	*Tam O'Shanter*	Sch	S	New Point Comfort, Va.
Mar 26	*Salisbury*	Sch	B	Cedar Point, Md.
Mar	*Mary Thomas*	Sch	F	Hooper Straits, Md.
Apr 18	*William T. Willing*	GSc	B	Kent Narrows, Md.
Apr 20	*Superior*	SWSF	B	Norfolk, Va.
May 19	*Chetolah*	StY	B	James River, Va.
May 20	*Nettie A. Ruark*	GSc	B	Poplar Island, Chesapeake Bay, Md.
May 21	*Palmetto*	Sch	F	Norfolk, Va.
Jun 9	*Plumie E. Smith*	Sch	C[55]	Alexandria, Va.
Jul 4	*Mary*	ScS	B	James River, Va.
Jul 8	*Harriet E. Ford*	Sch	S	Love Point Light, Md.
Jul 10	*River Queen*	St	B	Washington, D. C.
Sep 18	*Stella Kaplan*	Sch	S	Tail of the Horseshoe, Chesapeake Bay, Va.
Sep 29	*Itinerant*	Sch	C[56]	Great Wicomico River, Va.
Sep 29	*W. C. Kirwan*	Sch	F	Sandy Point, Chesapeake Bay, Md.
Oct 19	*Elizabeth E. Vane*	Brg	C[57]	Baltimore, Md.
Nov 6	*G. W. North*	Sch	C[58]	Baltimore, Md.
Nov 11	*Della May*	Slp	C[59]	Baltimore, Md.
Nov 20	*Joel F. Sheppard*	Sch	B	Harborton, Va.
Nov 24	*Joseph G. Ray*	Sch	S	Tail of the Horseshoe, Chesapeake Bay, Va.
Dec 17	*Katherine D. Perry*	Sch	S	37-02-20 N, 75-56-12 W
1912 Jan 5	*Lizzie Lane*	Slp	S	Piney Point, Potomac River, Md.
Jan 29	*Morris L. Keene*	ScS	F	Baltimore Harbor, Md.
Feb 22	*Caroline*	Brg	C[60]	Poplar Island, Md.
Feb 22	*Ellen S. Jennings*	Brg	C[61]	Poplar Island, Md.
Mar 1	*Float No. 1*	Brg	F	Mobjack Bay, Va.
Mar 5	*Helen Thomas*	Sch	S	Cape Charles Shoals, Va.
Mar 7	*Atlantic*	St	U	Baltimore, Md.
Jul 13	*Mary S. Bradshaw*	Brg	S	Elizabeth River, Va.
Jul 24	*C. W. Steward*	BSch	C[62]	Chesapeake Bay
Aug 4	*Grit*	ScS	B	Days Point, James River, Va.
Aug 29	*Florida*	Sch	S	Hampton Roads, Va.
Sep 5	*Anna I. Gale*	Sch	S	Sandy Point, Chesapeake Bay, Md.
Sep 15	*West Shore*	ScS	S	Chesapeake Bay

Date	Vessel	Rig	Cause	Location
Nov 2	Corona	ScS	B	Patapsco River, Md.
Nov 24	Nora	Sch	F	Horn Harbor, Va.
Dec 3	Charmer	SchBrg	S	36-58-42 N, 75-58-06 W
Dec 6	Bangor	Brg	C[65]	Hampton Roads, Va.
Dec 9	Carlie and Virginia	GScY	B	Kent Island, Md.
1913 Jan 13	Julia Luckenbach	ScS	C[66]	Near entrance to Chesapeake Bay, Va.
Feb 10	Lady Evans	BSch	A	Crisfield, Md.
Feb 26	John R. P. Moore	U	S	Near Plum Point, Chesapeake Bay, Md.
Mar 15	I. W. Padgett	Skj	A	Cape Charles Va.
May 22	Elisha	U	U	Baltimore, Md.
Aug 9	E. R. Gandy	Slp	F	Chesapeake Bay, Va.
Oct 10	Eureka	Sch	F	Nanticoke, Md.
Nov 24	Thomas H. Kirby	Sch	S	On Occohannock Bar, Occohannock, Va.
Dec 5	Mary Elvis	Slp	A	Washington, D. C.
Dec 7	Mabel	Slp	F	Governor's Run, Md.
1914 Jan 12	Currie and Bell	Sch	F	Off Cedar Point, near Solomons, Md.
Feb 14	Dom Pedro II	Brg	S	Tail of the Horseshoe, Chesapeake Bay, Va.
Jun 17	Fannie Shepard	Slp	A	Crisfield, Md.
Jul 15	Reliance	Gsc	B	Deep Creek, Va.
Sep 12	Reba Sterling	GSc	C[67]	Norfolk Pier, Norfolk, Va.
Oct 2	A. J. McIntosh	GSc	B	Severn Side, Annapolis, Md.
Oct 10	Daisie	Sch	A	Norfolk, Va.
Oct 29	Highland	GSc	S	Hampton Roads, Va.
Nov 14	Sea Otter	GSc	E	Curtis Bay, Md.
Nov 15	Massasoit	Sch	S	Smith Island, Va.
Nov 23	Starlight	ScS	B	Rock Creek, Md.
Dec 22	General J. A. Dumont	SWS	B	Severn Side, Annapolis, Md.
1915 Jan 9	Frank E. Swain	Sch	F	SE of Cape Henry, Va.
Jan 22	Maryland	SWS	B	Magothy River, Md.
Jan 30	Arasapha	Brg	S	Old Point Comfort, Va.
Feb 8	Seth M. Tuttle	Sch	S	Hunger's Creek, Chesapeake Bay, Va.
Mar 17	E. S. Booth	ScS	B	Spring Garden, Eastern Branch, Md.
Apr 3	Carrie Louise	Slp	S	James River, Va.
Apr 3	Emma	Sch	S	Hooper Island Bar, Md.
Apr 3	Mary S. Ewing	Sch	S	Point Lookout, Md.
Jun 3	Edwina H. Redmond	Sch	F	SE of Cape Henry, Va.
Jun 30	Father & Sons	Sch	B	Alexandria, Va.
Jul 5	Malcolm V. Clark	ScS	F	James River, Va.

DATE	VESSEL	TYPE	MANNER	LOCATION
Aug 4	Sturdy	GY	S	Off Fort McHenry, Md.
Aug 18	John Wethered	Sch	F	Mouth of Rock Creek, Md.
Sep 11	I. C. Ewell	GSc	B	Potomac River, Md.
Oct 4	E. Goldstrom	GSc	B	Chesapeake Bay
Nov 26	Tivoli	SWS	B	Kent Island, Md.
Nov 28	Laurie V. Grove	Brg	B	Walkerton, Va.
1916 Jan 17	Anna	Sch	F	York Spit, Va.
Feb 21	Shamokin	SchBrg	F	Cape Henry, Va.
Feb 24	Enterprise	T	C[68]	Mouth of Sassafras River, Md.
Feb 29	Robert F. Bratton	Sch	S	Rappahannock River, Va.
Mar 3	Carrie E. Wright	Sch	S	Cedar Point, Md.
Mar 5	Beulah M. Holland	Gsc	S	Nassawadox Creek, Va.
Apr 26	W. J. Townsend	Sch	S	New Point Comfort, Va.
Sep 16	Tangier	Brg	F	Off York River, Va.
Nov 30	Interstate	Brg	F	Three miles off Cove Point Light, Md.
1917 Jan 20	Samuel Wood	Sch	B	Rappahannock River, Va.
Jun 1	Carrie Revell	Sch	F	Alexandria, Va.
Jun 30	John Williams	Slp	A	Norfolk, Va.
Aug 7	James A. Garfield	Sch	C[69]	Cove Point, Md.
Sep 8	A. L. Barnett	Sch	F	Hampton, Va.
Sep 21	Tillie	Brg	F	1.5 miles ESE of Wolf Trap Light, Va.
Oct 9	A. W. Embrey	Brg	S	Wolf Trap Bar, Va.
Nov	Nellie Bly	BSch	F	Black Walnut Cove, Tilghman Island, Md.
Dec 8	Andrew Hicks	Brk	F	Off Cape Henry, Va.
Dec 16	Pilot	ScS	C[70]	Hampton Roads, Va.
Dec 19	Madcap	GY	S	Sewell's Point, Va.
Dec 22	Avery Gorman	GSc	C[71]	Mouth of Back River, Va.
Dec 31	Mary Mills	Sch	F	Choptank River, Md.
	Enola	Slp	F	Canoe Neck Creek, Md.
	Florence	Gsc	I	City Point, James River, Va.
1918 Jan 17	Claudia V	Sch	I	York River, Va.
Jan 22	Water Lilly	Slp	I	Tilghman Island, Md.
Mar 2	Castleton	SWS	B	Norfolk, Va.
Apr 1	Dorchester	Brg	F	Off Smith Point, Chesapeake Bay, Va.

Date	Vessel	Rig	Cause	Location
Apr 9	L. J. Muir	BSch	F	Tighman Island, Md.
Apr 11	Idelia A. Moore	Sch	F	Herring Bay, Md.
Apr 12	Florence O'Brien	Brg	S	Two miles off Stingray Point, Va.
Apr 12	Ida V. Seward	GSc	F	Pig Point, Va.
Apr	Carrie Marie	Slp	C[72]	Choptank River, Md.
Jun 2	Alice M. Guthrie	GSc	S	Three miles east of Cape Henry, VA.
Jun 22	James A. Parsons	Sch	C[73]	St. Jerome Creek, Md.
Sep 3	Manaway	Sch	S	Windmill Point, Va.
Sep 3	Warren B. Potter	ScS	C[74]	Cape Charles Va.
Sep 5	Dauntless	ScS	B	Hampton Creek, Va.
Oct 27	O. M. Clark	Sch	F	Lamberts Point, Va.
Dec 6	Laura A. Muir	Sch	S	Magothy River, Md.
Dec 14	Thomas C. Caton	Sch	S	Smith Point, Va.
1919 Jan 5	Aga Naut	ScS	F	Colonial Beach, Va.
Jan 24	Piedmont	Slp	B	Off Cape Henry, Va.
Mar 4	John W. Wright	GSc	B	Hampton, Va.
Mar 27	Sequoyah	Sch	B	Jamestown, Va.
Apr 7	I. R. Moffett	GY	B	Potomac River
Apr 16	Helen M.	Sch	F	Old Point, Va.
Apr 23	Wild Flower	Brg	B	South of Tilghman Island, Md.
Apr 23	Alice	CB	B	Portsmouth, Va.
May 24	Edward J. Berwind	ScS	B	Portsmouth, Va.
Jun 25	Virginia	Sch	C[75]	Smith Point, Va.
Jun 28	Dexter	Sch	F	Norfolk, Va.
Aug 10	Sally Purnell Beswick	GSc	F	Sandy Point Light, Md.
Aug 13	James B. Anderson	SchBrg	F	Potomac River
Aug 27	Caroline	Sch	F	Off Thimble Shoal Light, Va.
Sep 23	Sodonia Curley	Sch	F	Wolf Trap, Chesapeake Bay
Oct 6	Eva S. Cullison	SchBrg	F	Off Costing Flats, Va.
Oct 13	Pathway	GSc	F	Andrews, Md.
Oct 19	I. H. Addison	Brg	F	Smith Creek, Va.
Oct 31[76]	Waverly	Sch	B	Norfolk Harbor, Va.
Nov 8	Robert Grier	Sch	S	Elizabeth River, one mile below Great Bridge, Va.
Nov 30	Maggie E. Davis	GY	F	Plum Point, Md.
Dec 3	Mary and Alice	Brg	S	Cape Charles Harbor, Va.
Dec 11	Diana	Brg	B	Baltimore Harbor, Md.
Dec 16	Export		B	Aberdeen Proving Grounds, Md.
	Security		F	Chesapeake Bay

DATE		VESSEL	TYPE	MANNER	LOCATION
1920	Jan 30	Weent	GY	B	James River, Va.
	Mar 5	Lillie	GSc	F	Richmond, Va.
	Mar 7	William C. Curtin	Brg	F	Off Kent Island, Md.
	Mar 16	William Schmink	Sch	S	Poplar Island, Md.
	Mar 26	Brooklyn	Sch	S	St. Mary's River, Md.
	Mar 26	Margaret	GSc	B	Norfolk Harbor, Va.
	Apr 6	Juliet L. Hopkins	Sch	F	Off Old Plantation Creek, Va.
	Apr 23	George W. Hardesty	GSc	S	Kent Island, Md.
	Jun 8	Catherine	GSc	B	Crittenden, Va.
	Jun 11	Passaic	ScS	F	Off Old Point Comfort, Va.
	Jun 15	Winthrop	ScS	F	Off Cape Henry, Va.
	Aug 19	John F. Dougherty	GSc	B	Norfolk, Va.
	Aug 22	Old Point Comfort	SWS	B	Baltimore, Md.
	Aug 23	Okesa	ScS	B	Claremont, Va.
	Sep 7	Chino	ScS	B	Seven Mile Reach, Va.
	Oct 1	Thomas F. Pollard	Sch	F	Off Cape Henry, Va.
	Oct 27	George C. Vanderslice	GSc	C[77]	Norfolk, Va.
1921	Feb 3	Sayonara	GSc	B	Off Warwick Creek, Va.
	Apr 22	Golden Harp	GSc	B	Norfolk, Va.
	Jun 30	Raymond Oliver	Sch	A	Reedsville, Va.
	Aug 7	Cecelia Cohen	Sch	F	Off Cape Henry, Va.
	Sep 13	Express	GSc	B	Near Cranberry Island Light, Va.
	Oct 5	E. T. Williams	ScS	B	Drum Point, Va.
	Oct 11	Wandered	GSc	B	James River, Va.
	Oct 16	Willana	Sch	F	Chesapeake Bay
	Oct 25	Daisy May	GSc	S	Virginia Beach, Va.
	Oct 31	Atlantic	ScS	F	Elizabeth River, Va.
	Nov 8	W. H. Mohler	ScS	B	Dundalk, Md.
	Dec 17	Clara M. Leonard	Sch	S	Point Lookout, Md.
	Dec 24	Anna Camp	Sch	F	Chesapeake Bay
	Dec 31	Alberta	ScS	F	Between Jamestown Island and Battery Park, Va.
		Lake Calvenia	ScS	C[78]	Chesapeake Bay
1922	Jan 28	Morning Light	Sch	F	Beach Island, Pocomoke Sound, Md.
	Feb 16	Norge	GSc	B	Middle Ground Lighthouse, Va.
	Feb 20	Defender	GSc	S	Fort Eustis, Va.

Date	Vessel	Type	Cause	Location
Mar 7	*Balsa*	Sch	S	Smith Island, Va.
Apr 8	*Ada*	Sch	A	Richmond, Va.
Apr 13	*Buxton*	ScS	B	Berkley, Va.
Apr 13	*Campello*	ScS	B	Claremont, Va.
Apr 13	*Rosedale*	SWS	B	Berkley, Va.
Apr 13	*Watch Hill*	GSc	B	Berkley, Va.
Apr 21	*Brewster*	GSc	C[79]	James River, Va.
Jul 11	*No. 14*	GSc	B	Baltimore, Md.
Jul 14	*Ella Flaherty*	GSc	S	Below Cape Henry, Va.
Aug 25	*Harry Rayner*	GSc	B	Armistead Point, Hampton, Va.
Aug 26	*Helen*	Sch	B	Port of Baltimore, Md.
Nov 11	*Mary R. Carr*	ScS	B	West Norfolk, Va.
Dec 3	*Sarah M. Rooks*	GSc	B	Pig Point, Va.
Dec 8	*Phillips*	ScS	B	Fort Eustis, Va.
Dec 12	*Lucretia*	Brg	F	Off Portsmouth Flats, Elizabeth River, Va.
1923 Jan 30	*R. W. Blanchard*	GSc	B	In Potomac River, off Quantico, Va.
Jan 31	*Buttonwood*	ScS	B	Lynnhaven Roads, Va.
May 8	*I. A. Chelton*	Sch	A	Sparrows Point, Md.
May 12	*Diana II*	GY	B	Baltimore, Md.
Jun 2	*Glen Beulah*	Slp	C	Ten miles SE of Cape Charles Light, Va.
Jun 7	*Florence E. McNaughton*	Brg	F	Above Turkey Point, Elk River, Md.
Nov 21	*Bailey*	Brg	S	Chesapeake and Delaware Canal
1924 Mar 10	*Victor Lynn*	PB	B	Whitehaven, Md.
Apr 3	*Clinton*	ScS	F	Newport News, Va.
Jun 13	*M. W. Hunt*	ScS	B	Curtis Bay, Md.
Jun 24	*R. C. & T. CO. NO. 386*	Scw	F	Curtis Bay, Md.
Jul 4	*Three Rivers*	SWS	B	Cove Point, Md.
Jul 26	*Gratitude*	St	C[80]	Norfolk Harbor, Va.
Aug 10	*Delivery*	GSc	F	Berlin, Md.
Sep 5	*Senora*	Sch	F	Choptank River, Md.
Oct 12	*Jennie R. Foote*	Sch	B	Smith Island Light, Va.
Dec 8	*A. Woodall*	GSc	B	Turkey Point Light, Chesapeake Bay, Md.
Dec 20	*D. J. Whealton*	Sch	F	Fort Monroe, Va.
Dec 29	*Newport News*	SWS	F	Pearl Beach, Va.
1925 Jan 2	*Arrow*	StY	F	Baltimore, Md.
Jan 21	*Carisco*	ScS	F	James River, Va.
Feb 10	*Juniper*	Brg	C[81]	NE of North River Gas Buoy, Chesapeake Bay, Md.
Mar 25	*Southland*	GSc	C	Tangier Island, Va.

DATE	VESSEL	TYPE	MANNER	LOCATION
Apr 15	Endeavor	ScS	B	Weems, Va.
Jun 23	Clare	GY	B	Point Comfort, Va.
Jul 3	Pathfinder	ScS	B	East River, Va.
Jul 23	Thomas C.	GSc	F	Sassafras River, Md.
Jul 24	Thomas B. Webster	ScS	B	Elizabeth River, Va.
Oct 21	Frances Fuller	GSc	F	James Shore, Md.
Nov 16	Severn	ScS	B	Elizabeth River, Va.
Nov 20	Emily E. Burton	Sch	F	James Point, Md.
Dec 12	Helen	GSc	F	Norfolk, Va.
1926 Jan 6	Baltimore	SWS	B	Rock Hall, Md.
Feb 26	W. B. Miller	GSc	B	Nassawadox Creek, Va.
May 27	Service	GSc	B	Chesapeake and Albemarle Canal, Va.
Jun 20	Peggy H.	OSc	B	Hampton, Va.
Jun 30	Dorothy	GScY	B	Tilghman Point, Md.
Sep 12	Desdemonia	GY	B	Tolchester Beach, Md.
Sep 20	Emma R. Faunce	Sch	A	Back Creek, Annapolis, Md.
Oct 9	Ella Strickland	Sch	F	Old Point, Va.
Oct 10	Westmoreland	OSc	U	McGuire's Wharf, Va.
Nov 16	Patapsco	Brg	S	Cherryfield Point, St. Mary's River, Md.
Nov 19	Anna Camp	Sch	B	Mouth of Magothy River, Md.
Nov 20	Idleon	Gsc	B	Sandy Island, Md.
Nov 27	Celadon	GScY	B	South Branch of the Elizabeth River, Va., near Berkley
Dec 7	Edna M. McKnight	Sch	A	Cape Henry, Va.
Dec 16	Henkessel	GSc	B	Chesapeake Bay, Md.
1927 Jan 10	Louise Greer	ScS	C[82]	Craney Island Light, Va.
Feb 21	L. C. Quinn	GSc	B	Island Creek, Md.
Feb 24	City of Annapolis	ScS	C[83]	Smith Point, Va.
Mar 16	Eva W.	GSc	B	Elizabeth River, Va.
Apr 14	604 Steel	Brg	F	Cape Charles, Va.
May 31	Reveler	GY	B	Annapolis, Md.
Jun 29	Benny W. Baker	GSc	B	Plum Point Wharf, Plum Point, Md.
Aug 25	Osprey	GSc	B	Nansemond River, Va.
Sep 25	Dodiewel	GScY	B	Mummy (Mony?) Island, Md.
Oct 11	Morian	GScY	B	Bear Creek, Md.

Date	Vessel	Rig	Cause	Location
1928 Dec 19	*Alexander J. Gibson*	Brg	F	Ott Smith Point, Va.
Jan 1	*Lucie Wheatley*	Sch	C[84]	Baltimore, Md.
Jan 4	*Eastern Shore*	SwS	B	Bay Shore, Md.
Jan 20	*Byam*	Sch	F	Chesapeake Bay, Va.
Jan 20	*Washington*	OSc	B	Norfolk, Va.
Apr 6	*E. R. Gandy*	GSc	F	Old Point Comfort, Va.
Apr 15	*Emily*	OSc	F	Lynnhaven Bay, Va.
Apr 20	*Rachel G.*	GSc	B	James River, Va.
Jun 9	*E. S. Johnson*	Sch	F	Rock Point, Md.
Jun 16	*Egbert L. Quinn*	GSc	B	Tangier Sound, Chesapeake Bay
Jun 20	*Hampton*	OSc	B	Hampton Roads, Va.
Aug 12	*Walton*	Brg	F	Sandy Point, Md.
Aug 27	*Josephine II*	GScY	B	Georgetown, Md.
Aug 27	*Lillian*	GSc	B	Newport News, Va.
Sep 7	*Lauretta Curran*	GSc	B	South River, Md.
Nov 23	*M. E. Dennis*	GSc	F	Sharps Island, Md.
	James E. Trott	Sch	F	Jacks Bay, Patuxent River, Md.
1929 Mar 31	*Henrietta Hearn*	GSc	B	Potomac River, Md.
Jan 4	*George H. Meekins*	Sch	S	Point Lookout, Md.
Jan 18	*Unida*	GSc	B	Cambridge, Md.
Mar 16	*Willie F. Thomas*	Sch	F	Cove Point, Md.
May 27	*Hazel*	GSc	C	Ragged Point, Va.
Jun 29	*R. B. Speeden*	Sch	S	Ragged Point, Va.
Jun 30	*Ellen Charlotte*	GSc	B	Bennett's Creek, Va.
Jul 20	*N. P. 1*	OScY	B	Gwynn's Island, Va.
Aug 10	*C. O. Nichols*	OSc	B	Black Water Creek, Va.
Sep 1	*Dorothy*	ScS	C[85]	Smith Point, Va.
Sep 7	*George H. Bradley*	ScS	B	Ocran, Va.
Sep 9	*Pine Grove*	Brg	B	Norfolk, Va.
Sep 13	*Alexine*	BSch	B	Crisfield, Md.
Sep 22	*Shiloh*	GSc	B	Tolls Point, Va.
Sep 16	*Choptank*	Brg	B	Bayport, Rappahannock River, Va.
Sep 29	*Nepenthe*	GY	B	Tangier, Va.
Oct 12	*Dandy*	ScS	B	Worton Point, Md.
Oct 25	*John Bowen, Jr.*	GSc	B	Washington, D. C.
1930 Jan 29	*Calvin*	Brg	F	Patuxent River, Md.
Feb 13	*Margaret Lucy*	GSc	B	Chickahominy River, Va.
Feb 27	*America*	OSc	S	South Beach, Va.

DATE	VESSEL	TYPE	MANNER	LOCATION
	Mar 27	General Mathews	ScS	B	Norfolk, Va.
	Apr 17	L. B. Platt	Sch	A	Baltimore, Md.
	May 5	Sachem	Gsc	B	Kedges Strait, Md.
	May 14	Annie	ScS	S	Patapsco River, Md.
	May 19	Lannan	OSc	B	Chestertown, Md.
	Jun 6	America	ScS	B	Sandy Point, Md.
	Jun 6	S. J. Cooper	GSc	B	Tommy Hunt Creek, Va.
	Aug 14	Doris C.	GY	B	Chesapeake Bay, Md.
	Sep 27	C. L. & T. Co. No. 268	Scw	F	Love Point Lighthouse, Md.
	Oct 5	L. E. Williams	Sc	F	Travers Point, Md.
	Dec 9	Virginia	GSc	B	James Point, Md.
		Millie Frank	Sch	A	Three miles above Tappahannock, Va.
1931	Jan 13	Sandy Hook	Sch	A	Locust Point, Baltimore, Md.
	May 13	Louis Lee	GSc	B	Chesapeake Bay, Va.
	May 25	Speed	Sch	F	Seven Foot Knoll, Chesapeake Bay, Md.
	Jun 4	Machodoc	Brg	F	Off Mosquito Point, Rappahannock River, Va.
	Jun 7	Vamp	OSc	B	Chesapeake Bay, Md.
	Jun 7	Pilot No. 2	GSc	B	Norfolk, Va.
		Swan	GSc	B	Norfolk, Va.
	Oct 18	Antares	GSc	B	Handys Point, Worton Creek, Md.
		Beulah Land	Sch	A	Locust Point, Md.
		C	Sch	A	Locust Point, Md.
1932	Feb 12	Edna A. Pogue	Sch	F	Locust Point, Md.
	Aug 2	William F. Dunn	Gsc	C[86]	Tangier Island, Va.
	Aug 12	Milton S. Lankford	OSc	B	Potomac River, Md.
	Aug 25	Mary and Elizabeth	OSc	B	Kent Island, Md.
	Sep 8	Charlotte	ScS	C[87]	Occohannock Creek, Va.
	Oct 21	Ripogenus	Sch	S	Off Cape Henry, Va.
	Oct 21	Thomas Thomas	Brg	B	Rock Point Buoy, Md.
	Dec 21	Nellie	GY	B	Off Gibson Island, Md.
		Squire	Sch	A	Off Morgantown Light, Potomac River, Md.
		Annie Bell	Sch	A	Cambridge, Md.
		Eva D. Rose	Slp	A	Spring Garden, Baltimore, Md.
		Grape Shot	Sch	A	Lower Machodoc Creek, Va.
		William Franklin	Sch	A	Weems, Va.

Year	Date	Vessel	Rig		Location
1933	Mar 13	Victor	OSc	B	Near the Chesapeake Lightship
	May 8	Beauty St. Joseph	OSc	B	Off Cape Henry, Va.
	Jun 14	Smuggler	GSc	B	Willoughby Spit, Va.
	Jun 18	Curtis	GSc	B	Norfolk, Va.
	Jun 21	Coleen	OSc	B	James River, Va.
	Jun 29	Richmond Cedar Works No. 1	Brg	B	James River, Va.
	Jun 29	Washington	Brg	B	Fork Swam, James River, Va.
	Jun 30	Marguerite Egan	CB	B	Berkley, Va.
	Jul 7	Edna Ruth	GSc	B	Chesapeake Bay
	Jul	Harriet P. Ely	Sch	S	South of Bodkin Point, Md.
	Aug 20	Point Breeze	T	S	Seven Foot Knoll, Chesapeake Bay, Md.
	Aug 21	A. G. Bigelow	ScS	F	Chesapeake Bay
	Aug 22	Hercules	SWS	B	Stone Point, Va.
	Aug 23	Cap	GSc	C[88]	Curtis Bay, Md.
	Aug 23	Carrie L.	Sch	S	Bowlers, Va.
	Aug 23	Elwood	Sch	S	West Point, Va.
	Aug 23	Emma V. Wills	Sch	S	Breton Bay, Md.
	Aug 23	Emmett Arthur	Slp	F	Breton Bay, Md.
	Aug 23	Friendship	GY	F	Lafayette River, Va.
	Aug 23	W. J. Lockerman	GSc	S	York River, Va.
	Sep 14	Alexander Bond	GScSch	B	Old Point Comfort, Va.
	Sep 20	New Berne	Osc	B	Chesapeake Bay
	Oct 20	Arianna Bateman	Sch	C	Maryland Point, Md.
	Dec 10	Northern No. 29	Brg	F	Beach Haven, Va.
	Dec 15	Capital	OSc	B	Crisfield, Md.
		Cecelia B. Sheppard	Sch	A	Colonial Beach, Va.
		Elizabeth Ann	Sch	A	N.W. branch of Yeocomico River, Va.
		Francis J. Ruth	Pgy	F	Milltown Landing, Patuxent River, Md.
		H. K. Price	Sch	A	Curtis Bay, Md.
		Martin Wayner	U	F	Crisfield, Md.
		Stephen A. Douglas	Sch	A	Bellevue, Tred Avon, Md.
1934	May 3	Emma K. Reed	OSc	C	Hampton Roads, Va.
	May 15	Cecelia	Sch	S	Mattaponi River, Va.
	Jun 3	Martin Wagner	Sch	F	Crisfield, Md.
	Aug 9	Quo Vadis	GSc	B	Sillery Bay, Md.
		Matilda	Sch	A	Walnut Point, Va.
1935	Jan 26	Harriet	GSc	S	Wide Water Station, Potomac River
	Aug 23	John C. Baxter	Brg	E	Stoops Point, Fairlee Creek, Md.

DATE	VESSEL	TYPE	MANNER	LOCATION
Aug 26	Munnatawket	OSc	B	East River, Va.
Aug 29	Emma Temple	Sch	C[89]	Patapsco River, Md.
Sep 5	Co	OSc	B	Chestertown, Md.
Sep 5	Fannie Mae	ScS	F	A mile ESE of Windmill Point Lighthouse, Va.
Sep 29	Walter Robins	GSc	F	Three miles south of Smith Point, Va.
Sep	Charlotte	GSc	F	Anacostia River, Washington, D. C.
Oct 29	Annapolis	SWS	B	Baltimore, Md.
	Anna Lloyd	Sch	S	St. Michaels, Md.
	Hannah and Ida	Sch	F	Marley Creek, Md.
	J. W. Knowles	Sch	A	Weems, Md.
	John W. Bell	Sch	A	Colgate Creek, near Baltimore, Md.
	Mary A. Fisher	Sch	A	Near Baltimore, Md.
1936 Jan	Augusta	Sch	C	Curtis Creek, Md.
Feb 28	G. G. Bennett	Brg	F	2.5 miles NNE of Smith Point Light, Va.
May 4	James L. Lewis	OSc	B	Off Windmill Point, Va.
Jun 5	Thomas E. Taylor	GSc	S	James Island Light, Tangier Sound, Va.
Jun 15	Wilven	GY	B	Fort Carroll, Baltimore, Md.
Jul 27[90]	Edith Muir	BSch	A	Crisfield, Md.
Jul 30	I. R. Dixon	Sch	F	Mouth of Wicomico River, Md.
Sep 1	Willie	ScS	F	Two miles north of Poplar Island Buoy, Md.
Sep 18	Clemmie Travers	Sch	S	Norfolk, Va.
Oct 18	Maryland	ScS	F	Thimble Shoals Light, Chesapeake Bay
Oct 26	I. A. Crosswell	Sch	F	Eastern Bay, Md.
	James A. Whiting	Pgy	A	Walnut Point, Coan River, Va.
	Speed	Sch	F	Baltimore, Md.
1937 Jan 20	Accomac	Brg	S	Windmill Point Bar, Va.
Feb 6	Catonsville	Brg	F	17.5 miles east of Chesapeake Lightship
Feb 14	Seagull	OSc	S	Linen Island, Va.
Apr 3	Vuel II	OY	B	Wellingtonville, Va.
Jun 4	Edgar E.	OSc	B	Kinsale, Va.
Jun 14	Raiford	GSc	B	Ocean View, Norfolk, Va.
Jun 23	Cachalot	GY	B	Two miles NE of Point Lookout, Md.
Jul 3	Rosamer	GY	B	At dockside, Urbanna, Va.
Jul 29	City of Baltimore	ScS	B	Seven Foot Knoll, Chesapeake Bay, Md.
Aug 7	Augusta C.	GSc	B	Bodkin Point, Md.

Date	Vessel	Rig	Cause	Location
Dec 13	Junera	GSc	B	Shady Side, Md.
	Anna Sherman	Sch	A	Whitehaven, Md.
	J. A. Chelton	Sch	A	JonesCreek, near Sparrows Point, Md.
	Lucy May	GY	A	Northwest Branch of the Yeocomico River, Va.
	Elsie Mae	GY	B	Off Jones Island, Tangier Sound, Va.
	Estelle	OSc	B	Girdletree, Md.
	W. R. Lewis	Sch	S	Harborton, Va.
	Agnes S. Quillin	OSc	C[91]	Off Smith Point, Va., in Potomac River
	William D. Sanner	BSch	A	Two miles NW of Cape Henry Light, Va.
	Maguire	Sch	A	Newport News, Va.
1938 May 21	Edna Bright Haugh	Sch	F	Norfolk, Va.
Jul 2	Nellie Jackson	OSc	B	Fort Carroll, Patapsco River, Md.
Aug 12	J. V. Davenport	GSc	B	Terrapin Sand Point, Tangier Sound, Va.
Nov 16	Mary L.	GSc	B	Off Poquoson Flats Buoy, Chesapeake Bay, Va.
Dec 1	Priscilla	OSc	B	Dutch Gap, James River, Va.
Dec 29	Mary Ella	GSc	B	One mile off Poplar Island Gas Buoy, Md.
1939 Feb 6	Dahlia	GY	B	Ordinary Point, Sassafras River, Md.
Feb 8	Lucinda	GSc	B	Goose Creek, Va.
Feb 17	Richard Armstrong	GSc	B	Chesapeake Bay
Mar 14	Reyner & Son	BSch	A	Norfolk Harbor, Va.
May 9	Lola Taylor	OSc	B	Cross Roads, Va.
Jul 7	Loretta	Sch	F	Claremont, Va.
Aug 15	John R. P. Moore	Sch	A	Norfolk, Va.
Aug 17	Effie A. Chase	Sch	A	Arundel Boat Club, Baltimore, Md.
Sep 29	Mary Lee	Sch	A	Spring Garden, Baltimore, Md.
Oct 23	Stephen Chase		A	Curtis Bay, Md.
Oct 31	Thomas A. Jones		F	Baltimore, Md.
1940 Jan 30	Elisa C.	Brg	F	SE of Blackistone Island, Md.
Mar 29	Lexington	Frt	C	On San Marcos wreck, SW of Tangier Island, Va.
Apr 10	J. D. C. Hanna	GSc	F	Punch Island Creek, Md.
Apr 14	Monavana	GY	B	Bush Run, Md.
Jun 16	Araemo	GY	B	Hanover Sreet Bridge, Baltimore, Md.
Jun 26	William H. Killman	GSc	S	Tangier Bar, Va.
Aug 13	F. B. Scarbrough	OSc	C[92]	Five miles above Coles Point, Chesapeake Bay
Aug 20	Fannie Insley	Sch	F	Windmill Point, Va., at 37-38-00 N, 76-09-54 W
Sep 17	Bright	Brg	S	38-37-07N, 76-25-06W
Oct 15	G. W. Bennett	GSc	F	North Point Bar, Eastern Bay, Md.
Oct 16	A. E. Whiteaker	GY	S	Seven miles south of mouth of Potomac River

DATE	VESSEL	TYPE	MANNER	LOCATION
Oct 27	Tarpon	GY	B	Two miles NE of entrance to Eastern Bay, Md.
Dec 2	Miss Virginia	GSc	B	Sarah's Creek, York River, Va.
1941 Mar 1	Virginia	GSc	F	Norfolk, Va.
Apr 2	The Major	GSc	B	Fisherman's Island, Va.
May 12	Charles A.	GSc	B	Cedar Point, Md.
May 15	Tolchester	SWS	B	Pier 16, Light Street, Baltimore, Md.
Jul 5	Green Goose	GY	B	Chesapeake Bay, Md.
Sep 4	Cherokee	OSc	B	Hog Island, James River, Va.
Sep 27	Kooyong	GY	B	Fredericktown, Md.
Sep	Sea Lyon	GSc	S	Fort Wool, Hampton Roads, Va.
Nov 21	Olive M.	OSc	C[93]	Hampton Roads, Va.
	C. W. Willey	Sch	A	Town Creek, Oxford, Md.
	Federal Hill	Sch	A	Monroe Creek, Va.
	Minnie and Emma	Sch	A	Yeocomico River, Va.
	S. J. Delan	Sch	A	Bellevue, Md.
	Zora and Anna	Sch	A	Curtis Creek, Md.
1942 Jan 8	Charlotte	Brg	S	SW of Point Lookout, Md.
Jan 28	Lycoming	Brg	F	Thimble Shoals Light, Va.
Feb 3	Klondyke	Brg	S	Turkey Point, junction of Elk and Susquehanna rivers, Md.
Mar 31	E. Madison Hall	OSc	F	Turkey Point, Chesapeake Bay, Md.
Jun15	Panama	OSc	B	Mobjack Bay, Va.
Aug 30	Chief	GSc	B	Chesapeake Bay, Va.
Nov 8	Helen of T. II	GY	B	Cambridge, Md.
Nov 12	Rogist	OSc	C[94]	Seven miles SE of Cape Charles Lighthouse, Va.
Dec 16	Columbia	Brg	C[95]	Drum Point Light, Md.
	S-49	S	F	Point Patience, Patuxent River, Md.
1943 Jan19	J. W. Thompson	ScS	F	Baltimore Harbor, Md.
Jan	Avalonte	GSc	F	Monroe Bay, Va.
Feb15	Brownstone	Sch	F	Black Walnut Bar, Choptank River, Md.
Apr 13	Clidy Boy	GSc	F	Chesapeake Bay Channel, Md.
May 9	Juniata	Brg	F	Virginia Capes
Jun4	Vernon Daniel	Slp	F	¼ mile NW of Tangier Lighthouse, Va.
Aug 6	Monomoy	GY	B	Potomac River
Nov 2	Daisy	GSc	F	James River, Va.

Date	Vessel	Type		Location
Nov 18	*Vasa*	GSc	B	Baltimore, Md.
Dec 13	*Forrest*	OSc	F	Four miles SSE of York Spit Light, Va.
	Edward V. Henderson	Sch	A	Tred Avon River, Oxford, Md.
	Perseverance	OSc	F	Mouth of Lynnhaven River, Va.
	Undercliff	GSc	F	Smith's Boat Yard, Curtis Bay, Md.
1944 Mar 11	*Nansemond*	OSc	C[96]	Off Old Point Comfort, Va.
Mar 16	*John I. Clark*	ScS	F	Norfolk, Va.
Apr 11	*Maguire*	OSc	B	Worton Point, Chesapeake Bay, Md.
May	*Lewis C. Worrell*	Sch	A	Washington, D. C.
Aug 1	*Lolita*	GSc	B	Piney Point, Md.
Sep15	*May Dee*	GSc	F	Ocean View, Va.
Sep	*Mikawe*	OSc	B	Lafayette River, Va.
Dec 22	*Howard Wood*	Brg	F	Worton Point, Md.
1945 Feb 3	*Effie L.*	GSc	B	Jackson Creek, Va.
Mar 13	*Nancy Lee*	GSc	B	Anacostia River, Washington, D. C.
Jun 29	*Wilmington*	Drg	F	Cedar Point, Md.
Jun	*Echo*	OSc	B	Buckroe Beach, Chesapeake Bay, Va.
Sep 30	*Norfolk*	ScS	B	Claremont, James River, Va.
Sep 30	*Richmond*	ScS	B	Claremont, James River, Va.
Oct 29	*White Wing*	GSc	B	Norfolk, Va.
Nov 29	*Virginia Lee*	GSc	F	Between Tangier, Va., and Great Wicomico River
Dec 5	*Mary B.*	GSc	F	Turkey Point, Chesapeake Bay
	Marine	Sch	A	Locust Point, Md.
1946 Jan	*Charlotte*	GSc	F	City Point, Hopewell, Va.
Aug	*Student Prince*	OSc	B	Urbanna, Va.
Sep 2	*Hughes Bros.*	GSc	F	Pooles Island, Md.
Sep16	*Quick Time*	BSch	A	Weems, Va.
Oct 30	*Ruth Conway*	OSc	C[97]	Chesapeake and Delaware Canal Causeway
1947 Jan	*Marylin*	OSc	B	Off Norfolk, Va.
Feb 22	*Schoodic*	OSc	B	Drum Point, Md.
Mar 11	*Nettie B. Greenwell*	OSc	C[98]	Off C&O Pier 15, Newport News, Va.
Mar 23	*Saint James*	OSc	B	Farrar Island, off James River, Va.
Apr 1	*J. P. Huppman*	Brg	C[99]	Sewell's Point, Hampton Roads, Va.
Apr 12	*Seminole*	OSc	C[100]	1¼ miles north of Thimble Shoals Light, Va.
May 20	*Florence Rosenbaum*	Gsc	C[101]	James River, Newport News, Va.
Nov 20	*Mihar II*	GSc	B	Norfolk, Va.
	H.M. Rowe	Sch	A	Bellhaven, Md.
	Ruth Decker	Sch	F	Fort Howard, Md.

DATE	VESSEL	TYPE	MANNER	LOCATION
1948 Aug 14	William D. Michael	Sch	A	Chesman Creek, Va.
Sep	Diane	ScS	B	Elizabeth River, Norfolk, Va.
Oct 15	Josephine	GSc	F	Lafayette River, Va.
Oct 19	Milford	GSc	F	Bayport Bay on Rappahannock River, Va.
Oct	Columbia	OSc	C	North Point, Md.
Oct	Annie T. Haley	GSc	F	Portsmouth, Va.
Oct	Dare's	GSc	B	Dare's Beach, Maryland
Nov 15	Beverly	Brg	B	City Point, Hopewell, Va.
Nov 17	Cohasset	Brg	C[102]	Worton Point, Md.
	Kate H. Tilghman	Sch	A	Urbanna Creek, Va.
	William J. Stanford	Sch	A	Swan Creek, Rock Hall, Md.
1949 Apr 26	Eastern Shore	OSc	B	Great Bridge, Va.
Apr 26	Mariner	GSc	B	Sewell's Point, Norfolk, Va.
Apr	Tuckahoe	Brg	F	Smith Point, Va.
Jun 6	Hoosier VI	GSc	B	Smith Point Light, Va.
Jun 20	Isis	GSc	S	Virginia Beach, Va.
Sep	Caponka	Brg	B	Tappahannock, Va.
Oct 15	T. H. Anderson	OSc	C[103]	Tangier Sound, Va.
Dec 7	Matilda	GSc	F	Three miles east of Smith Point Light, Va.
	Florence	Sch	A	Bellevue, Md.
	Zingara	Slp	A	Bellevue, Md.
1950 Jan10	Marion	GSc	F	400 yards south of Middle Ground Buoy, Crisfield, Md.
Jan 26	Fisher No. 1	GSc	B	Sturgeon Point Dock, Charles County, Md.
Apr 9	Lorraine	OScT	F	Near Windmill Point Light, Va.
Sep17	Ethel Mae	GSc	S	James River, Va.
Sep 24	Teddy	GSc	S	Willoughby Beach, near Norfolk, Va.
Oct 3	E. E. Moore	OSc	F	Chesapeake Bay, 15 miles north of Cape Charles
Oct 6	Choptank	GSc	B	Farm Creek Inlet, Nanticoke River, Md.
	Bohemia	Sch	A	Sarah Creek, Va.
	Sand Snipe	GSc	F	Norfolk, Va.
1951 Jan 2	Maine	Brg	F	In Chesapeake and Delaware Canal, Md.
Jan 16	Catbird	OSc	B	Hawkins Point Pier, Baltimore, Md.
Mar 2	Del-Mar-Va	OSc	C[104]	Two miles east of Sandy Point, Md.
Nov 14	Voyager II	OSc	F	Myrtles Island, near Cape Charles, Va.

Date	Vessel	Rig	Cause	Location
Mar 11	*…*	Dg		Three miles north of Sharps Island, Md.
Mar 12	*Shad*	GSc	S	Near naval base, Hampton Roads, Va.
Sep 13	*Bobswoodie*	GSc	B	Off Chesapeake City, Md.
Sep 16	*Margaret A. Travers*	OSc	S[105]	Near Hoopers Island, Chesapeake Bay
Sep 29	*Dorothy May*	GSc	S	½ mile off Willoughby Beach, Va.
Dec 31	*Gladys Melba*	Slp	S	One mile SSE of Sharps Island Light, Md.
Dec	*Blanche*	GSc	S	Washington, D. C.
1953 Jan 1	*Donna*	GSc	B	Washington, D. C.
Feb 11	*Conoco*	GSc	B	Steamboat Creek, Elizabeth River, Va.
Apr 10	*Sterling Sisters*	GSc	B	Gibson Point, Md.
Apr 12	*Estelle*	OSc	F	James River, Va.
May 25	*Nina Palmer*	GSc	B	Little Creek, Va.
Jul 2	*Jeannie*	OSc	F	York Spit, Swash Channel Light, Va.
Jul 6	*Lula Scott*	Slp	A	Cape Charles, Va.
Sep 10	*Marynette*	GSc	B	Mouth of Yeocomico River, Va.
Sep 17	*Ione*	GSc	B	In Potomac River at Washington, D. C.
Nov 28	*Anna F.*	GSc	B	Swantown Creek, Sassafras River, Md.
Dec 8	*Camden*	OSc	F	Off Windmill Point, James River, Va.
Dec 13	*Tommy*	GSc	B	Between Stingray and Grays points, Rappahannock River, Va.
Dec 29	*Kent*	OSc	B	Love Point Light, Md.
1954 Jan 9	*Normandic*	OSc	B	Deals Island, Md.
Jan 22	*Louise*	OSc	F	SE of Cherrystone Buoy, Cape Charles, Va.
Mar 27	*G. T. Forbush*	OSc	B	Fox Island, on Md-Va borderline
Jun 23	*Celmar*	GSc	B	Rock Creek, Pasadena, Md.
Jul 3	*Flo*	GSc	B	Kentmore, Sassafras River, Md.
Jul 14	*James J.*	GSc	F	Hampton Bar, Old Point Comfort, Va.
Sep 12	*Sunset*	GSc	B	Curtis Creek, Md.
Oct 7	*Jane*	GSc	F	Kiptopeke, Va.
Oct 15	*Pirate*	GSc	NL	West Norfolk, Va.
Oct	*Grace G. Bennett*	RmSch	F	Crumpton, Chester River
Dec 15	*Sam Weller*	OSc	B	Arundel Boatyard, Fairfield, Md.
Dec 21	*Enchanter*	OSc	F	Mouth of York River, Va.
	Birdshot	Slp	A	Canoe Neck Creek, Md.
	Blue Wing	BSch	A	Canoe Neck Creek, Md.
	Dover	StBrg	C[106]	Curtis Creek, Md.
	Ida Mae	Ski	A	Deal Island Bridge, Md.
1955 May 10	*Mattie F. Dean*	Sch	A	Annapolis, Md.
Aug 12	*La Forrest L. Simmons*	OSc	Cap[107]	1½ miles north of Sharps Island Light, Md.

DATE	VESSEL	TYPE	MANNER	LOCATION
Aug 12	Levin J. Marvel	RmSch	F	Off Holland Point, Herring Bay, Md.
Sep 1	My Shadow III	GSc	B	Mago Vista, Magothy River, Md.
Sep 19	Edward R. Baird	RmSch	F	Tangier Sound, Va.
Sep	Miss Texaco	GSc	NL	Norfolk, Va.
Oct 14	Ella Covington	BSch	A	Baltimore, Md.
Oct 21	Torbatross	GSc	C[108]	San Marcos Buoy, Chesapeake Bay, Va.
Oct 29	Whiteport	Brg	F	SW side of Severn River, Md.
Nov	Miss Hoopers Island	OSc	F	Morgan Boat Yard, Washington, D. C.
	Ella F. Cripps	Sch	A	Back Creek, Annapolis, Md.
	Mayme	GSc	F	Near Maine Avenue, Washington, D. C.
	Richmond Cedar Works No.1	Brg	F	Bell's Mill Landing, Gilmerton, Va.
	Richmond Cedar Works No.3	Brg	F	Bell's Mill Landing, Gilmerton, Va.
	Richmond Cedar Works No.7	Brg	F	Bell's Mill Landing, Gilmerton, Va.
1956 Jan 20	Machipongo	GSc	B	Point Farm, Quimby, Va.
Mar 17	Bertie	Brg	B	Five miles south of Wolf Trap Light, Va.
Sep 14	Edward R. Baird	Sch	F	Tangier Sound, Va.
Sep 27	Mary Anne	GSc	NL	Hampton Roads Naval Base, Va.
Dec 14	Charles E. Olsen	OSc	B	Three miles off Crisfield, Md.
1957 Feb 7	Shangri-La	GSc	B	Solomons, Md.
Apr 2	The Five C's	GSc	B	Crisfield, Md.
Apr 6	Toreador	GSc	U	Two miles off Cove Point, Md.
Aug 31	Hi-Binder	GSc	B	Off Love Point Light, Md.
Sep 13	Ajax	OSc	C[109]	Chesapeake Bay, Md.
Nov 2	Mart Jean IV	GSc	F	Near Cape Charles Light, Va.
Dec 5	Francis Mae	GSc	F	South Branch, Elizabeth River, Va.
Dec 22	Joyce Ann	GSc	B	Richmond, Va.
1958 Jul 5	Gladys	GSc	F	Elizabeth River, Va.
Sep 23	Lorena	GSc	F	Onancock Creek, Va.
	Anna and Helen	Sch	A	Crisfield Harbor, Md.
1959	Nonie	GSc	S	1¼ miles north of Magothy, Va.
Mar 15	Leona	GSc	B	Urbanna Creek, Va.
May 12	Miss Sue	GSc	B	Northeast River, Md.
Jun 8	Anastasia	GSc	B	Mary Point, Va.
Aug 7	Blanch	GSc	F	One mile north of Kiptopeke, Va.

Year	Date	Vessel	Rig	Cause	Location
	Sep 17	*Minnie V*	Osc	W	Cape Henry, Va.
	Oct 2	*Daphine*	Osc	S	Occohannock Bar, Va.
	Oct 6	*Barbara Ann*	Osc	B	Watts Island, Pocomoke Sound, Va.
	Oct 19	*Phantom*	GSc	C[110]	Cape Charles Harbor, Va.
1960	Feb	*Frank & Theresa*	Sch	U	Smith Creek, Md.
	Jul 29	*Northampton*	Osc	W	Little Creek, Norfolk, Va.
	Sep 12	*Marion*	GSc	W	Carrollton, Va.
	Sep 12	*Peggy*	GSc	W	Norfolk, Va.
	Sep	*Tender*	Osc	W	Norfolk, Va.
	Sep	*Anthony R.*	Brg	F	Portsmouth, Va.
	Sep	*Fred R.*	Brg	F	Portsmouth, Va.
	Sep	*Pruitt Sisters*	GSc	W	Off Watts Island, Va.
	Oct 6	*Attie L.*	Osc	F	Five miles off Onancock, Va.
	Oct 17	*Brigadier*	Osc	C[111]	Chesapeake & Delaware Canal, Md.
	Oct 23	*B. S. Ford*	Brg	F	500 yards off Honga River, Md.
	Oct	*Stingaree*	GSc	W	Hollowing Point Pier, Lorton, Va.
		Rose Marie	GSc	F	In Chesapeake Bay, near Annapolis, Md.
	Dec 12	*Anna and Helen*	Sch	A	Crisfield, Md.
1961	Feb 16	*Sea Hag*	Osc	F	Edgewood Yacht Yard, Annapolis, Md.
	Mar 5	*Elmaria*	GSc	B	Hollywood, Md.
	May	*Seaweed*	GSc	B	Weems Creek, Annapolis, Md.
	Jun 22	*Louise I*	GSc	B	Port Covington Bar, Baltimore, Md.
	Jun 23	*John W. Brown*	Osc	B	Howells Point, Chesapeake Bay, Md.
	Jul 5	*Raven*	Osc	B	Richmond, Va.
	Aug 29	*Florida*	Drg	B	At Escort and Submarine Pier, Norfolk, Va.
1962	Mar 2	*Jennie D. Bell*	RmSch	A	In Wicomico River, Salisbury, Md.
	Apr 6	*Senora*	GSc	C[112]	SE of Chesapeake Lightship
	Jun	*Carol Ross*	GSc	F	Newport News, Va.
	Sep 20	*Tuna*	Osc	F	Front Street Pier, Norfolk, Va.
	Oct 9	*Gaynelle*	Osc	B	Pritchard Marine Railway, Portsmouth, Va.
1963	Jul 15	*Lotus II*	GSc	B	Pritchard Marine Railway, Portsmouth, Va.
	Jul 30	*Tucaway*	Osc	F	Norfolk and Kiptopeke Channels junction, Va.
	Oct 28	*Eddie G. Jr.*	GSc	S	Off Rock Hall, Md.
	Nov 2	*Elva*	GSc	F	Seashore State Park, Va.
	May 12	*Ruth*	Osc	B	Norfolk Tallow Company Dock, Norfolk, Va.
		Sea Saw IV	OscY	B	Five miles north of Sharps Island Light, Md.
1964	Jun 6	*Nancy B.*	GSc	B	Off Blackistone Island, Md.
	Nov 25	*Abogado*	Osc	B	Tebbston, Magothy River, Md.

DATE	VESSEL	TYPE	MANNER	LOCATION
1965 Jan 1	*Clarence and Eva*	U	B	Deal Island Harbor, Md.
Jul 9	*Somerset*	GSc	F	Weems Creek, Annapolis, Md.
Jul 18	*Gussum*	OSc	B	Pocomoke City, Md.
Jul 18	*Daddy's Boat*	GSc	B	Broad Creek, Choptank River, Md.
Oct 7	*Ruth Conway*	OScSh	F	One mile west of Thimble Shoal Light, Va.
Dec 16	*Petrolia No. 5*	OSc	F	Pier at 72 Rader St., Norfolk, Va.
	Miss Constance	OSc	F	Hopewell, Va.
1966 Jan 23	*Julia Ann*	GSc	W	Silver Beach, Va.
Apr 13	*Beryl Marie*	OSc	B	Tangier, Va.
Apr 21	*Staunton*	OSc	F	Six miles west of Tangier Light, Va.
May 11	*Brunswick*	Brg	F	Five miles south of Sharps Island Light, Md.
Jun 23	*Bobali*	OSc	B	Turkey Point, Northeast River, Md.
Jul 28	*Saint Arthur*	OSc	C[113]	Five miles south of Richmond, Va.
Jul	*Robeian*	GSc	U	Near White Rocks, Chesapeake Bay, Md.
Nov 8	*La Ronde*	GSc	B	Galesville, Md.
1967 May 21	*Deemon*	GSc	B	In Northeast River, off Northeast, Md.
Jun 1	*Miss Evelyn*	GSc	B	Mouth of Port Tobacco River, Md.
Jun 11	*June Sea*	GSc	F	Five miles south of Gwynn's Island, Va.
Jul 27	*Keno*	GSc	B	Lafayette River, Norfolk, Va.
Aug 2	*Cabiness*	OSc	B	Gloucester Point, Va.
Aug 2	*Hedo*	OSc	B	Gloucester Point, Va.
Sep 4	*Dutchess*	GSc	F	Norfolk, Va.
Sep 6	*Virginia*	OSc	B	Nelson Point, Mattawoman Creek, Md.
Nov 4	*Laurette*	GSc	B	Bay Marina, Norfolk, Va.
1968 Jan	*Emma Jean*	GSc	W	Olivet, Md.
Mar 22	*Klondike*	OSc	F	Off Grandview Beach, Va.
Apr 16	*Violet*	OSc	S	Near Craney Island, Norfolk, Va.
May 23	*Carol Diane*	OSc	U	Between York Spit and Grandview, Va.
May 23	*Kingfish*	GSc	W	Off Burles Bay, James River, Va.
May 27	*Tommie Boy*	GSc	W	James River, Va.
Jun 15	*Jo Ho So IV*	OSc	B	In Potomac River, off Washington, D. C.
Jul 20	*Swan*	OSc	S	West of Little Creek Inlet, Norfolk, Va.
Sep 1	*Playmate*	GSc	F	Off Fort Brady, in James River, Va.
Oct 5	*Marie*	OSc	F	Eleven miles south of Great Bridge, Va.

Date	Vessel	Rig	Cause	Location
Oct	Seabay Beach	Drg	B	Hoskins Creek, near Md-Va border
Dec 23	Hawalou	GSc	B	Pasadena, Md.
	Bella Siesta III	OSc	B	Turkey Point, Md.
	Dolly Marie	OSc	U	Shore Drive Marina, Norfolk, Va.
	Tunnel	GSc	S	Claremont, James River, Va.
1969 Feb 9	Dreamer	GSc	F	One mile SSE of Yeocomico River Light, Va.
Apr 3	Three Brothers	OSc	B	North of Onancock Channel, Onancock, Va.
Jul 4	Judy B.	GSc	S	Virginia Beach Marina, Virginia Beach, Va.
Jul 24	Skidbladnir	OSc	F	Off Chesapeake Beach, Md.
Aug 20	Leader	OSc	B	Four miles east of Cape Henry, Va.
Aug 30	Jay Cee Dee	GSc	C[115]	Pasadena, Md.
Sep 18	Hel Mar	OSc	B	Norfolk, Va.
Oct 22	Pas Vite	OSc	B	In Nansemond River, two miles below Suffolk, Va.
Oct	Lazy Lady	GSc	B	Off Rosehaven, Herring Bay, Md.
Nov 20	Myrtle Ann	OSc	B	In Tangier Sound, off Tangier Island, Va.
Dec 21	Selandia	GSc	B	Georgetown, Md.
	Senator	OSc	F	At Key Highway Pier, Baltimore, Md.
1970 Mar 22	Coastwise No. 1	Brg	F	Near Old Point Comfort, Va.
Apr 30	Mildred	OSc	F	Five miles north of Hooper Island Lighthouse
May 20	Billie Jean II	GSc	B	Eastern Branch, Elizabeth River, Va.
Jul 29	The Reub II	OSc	B	Between Howell and Meeks Point, Md.
Oct 10	Susan	GSc	F	In Onancock Creek, Onancock, Va.
Oct	South Wind	GSc	F	Port Tobacco, Md.
Nov 4	Summer Wind	OSc	F	Smith Point, Va.
Nov 25	Seven Dwarfs	OSc	B	In Chesapeake Bay, Va.
Dec 23	Miss Bunker Hill II	GSc	W	At wharf, Grasonville, Md.
Dec	Jo Mar III	GSc	F	Bellhaven Marina, Alexandria, Va.
1971 Feb 13	Nirvana	OSc	F	Fort McNair Yacht Basin, Washington, D. C.
Apr 7	Docs Out	GSc	B	West River Marina, Galesville, Md.
Apr 30	Calibria	GSc	B	West River Marina, Galesville, Md.
Apr 30	Kitten	GSc	B	West River Marina, Galesville, Md.
Apr 30	Lady Pat	GSc	B	West River Marina, Galesville, Md.
Apr 30	Safari	GSc	B	West River Marina, Galesville, Md.
Jul 11	Adventure	GSc	F	Craighill Front Range Light, Chesapeake Bay, Md.
Jul 28	Silver Spray	GSc	B	In Choptank River, Cambridge, Md.
Aug 1	Sea Dream	GSc	F	Curtis Creek, Md.
Aug 10	Briarwood	GSc	B	Near Thimble Shoal Light, Va.
Sep 11	Caroline Rebei	OSc	F	York River, Va.

DATE	VESSEL	TYPE	MANNER	LOCATION
Nov 2	Snook	OSc	F	In Chesapeake Bay at mouth of York River, Va.
Nov 7	Dolfin	GSc	F	Virginia Beach, Va.
Nov 22	Azucara II	GSc	F	In Chesapeake Bay at Hacksneck, Va.
1972 Feb 18	Argus II	GSc	B	Georgetown, Md.
Mar 4	Betty Anne II	OSc	U	Between Smith Point and Tangier Island, Va.
Apr 20	J. Lee	OSc	F	Blount Point, Newport News, Va.
May	Carrie A.	GSc	F	Heathsville, Va.
Jul 10	Weezie	GSc	S	Pooles Island, Md.
Aug 8	Miss Kris	GSc	F	Drum Point Light, Solomons, Md.
Aug 17	Katie II	GSc	F	Near Chesapeake Bay Bridge, Md.
Sep 17	Wander	GSc	B	Lynnhaven River, Va.
Oct 15	Seasalt II	OSc	C[116]	36-49-57 N, 75-41-24 W
Dec 6	Eugenia	OSc	F	Off Windmill Point, Va.
Dec 7	Mary Beth	GSc	C[117]	Near Chesapeake Bay Bridge-Tunnel, Va.
1973 Feb	Frank B.	OSc		Hopewell, Va.
Apr 4	Mina Crockett	OSc	F	37-14 N, 76-12 W
Jun	Jehu	GSc	F	Off Patuxent River, Md.
Jun	Laurie K.	GSc	B	Conflux of Occoquan Bay, Va., and Potomac River
Sep 12	La Voie Aller	OSc	F	Windmill Point Marina, Rappahannock River, Va.
Nov 13	Gypsy	GSc	B	Northeast River, Northeast, Md.
Nov 18	Patricia B.	GSc	F	Off Little Choptank River, Md.
Dec 30	Honey Kay	GSc	B	500 yards east of Yorktown, Va.
1974 Feb 5	Big Daddy III	GSc	B	Lord Calvert Marina, Solomons, Md.
Feb 5	The Val III	GSc	B	Lord Calvert Marina, Solomons, Md.
Feb 6	Caprice IV	OSc	B	Lord Calvert Marina, Solomons, Md.
Feb 6	Desire	GSc	B	Lord Calvert Marina, Solomons, Md.
Feb 6	Keck	OSc	B	Lord Calvert Marina, Solomons, Md.
Feb 6	Lady Pat	GSc	B	Lord Calvert Marina, Solomons, Md.
Feb 6	Suggie	GSc	B	Lord Calvert Marina, Solomons, Md.
Feb 6	True Love	GSc	B	Lord Calvert Marina, Solomons, Md.
Feb 6	Vauntie	OSc	B	Lord Calvert Marina, Solomons, Md.
Feb 6	Wild Blue	GSc	B	Lord Calvert Marina, Solomons, Md.
Mar 15	Malolo	OSc	F	Three miles south of Sandbridge, Virginia Beach, Va.
Mar 28	Thomas F. Jubb	OSc	F	Off Grand View Shores, Hampton, Va.

Date	Vessel	Rig	Cause	Location
Aug	Slip Away	GSc	F	in James River, off Rushmere, Va.
Sep 9	Tarus	GSc	B	Mars Marina, Turners Station, Dundalk, Md.
1975 Jan 12	Capt N Rick	OSc	F	14 miles ESE of Chesapeake Light Tower, Md.
Mar 17	ATC 3060	Brg	B	Allied Towing Corp. Dock, Norfolk, Va.
Mar 30	Helen	OSc	U	Chesapeake & Delaware Canal, Md.
Aug 13	Suntan	GSc	B	7 miles north of Little Creek Inlet, Va.
Aug 15	Devils Justice II	GSc	F[118]	Tilghman Island, Md.
	Inlet Queen	GSc	F[119]	In Chester River, Chestertown, Md.
1977 Feb 3	Manana	GScY	F	Bear Creek, Baltimore, Md.
Feb 16	Slopoke	GSc	F	West of Nelson Island, Choptank River, Md.
Apr	Larry Lee	GSc	F	Slaughter Creek, Md.
Jun 6	Dixie Lee	GSc	Cap	Near Norfolk, Va., in Chesapeake Bay
	Friendship	GSc	F	Wispering Cove, Cambridge, Md.
1978 Oct 17	U.S.C.G. Cuychoga	GSc	C[120]	Off Smith Point, Va.

NOTES

For fuller information on these references, see the Bibliography

1. THE TANGIER ISLAND WRECK

1. *Baltimore Sun*, 6 April 1926.
2. Ibid.
3. Ibid.
4. Ibid.
5. Ibid.
6. Ibid.
7. Ibid.
8. Ibid.
9. Kvarning, p. 22-29; Hopkins and Shomette, p. 6.
10. Lewis, pp. 9, 15-18, 39-57.

2. THREE HUNDRED SWITZERS

1. Dabney, pp. 91-92.
2. *Virginia Gazette*, 12 January 1738.
3. Hofstadter, pp. 37-42.
4. *Virginia Gazette*, 12, 19 January 1738.
5. Ibid.
6. Ibid.
7. Ibid.
8. Ibid.
9. Ibid.
10. Ibid.
11. Wust, p. 39.

3. A COLONIAL DISASTER LOG

1. *Virginia Gazette*, 24 February 1737.
2. Ibid., 21 April 1738.
3. Ibid., 14 April 1738.
4. *Maryland Gazette*, 14 January 1745.
5. Ibid., 29 April 1746.
6. Ibid., 31 March 1747.

7. Ibid., 15 September 1747.
8. Ibid., 15 January 1749.
9. Ibid., 18 October and 8 November 1749.
10. Ibid., 16 November 1752.
11. Ibid., 22 February 1752.
12. Ibid., 4 September 1751.
13. Ibid., 26 July 1753.
14. Ibid., 15 November 1753.
15. Ibid., 11, 18 May 1758.
16. Ibid., 10 May 1759.
17. *Virginia Gazette* (Purdie and Dixon), 10 October 1766.
18. Ibid., 4 December 1766.
19. Ibid., 22 December 1768.
20. *Maryland Gazette,* 19 October 1768
21. Marx, p. 165; Vaughn W. Brown, Appendix.
22. Ibid.
23. *Maryland Gazette,* 11 February 1773.
24. Ibid.

4. YOU HAVE MADE A BON FIRE

1. Gipe, pp. 4-5.
2. Ibid, p. 5.
3. Ibid.
4. Papenfuse, pp. 46-47.
5. Ibid., pp. 47-48.
6. *Maryland Gazette,* 17 February 1774.
7. Papenfuse, p. 49
8. "The Burning of the *Peggy Stewart,*" p. 235.
9. Wallace, Davidson, and Johnson Letter Book, 1:447.
10. Gipe, p. 6.
11. Ibid., p. 5.
12. "The Burning of the *Peggy Stewart,*" p. 239.
13. *Maryland Gazette,* 27 October 1774.
14. Ibid.
15. Ibid., 20 October 1774; "The Burning of the *Peggy Stewart,*" p. 236
16. "The Burning of the *Peggy Stewart,*" p. 236.
17. *Maryland Gazette,* 20 October 1774.
18. "The Burning of the *Peggy Stewart,*" p. 243.
19. Gipe, p. 6
20. Ibid.
21. "The Burning of the *Peggy Stewart,*" p. 236.
22. Ibid., pp. 236, 244.
23. Ibid., p. 243.
24. Gipe, p. 7.
25. "The Burning of the *Peggy Stewart,*" p. 240.
26. Ibid., p. 236.
27. Ibid.
28. Papenfuse, p. 50.
29. "The Burning of the *Peggy Stewart,*" p. 237.
30. Gipe, p. 7.

5. CONDUCT [TO] ADORN THE ANNALS OF FAME

1. Force, II, p. 1031.
2. *Maryland Journal,* 24 May 1775.
3. Ibid.
4. Force, II, p. 682.
5. Ibid., pp. 682-83.
6. Ibid., pp. 1104-5.
7. Ibid.
8. *Naval Documents,* I, pp. 1365, 1377; Vaughn W. Brown, Appendix.

9. Eden Transcripts, His Majesty's Officers for the Annapolis District to Robert Eden, Governor of Maryland, 18 August 1775.
10. Ibid.
11. *Naval Documents*, I, p. 995.
12. Ibid., pp. 865-66.
13. Ibid.
14. Ibid.
15. Ibid.
16. Eden Transcripts, His Majesty's Officers to Robert Eden, 18 August 1775.
17. Ibid.
18. *Naval Documents*, I, p. 903.
19. Ibid., p. 946.
20. Ibid.
21. Ibid.

6. LORD DUNMORE'S FLOATING TOWN

1. *Virginia Gazette* (Purdie), 21 April 1775.
2. *Naval Documents*, I, p. 212.
3. Ibid., p. 280.
4. Ibid., p. 635.
5. Ibid., p. 812.
6. *Virginia Gazette* (Pinkney), 7 September 1775; (Purdie), 8 September 1775.
7. *Naval Documents*, I, p. 1296. *Virginia Gazette* (Purdie), 8 September 1775 claimed *Mercury* had been stranded in barely two feet of water.
8. *Naval Documents*, I, p. 1296.
9. *Virginia Gazette* (Pinkney), 7 September 1775; (Purdie), 8 September 1775; (Dixon and Hunter), 9 September 1775.
10. Ibid., (Pinkney), 14 September 1775; (Purdie), 15 September 1775; (Holt), 20 September 1775.
11. *Naval Documents*, II, pp. 154-55; *Virginia Gazette* (Purdie), 22 September 1775; (Dixon and Hunter) 23 September 1775.
12. *Virginia Gazette* (Dixon and Hunter), 28 September 1775.
13. *Naval Documents*, III, pp. 579-80; Selby, pp. 46-49.
14. *Naval Documents*, III, p. 1187; Selby, p. 50.
15. *Naval Documents*, IV, pp. 401-2.
16. Ibid.
17. Ibid., V, p. 278.
18. Ibid., p. 258.
19. Ibid, p. 259.
20. Ibid., p. 278.
21. Selby, p. 58.
22. *Naval Documents*, V, p. 1094.
23. Selby, p. 59.
24. *Virginia Gazette* (Purdie), 19 July 1776.
25. Selby, pp. 59-60.
26. *Naval Documents*, V, p. 996.
27. *Virginia Gazette* (Purdie), 19 July 1776.
28. *Naval Documents*, V, p. 1312.
29. Ibid., p. 1094.
30. Ibid., p. 1079.
31. Ibid., pp. 1094, 1312.
32. Ibid., p. 1094.
33. Ibid., p. 1079, 1312.
34. Ibid., p. 1050.
35. Ibid., pp. 1094-95.
36. *Virginia Gazette* (Purdie), 19 July 1776.
37. *Naval Documents*, V, p. 1079; *Archives of Maryland*, XII, pp. 43-44.
38. *Archives of Maryland*, XII, pp. 43-44.
39. Ibid., p. 51.
40. *Naval Documents*, V, p. 1106; *Archives of Maryland*, XII, pp. 65-66.
41. *Naval Documents*, V, p. 1163.
42. Ibid., p. 1172.
43. Ibid., pp. 1206-7.

44. *Archives of Maryland*, XII, pp. 138-39; *Naval Documents*, V, p. 1314.
45. *Naval Documents*, V, p. 1314.
46. Ibid., p. 1315.
47. Ibid., p. 1316; VI, p. 66.
48. Ibid., VI, p. 173.
49. Ibid., p. 66.
50. Ibid., pp. 106-7.

7. *CATO, HAWK,* AND *NAUTILUS*

1. *Archives of Maryland*, XLV, p. 31.
2. Ibid., p. 113.
3. Ibid., pp. 125, 127-28.
4. Ibid., pp. 129-30.
5. Ibid., XLIII, p. 311.
6. Ibid., XLV, p. 173.
7. Ibid., pp. 182-83.
8. Ibid., p. 217.
9. Ibid., pp. 193-94.
10. Ibid., pp. 201-2.
11. Ibid., p. 258.
12. *Calendar*, p. 42.
13. *Archives of Maryland*, XLVII, pp. 37-38.
14. Ibid.
15. Ibid.
16. Ibid.
17. Ibid.
18. Ibid., p. 40.
19. Ibid.
20. Ibid.
21. Ibid., XLV, pp. 303-4.
22. Ibid., XLVII, p. 37.
23. Ibid., pp. 53-54.
24. Ibid., p. 94.

8. SO MANY ARMED VESSELS

1. *Naval Documents*, III, p. 737.
2. Ibid., V, pp. 94, 130.
3. Ibid., p. 1067.
4. Ibid., VI, p. 1426.
5. Stewart, p. 53.
6. *Naval Documents*, V, pp. 593-94, 1164; VI, p. 799.
7. Ibid., VI, p. 1282.
8. Ibid., VII, p. 633.
9. Ibid., p. 1148.
10. Stewart, pp. 54-55.
11. Ward, II, p. 538.
12. Lull, p. 9; Stewart, p. 77; Lossing, II, p. 538.
13. Lull, p. 9.
14. Ibid.
15. Stewart, p. 72.
16. Ibid.
17. Ward, II, pp. 868-70.
18. Ibid., pp. 870-71.
19. Ibid.
20. Simcoe, p. 199.
21. Ibid.
22. Ibid., pp. 199-200.
23. Ibid., p. 200.
24. Ibid., pp. 200-1.
25. Ibid., p. 201.
26. Ibid., pp. 200-1.
27. Stewart, p. 101.

9. THUNDER AND LIGHTNING

1. Chadwick, p. 141.
2. Ibid., pp. 141-42.
3. Ibid., p. 36.
4. Ibid., p. 37.
5. *Naval Documents*, I, p. 635.
6. The genealogies of *Nancy, Diana, Betsey,* and *Elizabeth,* as well as those of *Robert, Houston, Favorite, Bellona, Two Brothers, Lord Howe,* and *Neptune* may be traced through the voluminous Admiralty transcripts in the Library of Congress, Manuscript Division, Washington, D. C. Of particular note is the collection of Admiral's Dispatches for Admiral James Young (vol. 310), Admiral Samuel Graves (vol. 485), Admirals James Gambier and Thomas Graves (vol. 489), Admirals Molyneaux Shuldham, John Byron, Mariot Arbuthnot, and Commodore Peter Parker (vol. 486), and Lord Howe (vols. 487-88).
7. Chadwick, p. 149.
8. Davis, *Campaign*, p. 135.
9. Ibid., p. 136.
10. Chadwick, p. 126.
11. Ibid., p. 225.
12. Ibid., pp. 103, 106.
13. Davis, *Campaign*, p. 136.
14. Larrabee, p. 159.
15. Chadwick, p. 104; Davis, *Campaign*, p. 137.
16. Davis, *Campaign*, p. 169.
17. Chadwick, pp. 253-56.
18. Ibid., pp. 128-29; Davis, *Campaign*, pp. 141-42
19. Butler, pp. 107-8.
20. Acomb, p. 146; Davis, *Campaign*, pp. 217, 220.
21. Davis, *Campaign* p. 222.
22. Acomb, pp. 146-47.
23. Thacher, p. 283.
24. The identity of the transport fouled by *Charon* is assumed to have been *Shipwright* since she was the only victualler or transport vessel listed by Graves as being burnt. Von Closen, however, states that two transports were destroyed along with *Charon*. Chadwick, p. 149; Acomb, p. 147.
25. Chadwick, pp. 122, 140.
26. Ibid., p. 142.
27. Ibid., pp. 149, 151.
28. Ibid., pp. 141-42.
29. Ibid.

10. A DISASTER LOG CONTINUED

1. *Maryland Gazette,* 12 February 1784.
2. Ibid., 19 February 1784.
3. Ibid.
4. Ibid., 20 October 1785.
5. Ibid., 27 October 1785.
6. Ibid.
7. *The Daily Universal Register* (London), 8 May 1786.
8. Ibid., 25 November 1785.
9. Ibid., 26 November 1785.
10. Ibid., 10 July 1786.
11. *Maryland Gazette,* 21 May 1787.
12. *The Daily Universal Register* (London), 9 April 1787; Marx, p. 169.
13. *Maryland Gazette,* 7 June 1787.

14. *The Times*, (London), 8 October 1788.
15. *Maryland Gazette*, 19 May 1791.
16. *The Times*, (London), 4 January and 3 February 1792.
17. Ibid., 28 June 1797.
18. *Maryland Gazette*, 8 March 1798; *The Times*, 25 April 1798; Marx, p. 170.
19. *Maryland Gazette*, 3 May 1798.
20. *American and Commercial Daily Advertiser* (Baltimore), 20 December 1800.
21. Ibid., 1 February 1805.
22. Ibid., 5 February 1805.
23. Ibid., 14 January 1806.
24. Ibid., 16, 19 April 1806.
25. Ibid., 14 April 1806.
26. Ibid., 10 December 1806.
27. Ibid., 25 December 1806.
28. Ibid., 28 March 1807.
29. Ibid., 3 April 1807.
30. Ibid., 30 September 1807.
31. Ibid., 28 November 1807.
32. Marx, p. 170.
33. Ibid., p. 171.
34. Ibid., p. 166.
35. Ibid.
36. Ibid.
37. Ibid.

11. THE MUCH VAUNTED FLOTILLA

1. Joshua Barney to Secretary of the Navy William Jones, 4 July 1813, Manuscript Division, Library of Congress.
2. Footner, pp. 262, 263, 264; Defense of Baltimore Papers, MS 2304, R2; Chapelle, pp. 222, 223, 225.
3. Shomette, *Flotilla*, p. 35.
4. Captain Robert Barrie to Admiral Sir George Cockburn, 1 June 1814, Cockburn Papers, XXVIII; *American and Commercial Daily Advertiser* (Baltimore), 8 June 1814.
5. Shomette, *Flotilla*, pp. 42-55.
6. Ibid., pp. 57-78, 118-21.
7. Ibid., pp. 89-97, 102-4.
8. Cockburn to Vice Admiral Sir Alexander Cochrane, 7 June 1814, Cockburn Papers, XXIV.
9. Shomette, *Flotilla*, pp. 170, 179-80
10. Cockburn to Cochrane, 22 August 1814, Cockburn Papers, XXIV.
11. Hopkins and Shomette, p. 4.
12. Letter from the Secretary of War, Transmitting, With a Letter from the Chief of Engineers, Report of Examination of Patuxent River, Maryland, House of Representatives Document No. 531, 60th Congress, 1st Session, p. 2.
13. Shomette and Eshelman, I, pp. 138-41.
14. Hopkins and Shomette, pp. 5-7.

12. A GOLGOTHA OF HORROR

1. Flexner, pp. 129-31.
2. Robins, p. 16.
3. Tilp, p. 55.
4. Burgess and Wood, pp. xvii, xix.
5. Robins, p. 19.
6. Lytle, p. 291.
7. Burgess and Wood, p. xix; Elliott, pp. 3, 4; Alexander Crosby Brown, pp. 10, 11-12.
8. Lytle, p. 288.
9. *Alexandria Gazette,* 14 July 1837
10. Ibid., 18 July 1837.
11. Lytle, p. 270.
12. Alexander Crosby Brown, p. 158.
13. *American and Commercial Advertiser* (Baltimore), 15, 16 April 1842.
14. Ibid.
15. *Dixon's Letter* (Supplement) (Virginia), 14 April 1842.
16. Ibid.
17. Ibid.
18. Alexander Crosby Brown, p. 40.
19. Lytle, p. 288.
20. Burgess and Wood, pp. 4, 11; Lytle, p. 262.
21. Burgess and Wood, p. 1; Alexander Crosby Brown, pp. 16, 24; Lytle, p. 252.
22. Burgess and Wood, pp. 2, 9, 12, 16.
23. Lytle, pp. 19, 145.
24. Burgess and Wood, pp. 18, 147; Lytle, pp. 148, 282.

13. PEACEMAKER

1. *Dictionary of American Naval Fighting Ships,* V, p. 383.
2. Tilp, p. 113.
3. *Dictionary of American Naval Fighting Ships,* V, p. 383; *Baltimore American,* 1 March 1844.
4. Ibid.
5. Tilp, p. 114.
6. *Dictionary of American Naval Fighting Ships,* V, p. 383.
7. Ibid.
8. *Baltimore American,* 1, 2 March 1844.
9. Ibid., 1 March 1844.
10. Ibid.
11. Ibid.
12. Ibid.
13. Ibid.; Tilp, p. 113.
14. *Baltimore American,* 1 March 1814.
15. Tilp, p. 114.
16. Ibid.
17. Ibid.; *Baltimore American,* 1 March 1814.
18. Ibid.; *Dictionary of American Naval Fighting Ships,* V, p. 383.
19. *Baltimore American,* 4 March 1844.
20. Ibid., 2 March 1844.
21. Ibid., 1 March 1844.
22. Tilp, p. 114.
23. *Baltimore American,* 1, 2, 4 March 1844.
24. Ibid., 4 March 1844.
25. Tilp, p. 114.
26. *Baltimore American,* 1, 2 March 1844.
27. Ibid., 4 March 1844.
28. Tilp, p. 114.
29. *The American Peoples Encyclopedia,* XVII, p. 323.
30. Ibid., XVIII, p. 311.

14. A COMFORTABLE NIGHT'S REST

1. Alexander Crosby Brown, p. 53.
2. Ibid.
3. Ibid.
4. Ibid., p. 50.
5. Ibid.; *Baltimore American,*
   31 January 1859.
6. *Baltimore American* of January
   31, 1859 reports that the ship's
   net tonnage was given as 900,
   and that her vertical beam engine possessed a diameter of 54
   inches. Alexander Crosby Brown,
   p. 159, notes that *North Carolina*'s net tonnage was 861, and
   the diameter of her vertical beam
   engine measured in at 60 inches.
7. *Baltimore American,* 1 February 1859.
8. Ibid.
9. Ibid.
10. Ibid., 31 January, 1 February
    1859.
11. Ibid., 1 February 1859.
12. Ibid.
13. Ibid.
14. Ibid.
15. Ibid.
16. Ibid.
17. Ibid.
18. Ibid.
19. Ibid.
20. Ibid.; 31 January, 1 February
    1859.
21. Ibid., 1 February 1859.
22. Alexander Crosby Brown, pp. 54-
    55

15. THE STUFF OF WAR

1. Lull, pp. 45-46.
2. Ibid., pp. 46-47.
3. Ibid., p. 47.
4. Ibid., p. 53.
5. Ibid.
6. Ibid.
7. Ibid., p. 48.
8. Ibid., p. 49.
9. Stern, p. 24.
10. *Civil War Naval Chronology*, I,
    pp. 7-9.
11. Lull, p. 49.
12. Ibid., p. 50.
13. Ibid.
14. Ibid.
15. Ibid.
16. *Civil War Naval Chronology*, I,
    p. 9.
17. Lull, p. 52.
18. Ibid.
19. Ibid.
20. Ibid., p. 54.
21. Ibid., p. 52.
22. Ibid., p. 51.
23. Ibid., p. 55.
24. Ibid.
25. Ibid.
26. Ibid., pp. 55-56.
27. Ibid., p. 56.
28. Ibid., pp. 56-57.
29. Ibid., p. 57.
30. Ibid.
31. Ibid., p. 58.
32. Ibid., pp. 58-59.
33. Stern, p. 24; *Civil War Naval
    Chronology*, VI, pp. 241, 288,
    318, 320-21.

16. IRON AGAINST WOOD

1. Still, p. 8.
2. *Official Records*, Series 1, V, p. 806.
3. Still, p. 10.
4. *Civil War Naval Chronology*, II, p. 23.
5. Wood, pp. 696, 702.
6. *Official Records*, Series 2, I, p. 270; Still, p. 31.
7. Ibid., Series 1, VI, pp. 10, 19-20.
8. Wood, p. 698.
9. *Official Records*, Series 1, VI, p. 44.
10. Ibid., Series 1, VI, pp. 22-23; Wood, pp. 698-99.
11. *Official Records*, Series I, VI, pp. 23-24; 44-46; *Civil War Naval Chronology*, II, pp. 29-30.
12. *Official Records*, Series 1, VI, p. 45
13. Ibid.; Wood, pp. 699-700.
14. Ibid.
15. Ibid.
16. Francis Trevelyan Miller, p. 168.
17. Stern, p. 84.
18. Wood, p. 709; *Official Records*, Series 1, VI, pp. 793-94.
19. Wood, p. 709.
20. Ibid., pp. 709-10; *Official Records*, Series 1, VI, pp. 793-94.
21. Ibid.
22. Wood, p. 710; *Official Records*, Series 1, VI, pp. 791-93.
23. Wood, p. 710.
24. *Civil War Naval Chronology*, II, p. 62.

17. THE PRESIDENT DEEMED IT ADVISABLE

1. Cochran, p. 13.
2. *Civil War Naval Chronology*, I, p. 12.
3. Ibid, p. 13.
4. Ibid., pp. 14, 15.
5. Ibid, p. 16; *Official Records*, Series 2, I, p. 191.
6. *Civil War Naval Chronology*, I, p. 16; *Official Records*, Series 1, IV, pp. 516, 517, 533.
7. *Civil War Naval Chronology*, I, p. 18; *Official Records*, Series 1, IV, p. 556.
8. *Civil War Naval Chronology*, I, p. 19; *Official Records*, Series 1, IV, p. 577.
9. *Official Records*, Series 1, IV, pp. 594, 615-17.
10. Ibid., pp. 615-17.
11. Wills, p. 61.
12. *Civil War Naval Chronology*, I, p. 31; Shomette, *Shipwrecks*, p. 401.
13. *Civil War Naval Chronology*, I, p. 38.
14. Ibid., II, p. 7.
15. Ibid., VI, p. 327; Wills, pp. 30-31, 106-7.
16. *Civil War Naval Chronology*, II, p. 31; Wills, p. 147.
17. *Civil War Naval Chronology*, II, p. 97.
18. Shomette, *Shipwrecks*, pp. 417-18.
19. Ibid., p. 474; *Civil War Naval Chronology*, III, p. 45.
20. *Civil War Naval Chronology*, III, p. 87.
21. Ibid., p. 93.
22. Ibid., IV, p. 31.
23. Ibid., p. 90.
24. *Official Records*, Series 1, V, p. 685.
25. *Civil War Naval Chronology*, V, p. 80.

18. A PRIZE TO THE SOUTHERN CONFEDERACY

1. *Official Records*, Series 1, V, pp. 140-41.
2. Ibid., p. 139.
3. Ibid., pp. 118, 119.
4. Ibid., p. 138.
5. Ibid., p. 140.
6. Ibid.
7. Ibid., p. 139.
8. Ibid., p. 157.
9. Ibid., p. 310.
10. Ibid.
11. Ibid.
12. Ibid., pp. 344-45.
13. Ibid.
14. Ibid.
15. Ibid., p. 336.
16. Ibid., Series 2, I, pp. 190, 202.
17. Ibid., Series 1, V, p. 336.
18. Ibid., p. 345.
19. Ibid., p. 339.
20. Ibid.
21. Ibid.
22. Ibid.
23. Ibid., p. 340.
24. Ibid.
25. Ibid.
26. Ibid., pp. 336, 345.
27. Ibid., p. 336.
28. Ibid
29. Ibid., p. 330.
30. Ibid., p, 345.
31. Ibid.
32. Ibid.
33. Ibid., p. 344.
34. Ibid.
35. Ibid., p. 323.
36. Ibid., p. 322.
37. Ibid., p. 327.
38. Ibid.
39. Ibid., p. 345.
40. Ibid., pp. 328, 345.
41. Ibid., p. 394.
42. Ibid.
43. Ibid.
44. Ibid.
45. Ibid., pp. 400, 401.
46. Ibid., p. 398.
47. Ibid.
48. Ibid.
49. Ibid., p. 583.
50. Ibid.
51. *Civil War Naval Chronology*, IV, p. 29.

19. *TULIP*

1. *Official Records*, Series 2, I, p. 226; *The Washington Evening Star*, 14 November 1864.
2. *Official Records*, Series 2, I, p. 226.
3. *Civil War Naval Chronology*, IV, pp. 5, 9.
4. *The Washington Evening Star*, 14 and 15 November 1864.
5. Ellicott, p. 4.
6. Ibid.
7. *The Washington Evening Star*, 15 November 1864.
8. Ibid.
9. Ibid.
10. Beitzell, *Point Lookout*, p. 84; *The Washington Evening Star*, 14 and 15 November 1864.
11. Ibid.
12. Ibid.; "U.S.S. Tulip," p. 14.
13. *The Washington Evening Star*, 15 November 1864.
14. "U.S.S. Tulip," pp. 13-15.

20. THE INFERNAL MACHINE

1. Soley, p. 705.
2. Ibid.
3. *Civil War Naval Chronology*, I, p. 19.
4. Ibid., II, p. 113; III, p. 34; IV, pp. 37, 95; V, p. 16.
5. Ibid., II, p. 113.
6. Ibid., III, p. 114.
7. Ibid., p. 123.
8. *Official Records*, Series 1, X, p. 9.
9. Ibid., p. 12.
10. Ibid., p. 9.
11. Ibid., pp. 14-15; Series 2, I, p. 63; *Civil War Naval Chronology*, IV, p. 56.
12. *Official Records*, Series 1, X, p. 14.
13. Ibid.
14. Ibid.
15. Ibid.
16. Ibid.

21. CHAINED BULLDOGS

1. *Civil War Naval Chronology*, V, p. 75.
2. Ibid.
3. Ibid.
4. Ibid.
5. *Official Records*, Series 1, XII, p. 181; *Civil War Naval Chronology*, VI, pp. 191-92, 306-7.
6. Davis, *To Appomattox*, pp. 103-4.
7. *Official Records*, Series 1, XII, pp. 93-94.
8. *Civil War Naval Chronology*, VI, pp. 229-30, 293, 314, 321.
9. Ibid., pp. 246-47, 275, 290.
10. Ibid., pp. 203-4, 302, 317.
11. Ibid., p. 280; *Official Records*, Series 1, XII, p. 50.
12. *Official Records*, Series 1, XII, p. 95.
13. Ibid., p. 191.
14. *Civil War Naval Chronology*, V, p. 76.
15. Davis, *To Appomattox*, p. 104.
16. *Civil War Naval Chronology*, V, p. 76.
17. Ibid.
18. Ibid., p. 78.
19. Ibid.
20. Ibid., p. 79.

22. THE PITCHER WRECK

1. *Baltimore Sun*, 28 February 1870.
2. Registry Papers of New Jersey, Records of the Bureau of Marine Inspection and Navigation.
3. Alexander Crosby Brown, pp. 73-74.
4. Ibid., p. 152.
5. *Baltimore Sun*, 28 February 1870.
6. Ibid.
7. Ibid.
8. Ibid.
9. Ibid.
10. Alexander Crosby Brown, p. 74.
11. Ibid., p. 143.

23. LOOK AFTER YOUR LIFE

1. *The Washington Evening Star,* 9 August 1873.
2. Ibid., 9, 15 August 1873; Lytle, p. 305.
3. Ibid., 11 August 1873.
4. Ibid., 9 August 1873.
5. The purser's list of passengers was destroyed when *Wawaset* burned. A total of 137 passengers can be accounted for from subsequent reports concerning the disaster, even though initial reports indicated there were no more than 110 persons aboard. Various eyewitness accounts suggested that as many as 150 persons were aboard when the ship burned.
6. *The Washington Evening Star,* 9 August 1873.
7. Ibid., August 15, 1873.
8. Ibid., 9 August 1873.
9. Ibid.
10. Ibid., 15 August 1873.
11. Ibid., 9 August 1873.
12. Ibid., 15 August 1873.
13. Ibid.
14. Ibid., 9, 18 August 1873.
15. Ibid., 9 August 1873.
16. Ibid.
17. Ibid., 15 August 1873.
18. Ibid., 9 August 1873.
19. Ibid.
20. Ibid., 9, 11, 12 August 1873.
21. Ibid., 9, 11, 18 August 1873.
22. Ibid., 11 August 1873.
23. Ibid., 9, 16 August 1873.
24. Ibid., 16 August 1873.
25. Ibid., 9, 15, 16 August 1873.
26. Ibid., 9, 11, 12, 15 August 1873.
27. Ibid., 9 August 1873.
28. Ibid.
29. Tilp, pp. 110-11.
30. *The Washington Evening Star,* 11 August 1873.
31. Ibid.
32. Ibid., 9 August 1873.
33. Ibid.
34. Ibid., 11 August 1873.
35. Ibid., 9 August 1873.
36. Ibid., 11 August 1873.
37. Ibid.
38. Ibid.
39. Ibid.
40. It was reported August 12, 1873 in *The Washington Evening Star* that 72 bodies had been recovered. However, a close count of casualties listed at various times in newspapers during the following week indicated that 76 persons perished in the catastrophe.
41. *The Washington Evening Star,* 15 August 1873.
42. Ibid., 15, 16, 18 August 1873.
43. Tilp, p. 112.
44. Ibid., p. 113.

24. A HORSE AND A CANARY

1. *Baltimore American & Commercial Advertiser,* 16 November 1874.
2. *Official Records,* Series 1, I, pp. 293, 296, 313.
3. *Civil War Naval Chronology,* V, pp. 11, 16; VI, p. 326.
4. Although Alexander Crosby Brown's work is accepted by this author (pp. 50, 159), the *Baltimore American & Commercial Advertiser,* 16 November 1874 reported the ship to be 305 feet in length, 52 feet abeam, 35 feet

deep in hold, 1800 tons burthen, and capable of accommodating up to 200 first class passengers.

5. Alexander Crosby Brown, p. 50.
6. *Baltimore American & Commercial Advertiser*, 16 November 1874.
7. Ibid.
8. Ibid.
9. Ibid.
10. The quote is composited from various newspaper accounts of the incident cited.
11. *Baltimore American & Commercial Advertiser*, 16 November 1874.

12. Ibid.
13. Ibid.
14. Ibid.
15. Ibid.
16. Ibid.
17. Ibid.
18. Ibid.
19. Ibid., 17 November 1874.
20. *Baltimore Sun*, 18 November 1874.
21. Ibid., 17 November 1874.
22. Ibid., 18 November 1874; *Baltimore American & Commercial Advertiser*, 16, 17 November 1874.

25. THE *EXPRESS* DISASTER

1. *The Washington Evening Star*, 24 October 1878; *Baltimore Sun*, 25 October 1878.
2. *The Washington Evening Star*, 26 October 1878; *Baltimore Sun*, 26 October 1878.
3. *The Washington Evening Star*, 24 October 1878;
4. *Baltimore Sun*, 25 October 1878.
5. *The Washington Evening Star*, 24 October 1878.
6. *Baltimore Sun*, 25 October 1878.
7. Ibid.; *The Washington Evening Star*, 24 October 1878.
8. *Baltimore Sun*, 25, 26 October 1878.

9. Ibid.
10. *Baltimore Sun*, 26 October 1878.
11. Ibid., 25, 26 October 1878.
12. Ibid.
13. Ibid., 26 October 1878.
14. Ibid., 25 October 1878.
15. Ibid., 25, 26, 28 October 1878.
16. Ibid., 26 October 1878.
17. Ibid., 25 October 1878.
18. Ibid.
19. Ibid.
20. *The Washington Evening Star*, 24, 25 October 1878.
21. Ibid.
22. *Baltimore Sun*, 28 October 1878.

26. CAPTAIN HALL'S PREMONITION

1. *The Washington Evening Star*, 6 July 1924.
2. Ibid.
3. Burgess and Wood, pp. 89, 98.
4. *The Washington Evening Star*, 6 July 1924.
5. Ibid., 5, 6 July 1924.

6. Ibid.
7. Ibid., 5 July 1924.
8. Ibid., 6 July 1924.
9. Ibid.
10. Ibid., 5, 6 July 1924.
11. Ibid., 5 July 1924.

27. THE LAST CRUISE OF *LEVIN J. MARVEL*

1. Burgess, *This Was Chesapeake Bay*, p. 130; *The Washington Post*, 17 August 1955; *The Washington Evening Star*, 13 August 1955.
2. *The Washington Post*, 13 August 1955; *The Sunday Star*, 14 August 1955.
3. Ibid.
4. *The Washington Evening Star*, 13 August 1955.
5. *The Washington Post*, 13 August 1955.
6. Ibid.
7. *The Sunday Star*, 14 August 1955.
8. *The Washington Evening Star*, 12 August 1955.
9. Ibid., 11, 12 August 1955.
10. *The Sunday Star*, 14 August 1955.
11. *The Washington Post*, 14 August 1955; *The Sunday Star*, 14 August 1955.
12. *The Washington Post*, 14 August 1955; *The Washington Evening Star*, 13 August 1955.
13. *The Washington Post*, 14 August 1955.
14. Ibid.
15. Ibid.
16. Ibid.
17. Ibid.
18. *The Sunday Star*, 14 August 1955.
19. Ibid.
20. *The Washington Post*, 14 August 1955.
21. Ibid.; *The Sunday Star*, 14 August 1955.
22. Ibid.
23. *The Sunday Star*, 14 August 1955.
24. *The Washington Post*, 14 August 1955.
25. Ibid.
26. Ibid.
27. Ibid.
28. Ibid.
29. Ibid.
30. Ibid.
31. Ibid.
32. *The Sunday Star*, 14 August 1955.
33. Ibid.
34. *The Washington Post*, 13 August 1955.
35. *The Washington Evening Star*, 13 August 1955.
36. *The Washington Post*, 14 August 1955; *The Washington Evening Star*, 13 August 1955.
37. *The Washington Post*, 13 August 1955.
38. Ibid., 14 August 1955; *The Washington Evening Star*, 13 August 1955.

28. *CUYAHOGA*

1. *Marine Casualty Report*, pp. 3, 7; *The Washington Post*, 22, 23, 26 October 1978.
2. *Marine Casualty Report*, pp. 2, 34; *The Washington Post*, 25, 26 October 1978.
3. *The Washington Evening Star*, 2 November 1978.
4. *Marine Casualty Report*, pp. 32-33
5. Ibid., pp. 4, 7, 8, 9, 24; *The Washington Evening Star*, 27 October 1978.

6. *Marine Casualty Report*, p. 7; *The Washington Post*, 23 October 1978.
7. *Marine Casualty Report*, pp. 12-14; *The Washington Post*, 21, 22 October 1978.
8. *The Washington Evening Star*, 27, 28 October 1978.
9. *The Sunday Star*, 29 October 1978; *The Washington Evening Star*, 7 November 1978; *Marine Casualty Report*, p. 16
10. *Marine Casualty Report*, p. 29; *The Washington Evening Star*, 26, 27 October 1978; *The Sunday Star*, 29 October 1978.
11. *Marine Casualty Report*, p. 45; *The Washington Post*, 21, 22, 28 October 1978; *The Washington Evening Star*, 22, 26 October 1978.
12. *Marine Casualty Report*, pp. 1, 3, 9-11; *The Washington Evening Star*, 22, 26 October 1978; *The Washington Post*, 21, 22, 28 October 1978.
13. *Marine Casualty Report*, p. 10.
14. *The Washington Post*, 27 October 1978.
15. *Marine Casualty Report*, pp. 10-11.
16. Ibid., p. 17.
17. *The Washington Evening Star*, 26 October 1978; *The Washington Post*, 26 October 1978.
18. *Marine Casualty Report*, pp. 17-18.
19. Ibid., p. 11; *The Washington Evening Star*, 27 October 1978.
20. *Marine Casualty Report*, p. 18; *The Washington Post*, 22 October 1978.
21. *Marine Casualty Report*, pp. 42-43.
22. Ibid.; *The Washington Post*, 22 October 1978; *The Washington Evening Star*, 22 October 1978.
23. *Marine Casualty Report*, pp. 19-20.
24. Ibid., pp. 11, 24; *The Washington Evening Star*, 22 October 1978; *The Washington Post*, 25 October 1978.
25. *The Washington Evening Star*, 22 October and 7 November 1978.
26. Ibid., 22 October 1978.
27. Ibid., 31 October 1978.
28. Ibid., 30 October 1978.
29. Ibid., 31 October 1978.
30. Ibid.
31. Ibid.
32. Ibid.; *The Washington Post*, 22 October 1978.
33. *The Washington Evening Star*, 31 October 1978; *The Washington Post*, 23 November 1978.
34. *The Washington Evening Star*, 30, 31 October 1978.
35. Ibid.; *Marine Casualty Report*, p. 23.
36. *The Washington Post*, 27 November 1978.

APPENDIX

1. Also cited in some sources as lost in 1845
2. With Bgt *Windward*
3. With *George Peabody*
4. With St *General Meigs*
5. With St *Alliance*
6. With St *Allison*
7. With U. S. Army Transport *Massachusetts*
8. With *Mary Augusta*
9. With St *Falcon*
10. With St *Old Dominion*
11. With St *Phlox*
12. With St *Leverson*

13. With St *Mason L. Weems*
14. With T *Fortune*
15. With St *Luray*
16. With St *Elizabeth*
17. With St *William Lawrence*
18. With St *Enoch Pratt*
19. With St *Conoho*
20. With unknown vessel
21. With unknown schooner
22. With Sch *Industry*
23. With T *Camilla*
24. In battle with Maryland Oyster Navy steamer
25. With St *Main*
26. With unknown vessel
27. With Sch *Elwood Harow*
28. With St *Virginia*
29. With *Patapsco*
30. With Sch *Henry L. Little*
31. With submerged wreck
32. With Sch *Red Wing*
33. With *Mary Roberta*
34. With obstruction
35. With unknown vessel
36. With St *Cambridge*
37. With unknown vessel
38. With Sch *William and James*
39. Struck a buoy
40. With wreck of the Brg *Oak*
41. With unknown barge
42. With pier
43. With unidentified vessel
44. With St *Dorchester*
45. With Brg *Arthur*
46. Struck dock
47. With steam tug *Dauntless*
48. With St *Alabama*
49. With St *Ericsson*
50. With St *Gloucester*
51. With St *Everett*
52. With Slp *Enola*
53. With St *Fortune*
54. Blown up as shelling target by battleship *New Hampshire*
55. With St *City of Milford*
56. With Brg *Keystone*
57. With St *Columbia*
58. With obstruction
59. With Sch *Au Revoir*
60. With Brg *Ellen S. Jennings*
61. With Brg *Caroline*
62. With St *City of Norfolk*
63. With St *Kenwood*
64. With St *Essex*
65. With unknown vessel resulting in stranding
66. With St *Indrakula*
67. Struck a pier
68. With wreck
69. With St *Chespton Castle*
70. With St *Berkshire*
71. Struck obstruction
72. With St *Anson M. Bangs*
73. With St *G. S. Allyn*
74. With an unidentified scow
75. With St *Lizzie Colburn*
76. Also given as 10/31/21
77. With St *Norfolk*
78. With St *H. H. Roper*
79. With *Lady Stirling*
80. Run on unidentified wreck and foundered
81. With St *City of Atlanta*
82. With St *Howard*
83. With St *City of Richmond*
84. With St *Anne Arundel*
85. With St *Eurana*
86. With St *State of Maryland*
87. With St *Evansville*
88. Crushed between two unidentified vessels
89. With T *Columbia*
90. Also given as 7/27/37
91. With St *Levenband*
92. With St *Pocahontas*
93. With unidentified barge
94. With navy pilot *SC-330*
95. With *Lillian Anne*
96. With U. S. S. *Catbird*
97. With *Hustler* and *110*
98. With St *Virginia*
99. With unidentified vessel
100. With St *Elisha Lee*
101. With T *F. M. Whitaker*
102. With T *Tern*
103. With *San Marcos* wreck
104. With unidentified vessel
105. Stranded on a bombing target
106. With bridge
107. During Hurricane Connie
108. With submerged wreck
109. With unidentified tugboat

110. With *W. R. Rowe*
111. With *Bethcoaster*
112. With St *Esso New York*
113. With a tow barge
114. With unidentified barge
115. With *Southern Kraft No. 3*
116. With unidentified vessel
117. With unidentified vessel
118. Foundered after being struck by a tornado
119. Date unknown but reported in 1976 *Merchant Vessels of the U. S.*
120. With *Santa Cruz II*

BIBLIOGRAPHY

Acomb, Evelyn M., ed. *The Revolutionary Journal of Baron Ludwig Von Closen, 1780-1783.* Chapel Hill, 1958.

Alexandria Gazette, Alexandria, Virginia.

American and Daily Commercial Advertiser, Baltimore.

Annual Report of the Operations of the United States Life-Saving Service. Washington, D. C., 1878-1913.

Archives of Maryland. Baltimore, 1883-   .

Baltimore Sun Almanac. Baltimore, 1876-1923.

Beitzell, Edwin W. *Life on the Potomac River.* Abell, Maryland, 1968.

———. *Point Lookout Prison Camp for Confederates.* Abell, Maryland, 1972.

Berman, Bruce D. *Encyclopedia of American Shipwrecks.* Boston, 1972.

Brewington, M. V. *Chesapeake Bay Log Canoes and Bugeyes.* Cambridge, Maryland, 1963.

Brown, Alexander Crosby. *The Old Bay Line 1840-1940.* New York, 1950.

Brown, Vaughn W. *Shipping in the Port of Annapolis 1748-1775.* Annapolis, Maryland, 1965.

Burgess, Robert H. *Chesapeake Circle.* Cambridge, Maryland, 1965.

———. *Chesapeake Sailing Craft: Part I.* Cambridge, Maryland, 1975.

———. *This was Chesapeake Bay.* Cambridge, Maryland, 1963.

Burgess, Robert H., and Wood, H. Graham. *Steamboats Out of Baltimore.* Cambridge, Maryland, 1968.

"The Burning of the *Peggy Stewart.*" *Maryland Historical Magazine,* V, No. 3, September 1910.

Butler, Colonel Richard. "Journal of the Siege of Yorktown." *Historical Magazine*, VIII.

Calendar of the General Otho Holland Williams Papers in the Maryland Historical Society. The Maryland Historical Records Survey Project, November 1940. Baltimore, Maryland.

Chadwick, French Ensor, ed. *The Graves Papers and Other Documents Relating to the Naval Operations of the Yorktown Campaign July to October, 1781.* New York, 1916.

Chapelle, Howard I. *The History of the American Sailing Navy: The Ships and Their Development.* New York, 1949.

Civil War Naval Chronology 1861-1865. 6 vols. Washington, D. C., 1961-1966.

Cochran, Hamilton. *Blockade Runners of the Confederacy.* Indianapolis and New York, 1958.

Cockburn Papers. Manuscript Division, Library of Congress, Washington, D. C.

Cooledge, J. J. *Ships of the Royal Navy: And Historical Index*, I. New York, 1969.

Customs Reports of Casualties for Annapolis, for Alexandria, for Baltimore, for Newport News, for Norfolk, and for Portsmouth. National Archives, Washington, D. C.

Dabney, Virginius. *Virginia: The New Dominion.* Garden City, New York, 1971.

Daily Universal Register, (London)

Davis, Burke. *The Campaign That Won America: The Story of Yorktown.* New York, 1970.

———. *To Appomattox: Nine April Days, 1865.* New York and Toronto, 1959.

Defense of Baltimore Papers. Maryland Historical Society, Baltimore, Maryland.

Dictionary of American Naval Fighting Ships. Washington, D. C., 1959-

Dixon's Letter (Supplement). Virginia.

Eden Transcripts. Maryland Historical Society, Baltimore, Maryland.

Ellicott, Captain J. M. "A Child's Recollections of the Potomac Flotilla," *Chronicles of St. Mary's*, X, No. 9, September 1962.

Elliott, Richard V. *Last of the Steamboats: Saga of the Wilson Line.* Cambridge, Maryland, 1970.

Flexner, James Thomas. *Steamboats Come True.* Boston and Toronto, 1978.

Footner, Hulbert. *Sailor of Fortune: The Life and Adventures of Commodore Barney, U. S. N.* New York and London, 1940.

Force, Peter, ed. *American Archives*, 4th Series, Vol. II. Washington, D. C., 1837-1853.

Gipe, George A. "The Day They Burned the *Peggy Stewart*," *Maryland in the Revolution*. Annapolis, 1976.

Hall, Clayton Colman, ed. *Narratives of Early Maryland, 1633-1684*. New York, 1910.

Henry G. Granofsky Customs Collection. Maryland Historical Society, Baltimore, Maryland.

Hofstadter, Richard. *America at 1750: A Social Portrait*. New York, 1973.

Hopkins, Fred W., Jr., and Shomette, Donald G. *War on the Patuxent 1814: A Catalog of Artifacts*. Solomons, Maryland, 1981.

Kvarning, Lars °Ake, and Ohrelius, Bengt. *The Swedish Warship Wasa*. Basingstoke, Hampshire, England, 1973.

Larrabee, Harold A. *Decision at the Chesapeake*. New York, 1964.

Letter from the Secretary of War, House of Representatives Document No. 531, 60th Congress, 1st Session. Washington, D. C.

Lewis, Clifford M., S.J., and Loomie, Albert J., S.J. *The Spanish Jesuit Mission in Virginia, 1570-1572*. Chapel Hill, 1953.

Lloyds Register. London, 1776-1800.

Lonsdale, Lieutenant Commander Adrian L., and Kaplan, H. R. *A Guide to Sunken Ships in American Waters*. Arlington, Virginia, 1964.

Lossing, Benson J. *Pictorial Field Book of the Revolution*. 2 vols., New York, 1850-52.

Lull, Edward P. *History of the United States Navy-Yard at Gosport, Virginia*. Washington, D. C., 1874.

Lytle, William M., and Holdcamper, Forrest R. *Merchant Steam Vessels of the United States, 1790-1868*. Staten Island, New York, 1975.

Marine, William M. *The British Invasion of Maryland 1812-1815*. Hatboro, Pennsylvania, 1965.

Maritime Records Port of Philadelphia, Section IV, Record of Wrecks, Philadelphia District 1874-1934. 12 vols. Pennsylvania Historical Society, Philadelphia, Pennsylvania.

Marx, Robert F. *Shipwrecks of the Western Hemisphere: 1492-1825*. New York, 1971.

Maryland Gazette. Annapolis.

Maryland Journal and Baltimore Advertiser. Baltimore.

Merchant Vessels of the United States. Washington, D. C., 1875-

Miller, Bill. "Wrecks of the Chesapeake," *Bay Country Living*. August 1976.

Miller, Francis Trevelyan, ed. *The Photographic History of the Civil War: The Navies*. New York, 1957.

Naval Documents of the American Revolution. 8 vols. Washington, D. C., 1964-

New York Times.

Official Records of the Union and Confederate Navies in the War of the Rebellion. 31 vols. Washington, D. C., 1894-1927.

Papenfuse, Edward C. *In Pursuit of Profit: The Annapolis Merchants in the American Revolution 1763-1805*. Baltimore and London, 1975.

Pennsylvania Gazette. Philadelphia.

Rankin, Hugh F. *The Golden Age of Piracy*. New York, 1969.

Records of the Bureau of Marine Inspection and Navigation. Record Group 41 National Archives, Washington, D. C.

Robins, Peggy. "S-T-E-AM-BOAT A-C-OM-IN," *American History Illustrated*, XIV, No. 7, November 1979.

Scharf, J. Thomas. *History of Maryland*. 3 vols., Baltimore, 1879.

Selby, John E. *Dunmore*. Williamsburg, Virginia, 1977.

Shomette, Donald. *Flotilla: Battle for the Patuxent*. Solomons, Maryland, 81.

————. *Shipwrecks of the Civil War: The Encyclopedia of Union and Confederate Naval Losses*. Washington, D. C., 1973.

Shomette, Donald G., and Eshelman, Ralph E. *The Patuxent River Submerged Cultural Resource Survey, Drum Point to Queen Anne's Bridge, Maryland*. Solomons, Maryland, 1981.

Simcoe, Lieutenant Colonel J. G. *Simcoe's Military Journal*. New York, 1844.

Smith, John. *The General Historie of Virginia, New-England, and the Summer Isles*. London, 1624.

Soley, James Russell. "Closing Operations in the James River," *Battles and Leaders of the Civil War*, IV. New York and London, 1956.

Stern, Philip Van Dorn. *The Confederate Navy: A Pictorial History*. New York, 1962.

Stewart, Robert Armistead. *The History of Virginia's Navy of the Revolution*. Richmond, 1934.

Still, William N. *Confederate Shipbuilding*. Athens, Georgia, 1969.

Thacher, James. *A Military Journal During the American Revolutionary War, from 1775-1783; Describing interesting events and transactions of this period; With Numerous Historical Facts and Anecdotes, from the original manuscript. To which is added, an*

Appendix, Containing Biographical sketches of several general officers. Boston, 1827.

The Washington Evening Star. Washington, D. C.

The Baltimore Sun.

The Times. (London).

The Washington Post. Washington, D. C.

Tilp, Frederick. This Was Potomac River. Alexandria, Virginia, 1978.

U. S. Coast Guard, Department of Transportation. Marine Casualty Report: USCGC Cuyahoga, M/V Santa Cruz II (Argentina); Collision in Chesapeake Bay on 20 October 1978 With Loss of Life. U. S. Coast Guard Marine Board of Investigation Report and Commandant's Action. Report No. USCG 16732/92368.

"U.S.S. Tulip Centennial Commemoration Ceremony, November 11, 1964," Chronicles of St. Mary's, XII, No. 12, December 1964.

Wallace, Davidson, and Johnson Letter Book. Maryland Hall of Records, Annapolis, Maryland.

Ward, Christopher. The War of the Revolution. 2 vols., New York, 1952.

Wills, Mary Alice. The Confederate Blockade of Washington, D. C. 1861-1862. Parsons, West Virginia, 1975.

Wood, John Taylor. "The First Fight of Iron-Clads," Battles and Leaders of the Civil War, I. New York and London, 1956.

Wust, Claus. The Virginia Germans. Charlottesville, Virginia, 1969.

INDEX